WINE MAGAZINE

POCKET

WINE BUYER'S

GUIDE

2001

A Dorling Kindersley Book

Dorling Kindersley
LONDON, NEW YORK, SYDNEY, DELHI, PARIS,
MUNICH and JOHANNESBURG

First published in Great Britain in 2000
by Dorling Kindersley Limited,
9 Henrietta Street,
London WC2E 8PS

Copyright © 2000
Dorling Kindersley Ltd, London
Text and illustration
copyright © 2000
International WINE Challenge

A CIP catalogue record
for this book is available
from the British Library.

ISBN 0 7513 1271 1

see our complete
catalogue at
www.dk.com

CONTENTS

INTRODUCTION

N O SOONER HAVE YOU focused your attention on one bottle, another barges its way into your line of vision, screaming "Try me!". The merchant's shelf is a confusing battleground, where wines from around the world jostle for position and favour. Some rely on clever packaging and enticing label literature; others rely on reputation and word-of-mouth. The majority, however, can be an unknown quantity.

The citizens of many other nations are, however, never faced with quite the same dilemma. Their shelves are stocked mainly with national produce, offering little choice and even less scope for experiment. Britain, on the other hand, suffers from little national bias toward its own wines and where wines from around the world can be bought in the local high street.

So how should we find that elusive wine, that needle in the haystack?

REAPING THE REWARDS

Since its launch in 1983, WINE magazine's International WINE Challenge has become the world's largest, and most influential, wine competition. This year it brought together some 9,300 wines and over 550 finely-tuned palates. The results of those tasters' efforts appear on the following pages in the form of over 3,000 winners, descriptions of how they taste, where to buy them and how much they will cost. These will help you to find your way around all those shelves.

THE CHALLENGE

THE INTERNATIONAL WINE CHALLENGE was created in 1983 by Robert Joseph and Charles Metcalfe, co-Chairmen, as the basis for an article which examined how English wine

makers were doing compared to their counterparts in other countries. Neither had any idea at that stage that the Challenge would transform itself into the world's largest, most comprehensive and, increasingly, most respected wine competition.

WE CAN WORK IT OUT

The difficulty for retailers is that diversity is not enough; quality and value for money are the real selling points, especially to discerning British consumers. The same is true within the wine trade itself, where restaurateurs buying from importers are justly looking to make money from the wines they put on their lists. Consequently, both retail and

wholesale merchants quickly recognise the need for a fair method of evaluating the wines and, more importantly, for an effective way of merchandising them.

WITH A LITTLE HELP FROM OUR FRIENDS

Together with the support received from both the wine trade in this country and producers around the world, the IWC's success is undoubtedly due to the relentlessly hard-working team that unpack, label, organise, bag, tag and present every single bottle.

CREATING AN INTERNATIONAL BENCHMARK

This simple method of guiding people through the minefield of wine buying has gained the International WINE Challenge its support from the trade. Companies ranging from the retail giants such as Tesco, chains like Unwins and specialist merchants, Justerini & Brooks all

enter wines. Equally important is the support of such companies in the evaluation of the wines, for it is their representatives who judge each and every wine. Buyers from these companies, renowned for their experience and accuracy, together with winemakers from all over the world and Britain's most respected wine writers make up the tasting team which works so hard. It is their involvement that generates the unique trust in the results.

UNDER STARTER'S ORDERS

The process begins in January, when entry kits are distributed to thousands of companies worldwide, inviting them to submit their wines. Within a few weeks, the replies start pouring in, detailing information on every wine to be tasted, such as the principal grape varieties used and the regions in which the grapes were grown.

Once this information is logged in, the entire Challenge team descends to the venue to begin receiving the wines themselves, delivered by local companies, others are samples brought in specially by courier and not forgetting six articulated lorries.

GET READY

Next comes the 'flighting': placing entries into groups of 12-18 wines. Flights are grouped by origin, variety and retail price so that they can be evaluated fairly among equals. Bottles are then wrapped in special 'co-extruded' wine bags, tagged with tamper-proof seals and boxed. Sparkling wines are chilled, vintage ports decanted and wines with distinctive bottles transferred.

THEY'RE OFF!

It is now that the tasters arrive in droves, only to be split into tasting teams of five or six to tackle the wines. Flights are tasted, removed and recorded. Corked bottles are replaced within 90 seconds and corks pulled at an alarming rate and over 2,000 wines can be tasted in a day. Every wine is tasted once again by a 'Super Juror', an experienced and respected trade member, a Master of Wine, a wine maker or an international judge, whose task it is to ensure no worthy wine slips the net. Lurking beneath is the less glamorous process of control; all results are double-checked, every bottle is 'debagged'; a checking sheet, produced with the

original flight, is used to ensure that the right wine is in the right bag; tasting sheets proceed to the computer, the 'nerve-centre' and every result is recorded by helpers working in pairs, one reading, one inputting. The second-round flights are born, wines are re-flighted, re-bagged, re-tagged and re-tasted. This process will result in a Trophy wine being tasted by over 25 of the most experienced palates in the world.

WINES OF THE YEAR

O NE OF THE MAIN roles of the International WINE Challenge is to introduce the consumer to readily available, great-value wines. The Wines of the Year are the best Gold and Silver medal winners to fit two crucial criteria: widespread availability and reasonable price (under £8 for table wines and under £15 for sparkling). Wines are shortlisted by these criteria and then tasted by the Trophy panel, who choose their favourite wines in each category.

THE FIZZ

The Millennium celebrations have not caused the predicted shortage of sparklers, so cleverly hyped by some producers. From Australia the moreish, **Seaview Chardonnay Blanc de Blancs 1995** is brimming with ripe melons and cream, an amazing bargain considering the age and complexity offered. The next two wines fly the flag for Champagne, a region that continues to produce top-quality fizz at prices still accessible to all on the high street.

Sainsbury's Extra Dry Champagne NV is serious stuff. Packed with freshly baked biscuits and lemon meringue flowing to a rich palate. The final sparkler, **MHV The House Champagne NV** is full and fresh with citrus and leesy characters. It is perfect as a party starter. These sparkling wines show that there are quality bubbles on the shelves without having to pay for 'big name' brands.

THE WHITE WINES

Bordeaux shone this year with a stunning white full of character, **Laithwaite Sauvignon Blanc 1999** is laden with zippy fruit and wonderful stoney acidity, this is what everyday white Bordeaux is all about. From the southern Italian region of Puglia, bristles the refreshing **Trulli Chardonnay 1999.** Showing an inviting herbal approach and juicy melons, it is great value at under £5. From the sunny clime of South Australia bursts **Wolf Blass South Australia Chardonnay 1999** all rich, ripe guavas and exotic fruit with a polite lick of sweet oak. All three of these whites hold true to their origins and varieties used.

1998
BAROSSA
SHIRAZ

1998 *Metala*
Langhorne Creek

SHIRAZ CABERNET

Since the original plantings in 1891 the
Metala vineyards have produced wines of
character and distinction, including the
inaugural Jimmy Watson Trophy in 1962.

Matured in French and American oak for
15 months, the 1998 Metala is a balanced
full flavoured wine that will further improve
over the next few to eight years.

No 300048

A·MANO
1999
PRIMITIVO

THE RED WINES

Australia appears again, in the Red Wines of the Year with two awards reflecting this country's strength for producing action-packed, value wines. The inclusion of an Italian Primitivo signals this wine's ability to offer quality imbibing at keen prices.

Peter Lehmann Shiraz 1998, is almost as Barossan as the maker, oozing chocolate and dark fruit with plenty of style. From the Langhorne Creek region South of Adelaide **Stonyfell Metala Shiraz Cabernet Sauvignon 1998,** is brooding with deep, black fruit and eucalyptus lift. While wonderful now this wine will improve over the next few years. From Puglia again is **Primitivo di Puglia 1999, A Mano,** an invitingly spicy number that offers complex earth and mixed herbs.

The Wines of the Year have been tasted by some of the finest palates on this planet. We hope that you will find as much pleasure in trying these wines as the judges did in selecting them. All nine of these wines offer a taste of their origins as well as offering exceptional value for money.

THE TROPHIES

Having tasted the wines and chosen the Gold Medal Winners, the final task is to select the supreme champions from each category: the Trophy winners. At this stage considerations such as price and volume of production are disregarded; wines compete against each other on their intrinsic qualities alone. Unlike any other competition, the judges were not obliged to award trophies in every category. From the start they were told to award trophies only where they thought they were deserved. The following trophies were awarded by a selection of 16 of the UK's best palates, including 12 MWs.

Charles Heidsieck Blanc de Blancs (Oenothèque) 1982, a wine of amazing freshness, poise and style, won the Champagne & Sparkling White Wine Trophy.
Corbans Cottage Block Chardonnay 1997 and **Puligny-Montrachet Claude Chonion 1997** shared the Chardonnay Trophy with the latter showing enough classical sophistication and complexity to also receive the coveted honour of overall White Wine Trophy.

The French chimed in again, taking out the Aromatic White Wine Trophy with **Domaine Zind-Humbrecht Pinot Gris Heimbourg Grand Cru 1998.** Germany was next with two Riesling Trophies, the first, the lithe **Forster Pechstein Riesling Spätlese Trocken JL Wolf 1998** and the stylish **Brauneberger Juffer Sonnenuhr Riesling Auslese Fritz Haag 1997.**

To the reds, in the Burgundy and Pinot Noir section two wines from different hemispheres shared the gong. **Volnay 1er Cru Les Chevrets 1996** from **Boillot** flew the flag for Burgundy, while South Africa supplied the elegant and supple **Galpin Peak Pinot Noir Tête de Cuvée** from **Bouchard Finlayson.**

Italy, not to be outdone, offered another double of reds, the classically Tuscan **Flacianello 1997** and its highly attractive southern cousin **Primitivo Giordano 1997.**

The Bordeaux and Cabernet/Merlot Trophy proved to be a real dogfight with an Antipodean upstart, from the highly fancied Hawke's Bay subregion of Gimblett Road, **CJ Pask Reserve Merlot 1998,** emerging the victor.

America could not be left out of the line-up and Paul Draper delivered the goods, **Ridge Geyserville 1997** showing plenty of attitude to take the Zinfandel Trophy.

The Rhône and Syrah/Grenache Trophy was split between the two heavyweights of France and Australia. **Côte Rôtie 1998** from **Domaine Boucharey** displayed plenty of power and silky finesse further enhancing this region's place at the top of the vinous tree. From the laid-back Margaret River glides **Evans & Tate Shiraz 1999** a great example of carefully restrained fruit yet oozing its Australian character. This wine so impressed the judges that it also received the Red Wine Trophy, the second year in a row that a Shiraz from Oz has done so.

The final part of the day involved the choice of those hardest-to-judge wines, the fortifieds and sweeties. The first to be awarded was **Barbadillo Obispa Gascon Palo Cortado** a hedonistic mix of dried fruits and nuts displaying great depth and balance between age and freshness for the Sherry Trophy. The fortified wines of Jerez continue to be among the most under-valued wines in the world; remarkable complexity can be purchased for very little.

The Ports proved to be a hard bunch to split, single quintas vying with vintages and old tawnies. **Quinta de Vargellas 1987** from **Taylor's** full of Moroccan spice bazaars and intense young fruit was the winner. This port is still looking very young yet still approachable now.

The last of the fortified trophies was for Fortified Muscat. This was awarded to **Seppelt DP63 Rutherglen Show Muscat,** a wine offering an out-of-control ball-bearing of flavour in the mouth. This style of Australian "sticky" is unique to the region of Rutherglen in the north of Victoria. The judges were so taken with this wine that it was also the recipient of the overall Fortified Trophy.

To round off the set a Dessert Wine Trophy was awarded. From the German region of Franken **Lump Riesling Eiswein 1998** from **Weingut Horst Sauer** exhibited amazing purity of fruit matched by extraordinary acidity *"sur pointes"*. This collection of some of the very best wines to be found reflects only a small percentage of the array of styles available from around the world that meets the high standards expected by the trophy judges.

WINES OF THE YEAR AND TROPHY WINES

SPARKLING WINES OF THE YEAR

MHV The House Brut Champagne NV (£14.50) p134
Sainsbury's Champagne Extra Dry NV (£14.00) p133
Seaview Chardonnay Blanc de Blancs 1995 (£9.00) p87

WHITE WINES OF THE YEAR

Laithwaite Sauvignon Blanc 1999 (£5.80) *p119*
Trulli Chardonnay 1999 (£4.60) *p212*
Wolf Blass
   South Australian Chardonnay 1999 (£7.00) *p36*

RED WINES OF THE YEAR

Peter Lehmann Shiraz 1998 (£7.30) *p70*
Primitivo di Puglia A Mano 1999 (£6.00) *p188*
Stonyfell Metala
   Shiraz Cabernet Sauvignon 1998 (£7.50) *p52*

TROPHY WINES

Champagne and Sparkling White Wine Trophy
Charles Heidsieck
   Blanc de Blancs (Oenotheque) 1982 (£90.00) *p146*
Off-Dry Riesling Trophy
Brauneberger Juffer Sonnenuhr Riesling Auslese 1997,
   Fritz Haag (£18.50) *p175*
Dry Riesling Trophy
Forster Pechstein Riesling Spätlese Trocken 1998,
   JL Wolf (£13.30) *p175*

Aromatic White Wine Trophy
Pinot Gris Heimbourg Grand Cru 1998,
Zind-Humbrecht (£19.00)   *p108*

Chardonnay Trophy
Corbans Cottage Block Chardonnay 1997 (£13.00)   *p254*

Chardonnay & White Wine Trophy
Puligny-Montrachet Claude Chonion 1997 (£20.00) *p129*

Bordeaux & Cabernet/Merlot Trophy
CJ Pask Reserve Merlot 1998 (£14.00)   *p246*

Italian Red Wine Trophy
Flaccianello Della Pieve 1997 (£28.50)   *p211*
Primitivo 1997, F Giordano (£6.50) Not available in UK at time of print

Rhône & Syrah/Grenache Trophy
Côte Rôtie 1998, Domaine Boucharey (£17.90)   *p169*

Rhône & Syrah/Grenache & Red Wine Trophy
Evans & Tate Margaret River Shiraz 1999 (£9.00)   *p73*

Red Burgundy & Pinot Noir Trophy
Galpin Peak Pinot Noir Tête de Cuvée 1997 (£13.00) *p332*
Volnay 1er Cru Les Chevrets 1996, J Boillot (£25.00) *p123*

Zinfandel Trophy
Ridge Geyserville 1997 (£20.00)   *p240*

Late Harvest Wine Trophy
Lump Riesling Eiswein 1998 (£31.10) (37.5cl)
Not available in UK at time of print

Sherry Trophy
Barbadillo Obispo Gascon Palo Cortado (£22.00)   *p342*

Port Trophy
Quinta de Vargellas 1987, Taylor's (£21.10)   *p280*

Fortified Muscat & Fortified Wine Trophy
Seppelt DP63 Rutherglen Show Muscat (£8.00)   *p45*

THE
WINES

HOW TO USE THIS BOOK

Every wine in this guide has been awarded a medal at the 2000 International WINE Challenge. The wines are listed by country and region, with up to seven wine headings: red, white, sweet white, rosé, sparkling, sparkling rosé and fortified.

Under each heading the wines are listed in price order, from the least to the most expensive. Wines of the same price are listed in medal order: Gold, Silver and Bronze. Each wine carries the same range of information: its name (and vintage where applicable), a tasting note, average retail price, three-letter stockist's code (see page 391), and the medal it was awarded. Below is an explanation of how wines are listed, for example:

The wine name, vintage, producer and region	*The average retail price*	*The Medal:* **G** *Gold,* **S** *Silver, or* **B** *Bronze*	
PETER LEHMANN SHIRAZ, PETER LEHMANN South Australia	*Full intense profound spice aroma, well structured palate, layers of fruit, spice and oak complexity.*	**£7.30**	Widely Available	**(S)**

WINE OF THE YEAR

A tasting note provided by Challenge tasters

Codes for stockists (see page 391)

Gold medal winning wines are shaded gold

These symbols indicate a Wine of the Year or Trophy Wine

Silver medal winning wines are shaded silver

TROPHY WINE

AUSTRALIA

Yet again this leading wine producer has much to be proud of, they hold the record for the highest proportion of wines entered, winning prestigious medals, trophies and Wines of the Year. Along with flying the flag for excellent classic French grape wine styles, the Australian wine industry as a whole has branched out in recent years, with bounding success, offering varieties such as Viognier and Sangiovese of the Old World. These styles are providing a wonderful new direction away from the big bold styles with which Australia has made its name.

AUSTRALIA • CABERNET SAUVIGNON

SANDFORD ESTATE CABERNET SAUVIGNON 1998, WINGARA Victoria	*Nice fragrant fruit with cherries on the nose and palate, great tannins, well balanced with a long finish.*	£5.80	HOT	**B**
JACOB'S CREEK RESERVE CABERNET SAUVIGNON 1998, ORLANDO WYNDHAM South Eastern Australia	*Inviting warm blackberry nose, soft ripe mouthfeel with elegant firm fruited finish and good length.*	£6.00	WTS OWC	**B**
PARSONS BROOK CABERNET SAUVIGNON 1999, ESSINGTON ESTATES South Eastern Australia	*Big extract of savoury eucalyptus on the nose, huge mouthfeel with blackcurrants, intense concentration.*	£6.00	CTC	**B**
HANWOOD CABERNET SAUVIGNON 1997, MCWILLIAMS New South Wales	*Minty cherry chocolate and toasty oak on a nice full palate with a hint of plum.*	£6.20	CAM CTC	**S**
DEEN DE BORTOLI VAT 9 CABERNET SAUVIGNON 1998, DE BORTOLI New South Wales	*Lifted and complex, delicious ripe fruit and oak nose, balanced tannins and fruits with a drying long finish.*	£6.20	BNK QWW RHV	**B**

HIGH COUNTRY CABERNET SAUVIGNON 1998, MIRANDA Victoria	*Deep classy minty nose, big blackcurrants in a herbal palate, new oak and great acidity.*	£6.60	AVB CTC	(S)
E&C MCLAREN VALE CABERNET SAUVIGNON 1998, SOUTHCORP South Australia	*Excellent savoury ripe fruit palate, very rich and concentrated, well balanced sweet black fruit finish.*	£7.00	ODD	(S)
ROSEMOUNT ESTATE CABERNET SAUVIGNON 1999, ROSEMOUNT ESTATE South Eastern Australia	*Vivid, robust, baked fruits on palate, dry tannins and great structure, spicy jam finish.*	£7.20	Widely Available	(B)
ROVALLEY RIDGE CABERNET SAUVIGNON 1998, MIRANDA WINES Victoria	*Gamey, sweet cherry fruit leads to a smooth oak fruit palate, delicate structure and a pleasant finish.*	£7.20	AVB QWW CTC	(B)
WYNDHAM ESTATE BIN 444 CABERNET SAUVIGNON 1998, ORLANDO WYNDHAM South Eastern Australia	*Very attractive ruby colour, vanilla nose followed by ripe cassis fruit and a soft, long finish*	£7.40	MWW CVR A&A OWC COM FEN	(B)
WAKEFIELD ESTATE CABERNET SAUVIGNON 1998, WAKEFIELD ESTATE South Australia	*Attractive complex nose, clean intense oak and fruits with some vanilla tones. Balanced and enjoyable.*	£7.50	ODD DBY GHL BTH WRW	(B)
JJ MCWILLIAMS CABERNET SAUVIGNON 1997, MCWILLIAMS New South Wales	*Lifted strawberry nose, sweet ripe fresh red berries on the palate, well balanced, elegant finish.*	£7.90	BBO ASH CTC	(B)
THREE VALLEYS CABERNET SAUVIGNON 1998, MIRANDA Victoria	*Deep oak nose, very concentrated black fruit with delicious balanced acidity and a long satisfying fruit finish.*	£8.00	BDR	(S)

YARRA GLEN CABERNET SAUVIGNON 1998, ANDREW GARRETT Victoria	*Delicate, clean savoury nose, lots of juicy fruit, very well balanced structure, firm long tannic finish.*	**£8.00**	THI	S
BLEASDALE MULBERRY TREE CABERNET SAUVIGNON 1998, BLEASDALE South Australia	*Subtle toasted oak on the nose, sweet fruit to the fore in the mouth, lovely grippy conclusion.*	**£8.00**	ODD	B
RYMILL CABERNET SAUVIGNON 1997, RYMILL COONAWARRA South Australia	*Intense ripe fruit on the nose, big and round supported with lovely acidity and balanced tannins.*	**£8.00**	MWW	B
BROWN BROTHERS CABERNET SAUVIGNON 1998, BROWN BROTHERS Victoria	*Dense black fruit and sweet oak nose, good weight, balanced tannins and concentration of blackfruit flavours.*	**£8.20**	Widely Available	S
PETER LEHMANN CABERNET SAUVIGNON 1998, PETER LEHMANN South Australia	*Fresh juicy mulberry nose harmonising with succulent brambly fruit, depth to the palate and lovely structure.*	**£8.30**	JSM ODD JMC VDV WCR G&M	S
ROUGE HOMME CABERNET SAUVIGNON 1997, SOUTHCORP South Australia	*Juicy fruit aroma followed by a rich spiced palate, subtle oak provides support and grip.*	**£8.40**	DBY AMW WRW RHV	B
WESTEND PREMIUM RESERVE OAK AGED CABERNET SAUVIGNON 1999, WESTEND WINES New South Wales	*Green pepper and smokey fruits on nose, redcurrant, red cherries and great tannins finish slowly.*	**£8.40**	BDR	B
NORMANS COONAWARRA CABERNET SAUVIGNON 1998, NORMANS South Australia	*Delicate wet leaf nose, soft ripe fruit well balanced with very nice tannins. Good length.*	**£8.50**	PLB	B

TATACHILLA MCLAREN VALE CABERNET SAUVIGNON 1998, TATACHILLA South Australia	*Dense concentrated palate of fruit, cassis and mint on the finish which lasts forever.*	£8.60	JSM MWW ODD CAM QWW	(B)
ROSEMOUNT ESTATE HILL OF GOLD CABERNET SAUVIGNON 1998, ROSEMOUNT ESTATE New South Wales	*Herbaceous notes on a full upfront red berry palate, lush tannins and great backbone.*	£8.70	WTS	(B)
BEST'S VICTORIA CABERNET SAUVIGNON 1998, BEST'S GREAT WESTERN Victoria	*Deep plumstones on the nose, figs and black fruit on the palate with hints of cracked pepper.*	£8.80	GRT JNW WCR BOO	(S)
MAGLIERI CABERNET SAUVIGNON 1998, MAGLIERI South Australia	*Thick ripe and jammy, a bold character holding raspberries and spicy plums to the finishing line.*	£9.00	PLB	(B)
MARIENBERG RESERVE CABERNET SAUVIGNON 1998, MARIENBERG South Australia	*Minty nose with fresh raspberries and gaminess, high acidity, firm tannins and a lengthy tail.*	£9.00	ASH	(B)
SARNIA FARM CABERNET SAUVIGNON 1998, ANGOVE'S South Australia	*Huge in the face aroma with eucalyptus and blueberries, delicious fruity palate, lovely grippy ending.*	£9.00	TMW	(B)
SEPPELT HARPERS RANGE CABERNET SAUVIGNON 1997, SEPPELT Victoria	*Attractive cedary black-currant nose, ripe sweet firm black fruit on the palate, supported by lovely acidity.*	£9.00	PEF	(B)
MAMRE BROOK CABERNET SAUVIGNON 1997, SALTRAM South Australia	*A wealth of fruit preserves, cooling in the kitchen, huge weighty style with a smooth finish.*	£9.10	MWW ODD NRW SAF PBA WRK	(S)

TATACHILLA PADTHAWAY CABERNET SAUVIGNON 1998, TATACHILLA South Australia	*Light cassis and smoky oak nose, full bodied sweet cassis with intense fruit and delicious finish.*	**£9.10**	BDR SAF	**S**
MAMRE BROOK CABERNET SAUVIGNON 1998, SALTRAM South Australia	*Bold and full bodied wine of complex fruit flavours and classic varietal characteristics with good length.*	**£9.20**	DBY CPR SAF PBA WRK WCS	**B**
TIM ADAMS CABERNET SAUVIGNON 1998, TIM ADAMS South Australia	*Quintessential Aussie cabernet, warm ripe fruit flavours, with excellent structure and balance.*	**£9.50**	DBY AUC WSO	**S**
SANDALFORD CABERNET SAUVIGNON 1997, SANDALFORD WINES Western Australia	*Big tarry red fruit nose, lots of body and character, liquorice kick at the finishing line.*	**£9.50**	HBJ	**B**
ORANGE VINEYARD CABERNET SAUVIGNON 1997, ROSEMOUNT ESTATE New South Wales	*Perfumed fruit nose, deep and complex plum fruit on the palate, with tidy tannins.*	**£9.60**	ROS	**S**
WYNNS COONAWARRA CABERNET SAUVIGNON 1997, WYNNS ESTATE South Australia	*Deep and luscious velvety texture with cassis and spearmint palate, a big and powerful finish.*	**£9.90**	Widely Available	**B**
CHAPEL HILL CABERNET SAUVIGNON 1998, CHAPEL HILL South Australia	*A dish of baked fruit aromas, vanilla and blackcurrant finishes this wine off in true style.*	**£10.00**	DBY TOS AUC	**B**
E&C SECTION 353 CABERNET SAUVIGNON 1997, SOUTHCORP South Australia	*Mulberry and herb aroma with blackfruit, liquorice and chocolate on the delicious finish.*	**£10.00**	ODF	**B**

PHOENIX CABERNET SAUVIGNON 1998, PENLEY ESTATE South Australia	*Fragrant gamey aromas with robust spicy berry flavours, nice depth and length, supple tannins.*	£10.80	JLW N&P	(B)
PENFOLDS BIN 407 CABERNET SAUVIGNON 1997, PENFOLDS South Australia	*Herbaceous berry aroma with vivid mint and blackberry flavours surrounded by nice tannins.*	£11.00	Widely Available	(B)
REYNOLDS ORANGE CABERNET SAUVIGNON 1998, REYNOLDS New South Wales	*Lovely mocha and cool fruit nose, fine grained tannins provide good grip on the long finish.*	£11.00	JLW	(B)
STEVE HOFF CABERNET SAUVIGNON 1998, STEVE HOFF WINES South Australia	*Stewed plum nose leading to bags of character full of gamey fruit, vibrant tannins. Lush savoury wine.*	£11.00	AUC	(B)
YARRA GLEN GRAND CABERNET SAUVIGNON 1997, ANDREW GARRETT Victoria	*Warm stewed fruit nose with plummy fruit compote with some meatiness and good length.*	£11.00	THI	(B)
LONG GULLY CABERNET SAUVIGNON 1996, LONG GULLY ESTATE Victoria	*Grassy nose with mature complex ripe plum jam palate, grainy tannins and good backbone.*	£11.30	DBY REN WCR BOO	(B)
SIMON HACKETT FOGGO ROAD CABERNET SAUVIGNON 1997, SIMON HACKETT South Australia	*Fresh nose of redcurrants, clean berry palate with good concentration and toasty oak.*	£11.40	CPW GHL NYW WRW	(S)
BRIAN BARRY CABERNET SAUVIGNON 1998, BRIAN BARRY South Australia	*Leafy white pepper nose, rich ripe blackcurrant flavours with lithe tannins and a vibrant finish.*	£11.50	VRS	(S)

Wine	Tasting Note	Price	Stockists	
WOLF BLASS PRESIDENTS SELECTION CABERNET SAUVIGNON 1996, MILDARA BLASS South Australia	Soft vanilla nose with some mintiness fusing with gamey cassis fruits with a long tail.	£11.60	Widely Available	S
KATNOOK ESTATE CABERNET SAUVIGNON 1998, KATNOOK ESTATE South Australia	Leathery damson nose with spicy brambles, mint and blackcurrant flavours, and chewy tannins.	£11.70	ODD DBY BWL NYW	S
SIMON HACKETT FOGGO ROAD CABERNET SAUVIGNON 1996, SIMON HACKETT South Australia	Leathery plum nose, leafy savoury elements, some toffee, and a chewy dry finish.	£11.70	CPW GHL WRW	S
LANGHORNE CREEK CABERNET SAUVIGNON 1997, NORMANS South Australia	Great jammy berry fruits on the nose, ripe concentrated fruit palate that offers good length.	£12.00	PLB	B
LECONFIELD ESTATE CABERNET SAUVIGNON 1997, LECONFIELD ESTATE South Australia	Open leather and berry aroma followed by rich chocolate and fruitcake flavours with firm tannins.	£12.00	J&B	B
HAYSHED HILL CABERNET SAUVIGNON 1997, HAYSHED HILL Western Australia	Smoky cassis aroma with rich blackcurrant and milk chocolate flavours, elegant style and good length.	£12.40	NYW WRK	B
PLANTAGENET CABERNET SAUVIGNON 1997, PLANTAGENET Western Australia	Wet leaf nose mingling with spicy oak fruit, lovely firm tannins and a structured backbone.	£12.40	V&C DBY NRW NYW VDV CTC	B
XANADU CABERNET SAUVIGNON 1998, CHATEAU XANADU Western Australia	Stalky blackcurrant nose with balanced juicy red fruit, chewy tannins and an agreeable finish.	£12.50	ODD	B

GEOFF MERRILL RESERVE CABERNET SAUVIGNON 1996, GEOFF MERRILL South Australia	*Tobacco and bramble fruit aroma with spicy full fruit flavours, tight tannins with weight and acidity.*	**£13.00**	ODD SAF	**B**
YARRA VALLEY CABERNET SAUVIGNON 1995, DE BORTOLI Victoria	*Mature gamey nose with blueberry and cassis flavours, lovely velvety mouthfeel and great length.*	**£13.40**	QWW VDV N&P WRW	**S**
SHOW RESERVE CABERNET SAUVIGNON 1997, ROSEMOUNT ESTATE South Australia	*Fresh grassy and fruity aroma mixed into ripe plum flavours excellent balance and style.*	**£13.80**	ROS BNK SAF	**S**
SEPPELT DORRIEN CABERNET SAUVIGNON 1996, SEPPELT South Australia	*Leathery aromas with blueberries dipped in chocolate and spice wrapped in velvety tannins. A winter warmer!*	**£14.00**	PEF	**S**
SEPPELT DRUMBORG CABERNET SAUVIGNON 1996, SEPPELT Victoria	*Eucalyptus and deep berry nose with cool summer fruits, clean acid and brooding length.*	**£14.00**	PEF	**S**
ELDERTON CABERNET SAUVIGNON 1997, ELDERTON WINES South Australia	*Subtle blackberry leaf aroma with spicy peppery fruit, elegant oak and a lengthy finish.*	**£14.30**	ODF DBY	**B**
JOANNA LIMESTONE COAST CABERNET SAUVIGNON 1998, MOUNT LANGI GHIRAN South Australia	*Youthful jammy oak nose with tobacco, chocolate and black cherries, an explosive delicious wine.*	**£14.50**	CTC	**S**
LINDEMANS ST GEORGE CABERNET SAUVIGNON 1996, LINDEMANS South Australia	*Minty nose of blackcurrants, mouth coating tannins and good acidity, with backbone and a long finish.*	**£14.50**	MWW ODD WCR HVW	**B**

WIRRA WIRRA **THE ANGELUS 1997,** **WIRRA WIRRA** South Australia	*Inviting nose with liquid chocolate, stewed plums and strawberry flavours, firm acidity and lovely balance.*	£15.00	ODF DBY WSO BBO	B
WIRRA WIRRA **THE ANGELUS 1996,** **WIRRA WIRRA** South Australia	*Ripe blackcurrant nose fusing with a velvety texture of raspberries, currants and full tight tannins. Beautiful.*	£15.10	ODF WTS DBY BBO ESL	G
THE MENZIES **COONAWARRA** **CABERNET SAUVIGNON** **1997, YALUMBA** South Australia	*Herbaceous nose, rich mulberry and toffee flavours, with clean tight tannins and a glowing finish.*	£15.10	Widely Available	B
COPPERMINE ROAD **CABERNET SAUVIGNON** **1998, D'ARENBERG** South Australia	*Big smoky nose, dense dark fruit, rather chewy tannins leading to a strong brash end.*	£15.30	ODD CTC DBY HST COM	B
PETALUMA COONAWARRA **CABERNET SAUVIGNON** **1998, PETALUMA** South Australia	*Exotic spicy nose, intense minty liquorice flavours with a great structure and a hint of oak.*	£15.60	Widely Available	B
PENLEY ESTATE **CABERNET SAUVIGNON** **RESERVE 1994,** **PENLEY ESTATE** South Australia	*Excellent floral red berry nose, a concentrated fruit palate with velvety texture and firm tannins.*	£15.90	JLW VDV OWC	S
ARTHUR'S CREEK **CABERNET SAUVIGNON** **1994, ARTHUR'S CREEK** **ESTATE** Victoria	*Nice mellow plum fruit on a medium bodied palate with good grip. Showing nice maturity.*	£16.00	BBR	B
SUMMERFIELD **CABERNET SAUVIGNON** **1997, SUMMERFIELD** Victoria	*Herbaceous ripe cassis nose leading to vanilla and blackberry, young tannins and mellow acid.*	£16.50	BBR	S

LEASINGHAM CLASSIC CLARE CABERNET SAUVIGNON 1997, BRL HARDY South Australia	*Minty berry nose with spicy crushed raspberry fruit, beautiful structure and a pleasant acid tail.*	£18.40	ODD DBY NYW VDV WCR VIL	(S)
H SERIES CABERNET SAUVIGNON 1998, HASELGROVE South Australia	*A blockbuster of damsons and dark berries on this youthful wine with a drying smooth finish.*	£18.40	LIB NYW DIC VIL	(B)
MOUNTADAM CABERNET SAUVIGNON 1995, MOUNTADAM South Australia	*Chocolate mints on the nose fusing with dusty ripe plums with lithe structure and a lingering finish.*	£18.40	ADN MAD NYW JNW DBY	(B)
MOUNTADAM CABERNET SAUVIGNON 1996, MOUNTADAM South Australia	*Liquorice allsorts nose with spicy oak and currants displaying elegant structure and balance.*	£18.90	ADN ODF DBY MAD NYW JNW	(G)
HOLLICK RAVENSWOOD CABERNET SAUVIGNON 1994, HOLLICK South Australia	*Rich raspberry nose with some leafiness, good tannin and full ripe fruit. Elegant wine.*	£19.80	NYW JNW VDV HST AMW HVW BEL	(B)
ST ANDREWS CABERNET SAUVIGNON 1997, WAKEFIELD ESTATE South Australia	*Soft integrated cracked black pepper, spice and sweet blackcurrants, good mouthfeel and length.*	£20.00	SWS	(B)
LAGAN ESTATE RESERVE CABERNET SAUVIGNON 1997, CHATEAU XANADU Western Australia	*Menthol camphor nose, rich warm cassis fruit and good acidity with chewy tannins.*	£23.00	ODD	(B)
GRANT BURGE SHADRACH 1996, GRANT BURGE South Australia	*Dusty cedar nose blending with rich big style fruit palate ,some spiciness and fine tannins.*	£30.90	BDR COM DBY MAD BLS OWC WRW	(B)

CABERNET SAUVIGNON • AUSTRALIA

PENFOLDS BIN 707 CABERNET SAUVIGNON 1997, PENFOLDS South Australia	*Luscious blackcurrant with smoky vanilla on a polished palate, ripe tannins and lovely length. Class.*	**£35.90**	Widely Available	(G)
JOHN RIDDOCH CABERNET SAUVIGNON 1997, WYNNS ESTATE South Australia	*Minty plummy nose with baked summer fruits balancing well with ripe tannins and good acidity. Just scrumptious.*	**£36.20**	Widely Available	(S)
CYRIL HENSCHKE CABERNET SAUVIGNON 1996, HENSCHKE South Australia	*Mocha blackcurrant nose complimented by rich bramble fruit flowing to a tidy tail. Plenty of life left.*	**£39.30**	JLW NYW VDV HST	(S)

AUSTRALIA • CHARDONNAY

PARSONS BROOK CHARDONNAY 1999, ESSINGTON ESTATE South Eastern Australia	*Lemony nose, lovely ripe fruit palate, great length, some light oak brings out lots of flavour.*	**£4.30**	CTC	(B)
WOOLPUNDA CHARDONNAY 1998, THOMSON VINTNERS South Australia	*Fig preserve on toast aroma, buttery smooth mouthfeel of juicy fruits and creamy acid.*	**£4.50**	AHW TOS	(S)
BANROCK STATION CHARDONNAY 1999, BRL HARDY South Eastern Australia	*Attractive soft fruity nose, pleasant clean, fresh green apples and peaches, good enjoyable length.*	**£4.70**	Widely Available	(B)
HARDY'S NOTTAGE HILL CHARDONNAY 1999, BRL HARDY South Eastern Australia	*Delightful fruity nose leads to lovely clean, fresh and well balanced tropical citrus grapefruit flavours.*	**£4.90**	Widely Available	(S)

JINDALEE CHARDONNAY 1998, JINDALEE ESTATE South Eastern Australia	*Warm inviting ripe fruit nose, excellent integration of vanilla and acid fruits. Full bodied, long finish.*	£5.00	SAF	(S)
ANDREW PEACE CHARDONNAY 1999, ANDREW PEACE Victoria	*Green pears and dry oak nose, hints of butter, attractive full bodied palate of juicy fruits, refreshing acidity.*	£5.00	BGL	(B)
ANGOVE'S CLASSIC RESERVE CHARDONNAY 1999, ANGOVE'S South Australia	*Honeyed fruit nose, full bodied delicious buttery fruit palate, creamy mouthfeel and vanilla characters.*	£5.00	MWW JAG CAM	(B)
LINDEMANS BIN 65 CHARDONNAY 1999, LINDEMANS South Eastern Australia	*Fresh green aromas, integrated oak with citrus juicy fruit on a soft creamy palate and good length.*	£5.00	Widely Available	(B)
NORMANS PENDULUM CHARDONNAY 1999, NORMANS South Eastern Aust	*Ripe fruit on the nose, creamy grapefruit and pears on palate, full bodied citric acidity, pleasant finish.*	£5.00	WTS	(B)
NORMANS UNWOODED CHARDONNAY 1999, NORMANS South Eastern Australia	*Interesting green fruits and creamy aromas, gorgeous creamy texture of ripe fruit with nice acidity.*	£5.00	TOS	(B)
SAFEWAY AUSTRALIAN OAKED CHARDONNAY 1999, BRL HARDY South Eastern Australia	*Rich lifted tropical fruit with creamy oak palate, funky fruit acid, firm tannins on a crisp finish.*	£5.00	SAF	(B)
JACOB'S CREEK CHARDONNAY 1999, ORLANDO WYNDHAM South Eastern Australia	*Lots of melon and citrus on the nose, well balanced, complex, great citrus on the finish.*	£5.10	Widely Available	(B)

NEW WORLD SOUTH EASTERN AUSTRALIA CHARDONNAY 1999, NEW WORLD WINES South Eastern Australia	*Tropical pineapple nose, rich flirty tropical fruit in full bodied palate, delightful long finish.*	**£5.10**	QWW BOO	**B**
NORMANS LONE GUM CHARDONNAY 1999, NORMANS South Eastern Australia	*Smooth honey, silky texture, good fruits, rich, full bodied, attractive wine, well integrated acidity.*	**£5.10**	ODD CAM DIC	**B**
MIRANDA CHARDONNAY 1999, MIRANDA South Eastern Australia	*Hot tropical vanilla nose with pineapple, citrus flavours fusing with clean acidity and a pleasant finish.*	**£5.30**	AVB RNS QWW NYW WCS CTC	**S**
MIRANDA CHARDONNAY 1998, MIRANDA South Eastern Australia	*Citrus green nose with soft attractive peaches and cream flavours reaching to the end.*	**£5.40**	AVB RNS QWW NYW CTC	**S**
ANDREW MCPHERSON CHARDONNAY 1999, MCPHERSON South Eastern Australia	*Citrus peel and lovely oak on the nose, delicious creamy ripe fruit, beautiful balance.*	**£5.40**	BDR OWC	**B**
CRANSWICK ESTATES CASTLE CREEK CHARDONNAY 1999, CRANSWICK ESTATES South East Australia	*Appley candied fruit nose, very delicate apples and pear flavours with good acidity.*	**£5.40**	WAC	**B**
MITCHELTON THOMAS MITCHELL CHARDONNAY 1999, MITCHELTON Victoria	*Fresh green fruit nose, citrus well integrated to a full palate of ripe fruit developing into a lovely finish.*	**£5.40**	JWS RAV WCS	**B**
MIRANDA BROTHERS OAK AGED CHARDONNAY 1999, MIRANDA South Eastern Australia	*Fetching vanilla and fruit nose, good balance, enjoyable ripe fruit with peach notes and good length.*	**£5.50**	BDR WCS	**S**

AUSTRALIA • CHARDONNAY

KINGSTON ESTATE WILDLIFE CHARDONNAY 1998, KINGSTON ESTATE South Eastern Australia	*Inviting fresh fruit and nutty characters on the nose and palate, excellent fruit finish.*	£5.70	BNK OWC	(S)
DOUBLE BAY CHARDONNAY 1998, RIVERINA South Eastern Australia	*Great ripe fruit nose, fresh fruits and vanilla palate, pleasant oak and acidity, elegant extended finish.*	£6.00	WAV	(G)
E&C MCLAREN VALE CHARDONNAY 1999, SOUTHCORP South Australia	*Captivating fresh summer fruits on the nose, ripe pears on the palate, lovely enticing finish.*	£6.00	ODD	(S)
LINDEMANS LIMESTONE COAST CHARDONNAY 1998, LINDEMANS South Australia	*Tropical fruit nose with citrus flavours coming out on a well structured wine with balanced acidity.*	£6.00	JSM OWC	(B)
MALLEE POINT CHARDONNAY 1999, CASELLA South Australia	*Spiced pears on the nose, very good green fruit palate, pleasant long fresh finish.*	£6.00	SWS	(B)
TESCO MCLAREN VALE CHARDONNAY 1998, MAGLIERI South Australia	*Honey blossoms and herbaceous nose with lemons and melon flavours, fresh acidity and complexity.*	£6.00	TOS	(B)
WILLANDRA CHARDONNAY 1998, WILLANDRA South Eastern Australia	*Herbaceous tropical flavours with clean acidity balanced with firm tannins and a good length.*	£6.00	QWW NYW HDS GRO	(B)
THE MILL CHARDONNAY 1999, WINDOWRIE ESTATE New South Wales	*Gorgeous butterscotch and vanilla aromas on the nose, superb acidity gives freshness, great finish.*	£6.10	CPR RNS NYW PBA AMW	(S)

LENNARD'S CROSSING CHARDONNAY 1999, MCGUIGAN South Eastern Australia	*Charming fresh fruit on the nose, ripe peaches and lovely acidity on the palate and clean finish.*	£6.10	QWW ESL OWC CST	(B)
TATACHILLA MCLAREN VALE CHARDONNAY 1999, TATACHILLA South Australia	*Butterscotch nose with sunny pineapple and mango, hints of spice. Clean acid and refreshing.*	£6.20	MWW	(B)
WYNDHAM ESTATE BIN 222 CHARDONNAY 1999, ORLANDO WYNDHAM South Eastern Australia	*Zingy notes of orange peel and lime, good acidity, lovely weight with apricots on the tail.*	£6.40	CVR A&A OWC FEN	(B)
JACOB'S CREEK RESERVE CHARDONNAY 1998, ORLANDO WYNDHAM South Eastern Australia	*Nice light oak aromas, big powerful flavours of peach and delicious oak and soft finish.*	£6.50	OWC	(S)
BEST'S VICTORIA CHARDONNAY 1999, BEST'S GREAT WESTERN Victoria	*Good weight of fruit, well balanced, lightly toasted oak, refreshing finish, very simple and captivating.*	£6.50	SWS JNW	(B)
KINGSTON ESTATE CHARDONNAY 1998, KINGSTON ESTATE South Australia	*Lovely intense oak on the nose leads to very pleasant round fruit flavours on the palate.*	£6.50	BNK CVR JSS OWC	(B)
D'ARENBERG OLIVE GROVE CHARDONNAY 1999, D'ARENBERG South Australia	*Honey and melon nose with oak on the fruity palate and tannins flowing to the finish.*	£6.60	Widely Available	(B)
WARBURN ESTATE OAK AGED CHARDONNAY 1999, RIVERINA New South Wales	*Very strong fruity aromas, ripe tropical fruits on the palate, full bodied, enjoyable with good length.*	£6.60	BDR	(B)

AUSTRALIA • CHARDONNAY

TYRRELL'S OLD WINERY CHARDONNAY 1999, TYRRELL'S South Eastern Australia	*Rich pears on the nose, lovely well balanced apples and peaches, a rich, complex wine with good length.*	£6.70	JSM CPW VIL WCS CTC	**B**
HOPE ESTATE CHARDONNAY 1999, HOPE ESTATE New South Wales	*Full bodied wine with smooth creamy fruits on nose and palate, great length and fresh finish.*	£6.90	SWS CEB BOO	**B**
RIDDOCH ESTATE CHARDONNAY 1998, RIDDOCH ESTATE South Australia	*Warm butterscotch nose, ripe bananas and vanilla flavours beautifully incorporated to a delicious fruit structure.*	£7.00	BWL SAF CTC	**S**
WOLF BLASS SOUTH AUSTRALIAN CHARDONNAY 1999, MILDARA BLASS South Australia	*Creamy sweet grapefruit nose, elegant style, full structure, fresh fruits and well incorporated acidity.*	£7.00	Widely Available	**S** WINE OF THE YEAR
MAGLIERI CHARDONNAY 1999, MAGLIERI South Australia	*Lovely appley fruit nose, sweet peaches and peas on the palate, well balanced, a fine delicious finish.*	£7.00	Widely Available	**B**
PENFOLDS THE VALLEYS CHARDONNAY 1998, PENFOLDS South Australia	*Beautiful vanilla and oak on the nose followed by juicy fruit palate with very good weight.*	£7.00	Widely Available	**B**
PEPPER TREE RESERVE CHARDONNAY 1998, PEPPER TREE New South Wales	*Buttery toasted and flowery fruits on the nose and palate with attractive contribution of acidity.*	£7.00	VIL	**B**
CHATEAU TAHBILK CHARDONNAY 1998, CHATEAU TAHBILK Victoria	*Full rich style, depth of flavour, tropical and fruit driven and a long vanilla finish.*	£7.10	DBY JMC VDV	**B**

DIAMOND VALLEY CHARDONNAY BLUE LABEL 1998, DIAMOND VALLEY Victoria	*Light vanilla and lemony nose, good ripe apples on the palate with round finish and lovely length.*	**£7.20**	NYW	(S)
WYNNS COONAWARRA ESTATE CHARDONNAY 1997, WYNNS ESTATE South Australia	*Earthy melon aromas, a fully concentrated lovely wine of ripe citrus and apricots on a lengthy finish.*	**£7.20**	ODD GHL NYW WCR POR	(B)
WAKEFIELD ESTATE UNWOODED CHARDONNAY 1999, WAKEFIELD ESTATE South Australia	*Inviting floral nose, ripe fruit on the palate with hints of apples and peas, good length.*	**£7.30**	GHL WRW	(B)
ROUGE HOMME CHARDONNAY 1999, SOUTHCORP South Australia	*Delicious fresh raspberry nose followed by captivating ripe fruit, intense fresh acidity and long finish.*	**£7.40**	MAD NYW AMW RHV CTC	(G)
WAKEFIELD ESTATE CHARDONNAY 1998, WAKEFIELD ESTATE South Australia	*Intense fruit on the nose, full bodied, fresh flavours of melon and grapefruit, good balance.*	**£7.40**	NYW WRW	(S)
LEASINGHAM DOMAINE CHARDONNAY 1997, BRL HARDY South Australia	*Full mouthfeel of limes, lemons and butterscotch with hints of oak and a clean tannic end.*	**£7.40**	WTS DBY JMC WCR VIL	(B)
PETER LEHMANN CHARDONNAY 1998, PETER LEHMANN South Australia	*Toasted vanilla on the nose, creamy juicy fruit salad on the palate with lovely finish.*	**£7.40**	CFT G&M	(B)
CHAPEL HILL UNWOODED CHARDONNAY 1998, CHAPEL HILL South Australia	*Glorious lemon aroma with full bodied palate of citrus and a clean smooth finish.*	**£7.50**	TOS AUC	(S)

TRIALL HILL OAK AGED CHARDONNAY 1998, MIRANDA South Eastern Australia	*Oaky citrus fruit nose followed by good weight on the palate, good structure, lively firm finish.*	**£7.50**	Widely Available	**B**
ROSEMOUNT ESTATE YARRA VALLEY CHARDONNAY 1999, ROSEMOUNT ESTATE Victoria	*Special lemon and oak notes integrated in a fruity complex wine with a long acid finish.*	**£7.60**	ROS	**B**
JIM BARRY CLARE CHARDONNAY 1999, JIM BARRY South Australia	*Citrus and pear aromas lead to rich oak that supports well some apple and citrus flavours.*	**£7.70**	ODD DBY MAD QRW BEN	**B**
SEPPELT CORELLA RIDGE CHARDONNNAY 1998, SEPPELT Victoria	*Apple on the nose, fresh fruit notes of peach, pineapple with oak and good length.*	**£7.80**	TNI NYW OWC	**B**
BASEDOW CHARDONNAY 1998, BASEDOW South Australia	*Fabulous and tropical on the palate, with well balanced fruit flavours and a gentle oak finish.*	**£7.90**	HVW	**S**
COLDSTREAM HILLS CHARDONNAY 1997, COLDSTREAM HILLS Victoria	*Buttery apricot fruit on the nose, hints of vanilla mingling with citrus and ending with delightful acidity.*	**£8.00**	ODD WCR	**S**
ENDEAVOUR CHARDONNAY 1998, HEATHFIELD RIDGE South Australia	*Hints of sweet spice on the nose, with delicate citrus and pineapple fruit palate, good acidity.*	**£8.00**	SAF	**B**
MAMRE BROOK CHARDONNAY 1998, SALTRAM ESTATES South Australia	*Soft fruity nose is followed by fresh and well balanced vanilla and ripe grapefruit flavours.*	**£8.00**	Widely Available	**B**

ALLANDALE HUNTER VALLEY CHARDONNAY 1998, ALLANDALE New South Wales	*Complex and interesting perfumed nose, with notes of banana and pineapple on the finish.*	£8.20	AUC BEL	**B**
NEPENTHE UNWOODED CHARDONNAY 1999, NEPENTHE South Australia	*Fresh fruit nose, delicious light fruit well balanced with high acidity. Captivating finish and good length.*	£8.70	GRT ODD DBY EDC BOO	**S**
ST HALLETT CHARDONNAY 1998, ST HALLETT South Australia	*Forward and rich vanilla aromas with pleasant toasty notes on a spicy finish.*	£8.70	AUC NRW HVW	**B**
HEGGIES VINEYARD CHARDONNAY 1997, YALUMBA South Australia	*Smoky bacon oak and hints of ripe pears on the nose and palate with a delicate finish.*	£9.00	ODF JNW	**B**
MARIENBERG RESERVE CHARDONNAY 1998, MARIENBERG South Australia	*Lively tropical ripe fruit on nose and palate with good fruity acid and a long finish.*	£9.00	HFI	**B**
TATACHILLA ADELAIDE HILLS CHARDONNAY 1998, TATACHILLA South Australia	*Delicious fruit nose followed by long fruity mouthfeel with very good intensity and juicy finish.*	£9.00	SAF	**B**
HOLLICK CHARDONNAY 1996, HOLLICK South Australia	*Toasty aromas develop into buttery fruits on the palate with notes of pears and tropical fruit.*	£9.10	JNW VDV HDS AMW	**B**
MITCHELTON ESTATE CHARDONNAY 1997, MITCHELTON Victoria	*Strong tropical nose leads to a palate of round and ripe sweet fruits with toasty oak.*	£9.10	JEF AMW WCS	**B**

WIRRA WIRRA CHARDONNAY 1998, WIRRA WIRRA South Australia	*Plenty of good ripe fruit on the nose and palate, well balanced oak and acidity. Smooth finish.*	£9.20	ODD WTS BBO	**B**
CHATEAU REYNELLA CHARDONNAY 1998, BRL HARDY South Australia	*Elegant, well balanced lemony fruits and pleasant wood, interesting warm mouth feel with long finish.*	£9.30	ESL WCR VIL FEN	**S**
CHATSFIELD CHARDONNAY 1998, CHATSFIELD Western Australia	*Great fruity nose with lovely sharp lemon hints in a bed of well balanced ripe fruit flavours.*	£9.50	HOT	**B**
PAUL CONTI CHARDONNAY 1998, PAUL CONTI Western Australia	*Young flavour of balanced and integrated fruits and oak with notes of butter and good acidity.*	£9.50	OWC	**B**
ROSEMOUNT ESTATE SHOW RESERVE CHARDONNAY 1998, ROSEMOUNT ESTATE New South Wales	*Subtle vanilla nose followed by tropical ripe fruit balanced with clean acid and fine tannins.*	£9.80	Widely Available	**B**
E&C SECTION 353 CHARDONNAY 1997, SOUTHCORP South Australia	*Toasty ripe fruits and vanilla nose, intense round fruit palate with extremely pleasant finish.*	£10.00	ODF	**S**
GEOFF MERRILL RESERVE CHARDONNAY 1997, GEOFF MERRILL South Australia	*Smoky honey nose leads to a full bodied palate with delicious fruit and oak balance.*	£10.00	PLE	**B**
EBENEZER CHARDONNAY 1999, BRL HARDY South Australia	*Well balanced fresh acidity and well integrated oak to lemony fruits, long tasteful finish.*	£10.30	ESL VIL	**B**

PLANTAGENET CHARDONNAY 1998, PLANTAGENET Western Australia	*Very aromatic wine with nectar palate and pleasant oak, creamy almondy finish and very good balance.*	£10.30	V&C NRW NYW VDV HDS GRO CTC	**B**
BLUE PYRENEES ESTATE CHARDONNAY 1998, BLUE PYRENEES ESTATE Victoria	*Fresh nose, hints of apples and pears with lovely presence of oak and a long fresh finish.*	£10.60	TOS QWW COM	**S**
ROSEMOUNT ESTATE GIANTS CREEK CHARDONNAY 1998, ROSEMOUNT ESTATE New South Wales	*Lovely oak on the nose, ripe pear and peaches on the palate with good length.*	£10.70	BNK	**B**
KATNOOK ESTATE CHARDONNAY 1998, KATNOOK ESTATE South Australia	*Very attractive honeyed nose, restrained pleasant fruit intensity with notes of pepper, zesty acidity, finishes delicately.*	£11.00	BWL	**B**
BEST'S GREAT WESTERN CHARDONNAY 1998, BEST'S GREAT WESTERN Victoria	*Ripe clean fruit, slightly honeyed attractive nose and ripe fruit flavour with citrus notes.*	£11.20	GRT DBY	**B**
NEPENTHE CHARDONNAY 1998, NEPENTHE South Australia	*Very pleasant tropical melons on the nose followed by rich zesty fruits and vanilla tones.*	£11.30	GRT ODD DBY BOO COM	**S**
YARRA VALLEY CHARDONNAY 1998, DE BORTOLI Victoria	*Delicate peach nose, well balanced acidity on the palate with vanilla scents, giving warm mouthfeel and clean finish.*	£11.50	WTS DBY BNK QWW VDV N&P WRW	**S**
TUNNEL HILL CHARDONNAY 1999, TARRAWARRA Victoria	*Fresh, chewy and appetising nose, great structure, full bodied providing excellent company for food.*	£11.50	BBO ASH CTC	**B**

MIRANDA FAMILY RESERVE CHARDONNAY 1998, MIRANDA WINES Victoria	*Complex, toasted oak and butterscotch, generous refreshing acidity in a bed of sweet fruit.*	£11.60	AVB QWW NYW WCS CTC	**G**
NEPENTHE CHARDONNAY 1997, NEPENTHE South Australia	*Subtle oak nose, full ripe tropical peachy characters, delicate firm tannins, long elegant finish.*	£11.60	ODD BOO	**B**
PENFOLDS ADELAIDE HILLS CHARDONNAY 1998, PENFOLDS South Australia	*Light nose followed by mineral fruit, subtle oak and balanced complexity. Good length.*	£12.00	Widely Available	**B**
RED HILL CHARDONNAY 1999, RED HILL Victoria	*Pronounced appley nose, strong buttery oak with nice acidity and ripe fruit, good length.*	£12.00	NWG	**B**
LENSWOOD KNAPPSTEIN CHARDONNAY 1997, LENSWOOD KNAPPSTEIN South Australia	*Exciting ripe oak fruit on the nose and palate leads to a big round finish.*	£12.60	BWC VDV	**B**
MOUNTADAM CHARDONNAY 1997, MOUNTADAM South Australia	*Citrus aromas on the nose, toasty buttery palate with lots of complex and ripe flavours.*	£13.10	Widely Available	**S**
EILEEN HARDY CHARDONNAY 1997, BRL HARDY South Australia	*Fantastic nose with good fruit and a honeyed complex palate produces a rich mouthfeel.*	£13.70	DBY ESL VDV JSS VIL	**B**
PETALUMA CHARDONNAY 1998, PETALUMA South Australia	*Lovely inviting fruity nose followed by amazing rich full bodied structure with refreshing acidity.*	£14.00	Widely Available	**S**

ROSEMOUNT ESTATE ORANGE VINEYARD CHARDONNAY 1999, ROSEMOUNT ESTATE New South Wales	*Rich fruity nose, pleasant full bodied stonefruits on the palate with a good balance of acidity.*	£14.20	WCR BEL	**B**
STONIER RESERVE CHARDONNAY 1998, STONIER Victoria	*Lovely sugar in nose, very nice fruit on palate, pleasant weight and good length.*	£14.30	ODF MZC VIL	**B**
PETALUMA CHARDONNAY 1997, PETALUMA South Australia	*Big ripe fruit aroma leads to a pleasant ripe tropical creamy texture. Seductive extended finish.*	£14.40	Widely Available	**B**
DEVILS LAIR CHARDONNAY 1998, DEVILS LAIR Western Australia	*Pineapple and vanilla on the nose leads to rich round melons and gooseberry flavours with creamy mouthfeel.*	£14.60	Widely Available	**S**
VASSE FELIX HEYTESBURY CHARDONNAY 1999, VASSE FELIX Western Australia	*Nice intensity in this very fruity and balanced oak nose and palate with toasty notes.*	£14.60	DBY QWW NYW VDV HST HVW	**B**
DROMANA RESERVE CHARDONNAY 1998, GARRY CRITTENDEN Victoria	*Interesting integration of oak, vanilla and fruit. Seriouspalate of well meshed cashews and cantelope.*	£14.70	COM QWW NYW PIM BOO	**B**
COLDSTREAM HILLS RESERVE CHARDONNAY 1998, COLDSTREAM HILLS Victoria	*Subtle oak in a very well balanced honey and citrus fruit structure with a hint of greenness*	£15.00	ODD	**B**
ST ANDREWS BARREL FERMENTED CHARDONNAY 1998, WAKEFIELD ESTATE South Australia	*Creamy and sweet nose, good structure, fresh subtle acidity supporting fruit flavour with a pleasant finish.*	£15.00	SWS	**B**

AUSTRALIA • CHARDONNAY

TarraWarra Chardonnay 1998, TarraWarra Victoria	*Baked apples on the nose, excellent weight on the palate, plenty of juicy ripe fruit characters.*	£15.30	ODF DBY BBO CTC	**S**
Dalwhinnie Estate Chardonnay 1998, Dalwhinnie Estate Victoria	*Fresh smokey nose leads to vanilla pudding flavours in the mouth with a beautiful finish.*	£15.50	J&B NYW	**B**
Tyrrell's Vat 47 Pinot Chardonnay 1999, Tyrrell's New South Wales	*Attractive fresh citric nose, subtle cheese palate with melon characters and a pleasant long finish.*	£16.30	Widely Available	**S**
Pipers Brook Summit Chardonnay 1998, Pipers Brook Tasmania	*Lovely smooth fruity nose, ripe raspberries and peaches and hints of tobacco, with wonderful acidity.*	£18.80	CPR PBA JSS VIL HVW WCS BOO	**B**
Other Side Chardonnay 1998, d'Arenberg South Australia	*Spicy oak and herbaceous characters on the nose, luscious pineapple and cantaloupe melons on the finish.*	£20.40	CTC VDV HST COM	**B**
Rosemount Estate Roxburgh Chardonnay 1997, Rosemount Estate New South Wales	*Fresh raspberries on the nose and palate with elegant oak integration, smooth fruity finish.*	£30.40	UNS POR	**S**

AUSTRALIA • FORTIFIED

Penfolds Magill Tawny, Penfolds South Australia	*Smacked in the face with this candied peel and walnut style, good high acidity and length.*	£6.00	Widely Available	**S**

STANTON & KILLEEN RUTHERGLEN MUSCAT, STANTON & KILLEEN Victoria	*Deep rich aromas of ripe mellow fruit, clean and balanced, very attractive blend with good acidity.*	£7.00	WSO BNK NYW VDV AMW HVW	(S)
CAMPBELLS RUTHERGLEN MUSCAT, CAMPBELLS Victoria	*Deep gold colour, attractive ripe fruit nose, deep muscat with some acidity, clean balanced stylish structure.*	£7.20	Widely Available	(S)
SEPPELT DP63 RUTHERGLEN SHOW MUSCAT, SEPPELT Victoria	*Amazing nose melding freshnes with age, lovely rancio poise and length to die for.*	£8.00	ODD NYW OWC	(G) TROPHY WINE
YALUMBA MUSEUM MUSCAT, YALUMBA South Australia	*Golden brown with red hues, warm caramel aromas, lovely rich syrupy style with some nice acidity.*	£8.90	QRW QWW TNI NYW	(B)
SANDALFORD SANDALERA, SANDALFORD Western Australia	*Amber gold, rich nutty caramel nose with toffee and raisins, wonderful intensity and excellent balance.*	£10.00	HBJ	(B)
NOSTALGIA RARE TAWNY, D'ARENBERG South Australia	*Blue mountain coffee and dried fruit aromas, intense sweet lemon peel on the finish.*	£10.70	ODD NYW	(S)
BROWN BROTHERS LIQUEUR MUSCAT, BROWN BROTHERS Victoria	*Very deep brown colour, balanced delicate muscat aromas and taste, mellow rich ripe fruit.*	£13.00	Widely Available	(B)
DE BORTOLI BLACK NOBLE, DE BORTOLI New South Wales	*Deep amber colour, fantastic style on the nose, concentrated silky, nutty, pruney flavours. Full on sweetness.*	£14.10	Widely Available	(B)

AUSTRALIA • FORTIFIED

ANTIQUE TAWNY, YALUMBA South Australia	*Mature rich notes with a well balanced structure, complex figs and nuts on the finish.*	£18.20	ODF DBY QWW NYW VDV BEN	S
CAMPBELLS MERCHANT PRINCE RARE RUTHERGLEN MUSCAT, CAMPBELLS Victoria	*Inviting olive rim, intense ripe fruit flavours and good acidity. Rich warm mouthfeel.*	£31.90	ODF TNI RHV	S

AUSTRALIA • MERLOT

MCGUIGAN BLACK LABEL MERLOT 1999, MCGUIGAN WINES South Australia	*Good honest fruit with mint and plumpudding on the nose, brimming with style and character.*	£5.20	Widely Available	G
JJ MCWILLIAM MERLOT 1998, MCWILLIAMS New South Wales	*Savoury rich nose with blackcurrant and bramble leaves, smooth on the palate, long firm finish.*	£7.70	BBO UNS ASH CTC	B
JAMIESONS RUN MERLOT 1998, MILDARA BLASS South Australia	*Smokey, spice nose with full bodied plums and currants, celebrated with soft tannins and an elegant finish.*	£8.00	ODD VIL	S
WOLF BLASS MERLOT 1998, MILDARA BLASS South Australia	*Fruit cake aromas with sun baked strawberries and plums, balanced structure and velvety tannins.*	£8.00	Widely Available	B
MAGLIERI MERLOT 1998, MAGLIERI South Australia	*Sweet mint aromas on an inviting palate of cassis and plums with roasted coffee hints.*	£9.00	Widely Available	B

CERAVOLO MERLOT 1999, ST ANDREW'S ESTATE South Australia	*Stylish black fruit, intriguing earthy nose with warm juicy plums wrapped in silky tannins and a lovely tail.*	£10.00	ECA	**B**
TEMPLE BRUER RESERVE MERLOT 1997, TEMPLE BRUER South Australia	*Juicy red currant aromas, captivating black cherry flavour with toastiness, good acid and firm tannins.*	£10.00	TOS	**B**
OAKRIDGE ESTATE MERLOT 1998, OAKRIDGE ESTATE Victoria	*Juicy herbal fruit mingling with smokey warm black cherries with firm tannins and good length.*	£10.70	GRT	**B**
HEGGIES MERLOT 1996, YALUMBA South Australia	*Smokey warm young berries hinting of mint with soft tannins, fresh acidity and a big finish.*	£12.50	ODF QWW NYW VDV BEN WRW	**B**
KINGSTON RESERVE MERLOT 1997, KINGSTON ESTATE South Eastern Australia	*Tempting plummy nose with eucalyptus hints. Good concentration of fruit flavour on palate with firm finish.*	£12.60	BBO BNK OWC	**B**
TATACHILLA CLARENDON VINEYARD MERLOT 1998, TATACHILLA South Australia	*Mint julep and dark plum inviting nose cascading onto a fruit laden palate, green tannins and good length.*	£12.80	ODD DBY CAM QWW NYW	**S**
ROSEMOUNT ESTATE ORANGE VINEYARD MERLOT 1998, ROSEMOUNT ESTATE New South Wales	*Gentle minty fruit nose with full rich juicy fruit palate of lovely intensity and length.*	£13.70	Widely Available	**S**
BRIAN BARRY MERLOT 1998, BRIAN BARRY South Australia	*Luscious entry of black-currants hinting at pep-permints wrapped in vel-vety tannins. Wonderful structure and finish.*	£15.00	VRS	**S**

AUSTRALIA • MERLOT

COLDSTREAM HILLS MERLOT 1998, COLDSTREAM HILLS Victoria	*Green leafy aromas fusing with cassis fruit and hints of chocolate with balance and style.*	**£15.00**	ODD	**B**
ELDERTON MERLOT 1997, ELDERTON South Australia	*Green leafy plum nose with attractive mature fruit and lovely balanced tannins and acid.*	**£18.00**	ODF DBY	**B**

AUSTRALIA • RED • OTHER

SOMMERFIELD AUSTRALIAN DRY RED 1999, SOUTHCORP South Eastern Australia	*Lovely raspberry nose, creamy oak and tart fruit, structured tannins and good acidity, light fruity finish.*	**£4.00**	SMF	**B**
BANROCK STATION SHIRAZ MATARO 1999, BRL HARDY South Eastern Australia	*Subtle fruit nose, oak intensity on the palate but some underlying clean fruit character.*	**£4.10**	Widely Available	**B**
MIRANDA OPAL RIDGE SHIRAZ CABERNET 1999, MIRANDA South Eastern Australia	*Young and fresh with upfront fruit, offering instant pleasure this friendly little number is ready to go.*	**£4.60**	AVB QWW JSS WCS CTC	**B**
MHV NINE PINES AUSTRALIAN SHIRAZ 1998, CRANSWICK ESTATE New South Wales	*Seriously structured enticing wine with great depth of fruit flavour and a lovely satin balanced feel.*	**£5.00**	MHV	**B**
McGUIGAN BLACK LABEL 1999, McGUIGAN South Australia	*Smokey bacon nose, spicy, tobacco and cedar oak flavours. Underlying fruit character needs time to develop.*	**£5.20**	Widely Available	**S**

MIRANDA CABERNET SHIRAZ 1999, MIRANDA South Eastern Australia	*Attractive sweet fruit nose, intense depth of flavour on palate, very stylish with cherry finish.*	**£5.40**	AVB QWW WCR WCS CTC	**S**
KINGSTON WILDLIFE MOURVEDRE 1998, KINGSTON ESTATE South Eastern Australia	*Inviting concentrated spicy tannin, smokey, earthy, redcurrant fruit flavours with a pleasing length and structure.*	**£6.00**	Widely Available	**B**
ROSEMOUNT NEW AUSTRALIAN RED 1999, ROSEMOUNT ESTATE New South Wales	*Light and fresh fruit on the nose, pleasant easy drinking style, nice long fruity character.*	**£6.00**	PFC	**B**
SAMUELS BAY GRENACHE 1997, ADAM WYNN South Australia	*Savoury, developed nose, sweet strawberry fruit, lighter style of wine that is ready for consumption.*	**£6.00**	FQU	**B**
TESCO MCLAREN VALE GRENACHE 1998, MAGLIERI South Australia	*Light dark cherry and chocolate aroma, traces of sweetness assist fruit character, good acidity.*	**£6.00**	TOS	**B**
BLEASDALE MALBEC 1999, BLEASDALE South Australia	*Tobacco nose with jammy ripe black plums and cherries with spiciness and a dry tail.*	**£6.20**	TOS	**S**
ROUGE HOMME SHIRAZ CABERNET 1998, SOUTHCORP South Australia	*Well evolved bouquet of jam, earth and spice with soft rounded tannins, quality fruit flavours, memorable finish.*	**£6.20**	ODD DBY AMW POR RHV	**S**
DEEN DE BORTOLI VAT 1 DURIF 1998, DE BORTOLI New South Wales	*Strong spicy fruit character, good use of oak, full ripe fruit palate with fine tannins.*	**£6.30**	BNK CAM VDV WRW RHV	**S**

WATTLE PARK MCLAREN VALE GRENACHE SHIRAZ 1999, TATACHILLA South Australia	*Good varietal lift, chewy and juicy fruit weight on the palate, interesting bitter sweet finish.*	**£6.40**	CAM QWW NYW	(B)
WOLF BLASS RED LABEL SHIRAZ CABERNET 1998, MILDARA BLASS South Australia	*Spice and leather nose, full fruit on a dry austere palate with many layers, round texture.*	**£6.60**	Widely Available	(B)
JACOB'S CREEK LIMITED RELEASE SHIRAZ CABERNET 1995, ORLANDO WYNDHAM South Eastern Australia	*Full of mouthfilling big, ripe, red fruits consistent on both the nose and palate. Amazing.*	**£6.80**	OWC	(S)
PENFOLDS BIN 2 1998, PENFOLDS South Eastern Australia	*Lovely vanilla nose, good quality fruit on a lingering palate, layered oak and silky fruit tannins.*	**£6.80**	Widely Available	(B)
WAKEFIELD ESTATE SHIRAZ CABERNET 1999, WAKEFIELD ESTATE South Australia	*Rich leather nose, supple red fruits, rounded and soft tannins with a dash of spice.*	**£6.90**	DBY	(B)
BETHANY GRENACHE 1999, BETHANY South Australia	*Dark cherry and pepper nose, nice balance, interesting fruit character, long cherry fruit finish.*	**£7.00**	MWW CAM UNS WCR COM	(B)
ESSINGTON CABERNET SHIRAZ 1998, ESSINGTON ESTATE New South Wales	*Plenty of plums and quite young fruit, very pleasant and rich texture, delicious cherries on finish.*	**£7.00**	CTC	(B)
LARAGHY'S GRENACHE SHIRAZ 1998, LARAGHY South Australia	*Lovely weight and intensity, ripe raspberry fruit ahead of fine tannins with strawberry on the finish.*	**£7.00**	AUC	(B)

TEMPLE BRUER SHIRAZ MALBEC 1997, TEMPLE BRUER South Australia	*Earthy and vegetal, bonfire smoke aromas, fat and meaty, richly balanced on a well weighted palate.*	**£7.00**	TOS	**B**
IRONSTONE SHIRAZ GRENACHE 1998, CAPE MENTELLE Western Australia	*Smokey, gamey nose, full ripe intense palate of tar and spice, silky tannins on finish.*	**£7.10**	Widely Available	**B**
PETER LEHMANN GRENACHE SHIRAZ 1999, PETER LEHMANN South Australia	*Good varietal lift, chewy and juicy fruit weight on the palate, interesting bitter sweet finish.*	**£7.10**	ODD G&M	**B**
WILLOW PARK CABERNET SHIRAZ 1998, PLUNKETT WINES Victoria	*Warm plum and mint nose, good intensity of minty blackberry jelly flavours, clean long finish.*	**£7.20**	ALL	**B**
D'ARRY'S ORIGINAL GRENACHE SHIRAZ 1998, D'ARENBERG South Australia	*Interesting violet and blackcurrant nose, good fruit definition, acidity provides elegance and balance. Will last.*	**£7.30**	CTC DBY NYW BTH VDV COM WES	**S**
BROWN BROTHERS BARBERA 1998, BROWN BROTHERS Victoria	*Sweet berries and a smokey nose, mouthful of rich fruit compote, well integrated clean finish.*	**£7.30**	Widely Available	**B**
WYNNS COONAWARRA ESTATE CABERNET SHIRAZ MERLOT 1997, SOUTHCORP South Australia	*Complex nose with some age, soft earthy characters on a nice fruit palate, drying slowly.*	**£7.30**	ODD TOS NRW NYW WBR POR	**B**
YALDARA RESERVE CABERNET MERLOT 1998, YALDARA South Australia	*Very attractive maturing nose, gorgeous structure, lots of sweet vanilla, concentrated jam and an oaky finish.*	**£7.40**	GRT RAV NYW VDV VIW BOO	**B**

JACOB'S CREEK LIMITED RELEASE SHIRAZ CABERNET 1996, ORLANDO WYNDHAM South Eastern Australia	*Concentrated spice, mint and liquorice aroma, warm feel with soft and supple tannins, round lasting finish.*	£7.50	OWC	**S**
STONYFELL METALA SHIRAZ CABERNET 1998, SALTRAM South Australia	*Spicy, earthy and meaty nose with strong tannin and acid composition compliments the generous fruit flavours.*	£7.50	ODD SAF DBY NRW NYW AMW HVW	**S** WINE OF THE YEAR
HASELGROVE GRENACHE SHIRAZ 1998, CRANSWICK ESTATE South Australia	*Leather and plum nose, juicy fruit, not overly complex but contains good quality fruit.*	£7.50	BDR	**B**
ROVALLEY RIDGE BAROSSA VALLEY SHIRAZ 1996, MIRANDA South Australia	*The nose is rich and opulent with signs of maturity, the palate is ripe, luscious and mouthfilling.*	£7.50	Widely Available	**B**
BEST'S GREAT WESTERN DOLCETTO 1996, BEST'S GREAT WESTERN Victoria	*Lively red fruits on the nose with old fashion toffee and a strong blasting end.*	£7.60	DBY SWS JNW	**B**
FOUR SISTERS GRENACHE SHIRAZ 1998, FOUR SISTERS South Australia	*Sweet plums and violets on the nose, juicy fruit, light balance and clean finish.*	£7.60	V&C NYW JNW VIL WRW CTC	**B**
TATACHILLA PARTNERS CABERNET SAUVIGNON SHIRAZ 1999, TATACHILLA South Australia	*Smooth fruit nose, complex, ripe berries and rich cabernet characters, lovely fresh fruit finish.*	£7.60	BDR	**B**
PIRRAMIMMA PETIT VERDOT 1997, AC JOHNSTON South Australia	*A tempting savoury nose with soft ripe strawberries and spice flavours with a long peppery finish.*	£7.70	MWW DBY	**S**

STONYFELL METALA SHIRAZ CABERNET 1997, SALTRAM South Australia	*Pencil shaving aromas, peppermint on the palate, great depth of flavour that has a layered structure.*	**£7.70**	Widely Available	**S**
ROVALLEY RIDGE BUSH VINE GRENACHE 1997, MIRANDA Victoria	*Plum and leather aroma, well integrated fruit and oak, quality tannins with signs of ageing complexity.*	**£7.80**	AVB WCR JSS CTC	**B**
OMRAH MERLOT CABERNET SAUVIGNON 1998, PLANTAGENET Western Australia	*Rich and velvety style with complex fruit layers showing a fine long lingering finish.*	**£8.00**	V&C ESL NYW VDV GRO POR CTC	**B**
TEMPLE BRUER CABERNET MERLOT 1996, TEMPLE BRUER South Australia	*Minty, blackcurrant nose, vanilla and sweet fruit on the palate with lovely tannins and good length.*	**£8.00**	SPR	**B**
PETER LEHMANN CLANCY'S RED 1998, PETER LEHMANN South Australia	*Invigorating fruit aroma, assertive spicy flavours that give a pleasant mouthfeel and a lasting flavour.*	**£8.10**	Widely Available	**B**
KNAPPSTEIN CABERNET MERLOT 1998, KNAPPSTEIN South Australia	*Delicate perfumed nose, big wine with plenty of tannins, well balanced into lovely long berry flavours.*	**£8.20**	ODD MZC SAF VDV OWC	**G**
NINTH ISLAND PINOT NOIR 1999, PIPERS BROOK Tasmania	*Bramble and raspberry jam nose, a hint of spice on the palate, medium acidity with good lingering fruit.*	**£8.30**	Widely Available	**B**
PENFOLDS ORGANIC RED 1998, PENFOLDS South Australia	*Fresh fragrant berry fruit, hints of allspice blended with funky blackcurrant flavours. Good length.*	**£8.40**	Widely Available	**B**

Wine	Tasting Note	Price	Stockists	Medal
YALUMBA BAROSSA GROWERS CABERNET SAUVIGNON SHIRAZ 1998, YALUMBA South Australia	*Ripe black fruit with minty, eucalyptus nose, good complex palate, soft ripe fruit and long finish.*	£8.40	MAD QRW WSO JNW	**B**
NORMANS OLD VINES GRENACHE 1998, NORMANS South Eastern Australia	*Youthful, very intense dark cassis and marzipan aromas, creamy, subtle oak and velvety mouthfeel.*	£8.50	SAF	**S**
ROUGE HOMME CABERNET MERLOT 1996, SOUTHCORP South Australia	*Ripe cassis on nose, some berry fruits and oak with good length and firm tannic finish.*	£8.50	ODD WRW	**B**
THE TWENTY EIGHT ROAD MOURVÈDRE 1998, D'ARENBERG South Australia	*Distinctively peppery on the nose with a palate that has complex, ripe fruit characters.*	£8.80	ODD CTC DBY NYW BTH VDV COM	**S**
HILLSTOWE BUXTON MERLOT CABERNET 1998, HILLSTOWE South Australia	*Charming, good wood and a berry nose leads to a delicious warm fruit texture with a lovely warm, embracing finish*	£8.80	ODD WRK	**B**
CAPEL VALE CABERNET MERLOT 1998, CAPEL VALE Western Australia	*Elegant complex fruit nose, good weight and balance of strong tannins with a peppery blackcurrant finish.*	£8.90	CFT GRO WRW	**B**
MAWSONS YALUMBA 1998, YALUMBA South Australia	*Delicious blackcurrant nose, well structured palate, good depth of fruit with a very pleasant finish.*	£9.00	NEG	**B**
MT HELEN CABERNET MERLOT 1998, MILDARA BLASS Victoria	*Intense sweet blackberry aromas, good tannins and lots of oak, well balanced with delicious fruit.*	£9.00	ODD	**B**

PAUL CONTI PINOT NOIR 1999, PAUL CONTI Western Australia	*Vanilla, chocolate and red fruit aromas, persistent fruity length, a well balanced commercial style.*	£9.00	OWC	B
WILKIE ESTATE CABERNET MERLOT 1998, WILKIE ESTATE Victoria	*Lifted oak, herbal nose, very pleasant ripe blackcurrants on palate, interesting wine, easy to drink.*	£9.00	BGL	B
CHITTERING ESTATE CABERNET MERLOT 1998, CHITTERING ESTATE Western Australia	*Chocolate oak and berries on the nose, earthy palate, gripping tannins and a pleasant round texture.*	£9.10	WBR	S
'T' BARBERA 1999, GARY CRITTENDEN Victoria	*Fresh, rich cherry nose, a clean easy drinking style, long bitter dried fruit finish.*	£9.10	WTS PIM WRK BOO COM	B
MCLAREN VALE PICTURE SERIES GRENACHE 1998, HASELGROVE South Australia	*Elegant pepper, spice and plum aromas with flavours consisting of cassis and an intense raspberry complexity.*	£9.20	CTC NYW DIC OWC VIL CTC	S
EVANS & TATE BARRIQUE 61 CABERNET MERLOT 1999, EVANS & TATE Western Australia	*Sweet dark fruits on the nose and palate with smooth buttery hints. Good tannins.*	£9.20	OWC HVW	B
WIRRA WIRRA CHURCH BLOCK 1998, WIRRA WIRRA South Australia	*Rich cassis nose, contains very pleasant acidity and structure of warm juicy fruit. Hot to trot.*	£9.20	ADN ODD WTS DBY WSO BBO JSS	B
HUT BLOCK CABERNETS 1998, RICHARD HAMILTON South Australia	*Deeply fruited nose, blackberry palate with vanilla savoury elements and blueberry characters. Nicely balanced finish.*	£9.40	CTC	S

BLEASDALE FRANK POTTS 1997, BLEASDALE South Australia	*Very rich dark liquorice nose, giving generously to a refined and conservative style.*	£9.50	ODD	B
CHARLES CIMICKY DAYLIGHT CHAMBER GRENACHE 1998, CHARLES CIMICKY South Australia	*A prolific style of wine, herby and minty with ripe jammy fruit and an elegant edge.*	£9.70	BDR WRW BOO COM	S
DEVILS LAIR FIFTH LEG RED 1998, DEVILS LAIR Western Australia	*Smooth berry fruits on the nose followed by rich complex, blackcurrant flavours with deliciously good length.*	£9.70	GRT ODF NYW VDV	S
LEASINGHAM SHIRAZ MALBEC 1998, BRL HARDY South Australia	*Cinnamon and nutmeg nose, tarry berried fruit, dry grippy tannins, well structured to the end.*	£9.70	DBY VDV VIL	B
CORNERSTONE GRENACHE MOURVÈDRE SHIRAZ 1998, CORNERSTONE South Australia	*Each variety is well complimented, fine structure and balance, firm, juicy finish and delicate tannins.*	£9.90	DBY AUC	B
WIRRA WIRRA ORIGINAL BLEND 1998, WIRRA WIRRA South Australia	*Deep fruit and spicy nose merge to a delectable fruit palate offering quality oak integration.*	£9.90	ODD DBY WSO BBO	B
PRIMO ESTATE IL BRICONE 1998, PRIMO ESTATE South Australia	*Exquisite ripe cherries married with vanilla, producing a warm, black fruit attack on the palate.*	£10.00	DBY AUC NYW	G
RIDDOCH ESTATE SHIRAZ 1998, RIDDOCH ESTATE South Australia	*Intensely perfumed nose, fine concentration of flavour and strong tannin harmony. Finely tuned and balanced.*	£10.00	BWL CTC	S

TEMPLE BRUER CABERNET PETIT VERDOT 1998, TEMPLE BRUER South Australia	*Sweet, almost smokey nose, attractive oak and tannins are well integrated on the fruity palate.*	**£10.00**	Widely Available	(S)
BRIAN BARRY SHIRAZ MERLOT 1998, BRIAN BARRY South Australia	*A delightfully refreshing nose leads to a well balanced, bright, berry fruit palate.*	**£10.00**	VRS	(B)
TIM ADAMS THE FERGUS 1998, TIM ADAMS South Australia	*Intense ripe varietal character that deserves time to broaden and bloom to show its true character.*	**£10.00**	AUC FQU NYW	(B)
XANADU SECESSION SHIRAZ CABERNET 1999, CHÂTEAU XANADU Western Australia	*Aromas of toasted walnuts and white chocolate, bright creamy tart on palate with lovely acidity.*	**£10.00**	ODD	(B)
'T' SANGIOVESE 1998, GARY CRITTENDEN Victoria	*Bitter fruit aromas, soft ripe fruit on the finish with gripping tannins.*	**£10.20**	WTS PIM WRK COM	(B)
VASSE FELIX CABERNET SAUVIGNON MERLOT 1998, VASSE FELIX Western Australia	*Intense, rich plum and black fruit on the nose and palate with a smokey cedar hint. Very nice style.*	**£10.20**	QRW CPW VDV BEN WCR TAN HVW	(B)
YERING STATION PINOT NOIR 1998, YERING STATION Victoria	*Spicy red fruit aromas, well structured acid and fruity tannins flow through onto a long, luscious finish.*	**£10.30**	QWW NYW HDS COM	(S)
WILLOW CREEK PINOT NOIR 1998, WILLOW CREEK Victoria	*Slightly subdued redcurrant aromas, deep intense fruit palate offering high acidity and good length.*	**£10.30**	EOR	(B)

BETHANY CABERNET MERLOT 1998, BETHANY South Australia	*Mocha and hazelnut nose, hints of oak in a red and black fruity palate, good firm tannins.*	£10.50	MWW CAM COM	**B**
'T' NEBBIOLO 1997, GARY CRITTENDEN Victoria	*Herbaceous leafy fruit nose, touch of sweet cranberries on the palate, firm tannic structure.*	£10.60	PIM WRK BOO COM	**S**
LEASINGHAM CABERNET MALBEC 1998, LEASINGHAM ESTATE South Australia	*Sweet fruit on the nose, lifted blackcurrant on the palate, full of tannins but well balanced.*	£10.60	FQU VDV WCR VIL	**B**
GRANT BURGE FILSELL OLD VINE SHIRAZ 1997, GRANT BURGE South Australia	*Big, bright, raspberry fruit, good structure on palate, superb length with vanilla oak influence.*	£10.90	Widely Available	**B**
STONIER PINOT NOIR 1998, STONIER Victoria	*Good sweaty saddle nose yields to a well made, rich, concentrated fruit palate with good length.*	£11.00	ODF NYW VIL	**B**
COLDSTREAM HILLS PINOT NOIR 1999, COLDSTREAM HILLS Victoria	*Fresh, fruity nose is confirmed on the palate revealing lashings of strawberry fruit and vanilla oakiness.*	£11.20	ODD NYW WBR	**B**
BLUE PYRENEES ESTATE RED 1997, BLUE PYRENEES ESTATE Victoria	*Toasty blackberry aromas with full bodied chocolatey summer berry fruit with a spicy, textured finish.*	£11.30	TOS COM	**B**
FAMILY RESERVE SHIRAZ CABERNET 1996, MIRANDA Victoria	*A nose of blackcurrant fruit and oak aromas lead to a fine fruit driven finish.*	£11.40	AVB CTC	**B**

LAKE BREEZE BERNOOTA 1998, LAKE BREEZE South Australia	*A heady nose of vanilla and mint precedes a sweet vanilla oak palate with balanced acidity.*	£11.50	NYW	(S)
PENLEY ESTATE SHIRAZ CABERNET 1997, PENLEY ESTATE South Australia	*Quality fruit and clever oak handling has produced a wine of strong character with a bright future.*	£11.70	JLW PIM	(B)
HILLSTOWE UDY'S MILL PINOT NOIR 1998, HILLSTOWE WINES South Australia	*Oak driven nose with rich, meaty undertones, concentrated floral palate and nice persistent fruity finish.*	£12.00	ODD	(B)
PLANTAGENET PINOT NOIR 1998, PLANTAGENET Western Australia	*Beautiful new oak nose with fruit underneath is confirmed on the palate with a long intense finish.*	£12.10	V&C DBY BLU NRW VDV POR CTC	(S)
KINGSTON RESERVE PETIT VERDOT 1997, KINGSTON ESTATE WINES South Australia	*Dark summer pudding nose with spicy cherries and strawberries with crisp acidity and sweet finish.*	£12.40	WTS BBO OWC	(S)
NEPENTHE PINOT NOIR 1999, NEPENTHE South Australia	*Elegant brambly nose. Sweet, fat cranberry and orange juice palate with medium weight and decent length.*	£12.40	GRT ODF DBY NYW BOO COM	(B)
ROSEMOUNT ESTATE GSM 1998, ROSEMOUNT ESTATE South Australia	*Creamy vanilla, luscious spice and fruit nose is complimented by the subtle use of oak.*	£12.80	WTS DBY QWW FQU	(S)
PEACOCK NORMANS 1997, NORMANS	*Forward ripe black fruit with hints of spice and green pepper on the palate, delicious long finish.*	£13.00	Widely Available	(S)

RED HILL PINOT NOIR 1998, RED HILL Victoria	*Rich vegetal, strawberry and sweet red cherry nose, complex long spicy fruit palate and a long full finish.*	£13.00	NWG	(S)
SPRINGWOOD PARK PINOT NOIR 1997, ANDREW GARRETT South Australia	*Good vegetal, fruity nose gives way to a sweet tinned strawberry palate and nice length.*	£13.00	THI	(B)
PENFOLDS BIN 389 CABERNET SHIRAZ 1997, PENFOLDS South Australia	*Spicy clove nose, mixed berry flavours with a complex, well balanced structure. Elegant wine.*	£13.20	Widely Available	(S)
PELLION PINOT NOIR 1998, PIPERS BROOK Tasmania	*Chocolate and plumy aromas with hints of tastiness yield to soft red fruit and a full finish.*	£13.30	Widely Available	(B)
NEPENTHE THE FUGUE CABERNET MERLOT 1998, NEPENTHE South Australia	*Gorgeous gamey nose fusing with rich brambles and berries, well balanced and smooth tannins.*	£13.70	GRT ODF NYW BOO COM	(B)
LINDEMANS PYRUS 1997, LINDEMANS South Australia	*Toasty jammy nose leading to warm plums and spice, rich, dense and balanced. Wonderful complexity.*	£14.00	Widely Available	(G)
YARRA VALLEY PINOT NOIR 1998, DE BORTOLI Victoria	*Meaty, chocolate and oaky aromas, offers gripping tannins, toffee and strawberry flavours, good acidity.*	£14.00	DBY BNK QWW VDV WRW	(S)
OLD GARDEN MOURVEDRE 1998, HEWITSON South Australia	*Immense smokey and berry nose, chocolate, leather complexity, youthful tannins and a smooth finish.*	£14.00	WAW	(B)

CAMPBELLS **THE BARKLY DURIF** **1996, CAMPBELLS** Victoria	*Warm, jammy, spicy nose, palate displays an interesting blend of confected fruit and earthy liquorice notes.*	£14.10	ODF DBY MAD CPW VDV COM RHV	**B**
LINDEMANS **LIMESTONE RIDGE 1997,** **LINDEMANS** South Australia	*Aromas of sweet plum, pepper and spice, enveloped by rich dark chocolate, palate is soft and generous.*	£14.50	ODD DBY WBR WCR JSS	**S**
ROSEMOUNT ESTATE **TRADITIONAL 1998,** **ROSEMOUNT ESTATE** South Australia	*Juicy, spicy fruit with captivating savoury plums and berry flavours, good balance and bold tannins.*	£14.60	BNK FQU WCR POR	**S**
D'ARENBERG IRONSTONE **PRESSINGS GSM 1998,** **D'ARENBERG** South Australia	*An explosion of the senses. Earthy spiciness aromas and a palate filled with rich fruit flavours.*	£14.70	ODD CTC DBY VDV HST COM	**S**
VASSE FELIX SHIRAZ **1998, VASSE FELIX** Western Australia	*Tangy raspberry aromas precede a palate rich in oak with warm complexing flavours, nice clean finish.*	£14.90	DBY CPW NYW BEN HST	**B**
LENSWOOD **PINOT NOIR 1998,** **LENSWOOD KNAPPSTEIN** South Australia	*Sweet, red bramble fruit nose. Attractive silky palate, persistent tannins and nicely integrated oak finish.*	£15.00	BWC NYW VDV	**G**
BROWN BROTHERS **PINOT NOIR 1997,** **BROWN BROTHERS** Victoria	*Huge ripe red fruit, rhubarb and vegetal aromas. Full strawberry palate with subtle oak and good acidity.*	£15.00	BRB	**S**
CHARLES CIMICKY **THE RED BLEND 1997,** **CHARLES CIMICKY** South Australia	*Rich cassis fruit with chocolate and cedar hints on a concentrated palate with excellent fruit tannins.*	£15.00	SWS	**B**

MARGARET RIVER CABERNET MERLOT 1997, DEVILS LAIR Western Australia	*Dense ripe berry nose, hints of chocolate and earth, dark plum flavours, great acidity and length.*	£15.40	ODF NYW VDV CFT	(S)
STONIER RESERVE PINOT NOIR 1998, STONIER Victoria	*Hints of eucalyptus and mint on the nose, relatively intense strawberry palate, good structure and length.*	£16.50	ODF DBY VIL	(B)
TARRAWARRA PINOT NOIR 1998, TARRAWARRA Victoria	*Forest fruit hints with tarry, toasty oak are confirmed on a complex palate offering crisp acidity.*	£16.50	ODF DBY BBO GHC	(B)
THE SIGNATURE 1996, YALUMBA South Australia	*Smokey spice nose with full bodied berry and plum flavours with powerful tannins, ending well.*	£16.90	Widely Available	(S)
YERING STATION RESERVE PINOT NOIR 1998, YERING STATION Victoria	*Red berry fruit with oaky undertones are held together by alluring tannins. Opulent.*	£17.00	NYW HDS	(G)
TYRRELL'S VAT 8 SHIRAZ CABERNET 1997, TYRRELL'S South Eastern Australia	*Maturity on the nose, a palate of both red and black fruits and seamless oak integration.*	£17.10	ODF QWW NYW VDV WCS	(G)
JOSEPH MODA AMARONE 1998, PRIMO ESTATE South Australia	*Spicy high notes with warm sweet plum jam fruits, plenty of character and lively tannins.*	£17.30	DBY AUC NYW	(S)
COLDSTREAM HILLS RESERVE PINOT NOIR 1998, COLDSTREAM HILLS Victoria	*Subtle red fruit and smokey aromas with hints of pepper. Nice strawberry finish.*	£17.30	ODD NYW	(B)

ELDERTON CSM 1996, ELDERTON WINES South Australia	*Rich, ripe sweet berry nose, balanced warm palate with good intensity and lovely length.*	**£18.70**	ODF DBY POR	**B**
CLARENDON HILLS OLD VINES GRENACHE 1997, CLARENDON HILLS South Australia	*Stewed black cherries and wild fruit fragrances intensify on the palate and finish clean.*	**£19.00**	J&B	**B**
CHARLES MELTON NINE POPES 1998, CHARLES MELTON South Australia	*Subtle nose flows to a smooth, seamless palate and shows a remarkable persistence of flavour.*	**£19.40**	Widely Available	**S**
THE HOLY TRINITY 1996, GRANT BURGE South Australia	*Confected, spice and peppered fruit, apparent on both nose and palate, creates a well structured wine.*	**£20.70**	Widely Available	**B**
VASSE FELIX HEYTESBURY 1998, VASSE FELIX Western Australia	*Liquorice and spice nose with intense ripe brambly fruit, lively acidity and excellent length.*	**£23.30**	DBY QWW NYW VDV BEN HST	**S**
MOUNTAIN BLUE SHIRAZ CABERNET 1997, ROSEMOUNT ESTATE New South Wales	*Intense nose with powerful black fruit oak and pepper tones, medium weight palate, nice balance.*	**£25.10**	DBY POR	**B**
DIAMOND VALLEY ESTATE PINOT NOIR 1998, DR DAVID LANCE Victoria	*Young raspberries and fine hide leather aromas with a rich complex palate evoking a good beef wellington.*	**£25.50**	HOT	**S**
HOUGHTON JACK MANN 1996, BRL HARDY Western Australia	*Intense dried fruit and spice nose fusing with black crushed pepper and juicy plums. Awesome wine.*	**£28.80**	ODF WTS DBY NYW	**G**

AUSTRALIA • RIESLING

PENFOLDS BIN 202 RIESLING 1999, PENFOLDS South Australia	*Attractive and succulent style on the palate, a dry clean finish from this fruit driven wine.*	**£4.70**	Widely Available	(B)
TESCO OVERTLY AROMATIC WHITE NV, BRL HARDY South Australia	*Pleasant ripe fruit on the nose, rich mouthfeel with pineapples and lemons, long and lingering.*	**£5.00**	TOS	(B)
WYNNS COONAWARRA ESTATE RIESLING 1999, WYNNS ESTATE South Australia	*Rich and bursting with lime and lemon fruit, great acidity carrying this the whole nine yards.*	**£5.00**	Widely Available	(B)
PEWSEY VALE RIESLING 1997, YALUMBA South Australia	*Developed nose of apricots and dried fruits, good bite and length on the delicious palate.*	**£6.00**	FQU TOS	(B)
PEWSEY VALE RIESLING 1999, YALUMBA South Australia	*Attractive tropical fruit and limes, with a hint of residual sugar which provides the body and nice structure.*	**£6.10**	QRW TOS BEN	(B)
PETER LEHMANN EDEN VALLEY RIESLING 1999, PETER LEHMANN South Australia	*A fine example of true Riesling grown in a cool climate, showing limes ready squeezed.*	**£6.30**	ODD TMW G&M	(B)
WAKEFIELD ESTATE RIESLING 1996, WAKEFIELD ESTATE South Australia	*Easy and refreshing style, limes and richness with some residual sugar on the finish.*	**£6.40**	SWS VDV WRK	(S)

ELDERTON RIESLING 1999, ELDERTON South Australia	*Lime juice on the nose of this wine, a drier style, well balanced and pleasing.*	£7.50	ODF	**S**
MITCHELTON BLACKWOOD PARK RIESLING 1999, MITCHELTON Victoria	*Keylime Pie on the nose of this fresh floral crisp wine, a palate of pineapple notes, lush finish.*	£7.70	WSO ESL GHL WCS	**S**
TIM ADAMS RIESLING 1999, TIM ADAMS South Australia	*Richly aromatic, with good fruit development on the palate, subtle passionfruit tinges and well balanced.*	£7.70	AUC TOS	**B**
ANDREW GARRETT MARTINDALE HALL RIESLING 1998, ANDREW GARRETT South Australia	*Aged honeyed nose, pleasing richness in the mouth with crystallised pineapple notes on the conclusion.*	£8.00	THI	**S**
BROWN BROTHERS FAMILY RESERVE RIESLING 1997, BROWN BROTHERS Victoria	*Good aged character with hints of toast, touches of orange blossom on the syrupy finish.*	£8.50	MWW DBY CPW NRW OWC WRW	**S**
PENFOLDS EDEN VALLEY RIESLING 1999, PENFOLDS South Australia	*Refreshing spritz on the tongue, with lightweight body, grass and nettles on the finish.*	£8.60	ODD WTS SAF BTH	**B**
MOUNT LANGI GHIRAN RIESLING 1999, MOUNT LANGI GHIRAN Victoria	*Orange blossom nose with ripe pear fullness, hints of spice and steeliness, rich long finish.*	£8.90	V&C DBY NYW JNW VIL WRK CTC	**B**
CRAWFORD RIVER RIESLING 1998, CRAWFORD RIVER Victoria	*Full bodied and balanced, lime marmalade on freshly buttered toast appeal to the end.*	£9.60	J&B NYW	**B**

PIPERS BROOK RIESLING 1998, PIPERS BROOK Tasmania	*Bursting with over ripe fruit flavours, off dry and very stylish with subtle floral character.*	£10.50	Widely Available	**S**
MOUNT HORROCKS WATERVALE RIESLING 1999, MOUNT HORROCKS South Australia	*Almonds on the nose with green fruit hints on the palate, long enjoyable finish.*	£10.60	LIB NYW VDV CTC	**B**

AUSTRALIA • SEMILLON

BALLINGAL SEMILLON 1999, RIVERINA WINES New South Wales	*Crisp citrus aromas with lemon butteriness and tropical fruits on the palate with good length.*	£3.50	VKW	**B**
MHV AUSTRALIAN SEMILLON NV, REDELLO WINES New South Wales	*Delicious ripe tropical fruit nose, some oakiness on a pineapple and apricot palate with great acidity.*	£4.20	MHV	**S**
ROSEMOUNT ESTATE SEMILLON 1999, ROSEMOUNT ESTATE South Eastern Australia	*Subdued fruit nose, fresh citric and herbaceous palate, well balanced structure with good length.*	£5.30	MWW	**B**
PETER LEHMANN SEMILLON 1999, PETER LEHMANN South Australia	*Wonderfully structured wine. Light lemony nose followed through with lean citrus fruit and refined acidity.*	£5.80	Widely Available	**B**
BARRINGTON ESTATE PENCIL PINES SEMILLON 1999, BARRINGTON ESTATE New South Wales	*Hefty grassy, vegetal nose, lemon acidity with pineapple fruit, pea pod flavours with oaky undercurrents.*	£6.00	BGL	**B**

MAGLIERI SEMILLON 1999, MAGLIERI South Australia	*Attractive, grassy aromatics. Rich, clean concentrated citrus fruit with subtle acidity and reasonable length.*	£7.00	Widely Available	B
ANNIE'S LANE SEMILLON 1999, MILDARA BLASS South Australia	*Gentle, subtle grassy aromas give way to a palate of very ripe fruit with nice balancing acidity.*	£7.20	SAF	B
BETHANY SEMILLON 1998, BETHANY South Australia	*Ripe fruit nose is lifted on the palate by zippy acidity and clean fresh fruit.*	£8.00	CAM COM	B
FERNHILL ESTATE SEMILLON 1998, FERNHILL ESTATE South Australia	*Oily nutty nose, nice integrated wood and fruit palate with a full firm, persistent finish.*	£8.70	OWC ASH	S
TIM ADAMS SEMILLON 1998, TIM ADAMS South Australia	*Rich vanilla and zesty lemon with full fresh fruit with fantastic acidity and creaminess. Set for a long life.*	£8.70	AUC TOS WSO FQU	B
MOUNT PLEASANT ELIZABETH SEMILLON 1994, MCWILLIAMS New South Wales	*Rich toasty, honeyed nose, concentrated fruit ladened palate with subtle acidity and great depth of flavour.*	£8.80	TOS NYW CTC	S
ST HALLETT SEMILLON SELECT 1998, ST HALLETT South Australia	*Elegant citrus nose with buttery oak incorporated with the crisp green summer fruit palate.*	£9.00	AUC NRW	S
MARGAN FAMILY WINEGROWERS SEMILLON 1999, MARGAN FAMILY New South Wales	*Light grassy aromatics. Clean appley, slightly oaky flavour with a full rich dry finish.*	£9.00	MAD AMW RHV	B

AUSTRALIA • SEMILLON

MAXWELL TWENTY 20 SEMILLON 1999, MAXWELL WINES South Australia	*Pear drops and honey aroma with zesty lemon palate and crisp acidity at the end.*	£9.00	SWS	Ⓑ

AUSTRALIA • SHIRAZ

CO-OP JACARANDA HILL SHIRAZ 1999, ANGOVE'S South Eastern Australia	*Bramble open fruit character, fragrant, easy drinking style with clean, balanced acidity.*	£4.00	CWS	Ⓑ
TESCO AUSTRALIAN SHIRAZ 1999, GULLIN South Eastern Australia	*Displays classic telltale aromas and flavours of perfumed berries that mould the fine tannin tail.*	£4.30	TOS	Ⓑ
JINDALEE SHIRAZ 1999, JINDALEE ESTATE South Eastern Australia	*Amazing quality for its price bracket, ripe velvety wine with black fruit and full black cherry palate.*	£5.00	WTS SAF UNS	Ⓑ
WOODVALE SHIRAZ 1998, BRL HARDY South East Australia	*Great extraction, impressive depth of fruit and complex layered flavours and structure, pleasant flowing finish.*	£5.00	UNS NYW OWC	Ⓑ
GOSLING CREEK SHIRAZ 1998, HIGHLAND HERITAGE ESTATE New South Wales	*Powerful aromas of leather and spice, the dusty tannins enrich the fruit character leaving a complexing finish.*	£5.50	CHN	Ⓑ
ANGOVE'S CLASSIC RESERVE SHIRAZ 1998, ANGOVE'S South Australia	*Angove's reputation for value for money wines continues with this honest, clean and generous flavoured wine.*	£5.70	MWW JAG CAM QWW COM	Ⓑ

McGuigan Bin 2000 Shiraz 1999, McGuigan Wines South Australia	*Character and depth of fruit, well balanced with lots of ripe black cherry and plum.*	£5.90	Widely Available	**B**
Narrambla Shiraz 1998, Barrington Estate New South Wales	*Smokey mocha tones over dark fruit, nice dry balance, palate weight is rich and well integrated.*	£6.00	BGL	**B**
Three Brothers Shiraz 1999, Three Brothers New South Wales	*Leafy, peppery aroma, intense fresh raspberry and spice flavours. Nice, clean fruit acid finish.*	£6.00	BDR	**B**
The Mill Shiraz 1999, Windowrie Estate New South Wales	*Attractive floral aroma, nice dry balance, good acid and tannins, palate richly flavoured.*	£6.10	CPR RNS NYW PBA AMW	**B**
Essington Shiraz 1999, Essington Estate Adelaide Plains	*Open, leafy plummy aroma, concentrated and up front blackberry flavours with hints of violet.*	£6.20	DIC CTC	**S**
Seppelt Terrain Shiraz 1999, Seppelt South Eastern Australia	*Medium bodied, generous, dark cherry palate immersed in fine tannins and flowing to a lingering finish.*	£6.20	NYW CTC	**S**
Deen de Bortoli Vat 8 Shiraz 1999, de Bortoli New South Wales	*Fruit rich nose of cherry and smokey wood, powerful palate in harmony with the firm tannin structure.*	£6.30	BNK CAM QWW WRW RHV	**S**
Echo Point Shiraz 1998, 1896 Wine Co South Australia	*Good depth of colour, fine attractive berry, vanilla nose, palate has good weight and persistent flavour.*	£6.50	FTH	**B**

AUSTRALIA • SHIRAZ

Wine	Tasting Notes	Price	Stockist	
KINGSTON WILDLIFE SHIRAZ 1998, KINGSTON ESTATE South Eastern Australia	*Jammy scented nose, subtle peppery notes, mid palate complexity, lovely clean black fruit flavours.*	£6.60	BNK OWC	**B**
WYNNS COONAWARRA ESTATE SHIRAZ 1998, WYNNS ESTATE South Eastern Australia	*Subdued, warm nose, spicy oak, full bodied, sweet plum fruit attack, good honest wine.*	£6.90	Widely Available	**B**
HOPE ESTATE SHIRAZ 1999, HOPE ESTATE New South Wales	*Striking aromas that are complex and dense with flavours of lush ripe berries and balanced oak.*	£7.00	BOO	**B**
TESCO MCLAREN VALE SHIRAZ 1997, MAGLIERI South Australia	*Gentle spicy tea and leather notes on nose, fruit driven palate, refreshing style of wine.*	£7.00	TOS	**B**
WOLF BLASS GREEN LABEL SHIRAZ 1998, MILDARA BLASS South Australia	*Seamless concentrated aroma, lovely balance with good tannins and quite prominent acidity. Youthful but well integrated*	£7.00	Widely Available	**B**
HOUGHTON SHIRAZ 1998, BRL HARDY Western Australia	*Quite full and fruity with controlled acid and tannins. Nice dry fruit finish is its best asset.*	£7.10	DBY JMC	**B**
BAILEYS SHIRAZ 1998, BAILEYS ESTATE Victoria	*The acidity is the shining light keeping the fruit up and the tannins finely tuned.*	£7.30	Widely Available	**S**
PETER LEHMANN SHIRAZ 1998, PETER LEHMANN South Australia	*Full intense profound spice aroma, well structured palate, layers of fruit, spice and oak complexity.*	£7.30	Widely Available	**S** WINE OF THE YEAR

ROSEMOUNT ESTATE SHIRAZ 1999, ROSEMOUNT ESTATE South Eastern Australia	*Robust but supple, with spicy oak, leather and great depth of dark berry fruit with earthy undertones.*	£7.30	Widely Available	(S)
WYNDHAM ESTATE BIN 555 SHIRAZ 1998, ORLANDO WYNDHAM South Eastern Australia	*Complex fruit and rich scents of polished wood and spice, lovely smooth, silky balance and ripe fruit flavours.*	£7.30	MWW CVR A&A JSS OWC COM FEN	(S)
HASELGROVE SHIRAZ 1998, HASELGROVE South Australia	*Subtle hints of fruit and spice on the nose precedes a modest palate full of fruit flavour.*	£7.30	Widely Available	(B)
LINDEMANS LIMESTONE COAST SHIRAZ 1999, LINDEMANS South Australia	*Extracted full fruit driven nose, soft tannins mixed with full bodied fruit, easy drinking wine.*	£7.30	JSM GRO	(B)
WAKEFIELD ESTATE SHIRAZ 1999, WAKEFIELD ESTATE South Australia	*Vanilla pudding nose, good lift of flavour, spice and pepper character with fine grade tannins.*	£7.30	ODD UNS NYW WRW	(B)
BANKSIDE SHIRAZ 1998, BRL HARDY South Australia	*Animal aromas, intense, rounded and complex flavours stemming from quality fruit, earthy medium finish.*	£7.40	Widely Available	(B)
BLEASDALE BREMMERSVIEW SHIRAZ 1998, BLEASDALE South Australia	*Tobacco nose, forward fruit style, big earthy, smokey fruit, silky tannins, a mouthfilling wine.*	£8.00	ODD	(S)
NORMANS OLD VINES SHIRAZ 1998, NORMANS South Eastern Australia	*Soft black fruit and spice nose, layers of smooth summer fruit achieve a persistent length of flavour.*	£8.00	Widely Available	(S)

SEPPELT CHALAMBAR SHIRAZ 1997, SEPPELT Victoria	*Fresh and vibrant spicy black fruit and pepper nose, blackcurrant and green leaf fruit intensity.*	£8.00	UNS NYW	(S)
PLANTAGENET OMRAH SHIRAZ 1998, PLANTAGENET Western Australia	*Green pepper and blackberry nose, concentrated black cherries and redcurrant flavours, deft use of oak.*	£8.20	Widely Available	(G)
WINDOWRIE SHIRAZ 1999, WINDOWRIE ESTATE New South Wales	*Eucalyptus, violets and spice nose, ripe and sweet pear like flavours, oak is well integrated.*	£8.20	PBA	(S)
D'ARENBERG FOOTBOLT OLD VINE SHIRAZ 1998, D'ARENBERG South Australia	*Layers of complexity, a very fine balance, grippy tannins and a firm lingering finish.*	£8.20	Widely Available	(B)
BROWN BROTHERS SHIRAZ 1997, BROWN BROTHERS Victoria	*'Sweet shandy' summer nose into ripe jam, good extraction of acid and tannins, rounded texture.*	£8.40	Widely Available	(S)
ROTHBURY HUNTER VALLEY SHIRAZ 1998, MILDARA BLASS New South Wales	*Medium body in style with a lovely ripe fruit character. Certainly very approachable in its youth.*	£8.40	ODD DBY WBR WCR VIL FEN	(B)
KNAPPSTEIN SHIRAZ 1997, KNAPPSTEIN South Australia	*Pepper and spice and all things nice, ripe fruit tannins provide lovely structure on this hardy wine.*	£8.50	ODD	(S)
ANNIE'S LANE SHIRAZ 1998, MILDARA BLASS South Australia	*Restrained nose exudes class, sweetish berry fruits, lingering powerful flavours, full bodied, extracted mouthfeel.*	£8.50	ODD	(B)

CAPEL VALE SHIRAZ 1998, CAPEL VALE Western Australia	*Dried and peppery fruit characters on nose and palate with a creamy vanilla oak influence.*	£8.50	SAF BTH WCR CFT WRW	**B**
RYMILL SHIRAZ 1997, RYMILL COONAWARRA South Australia	*Prestigious Coonawarra wine with flavours that shows depth, complexity and great extraction of fruit flavour.*	£8.50	MWW	**B**
LINDEMANS PADTHAWAY SHIRAZ 1997, LINDEMANS South Australia	*Ripe, lifted blackberry nose becomes more apparent on the palate with a dry, raspberry fruit intensity.*	£8.60	ODD FQU NYW	**S**
ST HALLETT BAROSSA SHIRAZ 1998, ST HALLETT South Australia	*Chocolate and plums smells of the Barossa, rich with plenty of depth. Lovely wine.*	£8.70	AUC NRW FQU	**S**
GEOFF MERRILL SHIRAZ 1998, GEOFF MERRILL South Australia	*Spirited nose, rich, warm black fruit, ripe tannins, marked acidity and a nice fruit finish.*	£8.70	ODD DIC HVW	**B**
MOUNT PLEASANT PHILIP SHIRAZ 1994, MCWILLIAMS Victoria	*Developing characters, earthiness on the nose, balance of fruit and acidity holds the wine together nicely.*	£8.70	CTC	**B**
ANTHONY'S RESERVE SHIRAZ 1998, SIMON HACKETT South Australia	*Modern and fruit driven style with a palate consisting of eucalyptus and enticing peppermint character.*	£8.90	DBY CPW ESL GHL NYW WRW	**B**
EVANS & TATE MARGARET RIVER SHIRAZ 1999, EVANS & TATE Western Australia	*Nose is all thick black fruit and pepper, the palate is similarly full and fat fruited.Luvely stuff!*	£9.00	OWC SAF	**G** TROPHY WINE

MAGLIERI SHIRAZ 1998, MAGLIERI South Australia	*Dark chocolate and vanilla mix on the nose, ripe palate with lots of sweet fruit.*	£9.00	Widely Available	(S)
PENFOLDS BIN 28 SHIRAZ 1997, PENFOLDS South Australia	*Damson and bramble nose, creamy toffee, black and red fruit flavours with an enduring finish.*	£9.00	Widely Available	(S)
BRIGHT BROTHERS McLAREN VALE SHIRAZ 1999, BRIGHT BROTHERS South Australia	*Fabulous aromas of dark fruits, spice and strawberry, splendid mouthfeel with a silky smooth finish.*	£9.00	L&S	(B)
PIRRAMIMMA SHIRAZ 1997, AC JOHNSTON South Australia	*Pleasing plum aroma, good concentration and intensity of fruit on the palate with nice acidity.*	£9.00	MWW	(B)
CHATSFIELD SHIRAZ 1997, DR KEN LYNCH Western Australia	*Nose shows some maturity and complexity, round, full and well balanced with pleasing finish.*	£9.10	BTH VDV	(B)
CAMPBELLS BOBBIE BURNS RUTHERGLEN SHIRAZ 1998, CAMPBELLS Victoria	*Light strawberry and leafy nose, attractive summer berry fruit with hints of gaminess and good intensity.*	£9.30	Widely available	(S)
HASELGROVE BENTWING WRATTONBULLY SHIRAZ 1998, HASELGROVE South Australia	*Red and black plums with a faint peppery nose, developing rich fruit cake and peppery finish.*	£9.30	SAF VIL	(S)
BRIDGEWATER MILL SHIRAZ 1997, PETALUMA South Australia	*An unconstrained wine rich in red fruit aromas, minty, spicy pepper flavours and ready to consume.*	£9.40	JSM OWC WRW	(S)

ROSEMOUNT ESTATE HILL OF GOLD SHIRAZ 1998, ROSEMOUNT ESTATE New South Wales	*Rich black currant aromas, powerful grippy tannins, damsons and bramble fruit with hints of white pepper.*	**£9.40**	SAF	(S)
MARGAN FAMILY WINEGROWERS SHIRAZ 1999, MARGAN FAMILY New South Wales	*Light strawberry fruit aroma with hints of toffee, good tannin grip and balanced acidity.*	**£9.40**	MAD NYW RHV	(B)
MAMRE BROOK SHIRAZ 1998, SALTRAM South Australia	*Attractive perfumed nose, savoury red berry fruit, slight hint of bacon, mint and rolling finish.*	**£9.50**	DBY CPR NRW PBA WRK WCS	(S)
PENFOLDS BIN 128 COONAWARRA SHIRAZ 1997, PENFOLDS South Australia	*Cedar and mint to the fore, plummy fruit and hints of tobacco signal serious stuff.*	**£9.50**	Widely Available	(S)
SANDALFORD SHIRAZ 1997, SANDALFORD Western Australia	*Nicely developed nose, spice and dark berries mingle with softened oak to give a velvety finish.*	**£9.50**	HBJ	(S)
WOODSTOCK SHIRAZ 1998, WOODSTOCK South Australia	*Broody plums and chocolate and touch of smoked meat on the nose, soft red berry fruit.*	**£9.70**	BDR MWW	(B)
ROTHBURY BROKENBACK SHIRAZ 1998, MILDARA BLASS New South Wales	*Aromas of forest fruits and sweet, spicy flavours are beautifully entwined showing deft use of oak.*	**£9.80**	ODD WTS DBY BNK CVR	(G)
TIM ADAMS SHIRAZ 1998, TIM ADAMS South Australia	*Perfumed with red cherries and strawberries, the palate shares the same intensity of sweet Clare Valley fruit.*	**£9.80**	AUC TOS NYW	(G)

ANTHONY'S RESERVE SHIRAZ 1997, SIMON HACKETT South Australia	*Red berry, herbal and lavender aromas, slightly meaty, concentrated ripe red berry fruit on a complex palate.*	£9.80	DBY CPW GHL WRW	(S)
CHAPEL HILL SHIRAZ 1998, CHAPEL HILL South Australia	*Ripe plums and freshly turned earth flow with expert oak handling, dancing balance mixed with underlying power.*	£10.00	WTS AUC FQU	(S)
E&C SECTION 353 SHIRAZ 1997, SOUTHCORP South Australia	*Powerful leather and spice nose, strong varietal character, ripe full intensity, good extraction, firm tannins.*	£10.00	ODF	(S)
MCLAREN VALE PICTURE SERIES SHIRAZ 1998, HASELGROVE South Australia	*Upfront fruit with rich ripe cherries and plums leads to a full palate showing nice balance.*	£10.00	Widely Available	(S)
CERAVOLO SHIRAZ 1999, ST ANDREW'S ESTATE South Australia	*Herby, raspberry and cinnamon aroma, attractive spicy, summer fruit with good, balanced acidity.*	£10.00	ECA	(B)
HUNTER SHIRAZ 1998, REYNOLDS New South Wales	*Here is your classic Hunter style, earthy, spice and with a good grip of fruit and tannin.*	£10.00	V&C JLW	(B)
YALUMBA BAROSSA GROWERS SHIRAZ 1998, YALUMBA South Australia	*Green pepper and black cherry aromas, sweet black fruit laced with subtle tannins and acidity.*	£10.10	QRW WSO QWW NYW JNW VDV	(S)
HYLAND SHIRAZ 1998, PENLEY ESTATE South Australia	*Slightly closed medicinal nose, concentrated, spicy fruit, firm tannins, pleasant easy drinking style.*	£10.10	JLW PIM	(B)

LEASINGHAM SHIRAZ 1996, BRL HARDY South Australia	*Strawberry, savoury smoked meat complex aroma, well balanced and lovely ripe soft berry fruit flavours.*	**£10.30**	JSM DBY VDV VIL	(S)
BAILEYS 1920's BLOCK SHIRAZ 1998, BAILEYS ESTATE Victoria	*Red berry, almond and marzipan aroma, rich ripe raspberry fruit, well balanced and savoury finish.*	**£10.40**	Widely Available	(B)
MT IDA SHIRAZ 1998, MILDARA BLASS Victoria	*Dusty, vanilla nose, ripe warm fruit on the palate with tobacco and jam characters.*	**£10.70**	ODD NYW	(G)
BETHANY SHIRAZ 1997, BETHANY South Australia	*Generous spicy and berry aromas flow towards a palate consistent with its warm climatic region.*	**£10.80**	MWW CAM WCR COM	(S)
GRANT BURGE OLD VINE SHIRAZ 1998, GRANT BURGE South Australia	*Minty, lifted strawberry, chocolate and leather aroma, purity of flavour, classy use of oak.*	**£10.80**	Widely Available	(S)
PAUL CONTI MANJIMUP SHIRAZ 1997, PAUL CONTI Western Australia	*Intensely concentrated fruit with a level of acidity that provides good fruit balance and tannin structure. Yum!*	**£11.00**	OWC	(G)
STEVE HOFF BAROSSA SHIRAZ 1998, STEVE HOFF WINES South Australia	*Youthful and slightly closed nose, hints of mint and herb, velvety texture, layers of spicy black fruit.*	**£11.00**	AUC	(S)
BEST'S GREAT WESTERN SHIRAZ 1997, BEST'S GREAT WESTERN Victoria	*Fresh minty, herbaceous nose, layers of juicy fruit including currants and raspberries with good intensity.*	**£11.00**	Widely Available	(B)

CHAPEL HILL SHIRAZ 1997, CHAPEL HILL South Australia	*Plump fruit and some savoury flavours on the nose flow to a richly textured and inviting palate.*	**£11.00**	AUC BLU FQU	**B**
WOLF BLASS PRESIDENTS SELECTION SHIRAZ 1996, MILDARA BLASS South Australia	*A fine expression of fruit and oak integration that provides a lively, fresh and delicious palate.*	**£11.20**	Widely Available	**G**
BOWEN ESTATE COONAWARRA SHIRAZ 1997, BOWEN ESTATE South Australia	*Damson, spicy oak aromas, ripe chocolatey fruit, good length, a unique yet attractive style.*	**£11.50**	AUC	**B**
TIM ADAMS SORBY SHIRAZ 1998, TIM ADAMS South Australia	*Rose and violet aromas precede a palate of tarry, berry fruit and supple tannins.*	**£11.50**	AUC	**B**
CHATEAU REYNELLA SHIRAZ 1997, BRL HARDY South Australia	*Lifted coffee and chocolate on the nose, round soft and fleshy tannins with supreme oak integration.*	**£12.00**	ODF WTS DBY NYW VDV WCR	**G**
CHATEAU REYNELLA SHIRAZ 1996, BRL HARDY South Australia	*Earthy nose opens to reveal black fruit and liquorice aromas. Astringent tannins commend the fruit flavours.*	**£12.00**	ODD WTS DBY VDV EDC VIL FEN	**B**
MILBROVALE OWENS FAMILY HUNTER VALLEY SHIRAZ 1999, MILBROVALE VINEYARDS New South Wales	*Rich, sweet plummy nose, medium weight, balanced tannins and smokey oak fruit with persistent length.*	**£12.00**	MKV	**B**
PLUNKETT RESERVE SHIRAZ 1998, PLUNKETT Victoria	*Menthol, berry fruit, chocolate aroma, sweet velvety oak, liquorice and spice flavours, cool climate style.*	**£12.00**	ALL	**B**

MAXWELL ELLEN STREET SHIRAZ 1998, MAXWELL South Australia	*Inky, spicy, intensely ripe fruit offering attractive cherry aromas with jammy fruit and sweet oak.*	£12.20	DBY NYW BOO	(S)
KINGSTON RESERVE SHIRAZ 1997, KINGSTON ESTATE South Australia	*A frisky nose of strawberries and vanilla oak, peppery palate with bramble fruit and spice.*	£12.40	BBO OWC	(S)
ST HALLETT BLACKWELL SHIRAZ 1996, ST HALLETT South Australia	*Minty nose, lovely juicy mouth filling fruit, ripe, silky tannins, vibrant structure and length.*	£12.60	AUC NRW FQU POR	(S)
HILLSTOWE MARY'S HUNDRED SHIRAZ 1998, HILLSTOWE South Australia	*Very rich and opulent nose, big mouth filling and multidimensional, lovely well balanced wine.*	£12.80	ODD WRK	(S)
OLD ADAM SHIRAZ 1997, BREMERTON South Australia	*Peppermint, chocolate and jam nose, intense ripe fruit, good acid balance, profound new oak flavours.*	£12.80	NYW VDV HDS AMW HVW COM	(S)
YARRA VALLEY SHIRAZ 1998, DE BORTOLI Victoria	*Blackberry, lifted leather character and prominent oak on the nose, soft round bramble fruit flavours.*	£12.80	DBY BNK QWW VDV N&P CFT	(S)
EBENEZER SHIRAZ 1997, BRL HARDY South Australia	*Spicy new oak nose with lots of berry fruit, excellent ripe mouthfeel, slightly dry on finish.*	£12.90	ODF DBY NYW EDC VIL	(B)
ROSSCO'S SHIRAZ 1998, STEVE HOFF South Australia	*Herb and smooth cherry fruit aroma, intense wine with quality fruit tannins and ripe strawberry flavour.*	£13.00	AUC	(S)

AUSTRALIA • SHIRAZ

MIBROVALE MV2 HUNTER VALLEY SHIRAZ 1998, MILBROVALE VINEYARDS New South Wales	Red fruit and liquorice nose, dry tannic palate with big fruit characters underneath. Good weight at finish.	£13.00	MKV	B
ROSEMOUNT ESTATE SHOW RESERVE SHIRAZ 1997, ROSEMOUNT ESTATE South Australia	Rich ripe berry fruit aromas, harmonious fruit and oak that is highly complex and needs time.	£13.30	WCR	S
GEOFF MERRILL RESERVE SHIRAZ 1996, GEOFF MERRILL South Australia	Rounded and spicy with a grip of fruit tannins that entice the intensity of flavours.	£13.50	ODD	G
GEOFF MERRILL RESERVE SHIRAZ 1995, GEOFF MERRILL South Australia	Round, rich cassis aromas flow towards the palate and mingle with tobacco and spice flavours.	£13.50	ODD	S
PLANTAGENET SHIRAZ 1997, PLANTAGENET Western Australia	Strong black pepper nose, palate displays a savoury syrah aroma of black pepper and leather.	£13.70	Widely Available	S
DAVID WYNN PATRIACH SHIRAZ 1997, ADAM WYNN South Australia	White pepper approach indicates cool climate fruit, nice oak integration gives a fine balance and tail.	£14.00	ADN DBY NYW HVW WRW PFT	S
MCGUIGAN PERSONAL RESERVE SHIRAZ 1998, MCGUIGAN South Eastern Australia	Pronounced new oak and rich varietal aroma, palate consists of cherries and a vanilla oak character.	£14.00	DBY JAG QWW JSS OWC	S
HEWITSON BAROSSA SHIRAZ 1998, HEWITSON South Australia	Some new oak and a high tone of fruit, palate has nice upfront berry fruit flavour.	£14.00	WAW	B

H SERIES MCLAREN VALE SHIRAZ 1998, HASELGROVE South Australia	*Floral and fruit aromas explode from the glass and accompany the concentrated dark berry fruit flavours.*	£14.10	CTC NYW DIC VIL	(S)
DAVID WYNN PATRIACH SHIRAZ 1996, MOUNTADAM South Australia	*Rich cassis nose, sweet impression on the palate, dries on the finish due to firm tannin structure.*	£14.20	ADN V&C DBY JNW NYW EDC WRW	(S)
SEPPELT GREAT WESTERN SHIRAZ 1997, SEPPELT Victoria	*Concentrated aroma of sweet stewed fruit, acidity is high but it balances with the ripeness of fruit.*	£14.90	ODD TAN N&P OWC	(G)
ANNIE'S LANE CONTOUR VINEYARD SHIRAZ 1997, MILDARA BLASS South Australia	*Buxom aromas of juicy fruit and spice, modern fruit driven beast with well integrated spicy new oak.*	£15.00	ODD	(G)
WIRRA WIRRA RSW 1997, WIRRA WIRRA South Australia	*Marvellously inviting wine that delivers an elegant sweetness, leather and spice palate and fine grade tannin.*	£15.00	ODD DBY BBO	(S)
BROWN BROTHERS DINNINGS SHIRAZ 1997, BROWN BROTHERS Victoria	*Blackberry and rich oak nose, nice balance of fruit and tannins with distinctive wood character.*	£15.00	BRB	(B)
SALTRAM NO1 SHIRAZ 1997, SALTRAM South Australia	*Bouquet of redcurrant, blackberry, fresh mint and spicy cedar oak carries over to the palate.*	£15.10	DBY NRW NYW PBA AMW WCS	(S)
TATACHILLA FOUNDATION SHIRAZ 1998, TATACHILLA South Australia	*Fantastic colour, almost black, upfront spiciness, mint and wild berry nose, rich, concentrated, loads of potential.*	£15.20	Widely Available	(G)

CHARLES CIMICKY SIGNATURE SHIRAZ 1997, CHARLES CIMICKY South Australia	*Succulent ripeness, seriously smokey notes, soft underbelly, intense but not over extracted, beautiful balance.*	£15.20	DBY SWS VDV EDC JSS BOO COM	S
GEOFF MERRILL HENLEY SHIRAZ 1996, GEOFF MERRILL South Australia	*Strong oak intensity on nose with notes of spice, mint and wild berry, vanilla oak, medium tannins.*	£15.50	ODD	S
JIM BARRY MCCRAE WOOD SHIRAZ 1997, JIM BARRY South Australia	*Very concentrated young style nose consisting of blackberry and spice, soft tannins compliment the dark fruit flavours.*	£15.50	Widely Available	S
SUMMERFIELD SHIRAZ 1997, SUMMERFIELD Victoria	*Dark fruit, leather and tar flavours, lovely integrated herbs, pleasing tannins and good acid structure.*	£15.70	BBR	S
BALLANDEAN SHIRAZ 1997, BALLANDEAN ESTATE Queensland	*Cigar smoke and red cherry fruit nose, smokey and raspberry, spice palate showing good concentration.*	£15.70	DBY REN	B
PETER LEHMANN STONEWELL SHIRAZ 1995, PETER LEHMANN South Australia	*Rich, ripe new world style with concentrated fruit, strong tannin structure and good finish.*	£16.00	JSM ODF	B
EVANS & TATE SHIRAZ 1998, EVANS & TATE Western Australia	*Subtle nose displaying pleasant cherry and tobacco, delicious sweet raspberry palate, complex and grippy palate.*	£16.20	OWC	S
TIM ADAMS THE ABERFELDY 1998, TIM ADAMS South Australia	*Cedary oak, berry nose, balanced fruit acid that takes up the intense oak flavoured challenge.*	£17.00	DBY AUC	S

WOLF BLASS VINEYARD SELECTION EDEN VALLEY SHIRAZ 1996, MILDARA BLASS South Australia	*An abundance of rich, ripe, big smokey damsons and plum fruit and quality tannins.*	**£17.00**	Widely Available	(B)
ELDERTON SHIRAZ 1997, ELDERTON South Australia	*Attractive floral notes accent the ripe berry fruit on the nose, spicy, chocolate and liquorice palate.*	**£17.70**	ODD DBY QRW	(S)
D'ARENBERG DEAD ARM SHIRAZ 1998, D'ARENBERG South Australia	*Lovely rich aromatic berries and tobacco on nose, complexity of fruit , oak, tar and tobacco flavours.*	**£17.80**	ODD CTC DBY NYW VDV HST COM	(S)
STEVE MAGLIERI SHIRAZ 1998, MAGLIERI South Australia	*The nose is powerful and inviting, the palate is beautifully poised between concentration, sweetness and elegance.*	**£18.00**	Widely Available	(G)
MOUNT LANGI GHIRAN SHIRAZ 1998, MOUNT LANGI GHIRAN Victoria	*Minty eucalyptus aromas achieve a fine balance with the well adapted oak, acid, fruit and tannin.*	**£18.10**	Widely Available	(S)
LEASINGHAM CLASSIC CLARE SHIRAZ 1997, BRL HARDY South Australia	*Spice and warm oaky character on nose, rich tight and tannic, touch of chocolate and mintiness.*	**£18.20**	ODD DBY NYW VDV VIL	(S)
DALWHINNIE ESTATE SHIRAZ 1998, DALWHINNIE ESTATE Victoria	*Spicy, violet and mint nose, mid weight palate, spicy, earthy, lovely raspberry fruit and spice flavours.*	**£18.50**	J&B NYW VDV	(S)
DALWHINNIE SHIRAZ 1997, DALWHINNIE ESTATE Victoria	*Warm, powerful, elegant and harmonious bouquet with a palate that is broad, balanced and concentrated.*	**£18.50**	J&B NYW VDV	(B)

CHARLES MELTON SHIRAZ 1998, CHARLES MELTON South Australia	*Warm spicy Rhône style, delicious mouthfeel, harmonious use of oak and a strong fruity finish.*	£19.40	Widely Available	(S)
STONEWELL SHIRAZ 1994, PETER LEHMANN South Australia	*Dense black cherry and menthol aromas compliment the full, round, rich dark chocolatey flavours.*	£20.20	BDR ODF DBY WTS VDV OWC	(G)
YALDARA FARMS SHIRAZ 1998, YALDARA South Australia	*Voluptuously aromatic nose full of berry fruits and these flavours carry on to the finish.*	£20.20	GRT BDR SWS WBR BOO	(G)
MITCHELTON PRINT LABEL SHIRAZ 1996, MITCHELTON Victoria	*Rich, fresh cherries and blackberries on the nose consistent with the palate including toffee and tobacco.*	£21.00	ODD JMC JSS WCS	(S)
ELDERTON COMMAND SHIRAZ 1996, ELDERTON South Australia	*Aromatic berries and cherries fill the glass, complex tar, tobacco and blackberry flavours are in abundance.*	£25.80	ODF DBY QWW POR	(G)
PETER LEHMANN EIGHT SONGS SHIRAZ 1996, PETER LEHMANN South Australia	*Faint berry and cherry aroma with a smokey oak influence, very generous flavours and great structure.*	£26.00	ODF WTS DBY VDV G&M	(S)
EILEEN HARDY SHIRAZ 1997, BRL HARDY South Australia	*Still a baby yet releasing aromas of plum and black current with a streak of spicy oak.*	£28.70	Widely Available	(G)

Pinpoint who sells the wine you wish to buy by turning to the stockist codes. If you know the name of the wine you want to buy, use the alphabetical index. If the price is your motivation, refer to the invaluable price guide index; red and white wines under £5, sparkling wines under £12 and champagne under £16. Happy hunting!

E&E BLACK PEPPER SHIRAZ 1997, BRL HARDY South Australia	*Inviting wine with nice complex soft fruit, firm rich clean style, ripe and luscious exotic spice flavours.*	£29.20	Widely Available	(G)
THE OCTAVIUS 1996, YALUMBA South Australia	*Attractive fruit basket on the nose with a vein of oak, balanced by clean fruit acidity.*	£29.80	ODF DBY QWW JNW VDV	(B)
BASEDOW JOHANNES SHIRAZ 1996, BASEDOW South Australia	*Warm Shiraz fruit nose, spearmint and vanilla oak mingles with red fruit, full of integrity.*	£30.00	HFI	(S)
ROSEMOUNT ESTATE BALMORAL SYRAH 1997, ROSEMOUNT ESTATE South Australia	*Mulberry fruit, mint and toasted spice compliment the palate that is solid in structure and length.*	£30.20	JSM QWW UNS	(G)
GRANT BURGE MESHACH 1991, GRANT BURGE South Australia	*Big concentrated wine with complexing maturity, strong, juicy chocolate flavours, layered oak and silky fruit tannins.*	£32.20	OWC VIL WRW	(G)
MICHAEL SHIRAZ 1997, WYNNS ESTATE South Australia	*Mellow dark berry fruit and a creamy vanilla richness flows from the nose towards the palate.*	£35.30	JSM MWW DBY NYW VDV TAN	(G)
PENFOLDS RWT SHIRAZ 1997, PENFOLDS South Australia	*The balance is unrivalled and the full complexing flavours will live for many years to come.*	£36.10	Widely Available	(G)
CLARENDON HILLS SHIRAZ PIGGOTT RANGE 1997, CLARENDON HILLS South Australia	*Gamey intensity on the nose, interesting fruit profile with a richly concentrated black fruit flavour.*	£44.50	J&B SEB NYW	(S)

AUSTRALIA • SPARKLING

SOMMERFIELD AUSTRALIAN SPARKLING BRUT NV, SOUTHCORP South Eastern Australia	*Clean and easy, attractive fruit driven style offering an unusual mix of flavours. Good guzzling fizz.*	£5.70	SMF	B
SEAVIEW BRUT NV, SOUTHCORP South Eastern Australia	*Creamy refreshing clean fruity nose, nicely balanced, lovely texture, clean finish with good acidity.*	£6.60	Widely Available	B
ICE CRYSTAL 1995, HIGHLAND HERITAGE ESTATE New South Wales	*Strawberry cream pie characters immersed in bubbles with a crisp acid tail and a cleansing finish.*	£7.00	CHN	B
ROSEMOUNT ESTATE KIRRI BILLI BRUT 1997, ROSEMOUNT ESTATE South Eastern Australia	*Rich toasty nose, lots of fruit on the palate with good sweetness, nice acidic finish.*	£7.60	Widely Available	S
YELLOWGLEN PINOT NOIR CHARDONNAY NV, MILDARA BLASS South-Eastern Australia	*Creamy nose followed by a light, delicate sweet palate to finish with balanced acidity.*	£8.70	MWW ODD JAG RAV VIL	B
SEAVIEW CHARDONNAY BLANC DE BLANCS 1996, SOUTHCORP South Eastern Australia	*Apples and pears under a ripe fruit palate. Elegant, lots of complexity, very long and a bargain.*	£8.80	ODD DBY NRW NYW	G
SEAVIEW PINOT NOIR CHARDONNAY 1997, SOUTHCORP South Eastern Australia	*Soft mousse, delicate lemon nose, some toasted biscuits on the palate, pleasant citrus on finish.*	£8.80	Widely Available	B

SEAVIEW CHARDONNAY BLANC DE BLANCS 1995, SOUTHCORP South Eastern Australia	*Apples on the nose, exquisite full creamy fruit palate, delicious refreshing finish.*	£9.00	ODD NRW NYW	**S** WINE OF THE YEAR
SEPPELT SPARKLING SHIRAZ 1995, SOUTHCORP South Australia	*Enticing earthy nose with cherry character and a wonderful mouthfeel with a clean finish. Enjoyable wine.*	£9.10	Widely Available	**B**
YELLOWGLEN VINTAGE 1997, MILDARA BLASS South Australia	*Nice clean fresh chardonnay nose, lovely apples, good smooth fruit length, complex.*	£10.50	ODD JAG VIL	**B**
GREEN POINT VINTAGE BRUT 1996, CHANDON ESTATES Victoria	*Mature fruit nose, rich fruit on the palate, nice smooth length with lively acidity.*	£12.20	Widely Available	**B**
MIDNIGHT CUVÉE NV, BLUE PYRENEES ESTATE Victoria	*Elegant fragrances lead to a stylish fresh fruit palate with a very long citrus finish.*	£12.70	QWW	**S**
GREEN POINT ROSÉ 1996, CHANDON ESTATES Victoria	*Wonderful cool wild strawberry characters integrating with the mellow mousse and a lingering lush finish.*	£12.70	JAG FQU NYW VII, FEN	**B**
ASHTON HILLS SALMON BRUT 1995, ASHTON HILLS South Australia	*Summer red berries and strawberry aroma with zingy bubbles and lengthy tail. Generous tangy wine.*	£12.90	VDV	**B**
SEPPELT SHOW SPARKLING SHIRAZ 1990, SEPPELT Victoria	*Toasty nose with developed spicy red fruit characters, creamy mousse and a powerful pleasing finish.*	£14.10	ODF WRW	**B**

CHARLES MELTON SPARKLING RED NV, CHARLES MELTON South Australia	*Rich spicy strawberry nose, some butter and deep plums on the palate, great length and complexity.*	£23.90	Widely Available	S

AUSTRALIA • SWEET

THE PIONEERS RAISINED MUSCAT 1998, MIRANDA WINES South Australia	*Luxurious rich sweetness of honey and fruit on the palate, with good texture and length.*	£4.10	Widely Available	B
KATNOOK ESTATE BOTRYTIS RIESLING 1997, KATNOOK ESTATE South Australia	*Attractive aroma with caramel undertones leading to a rich and complex palate balanced in acidity.*	£6.00	CTC BWL AMW CTC	B
WELLWOOD ESTATE BOTRYTIS SEMILLON 1997, HIGHLAND HERITAGE ESTATE New South Wales	*Pale golden in hue, advanced honey to the nose with rich, full and a sweet palate.*	£6.00	CHN	B
BROWN BROTHERS LATE HARVESTED MUSCAT 1999, BROWN BROTHERS Victoria	*Perfumed peppered nose with creamy tropical taste, good grapey acidity and surprising length.*	£6.20	Widely Available	B
LINDEMANS BOTRYTIS RIESLING 1998, LINDEMANS South Australia	*Lively rich citrus bouquet, with a broad yet well balanced acidity and vigorous fruity flavour.*	£6.20	CPW NRW UNS ESL VIL HVW	B
PENFOLDS BOTRYTIS SEMILLON 1998, PENFOLDS New South Wales	*Subtle honey teases the nose and tickles the palate of this rich and clean tasting wine.*	£7.00	JSM ODD QWW NYW HVW POR	B

YENDA VINEYARDS BOTRYTIS SEMILLON 1996, YENDA VINEYARDS New South Wales	*Golden wine of honeyed floral fragrance, bursts onto the palate with tropical fruits and balanced refreshing conclusion.*	**£7.20**	AMW	**S**
ELDERTON GOLDEN SEMILLON 1997, ELDERTON WINES South Eastern Australia	*Revel in the perfume of apricot and honey before experiencing this rich and rounded caramely wine.*	**£8.60**	ODF BBR DBY QWW	**S**
RARE DRY BOTRYTIS SEMILLON 1996, DE BORTOLI New South Wales	*Intriguing nose from this very rare dry botrytised wine, lovely waxy honeycomb with dried apricot finish.*	**£8.60**	DBY N&P	**B**
YALUMBA NOBLE PICK BOTRYTIS VIOGNIER 1998, YALUMBA South Australia	*Gentle grapefruit on the nose, moderate in depth with an excellent balance of acidity.*	**£9.00**	Widely Available	**S**
D'ARENBERG NOBLE RIESLING 1998, D'ARENBERG South Australia	*Molten amber tone, cheeky hints of orange flush the rich palate with exquisite finish.*	**£9.40**	ODD CTC DBY VDV COM WES	**S**
YALUMBA NOBLE PICK BOTRYTIS SEMILLON 1998, YALUMBA South Australia	*A lively nose rich in lemon in a well balanced fruity wine with citrus undertones.*	**£10.90**	QRW QWW NYW	**B**
CRANSWICK BOTRYTIS SEMILLON 1996, CRANSWICK ESTATE New South Wales	*Wonderful marmalade and heather honey on a complex palate of buttery flavours lingering on the end.*	**£11.10**	BDR JMC ODD GHL BTH OWC WRW	**S**
JJ MCWILLIAMS BOTRYTIS SEMILLON 1994, MCWILLIAMS New South Wales	*Savour the great, full tropical character washing over palate and a good lengthy finish.*	**£11.10**	BBO CTC	**B**

| **DE BORTOLI NOBLE ONE SEMILLON 1996, DE BORTOLI** New South Wales | *Zesty aromas of exotic tropical fruits cascading into floral citrus flavours with good complexity.* | £13.50 | ODF BEN DBY CAM VDV N&P | **S** |

AUSTRALIA • WHITE • OTHER

BALLINGAL SEMILLON CHARDONNAY 1999, RIVERINA New South Wales	*Ripe melons on the nose with rich balanced tropical fruit palate smoothly integrated to the end.*	£4.00	VKW	**B**
RIVERHILL SEMILLON CHARDONNAY 1999, RIVERINA New South Wales	*Rich buttery pear drop nose with a hint of spice and tropical fruit palate enticing you.*	£4.00	VKW	**B**
CASTLE CREEK SEMILLON 1998, CRANSWICK ESTATES South East Australia	*Firm pencil shaving oak, good fruit on a palate of pleasant texture and excellent weight.*	£4.60	CVR	**S**
HARDYS STAMP RIESLING GEWÜRZTRAMINER 1999, BRL HARDY South Eastern Australia	*Lovely ripeness and sweet notes on the crisp and powerful palate, with an off dry finish.*	£4.60	Widely Available	**B**
MIRANDA OPAL RIDGE SEMILLON CHARDONNAY 1999, MIRANDA South Eastern Australia	*Very good concentration of fruit on the palate with a touch of honey and balancing acidity.*	£4.60	AVB RNS QWW JSS WCS CTC	**B**
SACRED HILL SEMILLON CHARDONNAY 1999, DE BORTOLI New South Wales	*Nice boneyed fruit on the nose with hot tropical fruit palate and agreeable acidity.*	£4.70	Widely Available	**B**

Wine	Notes	Price	Stockists	
DEAKIN ESTATE COLOMBARD 1999, DEAKIN ESTATE Victoria	*Buttery rich aromas, well balanced acidity into round rich fruit palate, good crispy finish.*	**£4.90**	ODD CTC BWL NYW	**B**
BEST'S VICTORIA COLOMBARD 1999, BEST'S GREAT WESTERN Victoria	*Ripe fruit palate with good firm acidity from smooth green fruit aromas. Good length, fresh pleasant finish.*	**£5.30**	GRT NYW TNI RAV JNW HVW	**B**
LENNARD'S CROSSING SEMILLON SAUVIGNON 1999, McGUIGAN South Eastern Australia	*Clean upfront nose, with fresh lemony flavours refined with a hint of oak on the palate.*	**£5.50**	Widely Available	**B**
LONG TERRACE SEMILLON CHARDONNAY 1999, RIVERINA WINES New South Wales	*Warm citrus and honey aromas with melon on the palate and clean crisp acidity.*	**£5.60**	BDR	**S**
BROWN BROTHERS DRY MUSCAT 1999, BROWN BROTHERS Victoria	*Smooth ripe fruit palate with boiled sweet fruit characters and a delicate finish. Good balance.*	**£5.70**	Widely Available	**B**
McGUIGAN BIN 6000 VERDELHO 1999, McGUIGAN South Australia	*Pronounced fruit nose, folowed by herbal complexity with good enjoyable texture and reasonable length.*	**£6.00**	JAG QWW BTH JSS OWC	**B**
SUMMER HILL VERDELHO CHARDONNAY 1999, RIVERINA New South Wales	*Warm fruity aroma, creamy mouth with good balance and some elegance, well integrated acidity*	**£6.20**	BDR	**B**
PETER LEHMANN SEMILLON CHARDONNAY 1999, PETER LEHMANN South Australia	*Clean, attractive floral, honeyed nose. Nice citrus acidity to compliment the oaky character and big fruit flavours.*	**£6.30**	G&M	**B**

WAKEFIELD ESTATE WHITE CLARE CROUCHEN CHARDONNAY 1998, WAKEFIELD ESTATE South Australia	*Strong ripe fruity aromas, powerful floral characters blended with lots of fruit and medium acidity.*	£6.40	DBY GHL WRW	B
MITCHELTON THOMAS MITCHELL MARSANNE 1999, MITCHELTON Victoria	*Lifted citrus nose with white peach hints, soft fruity palate with nice acid balance, good length.*	£6.50	ODD WCS	B
CHÂTEAU TAHBILK MARSANNE 1998, CHATEAU TAHBILK Victoria	*Honeysuckle and beeswax aromas followed by nice lemon and lime flavours, very nicely balanced.*	£6.60	ADN WTS WSO JMC BTH VDV G&M	B
IRONSTONE SEMILLON CHARDONNAY 1999, CAPE MENTELLE Western Australia	*Pungent aromas of asparagus and cats pee precede a palate of refined fruit and balanced acidity.*	£6.80	Widely Available	B
HOUGHTON VERDELHO 1999, BRL HARDY Western Australia	*Fresh and lively with grassy characters, well balanced and good leafy palate, zingy style structure.*	£6.90	JMC VDV	B
BOTANY CREEK BLACK SEAL 1998, McGUIGAN South Eastern Australia	*Inviting fresh limey nose followed by fresh green fruits with hints of pears and melons.*	£7.00	OWC	S
PRIMO ESTATE LA BIONDINA 1999, PRIMO ESTATE South Australia	*Very clean tropical fruits on the nose, good mouthfeel of fresh fruit with delicious finish.*	£7.00	AUC	S
BROWN BROTHERS SAUVIGNON BLANC 1999, BROWN BROTHERS Victoria	*Pungent green and rich tropical fruit aromas, subdued acidity and soft ripe gooseberry fruit palate.*	£7.20	GDS ODD DBY CPW	B

CHAPEL HILL VERDELHO 1998, CHAPEL HILL South Australia	*Very interesting floral and fruity aroma, good limey acidity in the mouth. Pleasant texture, long finish.*	£8.00	WTS FQU AUC	**B**
GABBA WARRA PINOT GIGOLO 1998, BOND ESTATE WINES Queensland	*Italian playboy style with aroma of stud farm and sweaty pradas, slightly flabby in the middle and a tart palate.*	£8.70	Widely Available	**B**
CHENIN BLANC 1999, SETTLERS RIDGE Western Australia	*Zingy and fresh palate of quinces and ripe fruit with hints of honey and spice.*	£9.00	VER	**B**
COLDSTREAM HILLS SAUVIGNON BLANC 1999, COLDSTREAM HILLS Victoria	*Fabulous rich ripe fruit aromas follow through to a juicy sweet fruit palate with nice crisp acidity.*	£9.00	NYW	**B**
PETALUMA BRIDGEWATER MILL SAUVIGNON BLANC 1999, PETALUMA South Australia	*Sweet gooseberry nose, brassy edge, well rounded palate, even if acidity is quite restrained.*	£9.00	WCR OWC	**B**
KATNOOK ESTATE SAUVIGNON BLANC 1999, KATNOOK ESTATE South Australia	*Elegant pineapple, spice and smokey nose, with a ripe passion fruit mid palate, and wonderful clean length.*	£9.20	ODD CTC DBY BWT CTC	**B**
VASSE FELIX SEMILLON SAUVIGNON 1999, VASSE FELIX Western Australia	*Ripe fruit and grassy green aromas, complex palate of rich ripe fruit with hints of canned peas.*	£9.30	CPW VDV BEN TAN	**S**
NEPENTHE SAUVIGNON BLANC 1999, NEPENTHE South Australia	*Clean, pungent leafy aromas follow through to the palate with good herbaceous grip. Nice mineral acidity.*	£9.40	GRT ODD WTS NYW EDC BOO	**S**

SHAW & SMITH SAUVIGNON BLANC 1999, SHAW & SMITH South Australia	*Green, fruity aromas follow through onto the palate and balanced with nice, long zingy acidity.*	**£9.60**	Widely Available	**B**
MIBROVALE OWENS FAMILY HUNTER VALLEY VERDELHO 1999, MILBROVALE New South Wales	*Fresh grapey floral aroma, lively ripe fruit well balanced with mild acidity and pleasing length.*	**£10.00**	MKV	**B**
DEVILS LAIR FIFTH LEG WHITE 1998, DEVIL'S LAIR Western Australia	*Intense herbaceous nose, rich spicy oak, gentlepalate with good oak integration and pleasing length.*	**£10.40**	GRT ODF V&C H&H TAN BEL	**B**
HEGGIES VINEYARD VIOGNIER 1999, YALUMBA South Australia	*Lifted perfume nose with melon characteristics giving great intensity, zippy acidity and fruity length.*	**£12.20**	ODF NYW JNW VDV HST WRW	**B**
LAST DITCH VIOGNIER 1999, D'ARENBERG South Australia	*Powerful floral nose combining with confected summer fruits and spicy flavours with rose on the finish.*	**£14.00**	ODF	**B**
THE VIRGILIUS 1999, YALUMBA South Australia	*Melon and grapefruit floral nose with big hot tropical fruits and integrated acidity with an elegant ending.*	**£15.30**	ODF JNW	**S**
THE VIRGILIUS 1998, YALUMBA South Australia	*A toasty nose with warm summer fruits on the palate and a long lifted finish.*	**£15.60**	MWW ODF JNW VDV	**S**
H SERIES MCCLAREN VALE VIOGNIER 1999, HASELGROVE South Australia	*Pleasant lemony nose leads to harmonised acidity and ripe fruit palate with lovely floral finish.*	**£22.50**	VIL	**B**

AUSTRIA

D essert wines shine out as the most successful and appealing style from this fascinating country, which has marched at great speed to catch up with the rest of the vinous world. Its attitude and standards have given us these award winning wines to delight and surprise the sceptics, Beerenauslese has swept the board of medals, from the stunning region of Burgenland. With only a fifth of grapes being red, still great shakes have been made to native and noble varieties to exhibit excellent red wines.

AUSTRIA • SWEET

WEINGUT MÜNZENRIEDER SÄMLING BOUVIER TBA 1997, MÜNZENRIEDER Neusiedlersee-Hügelland	*Relish the apricot fragrance displayed by this fresh and intensely fruity, rather sophisticated wine.*	**£10.00**	WSO	**G**
EISWEIN MUSKAT OTTONEL 1999, HAFNER LOEINE HOUSE OF HAFNER Burgenland	*Lemon nose and young zingy grapefruit perfume, well balanced acidity, very pleasant lingering length.*	**£11.70**	OPW	**B**
TROCKENBEERENAUSLESE SCHEUREBE 1998, HAFNER LOEINE HOUSE OF HAFNER Neusiedlersee	*A delicious mixture of honey mingling with apricots and floral hints on a zesty ending.*	**£14.00**	OPW	**B**
TRAMINER EISWEIN ELITE 1999, GERHARD WOHLMUTH Styria	*Enjoy the smooth rich nose followed by the full botrytis characteristics of this wine. Sensational.*	**£16.00**	STH	**S**
MUSKAT NO 1 ZWISCHEN DEN SEEN BEERENAUSLESE 1997, ALÖIS KRACHER Burgenland	*This golden wine smacks of grapefruit and is clean, well balanced, lean and racy.*	**£18.50**	NYW	**S**

BOUVIER No 2 ZWISCHEN DEN SEEN BOUVIER BEERENAUSLESE 1997, ALÖIS KRACHER Burgenland	*A really refreshing nose, good clean citrus tones leading to a round and balanced wine.*	**£19.50**	NYW	(S)
SCHEUREBE No 3 ZWISCHEN DEN SEEN BEERENAUSLESE 1997, ALÖIS KRACHER Burgenland	*Scented with orange zest, lemon and oak skip off the tongue from this rich wine.*	**£21.50**	NYW	(S)
MUSKAT OTTONEL No 5 ZWISCHEN DEN SEEN BEERENAUSLESE 1997, ALÖIS KRACHER Burgenland	*An enticing palate of lemon which is rich and balanced with a fabulously long fruity finish.*	**£22.00**	NYW	(G)
GRANDE CUVÉE TROCKENBEERENAUSLESE 1996, ALÖIS KRACHER Burgenland	*An extravagantly ripe tangy pineapple aroma, this wine has great spicy characteristics cascading into the palate.*	**£26.00**	NYW	(B)
ZWISCHEN ROSÉ No 4 NOUVELLE VAGUE BEERENAUSLESE 1997, ALÖIS KRACHER Burgenland	*A bouquet of cherry and raspberry characteristics, a fine and somewhat juicy wine to boot.*	**£27.00**	NYW	(S)
WELSCHRIESLING No 4 NOUVELLE VAGUE TBA 1996, ALÖIS KRACHER Burgenland	*This wine displays a big nose rich in honey, and great acid foundation dancing with fruit.*	**£29.00**	NYW	(S)
WELSCHRIESLING No 7 ZWISCHEN DEN JEEN TROCKENBEERENAUSLESE 1997, ALÖIS KRACHER Burgenland	*Apricots tantalise the nose of this rich and balanced wine that oozes of cheeky lime zest.*	**£32.00**	NYW	(S)

Pinpoint who sells the wine you wish to buy by turning to the stockist codes. If you know the name of the wine you want to buy, use the alphabetical index. If the price is your motivation, refer to the invaluable price guide index; red and white wines under £5, sparkling wines under £12 and champagne under £16. Happy hunting!

AUSTRIA • WHITE

RIESLING SUMMUS 1999, GERHARD WOHLMUTH Styria	*Crisp and good acidity on this heavy tasting peppery palate, good fruit on the finish.*	£6.10	STH	**B**
SUMMUS CHARDONNAY 1999, GERHARD WOHLMUTH Styria	*Good green fruit with peardrops on the nose and palate, good weight, fresh elegant finish.*	£7.10	STH	**B**

EASTERN EUROPE

The countries that provide us with fanatastic value dessert and still wines continue to show well in the overall market, especially on the supermarket shelves.. The infamous Hungarian Bulls Blood yet again raises the eyebrows of the judges who cannot deny its appeal. On the sweet side of things, medals have been widely awarded to some of the world's best dessert wines such as Tokaji. This region can thank the coastline of the Red Sea and the banks of the River Danube for much of its success, along with modernization, foreign investments and the coming of the free market.

BULGARIA • RED

BOYAR LAMBOL MERLOT 1999, DOMAINE BOYAR LAMBOL Southern Region	Elegant, rich and rounded nose, plummy fruits on the palate, good length and character.	£3.70	UNS JMC	(S)
SUHINDOL CABERNET MERLOT RESERVE 1996, LOVICO SUHINDOL Northern Region	Attractive spicy nose, followed by lots of oak tannins and ripe fruit, good depth, nice herbal finish.	£4.00	SAF	(S)
SUHINDOL MERLOT RESERVE 1996, LOVICO SUHINDOL Northern Region	Refined and ripe nose with some cinnamon spice, warming long finish with good acidity.	£4.00	SAF	(S)
DOMAINE BOYAR CABERNET SAUVIGNON 1999, DOMAINE BOYAR SHUMEN Eastern Region	Morello cherry nose melding with crushed mulberries, chalky tannins and generous length. Vibrant style.	£4.00	WCR	(B)
STAMBOLOVO BULGARIAN RESERVE MERLOT 1994, VINPROM HASKOVO Southern Region	Maturing cedar and tobacco box aromas, strawberries and cassis fruit, long finish, drinking well.	£4.00	SMF WCR	(B)

PREMIUM CUVÉE CABERNET SAUVIGNON 1999, DOMAINE BOYAR SHUMEN Eastern Region	*Rich ripe fruit on the palate with very nice balancing acidity and well integrated tannins.*	£4.50	DBO	**S**
DOMAINE BOYAR PREMIUM CUVÉE MERLOT 1999, DOMAINE BOYAR SHUMEN Eastern Region	*Big sweet style, with tar and bitter chocolate on the palate, good support from the tannins.*	£4.50	DBO	**S**
AZBUKA MERLOT 1996, HASKOVO Southern Region	*Plummy cedar nose, some drying tannins, decent length with a creamy vanilla character.*	£6.00	SAF	**B**

BULGARIA • WHITE

COPPER CROSSING DRY WHITE BULGARIAN WINE NV, LOVICO SUHINDOL Northern Region	*Spicy and floral nose fusing with pears and lemons refreshing acidity and butteriness with a lengthy finish.*	£3.00	LUV	**B**
BOYAR CHARDONNAY 1999, DOMAINE BOYAR SHUMEN Eastern Region	*Balanced melon and gooseberry aromas, clean balance on palate, good length with a fresh melon finish.*	£3.50	WCR	**B**

HUNGARY • RED

SZEKSZARDI BULLS BLOOD 1998, VILLANY WINERY Szekszard	*Good structure and mouthfeel, rich red fruit flavours and lingering easy finish.*	£3.60	SAF	**B**

HUNGAROVIN BULLS BLOOD 1997, HUNGAROVIN Eger	*Perfumed aromas with vegetal and red berry fruit, pleasing fruit acidity and a generous finish.*	£4.00	MYL	B
HILLTOP NESZMELY CABERNET SAUVIGNON 1997, HILLTOP NESZMELY Villany	*Musky blackcurrants on the nose followed by lovely red fruit palate with good portion of tannins.*	£6.50	BGL	B

HUNGARY • SPARKLING

CHAPEL HILL SPARKLING CHARDONNAY NV, BALATONBOGLAR Del Balaton	*Biscuity, bready and nutty nose followed by ripe greengage fruit palate, very nice balance.*	£5.00	MYL	B

HUNGARY • SWEET

TOKAJI ASZÚ 5 PUTTONYOS 1993, HILLTOP NESZMELY Tokaj	*Delicious aged toffee bombards the nose and tickles the palate along with butterscotch and citrus.*	£8.00	BGL	S
TOKAJI ASZÚ 5 PUTTANYOS 1994, TOKAJKOVAGO Tokaj	*Heady scents of toffee and cherry follow through into the palate with a dry satisfying conclusion.*	£8.00	MYL	B
TOKAJI ASZÚ 5 PUTTONYOS 1990, HILLTOP NESZMELY Tokaj	*A really intense lemon and honey with golden syrup aroma exudes from this deep golden coloured wine.*	£10.00	SAF WTS TOS	B

TOKAJI ASZÚ 5 PUTTONYOS 1992, DOMAINE DE DISZNÓKŐ Tokaj	*Tantalisingly fresh caramelised fruits in aroma, with an intensely fresh, clean and zesty palate.*	**£15.30**	ODD	**S**
TOKAJI ASZÚ 5 PUTTONYOS 1994, BODEGAS OREMUS Tokaj	*Porcini, honeyed citrus fruit nose with complex round full fruit palate, well balanced and good length.*	**£17.20**	QWW DBY NYW HST	**G**

HUNGARY • WHITE

SPICE TRAIL WHITE 1999, SZOLSKERT CO-OP Nagyrede	*Spicy aromatic with floral hints, summer fruit palate blending with balanced acidity and dry finish.*	**£4.00**	BGN SAF	**B**
HILLTOP NESZMELY CHARDONNAY VIRGIN VINTAGE 1999, HILLTOP NESZMELY Neszmely	*Aromatic fruit nose with grapefruit and apricots, refreshing acidity, great structure and lengthy tail.*	**£6.00**	BGL	**B**
HILLTOP NESZMELY SAUVIGNON BLANC VIRGIN VINTAGE 1999, HILLTOP NESZMELY Neszmely	*Very smooth grassy nose and ripe fruit aromas, juicy fruit on the palate with persistent finish.*	**£6.00**	BGL	**B**

ROMANIA • RED

RESERVE MERLOT 1999, PRAHOVA WINE CELLARS Dealul Mare	*Shiny cassis fruit, soft juicy berries with decent length and tannins all the way through.*	**£4.00**	HAE	**B**

FRANCE

The Champagne houses have survived the excitement and over exaggeration of demand in the market, for the purpose of celebrating the Millenium in style. Both Grand Marques and the minions have all scooped up a gallery of medals to escort with pride back to France. Southern regions, with the upsergence of new world techniques and massive investment are now hot on the heels of the more classic wines of notoriety. Still ever the source of good value and eclectic produce. They will always rule the past, present and future?

ALSACE • RED

PINOT NOIR FURSTENTUM 1996, DOMAINE PAUL BLANCK Alsace	*Pepper and morello cherry aromas give way to a young, lean, green fruit palate, good length.*	**£14.00**	ADN JBF	**B**

ALSACE • SPARKLING

PIERRE LAROUSSE BLANC DE BLANCS BRUT NV, LES CAVES DE WISSEMBOURG Alsace	*Fresh nose with some baked bread aromas, balanced acidity, subtle creamy mouthfeel. Great long savoury finish.*	**£8.50**	THI	**B**

ALSACE • SWEET

GEWÜRZTRAMINER FURSTENTUM GRAND CRU SGN 1997, DOMAINE PAUL BLANCK Alsace	*An explosion of raisin, peach and citrus in fragrance with rich honeyed fruit in flavour.*	**£22.00**	JBF	**S**

RIESLING FURSTENTUM GRAND CRU SELECTION DE GRAINS NOBLES 1995, DOMAINE PAUL BLANCK Alsace	*Spices exude from this green gold wine, with sweet caramel and pineapple present on the palate.*	£22.00	JBF	**B**
GEWÜRZTRAMINER RANGEN DE THANN GRAND CRU SGN 1994, DOMAINE SCHOFFIT Alsace	*Frolic in the rose petal perfumes of this spicy, complex and delightfully seductive wine. Excellent balance and viscosity.*	£25.00	HBJ	**G**

ALSACE • WHITE

BARON DE HOEN GEWÜRZTRAMINER ISSU DE VIEILLES VIGNES 1998, BEBLENHEIM Alsace	*Baked pear aroma, rich and sweet palate with a dry finish, held together by good structure.*	£6.00	WTS	**B**
GEWÜRZTRAMINER GOLD MEDAL 1997, VINICOLE DE RIBEAUVILLE Alsace	*Delicate honeyed aroma, light flavours of subtle fruits on palate and a lingering elegant finish.*	£6.00	GSJ	**B**
GEWÜRZTRAMINER WEINGARTEN 1998, RIBEAUVILLE Alsace	*Rich sweet aroma, full floral and tropical fruit on the crisp palate, which holds itself.*	£6.00	GSJ	**B**
TOKAY PINOT GRIS CAVE DE RIBEAUVILLÉ 1997, RIBEAUVILLÉ Alsace	*Floral deep nose, very clean balanced lemony palate with nice acidity and great length.*	£6.00	MWW	**B**
TOKAY PINOT GRIS HEIMBOURG GRAND CRU 1998, TURCKHEIM Alsace	*Very pleasant limey nose, tropical fruit palate, intense mouthfeel with long finish. Highly recommendable.*	£7.80	PBA DBY WRK WES	**S**

FRANCE • ALSACE • WHITE

RIESLING HEIMBOURG GRAND CRU 1996, TURCKHEIM Alsace	*Pronounced fruity nose, full ripe fruit on the palate, a tantalising finish leads you on.*	£8.00	QRW PBA DBY WRK FEN WES	S
CHARLES KOEHLY ET FILS MUSCAT D'ALSACE 1998, CHARLES KOEHLY ET FILS Alsace	*Asparagus and grassy aromas, good limey acidity, warm effect on palate and good spicy length.*	£8.00	HWL	B
RIESLING WINECK-SCHLOSSBERG GRAND CRU 1997, MEYER-FONNÉ Alsace	*Honeysuckle aromas, dry medium bodied palate, giving generous richness and spice on the finish.*	£8.60	JLW	S
GEWÜRZTRAMINER 1998, MATERNE HAEGELIN ET SES FILLES Alsace	*Opulent weighty ripeness, a sweet entry finishes dry, with persistent flavours on the lingering finish.*	£8.70	MWW ABY VIL	B
RIESLING BRAND GRAND CRU 1997, DOMAINE FRANÇOIS BAUR Alsace	*Stunning freshness of palate, lemon and apricot fruit, finish cleansing with some austerity*	£8.90	3DW	B
RIESLING WIEBELSBERG GRAND CRU 1996, CH WANTZ Alsace	*Good spritz on the opening, raspberry canes on the nose, vivacious palate with terrific acidity.*	£9.00	CHN	B
TOKAY PINOT GRIS ALTENBURG GRAND CRU 1998, KIENTZHEIM-KAYSERSBERG Alsace	*Candied fruit nose, very easy to drink with good fruit balance, fine depth and sweet finish.*	£9.00	ABY	B
GEWÜRZTRAMINER VIEILLES VIGNES 1999, GRUSS Alsace	*Ripe rich honey, with well balanced sweetness and acidity gives a successful enjoyable finish.*	£9.30	3DW	S

RIESLING ROSACKER GRAND CRU 1997, VINICOLES DE HUNAWIHR Alsace	*Elegant and austere, limes on the palate with full acidity and a long pleasing finish.*	£9.40	BWL CTC	**B**
GEWÜRZTRAMINER BRAND GRAND CRU 1994, TURCKHEIM Alsace	*Lovely rich oily texture, with ripe lychee nose, shows signs of age and delicate mature characteristics.*	£10.20	PBA DBY NRW AMW WRK FEN	**B**
GEWÜRZTRAMINER 1991, ROLLY GASSMANN Alsace	*Delicate light spritz on the palate of lychees and deep rich complexity, ageing gracefully.*	£10.30	CAM DBY RHV	**B**
GEWÜRZTRAMINER ROSACKER GRAND CRU 1997, MITTNACHT FRERES Alsace	*Perfumed nose, rich intensity of flavours on the palate, balanced with pleasing acidity and structure.*	£10.40	DBY	**B**
GEWÜRZTRAMINER HERRENWEG GRAND CRU 1997, FRANÇOIS BAUR Alsace	*Powerful sweet fruity palate and superb balanced crisp acidity give us this enjoyable experience.*	£10.80	3DW	**B**
GEWÜRZTRAMINER COLLECTION 1998, KUENTZ BAS Alsace	*Passionfruit on the nose followed by complex fruit on the palate, with subtle mango character.*	£11.00	PNA	**S**
GEWÜRZTRAMINER CLOS ZISSER GRAND CRU 1997, KLIPFEL Alsace	*Elegant style with delicate fruit and exotic floral aromas, a top class wine with long length.*	£11.00	DLA	**B**
RIESLING ROSACKER GRAND CRU 1995, MITTNACHT FRÈRES Alsace	*Sherbet and citrus fruit on the nose, lasting full sweet hints on the fruit driven palate.*	£11.10	DBY NYW	**B**

FRANCE • ALSACE • WHITE

Wine	Tasting Note	Price	Code	
GEWÜRZTRAMINER ROSACKER GRAND CRU 1998, HUNAWIHR Alsace	*Exotic and tempting, well balanced elegant palate with layers of fruit flavours to discover.*	£11.40	CTC	(B)
GEWÜRZTRAMINER FURSTENTUM GRAND CRU 1997, KIENTZHEIM-KAYSERSBERG Alsace	*Freasias and fresh tropical fruits on the nose, complimented by a rich palate of fruit salad.*	£11.50	ABY	(B)
RIESLING WINTZENHEIM GRAND CRU 1997, ZIND-HUMBRECHT Alsace	*Cherry blossom on a warm spring day burst out of this wine, with zesty limes.*	£11.70	FQU DBY FQU	(G)
GEWÜRZTRAMINER HENGST GRAND CRU 1997, WUNSCH ET MANN Alsace	*Classic perfumed nose, with sweet dried orange peel and spicy fruit palate, fresh elegant finish.*	£11.80	MKV	(S)
RIESLING SCHLOSSBERG GRAND CRU 1998, ALBERT MANN Alsace	*Lemon zest aroma, full tropical honey character on the mouth with good dry acidity*	£11.90	NYW	(B)
RIESLING ALTENBERG DE BERGHEIM GRAND CRU 1997, CHARLES KOEHLY ET FILS Alsace	*A clean luscious nose, marmalade fruits and good acidity, make for a long pleasing finish.*	£13.00	HWL	(G)
RIESLING ALTENBERG DE BERGHEIM GRAND CRU 1996, CHARLES KOEHLY ET FILS Alsace	*Pale light gold, big rich mouthfeel, dry delicate fruit aromas, good acidity and length.*	£13.00	HWL	(S)
GEWÜRZTRAMINER STEINGRÜBLER GRAND CRU 1998, ALBERT MANN Alsace	*Moroccan spice market aromas, lime and mandarines on the sophisticated palate, with balancing acidity.*	£13.20	NYW	(S)

TOKAY PINOT GRIS FURSTENTUM GRAND CRU 1998, ALBERT MANN Alsace	*Rich honeyed fruits with lychee and tropical tones, finishing in a clean lingering end.*	£13.50	ACQ	**G**
GEWÜRZTRAMINER RANGEN DE THANN GRAND CRU 1997, SCHOFFIT Alsace	*Floral and spice aromas dominate this powerful wine, light dry excellent finish lingers on forever.*	£14.00	HBJ	**B**
RIESLING CLOS HAUSERER 1998, ZIND-HUMBRECHT Alsace	*Great memorable nose which lingers on through the rich and seductive palate to the cleansing finale.*	£15.10	ABY FQU	**S**
RIESLING SCHLOSSBERG GRAND CRU 1998, PAUL BLANCK Alsace	*Delicate floral nose, good texture and balance, sweet with high acidity carrying it through.*	£15.10	ADN JBF BLS	**B**
RIESLING SOMMERBERG GRAND CRU 1998, PAUL BLANCK Alsace	*Luscious and ripe, with medium sweet balanced palate, slightly late harvest character on the finish.*	£16.00	JBF	**G**
GEWÜRZTRAMINER ALTENBOURG GRAND CRU 1998, PAUL BLANCK Alsace	*Delightful floral aromas, full intense fruit flavours on the palate, quite long rich honeyed finish.*	£16.00	ADN JBF	**S**
PINOT GRIS HEIMBOURG GRAND CRU 1997, ZIND-HUMBRECHT Alsace	*Refreshing green fruit aroma followed by ripe green fruit flavours, balanced acidity, fruity long finish.*	£16.70	ABY	**B**
RIESLING RANGEN DE THANN GRAND CRU No 10 1997, SCHOFFIT Alsace	*Attractive colour and great fragrance, full spicy fruit on the palate, concentrated weight, long stylish finish.*	£18.00	HBJ	**G**

Pinot Gris Heimbourg Grand Cru 1998, Zind-Humbrecht Alsace	*Attractive creamy ripe apples with hint of peaches and sweet melons on nose and palate.*	£19.00	ABY	**G** TROPHY WINE
Riesling Furstentum Grand Cru Vielles Vignes 1998, Paul Blanck Alsace	*Delicious and elegant on the nose and palate, rich and well balanced with good lasting acidity.*	£20.30	JBF	**G**
Riesling Schlossberg Grand Cru 1997, Kientzheim-Kaysersberg Alsace	*Rich minerally fruit and lemons on the nose, complex and morish on the long finish.*	£20.60	ABY	**B**
Clos Windsbuhl Gewürztraminer 1998, Zind-Humbrecht Alsace	*Delightful young style, opulently aromatic, exotic flavours on the palate, medium bodied and good length.*	£24.90	ABY VIL	**B**
Riesling Brand Grand Cru 1998, Zind-Humbrecht Alsace	*Some marmalade tones on the nose, slight residual sugar on palate giving mouthwatering long finish.*	£25.90	ABY VIL	**B**
Riesling Schlossberg Grand Cru Cuvée Ste Catherine 1997, Weinbach Alsace	*Smokey stylish palate, good weight of fruit, complex and classy right to the end.*	£26.80	J&B TAN	**S**
Gewürztraminer Furstentum Grand Cru Vendanges Tardives 1997, Weinbach Alsace	*Heather honey intensity of aroma, good balance of weight and fruit, excellent long finish.*	£29.50	J&B	**B**
Gewürztraminer Furstentum Grand Cru Cuvée Laurence 1996, Weinbach Alsace	*Essence of exotic fruits bring this pleasant wine together to give good acidity and length.*	£30.00	J&B	**B**

GEWÜRZTRAMINER GOLDERT GRAND CRU VENDAGE TARDIVE 1998, ZIND-HUMBRECHT Alsace	*Citrus fruit and five spice aromas with ripe lychee on the palate, rich structure.*	**£32.60**	ABY	(B)
PINOT GRIS RANGEN DE THANN GRAND CRU 1996, ZIND-HUMBRECHT Alsace	*Broad attractive fruit nose followed by melon and grapefruit, ripe melons and bananas, long finish.*	**£35.00**	WTS	(S)
GEWÜRZTRAMINER HENGST GRAND CRU 1998, ZIND-HUMBRECHT Alsace	*Powerful stylish and honeyed, pretty fruit culminating in a full rich mouthfeel.*	**£56.50**	ABY	(S)

BEAUJOLAIS • RED

MHV HENRI LA FONTAINE BEAUJOLAIS 1999, FAYE & CIE Beaujolais	*Interesting clean fresh vegetal notes on the nose, strong tannins and lovely fruit. Good balance.*	**£4.30**	BNK MHV	(B)
CHÂTEAU DE LA BRUYÈRE 1999, QUINSON Beaujolais	*Lifted caramel nose, good acidity with red crushed berrie palate, elegant complex structure. Well balanced.*	**£4.50**	ALD	(S)
BEAUJOLAIS LA BAREILLE 1999, THORIN Beaujolais	*Deep and complex, rich aroma and full bodied texture, bursting with red fruit, fantastic long finish.*	**£5.00**	TOS	(G)
BEAUJOLAIS VILLAGES 1999, GEORGES DUBOEUF Beaujolais	*Pale red colour, delicious jammy fruit on the nose, sweet berries on the palate, nice finish.*	**£5.30**	GDS MWW BWC CTC	(B)

MHV Henri La Fontaine Beaujolais Villages 1999, Faye & Cie Beaujolais	*Sweet pure berries on the nose and palate, well integrated acidity, fresh fruity finish.*	**£5.80**	MHV	B
Beaujolais Villages 1999, Louis Jadot Beaujolais	*Pink purple colour, attractive fresh berry fruit with high ripe tannins, clean strong fruit flavours.*	**£6.00**	WTS MAD TOS DBY QWW SAF JSS	B
Regnie JC Braillon 1999, Eventail Beaujolais	*Attractive purple colour, light fruit aroma, pleasant ripe fruit flavours, very good balance, lovely finish.*	**£6.00**	Widely Available	B
Morgon 1999, Paul Sapin Beaujolais	*Light ripe fruit with developed strawberry hints on nose and palate, pleasant round mouthfeel.*	**£6.50**	ROG	B
Régnié 1999, Georges Duboeuf Beaujolais	*Very aromatic youthful character with soft ripe bramble fruit. Excellent balance and fine acidity.*	**£6.60**	JSM BWC BNK UNS	S
Brouilly Selection Paul Boutinot 1998, Chapelle de Cray Beaujolais	*Inviting red colour, ripe fruit aromas, lovely strawberries on the palate, nice acidity on the finish.*	**£6.70**	PBA DBY WES	B
Chenas Château de Chenas 1999, Eventail Beaujolais	*Gorgeous rich raspberry nose followed by classic bubble gum, fruits and pepper. Fresh raspberry finish.*	**£7.00**	Widely Available	S
Chiroubles 1999, Eventail Beaujolais	*Very appealing high acidity in a bed of fresh cherries, raspberry characters strong on the extended finish.*	**£7.00**	Widely Available	B

FLEURIE CLAUDE CHONION 1998, VAUCHER PÈRE ET FILS Beaujolais	*Pleasant strawberry on the nose and palate, lots of sweet fruit, good balance. Smooth long finish.*	£7.00	NTD	(B)
FLEURIE GRILLE MIDI 1999, EVENTAIL Beaujolais	*Lovely warmth of delicate fresh cherries on nose and palate. Nice integration of acidity.*	£7.00	Widely Available	(B)
MOULIN-À-VENT 1997, GEORGES DUBOEUF Beaujolais	*Very aromatic fruity nose, very ripe fruit palate with attractive freshness. Excellent finish and good length.*	£7.20	BWC UNS	(S)
MOULIN-À-VENT CLAUDE CHONION 1998, VAUCHER PÈRE ET FILS Beaujolais	*Very pale red, very clean soft cherries, dry tannins, good acidity. Subtle cherry fruit finish.*	£7.50	NTD	(B)
ST AMOUR GUY PATISSIER 1999, EVENTAIL Beaujolais	*Purple ruby bright colour, clean delicious cheery fruit characters, dry medium acid cherry finish.*	£8.00	Widely Available	(S)
FLEURIE PAUL SAPIN OWN LABEL 1999, PAUL SAPIN Beaujolais	*Clean bright pale colour, clean vanilla hints in strawberry and creamy flavour. Cherry fruit finish.*	£8.00	ROG	(B)
FLEURIE 1999, GEORGES DUBOEUF Beaujolais	*Deep ruby purple colour, clean fresh dry juicy structure. Medium acidity, plenty of cherry fruit.*	£8.20	GDS JSM MWW BWC TOS BNK JCP FEN	(S)
MOULIN-À-VENT C FLAMY 1999, EVENTAIL Beaujolais	*Elegant upfront floral bramble nose with complex structure allowing for development. Simply superb.*	£9.00	Widely Available	(S)

Wine	Description	Price	Stockist	
MOULIN-À-VENT 1998, LOUIS JADOT Beaujolais	*Pale ruby bright colour, cherries and plenty of fruit, full bodied, well balanced. Elegant finish.*	**£9.50**	JSM MAD	B
BROUILLY 1998, CHÂTEAU DES TOURS Beaujolais	*Clear bright pale colour, jammy bright cherry fruit palate, clean balanced acidity and cherries. Medium length.*	**£9.80**	CPW WSO DBY TNI	B
MOULIN-À-VENT DOMAINE DE LA TOUR DU BIEF 1996, GEORGES DUBOEUF Beaujolais	*Earthy firm nose followed by surprisingly rich delightful complexity on the palate, very pleasant finish.*	**£9.80**	JNW	B
FLEURIE PONCIE 1999, DOMAINE DU VISSOUX Beaujolais	*Cherries and strawberries blend in sweet soft palate followed by extremely pleasant round mouthfeel.*	**£10.50**	NYW CTC	S
FLEURIE 1999, LUCIEN TARDIEU Beaujolais	*Very good clean ripe strawberries on the palate with jammy presence. Elegant very grippy finish.*	**£12.90**	EUW	B
MOULIN-À-VENT CLOS DE ROCHEGRES 1997, LOUIS JADOT Beaujolais	*Vivacious aroma of freshly picked up fruits, boiled sweet characters on palate, gorgeous warm mouthfeel.*	**£13.70**	MAD DBY QWW	G
MOULIN-À-VENT CHAMP DE COUR 1997, LOUIS JADOT Beaujolais	*A real pleasure to nose and palate, rich delicious fabulous ripe fruit, stunning round finish.*	**£14.00**	MAD	S

Pinpoint who sells the wine you wish to buy by turning to the stockist codes. If you know the name of the wine you want to buy, use the alphabetical index. If the price is your motivation, refer to the invaluable price guide index; red and white wines under £5, sparkling wines under £12 and champagne under £16. Happy hunting!

BORDEAUX • RED

SEGNEURS D'AIGUILHE 1998, COMTES DE NEIPPERG Bordeaux	*Mulberry sweet nose with beetroot and black cherry plump silky palate and firm tannins.*	£3.80	WTS	(B)
CHÂTEAU L'ESTANG 1998, CHÂTEAU L'ESTANG Bordeaux	*Lots of vanilla and crème brulée, ripe fruit on the palate with pleasing finish.*	£5.60	CTC	(B)
CHÂTEAU JOININ 1997, MME MESTREGUILHEM Bordeaux	*Warm spice with earthy aromas, soft well balanced fruits on the palate, fine long finish.*	£5.80	WAC	(B)
CHÂTEAU LA FLEUR BELLEVUE PREMIERS CÔTES DE BLAYE 1998, CHÂTEAU LA FLEUR BELLEVUE Bordeaux	*Strawberry and vanilla icecream on the nose, layers of ripe fruit on the palate.*	£6.00	LVF	(B)
BRIDGE OVER THE RIVER MERLOT 1998, GINESTET Bordeaux	*Tightly structured, complex berry palate, delicious wine, sour cherry tannins on the pleusum finish.*	£6.00	IWS	(B)
CHÂTEAU PEVY-SAINCRIT 1997, ROLLY GASSMANN Bordeaux	*Herbaceous characteristics exude from this lean but developing wine, good fruit palate with integrated spicy tannins.*	£6.90	CAM	(S)
CHÂTEAU TOUR BELLEGRAVE 1998, J CALVET Bordeaux	*Slight porty nose with cascades of oak spice and tangy young berries and plums ending with big tannins.*	£7.70	GYW	(B)

FRANCE • BORDEAUX • RED

CHÂTEAU MERCIER CUVÉE PRESTIGE 1997, CHÂTEAU MERCIER Bordeaux	*Warm spicy earthy aromas invite you into a wine of long blackfruit and cigar box finish.*	£8.00	FQU	(S)
DUCLA PERMANENCE 1998, YVON MAU Bordeaux	*Deep and dark rich fruit on the palate, youthful and spritely with good weight of fruit.*	£8.00	YVM	(S)
CHÂTEAU DE BELCIER CÔTES DE CASTILLON 1997, CHÂTEAU DE BELCIER Bordeaux	*Rich warm fruit flavours with elegant dry finish on this light bodied easy drinking wine.*	£8.80	PBA DBY NRW JSS AMW	(B)
CHÂTEAU REYNON ROUGE 1998, DENIS ET FLORENCE DUBOURDIEU Bordeaux	*Dark chocolate with cascades of vibrant young red fruit flavours, grippy tannins with velvety texture.*	£9.00	ABY	(S)
CHÂTEAU DES GRAVIÈRES COLLECTION PRESTIGE 1996, CHÂTEAU DES GRAVIÈRES Bordeaux	*Strawberry coulis nose with stewed plums and cedar palate supported by supple tannins with velvety texture.*	£9.00	CTC	(B)
VIEUX CHÂTEAU CHAMPS DE MARS 1997, CHÂTEAU CHAMPS DE MARS Bordeaux	*Fresh mint and cassis fruit married well together in a youthful classy dry finish.*	£9.00	MWW	(B)
CHÂTEAU ROCHES GUITARD 1998, CHÂTEAU ROCHES GUITARD Bordeaux	*Warm red fruit nose with bitter chocolate and dark berries on a well structured palate.*	£9.30	BDR	(B)
CRU BOURGEOIS HAUT MEDOC 1996, CHÂTEAU RAMAGE LA BATISSE Bordeaux	*Mature herbaceous plum nose with bags of red fruit and a harmonious lengthy finish.*	£9.40	PBA DBY NRW WES	(B)

RED • BORDEAUX • FRANCE

Château Ludon-Pomies Agassac 1997, Château la Lagune Bordeaux	*High class and intense aromas with dense fleshy fruits and a elegant dry finale.*	£9.70	MWW DBY	(S)
Château de la Nauve 1998, Château de la Nauve Bordeaux	*Forest leaves with mineral aroma celebrating complex spicy plum flavours, rich luscious texture with black pepper hints.*	£10.00	BDR	(G)
Château Peychaud Misoneuve 1997, Château Peychaud Bordeaux	*Spicy black pepper nose with savoury notes of blackcurrants, good acid, slightly dry and expressive length.*	£10.00	FQU	(G)
La Grande Cuvée de Dourthe Margaux 1996, Dourthe Bordeaux	*Spicy new oak nose with minty liquorice and blackcurrant flavours enveloping lovely acidity and tannins.*	£10.00	GOU	(S)
Château Beau Site 1996, Borie Manoux Bordeaux	*Stylish oaky nose with meaty plums and berries mingling with green tannins, smooth ending.*	£10.00	WAV	(B)
Château Guibeau La Fourvieille 1998, SARL Henri Bourlon Bordeaux	*Warm stalky nose with full body of raspberry, velvety mocha with supple tannins and a fine finish.*	£10.00	BDR	(B)
Château la Clarière Laithwaite 1998, Direct Wines Castillon Bordeaux	*Ripe plum fruit abounds in dark chocolate softly textured integrated with oak on the finish.*	£10.20	BDR	(S)
Château la Clarière Laithwaite 1997, Direct Wines Castillon Bordeaux	*Vanilla, chocolate and spice aroma deep delicious plum fruit with textured silky tannins and tail.*	£10.20	BDR	(B)

Name	Tasting Note	Price	Code	
CHÂTEAU LA CARDONNE 1997, CHÂTEAU LA CARDONNE Bordeaux	*Wet leaf aromas with weighty juicy black berries with hints of meatiness, wonderful length.*	£10.40	ODD JAG WBR WCR VIL TMW G&M	B
CHÂTEAU DU SEUIL GRAVES ROUGE 1997, CHÂTEAU DU SEUIL Bordeaux	*Good oaky nose with a light style of berry fruit and velvet mocha with good medium weight.*	£10.50	CTC	B
CHÂTEAU LA VIEILLE CURE 1996, CHÂTEAU LA VIEILLE CURE Bordeaux	*Spirited plumy nose with a lovely oaky cassis palate, green tannins and elegant finale.*	£11.00	JSM	B
EMILIUS DE TRIMOULET 1997, YVON MAU Bordeaux	*Green pepper and sweet black fruit nose with spicey velvety blackcurrants, elegant acidity and fine tannins.*	£11.00	YVM	B
CHÂTEAU LA FREYNELLE BORDEAUX ROUGE EMOTION 1998, CHÂTEAU LA FREYNELLE Bordeaux	*Tobacco and lovely red fruit nose with full balanced fruit palate with a good chocolate end.*	£11.50	ENO	S
CHÂTEAU SOUDARS 1996, M MIAILHE Bordeaux	*Stewed plum, intense nose with olive greenness giving a balanced silky textured wine, lovely finish.*	£11.50	WCR	B
BERRYS OWN SELECTION ST JULIEN 1998, CHÂTEAU LEOVILLE POYFERRÉ Bordeaux	*Jammy blackcurrant aroma with intense cassis and spicy palate with firm tannins. Just lovely.*	£12.10	BBR	B
CHÂTEAU GARRAUD 1998, VIGNOBLES LÉON NONY Bordeaux	*Lovely intensity of blackcurrants with mocha notes, soft and rich in the mouth. A pleasurable wine.*	£12.30	CPW	B

CHÂTEAU CÔTES DU ROL 1998, ROBERT GIRAUD Bordeaux	*Rich and austere, classic style with and edge of structure and complexity with bountiful fruit.*	£13.30	AVB	(B)
No 2 DU CHÂTEAU LAFON ROCHET 1996, CHÂTEAU LAFON-ROCHET Bordeaux	*Exciting vanilla cedar nose with intense blueberry and liquorice flavours with tannins that grab you.*	£14.00	SAF	(B)
CHÂTEAU POUJEAUX 1997, VIEUX CHÂTEAU CERTAN Bordeaux	*Savoury gutsy aromas with velvety liquorice and red fruit, gripping tannins and lush lengthy ending.*	£16.10	ODD J&B MAD N&P RHV	(S)
CHÂTEAU L'ANCIEN 1998, VIGNOBLES LÉON NONY Bordeaux	*Dense blackcurrant, tobacco aroma integrated with chocolate dipped plums balanced with fine smooth tannins.*	£17.00	PAT	(S)
CUVÉE ANDRÉ 1996, ANDRÉ QUANCARD Bordeaux	*Spicy blackcurrant fruit with integrated complex liquorice plum fruit palate, good balance, elegant style.*	£17.00	WTS	(B)
CHÂTEAU BATAILLEY 1996, BORIE MANOUX Bordeaux	*Beautiful vanilla nose with concentrated plummy palate with grainy tannins, structured complex wine.*	£21.80	BBR CTC	(B)
CHÂTEAU TROTTEVIEILLE 1996, BORIE MANOUX Bordeaux	*Cigar box nose celebrating spicy strawberries and plums with vanilla complexity. Rich round, well balanced.*	£22.80	BBR	(G)
CHÂTEAU HAUT-BATAILLEY 1996, CHÂTEAU HAUT-BATAILLEY Bordeaux	*Rich spicy cassis nose with complex mid palate of red currants, fine tannins and elegant finish.*	£24.00	BDR J&B N&P WCS	(B)

FRANCE • BORDEAUX • RED

CHÂTEAU BEAUSEJOUR-DUFFAU-LAGARROUSE 1996, CHATEAU BEAUSEJOUR Bordeaux	*Sweet soft nose with ripe dusty plums with mouth coating tannins and great oak integration.*	**£50.00**	J&B	(S)
VIEUX CHÂTEAU CERTAN 1996, VIEUX CHATEAU CERTAN Bordeaux	*Intense savoury fruit nose with harmonious plums, cherry fruit and dry tannins, well structured. Serious.*	**£59.60**	MAD FRI JNW TAN HST GHC RHV	(G)
VIEUX CHÂTEAU CERTAN 1986, VIEUX CHÂTEAU CERTAN Bordeaux	*Vivid red summer fruits integrating with fine tannins and medium acid, great mouthfeel. Lovely mature Bordeaux.*	**£96.70**	J&B MAD JNW UBC	(G)
CHÂTEAU LA MISSION HAUT BRION 1990, CHÂTEAU LA MISSION BRION Bordeaux	*Ripe cassis leathery nose integrated with oak, mature style with fine tannins. Just dandy.*	**£132**	BBR JNW J&B	(S)

BORDEAUX • SWEET

SAUTERNES BARON MATHILDE 1994, BARON PHILIPPE DE ROTHSCHILD Bordeaux	*This is an interesting sauternes, honey and marzipan both tease and seduce the palate.*	**£15.50**	CTC	(B)
CHÂTEAU FILHOT 1989, CHÂTEAU FILHOT Bordeaux	*Burnt sugar and banana skins dominate the aroma whilst orange and candyfloss rule the palate. Foie gras?*	**£25.00**	WTS	(B)
CHÂTEAU FILHOT 1990, CHÂTEAU FILHOT Bordeaux	*This sauternes is fresh and appealing, savour the flavours of zesty lemons with hints of butterscotch.*	**£25.80**	Widely available	(B)

CHÂTEAU COUTET 1996, CHÂTEAU COUTET Bordeaux	*Pure pleasure, breath in the delicious crème brulée giving this wine a great creamy complexity.*	**£37.80**	MWW WTS BBO JAG TAN	(S)

BORDEAUX • WHITE

CHÂTEAU CHANTELOUP BORDEAUX BLANC SEC 1999, CHÂTEAU CHANTELOUP Bordeaux	*Green, herbaceous nose followed by lots of balanced acidity and hints of oak on palate.*	**£4.50**	FCA FRW	(B)
BARON DE LESTAC BLANC 1999, CASTEL FRÈRES Bordeaux	*Lovely, rich, restrainrd tropical fruit aromas followed by creamy palate of ripe gooseberries and hints of spices.*	**£5.00**	L&T	(B)
LAITHWAITE SAUVIGNON BLANC 1999, DIRECT WINES CASTILLON Bordeaux	*Nice lemon and lime aromas, good weight, palate of rich ripe fruit, elegant wine! A bargain.*	**£5.80**	BDR	(S) WINE OF THE YEAR
ENTRE-DEUX MERS CHÂTEAU DUCLA BLANC 1999, YVON MAU Bordeaux	*Stylish sauvignon with big gooseberry aromas, a big middle palate and nice crisp acidity.*	**£6.00**	YVM	(B)
RÉSERVE MOUTON CADET GRAVES SEC 1997, BARON PHILIPPE DE ROTHSCHILD Bordeaux	*Rushes of meadow perfumes, grassiness and violets fill the nose. Clean, traditional rich sauvignon palate.*	**£6.80**	FEN CTC	(B)
CHÂTEAU DU SEUIL GRAVES BLANC 1998, CHÂTEAU DU SEUIL Bordeaux	*Rich spicy citrus nose with elegant buttery fruit characters and well defined finish and length.*	**£9.50**	J&B	(S)

FRANCE • BORDEAUX • WHITE

CHÂTEAU DU SEUIL BORDEAUX BLANC 1998, CHÂTEAU DU SEUIL Bordeaux	*Pleasant grapefruit nose, good fruit balance on the palate with notes of apples, good length.*	£10.50	CTC	**B**
CLOS FLORIDENE BLANC 1998, DENIS DUBOURDIEU Bordeaux	*Sweet passion fruit nose integrating with hot spicy fruit and some butteriness with a polished finish.*	£12.90	ABY	**B**

BURGUNDY • RED

MHV HENRI LA FONTAINE MÂCON ROUGE 1999, FAYE & CIE Burgundy	*Soft fruit nose followed by smooth ripe fruit palate. Pleasant acidity, well balanced, good length.*	£5.20	MHV	**B**
TESCO RED BURGUNDY 1998, LOUIS JOSSE Burgundy	*Subtle savoury aromas with cherry undercurrents. Well balanced fruit, acidity and tannin.*	£5.70	TOS	**B**
BOURGOGNE HAUTES-CÔTES DE NUITS 1998, LOUIS JOSSE Burgundy	*Attractive rich, berried nose. Good jammy ripe fruit, gripping tannins on the finish.*	£6.00	TOS	**B**
TESCO OAK AGED RED BURGUNDY 1998, LOUIS JOSSE Burgundy	*Combined savoury and fruit aromas. Attractive palate yields to sour finish.*	£6.50	TOS	**B**
CÔTE DE BEAUNE VILLAGES CLAUDE CHONION1998, VAUCHER PÈRE ET FILS Burgundy	*Crushed strawberry and damson bouquet, while the palate offers soft fine tannin and elevated acidity.*	£8.50	NTD	**B**

CÔTES DU BEAUNE VILLAGES 1998, CHANSON PÈRE & FILS Burgundy	*Lovely, pure and elegant aromas follow through onto a well balanced, concentrated palate. Rich and lengthy.*	**£9.00**	ESL POR	(B)
CÔTE CHALLONAISE CHÂTEAU DU CRAY 1997, CAVE DES VIGNERONS DE BUXY Burgundy	*Wild strawberry characters follow through to a delicate, but persistent fruit palate of nice balance and length.*	**£9.00**	CTC	(B)
MERCUREY ROUGE 1ER CRU EN SAZENAY 1997, JEAN-MICHEL & LAURENT PILLOT Burgundy	*A subtle vegetal and mulberry nose gives way to a well structured tannic palate.*	**£10.00**	3DW	(B)
CHÂTEAU DE LA CHARRIÈRE 1ER CRU CLOS ROUSSEAU 1997, YVES GIRARDIN Burgundy	*Rich cherry fruit aromas, followed by complex raspberry coulis palate and a long lingering finish.*	**£11.00**	LCD	(B)
BEAUNE 1ER CRU LES AVAUX 1998, DOMAINE LUCIEN JACOB Burgundy	*Fresh strawberry and plumy aromas flow onto a concentrated red fruit palate and nice oaky finish.*	**£11.20**	3DW	(S)
MERCUREY 1ER CRU LES PUILLETS CHÂTEAU 1998, CHÂTEAU PHILIPPE LE HARDI Burgundy	*A complex array of delicate fruit on the palate of this austere but characterful lingering wine.*	**£11.50**	WTS LHP	(B)
FIXIN LES VILLAGES DE JAFFELIN 1997, JAFFELIN Burgundy	*Black cherry fruit on the nose, well integrated with the palate of length and finesse.*	**£12.70**	AVB CTC	(B)
MERCUREY CLOS L'EVÈQUE 1998, DOMAINE MAURICE PROTHEAU Burgundy	*Complex, integrated, mushroom and toasted oak flavours give fine tannin with a tart, juicy length.*	**£12.70**	VIW	(B)

CHÂTEAU DE CHAMIREY ROUGE 1997, ANTONIN RODET Burgundy	*Gentle earthy aromas. Pleasant fruit on middle palate offering good length and balancing acidity.*	£13.50	JSM CTC	**B**
MONTHELIE 1ER CRU LES CHAMPS FULLIOT 1997, DOMAINE PARENT Burgundy	*Pleasant fruity nose, follows through to lofty acidity, good ripe fruit palate. Sophisticated wine.*	£13.90	CAM ESL	**B**
SAVIGNY-LES-BEAUNE 1998, BOUCHARD PERE ET FILS Burgundy	*Cherry and strawberry nose persists onto a fresh fruity palate that is clean and immediately appealing.*	£14.00	WTS MAD	**B**
BEAUNE 1ER CRU 1996, LOUIS JADOT Burgundy	*Rich, sweet juicy fruit palate held up by mouth watering acidity. Nice new world style.*	£18.00	MAD TOS	**B**
ALOXE-CORTON 1ER CRU CLOS DU CHAPITRE 1996, FOLLIN-ARBELET Burgundy	*Delicate peppery, spice aromas give way to a honeyed fruit palate with medium length.*	£19.50	J&B	**B**
MONTHELIE 1ER CRU SUR LA VELLE 1997, DOMAINE J PARENT Burgundy	*Rich strawberry and oak nose, palate offers a wonderfully creamy texture and nice rounded tannins.*	£20.00	WIN	**S**
POMMARD 1ER CRU LE CLOS BLANC 1997, DOMAINE J PARENT Burgundy	*Spicy oak aromas, cherries enhanced by spicy, peppery flavours, developed fruit palate and firm tannins.*	£20.00	CAM	**S**
ALOXE CORTON 1997, FRANK FOLLIN Burgundy	*Red berry aromas flow on to a lean, juicy palate revealing a subtle and elegant finish.*	£21.00	J&B	**B**

VOSNE-ROMANEE 1ER CRU LES SUCHOTS 1997, OLIVIER LANVIN Burgundy	*Berry fruit and spicy, peppery aromas, palate reveals cherry fruit and elegant savoury flavours.*	£21.20	ABY	(S)
CHAMBOLLE MUSIGNY 1997, OLIVIER LANVIN Burgundy	*Rich intense ripe red fruit aromas, palate reveals great savoury flavours and long intense finish.*	£22.40	ABY	(S)
NUITS-SAINT-GEORGES 1ER CRU LES CAILLES 1997, OLIVIER LANVIN Burgundy	*Alluring summer fruits fallen in the orchards with rich rabbit casserole on the finish.*	£24.70	ABY	(B)
VOLNAY 1ER CRU LES CHEVRETS 1996, J BOILLOT Burgundy	*Splendid banquet of truffles and ripe fruit desserts, followed by excellent acidity and length.*	£25.00	WTS	(G) TROPHY WINE
SAVIGNY LA DOMINODE 1ER CRU 1996, BRUNO CLAIR Burgundy	*Charming array of soft summer pudding fruits, subtle acidity and very fine structure and length.*	£25.00	J&B	(B)
NUITS-ST-GEORGE 1ER CRU LES VAUCRAINS 1994, ROBERT CHEVILLON Burgundy	*Bold, beetroot aromas with raspberry hints. Youthful cherry fruits, robust acidity, firm and elegant finish.*	£28.20	J&B NYW	(G)
VOLNAY CLOS DES CHENES 1ER CRU 1997, DOMAINE THOMAS Burgundy	*Creamy, vanilla nose. Fine tannins and dry firm structure, nice acidity and good length.*	£28.50	CRI	(B)
VOLNAY 1ER CRU LES CAILLERETS CLOS DES 60 OUVRÉES 1996, GÉRARD POTEL Burgundy	*Up front intense orange and red fruit attack, good solid acidity. Well made, elegant wine.*	£32.00	WTS	(B)

VOSNE-ROMANEE 1997, ROUGET Burgundy	*Lashings of rich, ripe fruit aromas are reflected on the palate and follow through to the finish.*	£35.00	J&B	(G)
CHAMBOLLE MUSIGNY 1ER CRU LES FUÉES 1996, GHISLAINE BARTHOD Burgundy	*Cherry jam aromas with hints of dried fruit. Big, bold, gutsy fruit palate with excellent length.*	£35.00	J&B	(S)
VOLNAY CLOS DES DUCS 1997, MARQUIS D'ANGERVILLE Burgundy	*A pretty floral nose gives in to a light, lean peppery fruit palate with elevated acidity.*	£35.00	J&B	(B)
CORTON BRESSANDES 1997, TOLLOT BEAUT Burgundy	*Rich, sweet oak nose, lovely complex palate of juicy ripe fruit with oak and mineral undertones.*	£35.20	J&B	(G)
CORTON 1995, MAISON LOUIS JADOT Burgundy	*Farmyardy, sweet peppery nose, a young tannic wine, intense peppery fruit with raspberry and apple.*	£38.50	MAD FQU	(S)
VOSNE-ROMANÉE 1ER CRU LES MALCONSORTS 1997, DOMAINE THOMAS Burgundy	*Ripe cherry nose, with hints of strawberries, some raspberry fruit, medium bodied, well balanced wine.*	£39.00	CRI	(B)
CLOS DE TART 1996, MOMMESSIN Burgundy	*Beautiful concentrated fruit and vegetal aromas, big, young fruit palate with well integrated oak.*	£43.90	WTS HRF	(S)

Pinpoint who sells the wine you wish to buy by turning to the stockist codes. If you know the name of the wine you want to buy, use the alphabetical index. If the price is your motivation, refer to the invaluable price guide index; red and white wines under £5, sparkling wines under £12 and champagne under £16. Happy hunting!

BURGUNDY • SPARKLING

CREMANT DE BOURGOGNE CAVE DE VIRE NV, CAVE DE VIRE Burgundy	*Lovely mousse, well balanced, gentle vegetal hint in fruity full bodied palate, fresh and long.*	**£8.20**	CTC	(B)

BURGUNDY • WHITE

PONT NEUF MÂCON BLANC VILLAGES 1998, VAUCHER PÈRE ET FILS Burgundy	*Tropical fruit and marzipan nose, full well balanced juicy fruits on the palate and delicious long finish.*	**£5.00**	NTD	(B)
TESCO PETIT CHABLIS 1999, LA CHABLISIENNE Burgundy	*Smooth citrus nose, lovely fruity palate with notes of creamy vanilla. Fresh creamy finish.*	**£5.50**	TOS	(B)
CHABLIS 1ER CRU 1997, GEORGES DESIRE Burgundy	*Light fruit aroma takes you to toffee fruity palate with delicious acidity and charming finish.*	**£6.00**	TOS	(B)
MÂCON CHARDONNAY 1998, DOMAINE LES ECUYERS Burgundy	*Voluptuous ripe fruit on nose and palate, very seductive full round mouth feel and tasteful long finish.*	**£7.00**	JSM	(B)
CHABLIS 1999, J MOREAU & FILS Burgundy	*Gentle mineral bouquet followed by good fruit and light vanilla notes for a velvety mouthfeel.*	**£8.00**	WCR	(S)

Wine	Description	Price	Code	
CHABLIS ANDRÉ SIMON 1999, DOMAINE LAROCHE Burgundy	*Soft clean elegant style of apples and pears on nose and palate with enjoyable spicy finish.*	£8.00	WRT	S
CHABLIS VIELLES VIGNES TOUR DE ROY 1998, DOMAINE DES MALANDES Burgundy	*Excellent inviting green fruit nose, fruit palate with beautiful balance of acidity. Great fresh mouth feel.*	£8.00	CHN	S
BOURGOGNE CHARDONNAY EN SOL JURASSIQUE 1998, JEAN-MARC BROCARD Burgundy	*Fresh apples and some pears on nose, very smooth fruit compote with pleasant depth on palate.*	£8.00	JBF	B
CHABLIS SAINTE CÉLINE 1998, JEAN-MARC BROCARD Burgundy	*Tight green apples on nose, buttery fruit flavours with lime hints on the palate, lovely fresh finish.*	£8.00	JBF	B
SAINSBURY'S CLASSIC SELECT CHABLIS 1999, JEAN-MARCION BROCARD Burgundy	*Nose shows a lot of ripe fruit, seductive generous fruits on palate and lovely crisp acidity.*	£8.00	JSM	B
CHABLIS LES HAUTS VERSANTS 1998, VAUCHER PÈRE ET FILS Burgundy	*Tropical buttery lychees on nose with toasty hints continuing on palate with smooth fresh finish.*	£8.50	NTD	B
CHABLIS LES VIGNERONS DE CHABLIS 1998, LA CHABLISIENNE Burgundy	*Aromas of rich fruit, fresh hints of pear on the palate leading to a textured finish.*	£8.60	CWS VIL PFT	S
ST VERAN 1998, DOMAINE CORSIN Burgundy	*Well balanced citrus fruits and vanilla mixture with smooth sweet effect on the nose.*	£8.60	VRT	B

CHABLIS VIEILLES VIGNES 1998, JEAN DURUP PÈRE ET FILS Burgundy	*Good exotic fruit nose, crisp acid freshness in great strong delicious fruit on the palate. Good balance.*	£9.10	ABY JCP	B
MONTAGNY 1ER CRU CUVÉE SPÉCIALE 1998, LES CAVES DE BUXY Burgundy	*Subtle fruity nose, smooth young fruit on the palate with fine acidity and lovely finish.*	£9.30	ADN CPW BLS CTC	B
CHABLIS 1998, J DROUHIN Burgundy	*Lovely subtle fruit nose, soft fruity palate with notes of grapefruit. Well balanced structure.*	£10.50	MZC JNW TMW	B
CHABLIS VIEILLES VIGNES 1998, DOMAINE DE VAUROUX Burgundy	*Good toasty nose with ripe melons and good acidity on palate, very agreeable sweetness on finish.*	£11.00	NYW	B
LES VIEUX MURS 1998, LORON Burgundy	*Buttery fragrant fruits on the nose, well balanced and pleasant citrus fruit on the palate.*	£11.40	ESL TAN	B
SAINT ROMAIN LES VILLAGES DE JAFFELIN 1998, JAFFELIN Burgundy	*Buttery fruit aromas, good viscosity and soft vanilla in tropical ripe fruit flavours. Round structure.*	£11.90	AVB WES CTC	B
CHABLIS 1ER CRU BEAUROY 1998, JEAN-MARC BROCARD Burgundy	*Lovely green fruit nose with expressive enchanting freshness, good fruit on palate with elegant full finish.*	£12.00	JBF SAF	B
MARSANNAY BLANC 1996, LOUIS JADOT Burgundy	*Well balanced acidity in bed of fruits with notes of fresh citrus and lovely high oak.*	£12.00	MAD FQU DIC	B

POUILLY FUISSE VIGNE BLANCHE 1998, DOMAINE SAUMAIZE-MICHELIN Burgundy	*Lovely fresh citrus on nose, full round palate of green fruit with great acidity, excellent balance.*	**£13.30**	CTC	**B**
CHABLIS 1ER CRU BEAUROY 1998, ALAIN GEOFFROY Burgundy	*Complex creamy fruity nose followed by rich ripe flavours and good integration of acidity.*	**£13.40**	ODD GRO CTC	**B**
POUILLY FUISSE PIERREFOLLE 1998, CHÂTEAU DES RONTETS Burgundy	*Pleasant peachy nose followed by a well complex structure of fruits and oak, good length.*	**£13.50**	CTC	**B**
SAINT ROMAIN 1998, FRANCOIS D'ALLAINES Burgundy	*Subtle creamy nutty nose, sweet citrus fruit flavours with refreshing acidity and good length.*	**£13.70**	NRW	**B**
CHABLIS 1ER CRU MONT DE MILIEU 1997, LA CHABLISIENNE Burgundy	*Vanilla and pineapples on the nose and palate with lovely integration of oak and long finish.*	**£13.90**	FQU VIL PFT CTC	**B**
MERCUREY LES ROCHEUES 1998, DOMAINE LA MARCHE Burgundy	*Rich oak nose, palate of apricots and citrus with notes of vanilla, good balance and length.*	**£14.00**	JSM	**B**
POUILLY FUISSE 1999, LOUIS JADOT Burgundy	*Fresh peach nose, subtle creaminess on mid palate and greatly balanced acidity. Good lemony length.*	**£14.10**	MAD TOS BNK QWW	**B**
CHABLIS 1ER CRU MONT DE MILIEU 1996, LA CHABLISIENNE Burgundy	*Subtle creamy nose leads to refined and elegant ripe fruit flavours, great structure, creamy finish.*	**£14.50**	VIL PFT	**B**

POUILLY FUISSE LES BIRBETTES 1998, CHÂTEAU DES RONTETS Burgundy	*Juicy green fruit on nose, nice subtle herbaceous hints and big vanilla flavours with strong delicious acidity.*	£14.90	NYW CTC	(B)
MEURSAULT 1998, ANTONIN RODET Burgundy	*Clear creamy vanilla nose followed by great balance between fruit and oak, elegant persistence.*	£17.00	JSM	(S)
MEURSAULT CLAUDE CHONION 1997, VAUCHER PÈRE ET FILS Burgundy	*Nutty creamy nose followed by good citrus palate in delicate style texture. Great oak characters.*	£17.50	NTD	(B)
ST ROMAIN 1998, DOMAINE JEAN PILLOT Burgundy	*Very captivating green fruit nose, excellent round mouthfeel, generous fresh sweetness and spicy oak.*	£17.60	NYW CTC	(G)
CHABLIS GRAND CRU LES CLOS 1996, DOMAINE DES MALANDES Burgundy	*Very pleasant tropical fruits on the nose and palate with citrus notes, good length and great finish.*	£18.00	CHN	(B)
MEURSAULT 1997, LUCIEN TARDIEU Burgundy	*Very pleasant rich oak deliciously blended in delicate ripe fruit palate give gorgeous complexity.*	£19.00	EUW	(G)
PULIGNY MONTRACHET CLAUDE CHONION 1997, VAUCHER PÈRE ET FILS Burgundy	*Firm pleasant tropical nose, great pleasurable rich mouthfeel of oak, ripe fruit and lovely acidity. Outstanding*	£20.00	NTD	(G) TROPHY WINE
CHABLIS BOUGROS GRAND CRU 1998, JEAN-MARC BROCARD Burgundy	*Very seductive fragrance from a full bodied creamy texture full of ripe fruit and marvellous mineral backbone.*	£22.30	JBF PIM POR	(S)

FRANCE • BURGUNDY • WHITE

MEURSAULT 1997, REINE PEDAUQUE Burgundy	*Lovely oak on the nose followed by expressive ripe peaches and cream on a sophisticated finish.*	£22.70	QWW	(S)
CHÂTEAU DE MEURSAULT 1ER CRU 1996, DOMAINE DU CHÂTEAU DE MEURSAULT Burgundy	*Gorgeous powerful tropical and oak nose, delightful well integrated acidity and ripe fruit. Pleasant finish.*	£26.00	PAT	(S)
CHASSAGNE MONTRACHET 1997, MAISON LOUIS JADOT Burgundy	*Nice clean ripe flemons and tropical fruit on the nose and palate with lovely portion of oak.*	£27.50	MAD FQU	(B)
CHÂTEAU DE MEURSAULT 1ER CRU 1997, DOMAINE DU CHÂTEAU DE MEURSAULT Burgundy	*Rich inviting vanilla nose leads to good balance on palate tasting of delicious fruit and oak.*	£32.70	WBR VIW	(B)
CORTON CHARLEMAGNE 1996, BRUNO CLAIR Burgundy	*A masterpiece of citrus fruit on a palate of balanced acidity, tannins and a lingering tail.*	£55.00	J&B	(G)

CHAMPAGNE • ROSÉ

MHV PAUL LANGIER ROSÉ NV, CHAMPAGNE F BONNET Champagne	*Blushing hue with complex creamy fruit palate, slippery texture and gorgeous lush finish. Stylish.*	£16.90	MHV	(B)
BONNET ROSÉ NV, ALEXANDRE BONNET Champagne	*Pink onion hue with gentle floral red fruit nose, fine mousse and wonderful clean finish.*	£17.00	ODD WTS RHV	(B)

Name	Description	Price	Code	
OEIL DE PERDRIX NV, CHAMPAGNE DEVAUX Champagne	*Strawberry icecream blending with creamy mousse running away on the end with weightiness and good structure.*	£17.70	MWW VIL	B
CHAMPAGNE DEVAUX ROSÉ NV, CHAMPAGNE DEVAUX Champagne	*Fresh baked bread nose with peaches and cream character with a persistent mousse. Has finesse.*	£18.30	DBY WCR VIL	S
FLEUR DE CHAMPANGE ROSÉ DE SAIGNÉE NV, DUVAL LEROY Champagne	*Attractive yeasty nose with gentle redfruit and biscuity character with a tangy ending. Very enjoyable.*	£18.80	JSS	B
CHAMPAGNE DRAPPIER GRANDE SENDRÉE ROSÉ 1990, CHAMPAGNE DRAPPIER Champagne	*Delicate classic nose, cream and fresh berries on a soft conclusion and lovely mousse.*	£20.10	ABY	B
CHARLES DE CAZANOVE BRUT ROSÉ NV, CHARLES DE CAZANOVE Champagne	*A zesty lime and berries nose complimenting the biscuity ripe fruit flavours and fulfilling length.*	£21.50	WRW	S
JACQUART ROSE MOSAIQUE NV, CHAMPAGNE JACQUART Champagne	*Pale pink, spicy bread nose preludes strawberries and cream that dances on the tongue.*	£22.00	PAT	B
BESSERAT DE BELLEFON CUVÉE DES MOINES ROSÉ NV, BESSERAT DE BELLEFON Champagne	*Blushing biscuity aromas balanced with strawberries and savoury hints ending with lovely lush peachiness.*	£23.50	MCD	S
POMMERY BRUT ROSÉ NV, CHAMPAGNE POMMERY Champagne	*Yeasty fresh nose with peaches and cream mouthfeel elegant with big bubbles and excellent length.*	£23.50	TOS	S

CHAMPAGNE MUMM CORDON ROSÉ 1995, GH MUMM & CIE Champagne	*Yeasty cream nose hinting at strawberries, fine mousse and soft texture. Simply delicious.*	£23.70	ODD UNS RAV	**B**
LOUIS EUGÉNIE ROSÉ NV, PANNIER Champagne	*Vivid rhubarb and strawberry aroma with some toastiness, fine mousse and a lingering finish.*	£24.00	MAD	**B**
LANSON BRUT ROSÉ NV, LANSON PÈRE ET FILS Champagne	*Lovely delicate complex aromas with lime peachy flavours flowing with grace and style to the end.*	£25.10	BNK FQU UNS WCR JSS G&M CST	**B**
RÉSERVE ROSÉ BRUT PHILIPPONAT NV, CHAMPAGE PHILIPPONAT Champagne	*Nice yeasty leesy nose with some toastiness fusing with ripe berry fruit and fine mousse.*	£25.50	ENO	**B**
TAITTINGER BRUT PRESTIGE ROSÉ NV, CHAMPAGNE TAITTINGER Champagne	*Toffee cream and cherries infusing with zingy bubbles completed to a soft cream finish.*	£27.60	Widely Available	**B**
RUINART ROSÉ CHAMPAGNE NV, CHAMPAGNE RUINART Champagne	*Elegant strawberry nose with light summer fruits tickling the palate with fine mousse. Clean finish.*	£28.30	QRW MAD BLU BTH WCR	**S**
MOËT & CHANDON BRUT IMPÉRIAL VINTAGE ROSÉ 1993, MOËT & CHANDON Champagne	*Spoonfulls of strawberries and red berries with complex structure, weighty palate. Brilliant, improves with age.*	£31.50	Widely Available	**G**
VEUVE CLICQUOT ROSÉ RÉSERVE 1995, VEUVE CLICQUOT Champagne	*Strawberry candy with creamy characters concentrated with juicy fruit complexity dancing on the tongue.*	£37.30	Widely Available	**S**

POMMERY LOUISE ROSÉ 1990, CHAMPAGNE POMMERY Champagne	*Hints of chocolate and cream character laden with ripe berries on a finely balanced mature wine.*	£65.00	PFC	(B)
DOM PÉRIGNON ROSÉ 1990, MOËT & CHANDON Champagne	*Honeyed classic nose with caramelised berries on a gentle palate with balance and fulfilling length.*	£135	JAG VIW VIL	(B)

CHAMPAGNE • WHITE

CHAMPAGNE DRAPPIER CARTE D'OR DEMI-SEC NV, CHAMPAGNE DRAPPIER Champagne	*Fresh baked biscuits with juicy ripe fruits, cleansing crisp acidity and subtle lasting finish.*	£13.20	JSM ABY	(B)
SAINSBURY'S CHAMPAGNE EXTRA DRY NV, DUVAL LEROY Champagne	*Pleasant baked biscuits on the nose, nice sweetness on the finish, well balanced structure. Great drinking!*	£14.00	JSM	(S) WINE OF THE YEAR
JEAN DE PRAISAC BRUT CHAMPAGNE 1996, F BONNET Champagne	*Soft toffee on the nose and palate, rich sweet full bodied, delicious refreshing lemony finish.*	£14.00	FQU	(B)
MHV PAUL LANGIER BRUT NV, CHAMPAGNE F BONNET Champagne	*Seductive mousse, creamy lemony nose, incredible lovely ripe fruit on the palate, pleasing finish.*	£14.00	MHV	(B)
ANDRÉ SIMON CHAMPAGNE BRUT NV, MARNE ET CHAMPAGNE DIFFUSION Champagne	*Clean fresh pleasant mousse, good overall flavour with nice degree of sweetness and acidity.*	£14.10	GDS BFD FEN	(B)

MHV The House Brut Champagne NV, Champagne F Bonnet Champagne	*Very biscuity nose leads to broad aged palate with lots of flavours. Long, well balanced.*	£14.50	MHV	**G** WINE OF THE YEAR
Tesco Blanc de Blancs NV, Duval Leroy Champagne	*Clean ripe fruit and baked biscuits on the nose and palate. Smooth complexity, lovely finish.*	£14.70	TOS	**B**
Grande Cuvée Brut NV, Laurenti Père Et Fils Champagne	*Cascades of bubbles, creamy biscuity nose leads to a very crisp vegetal and fruity palate, clean finish.*	£15.00	CTC	**S**
Bouche Père et Fils Cuvée Réserve Brut NV, Bouche Père Et Fils Champagne	*Delicious biscuity nose followed by sweet lemons and toasted palate, very good concentration.*	£15.00	MAD CTC	**B**
Champagne Maison Lenique Cuvée de Réserve NV, Maison Lenique Champagne	*Very fresh nose with a hint of pineapple, fresh palate of peachy apples and great acidity. Good length.*	£15.00	3DW	**B**
Cheurlin Dangin Carte d'Or NV, Cheurlin-Dangin Champagne	*Subtle complex nose of oranges, vanilla and flowers, good acidity and delicate fruit finish.*	£15.00	NEV	**B**
Champagne Forget Brimont NV, Forget Brimont Champagne	*Lovely mousse, biscuity characters in subtle orange flavours, excellent finish, good length.*	£15.50	J&B	**S**
Jean Moutardier Brut NV Selection NV, Johnathan Saxby Champagne	*Some interesting mushroom characters on the nose, very sweet well balanced structure, complex wine.*	£15.50	GRT	**B**

BONNAIRE BLANC DE BLANCS NV, CHAMPAGNE BONNAIRE Champagne	*Lovely bouquet of ripe fruit, warm palate full of rich fruit and good balancing acidity.*	£15.70	J&B	**B**
LE BRUN DE NEUVILLE CUVÉE CHARDONNAY NV, LE BRUN DE NEUVILLE Champagne	*Hint of sweetness on the nose, rich creamy fruits on the palate, balanced acidity, long and refreshing.*	£16.00	TRO CST	**S**
PANNIER BRUT SÉLECTION NV, CHAMPAGNE PANNIER Champagne	*Stylish nose of ripe fruit, with elegant yeasty palate, good length and a pleasant finish.*	£16.00	HBJ	**S**
CHAMPAGNE GREMILLET BRUT GRANDE RÉSERVE NV, CHAMPAGNE GREMILLET Champagne	*Lovely creamy nose, gentle mousse, superb acidity gives freshness to warm mouthfeel of ripe fruit.*	£16.10	PBA CPW NRW N&P	**B**
CHAMPAGNE BLANC DE BLANCS 1ER CRU NV, CHAMPAGNE VIUVE FOURVY ET FILS Champagne	*Fresh, complex, delicious appley nose, elegant palate of ripe fruit with very good length.*	£17.00	TNH	**S**
SAFEWAY ALBERT ETIENNE VINTAGE 1993, MARNE ET CHAMPAGNE Champagne	*Sweet inviting appley nose leads to exquisite honeyed fruits on the palate with very nice acidity.*	£17.00	SAF	**S**
CHAMPAGNE AMYOT BRUT RÉSERVE NV, AMYOT Champagne	*Fresh inviting melon on the nose, soft pleasant acidity, exotic fruit palate, very good length.*	£17.00	WIN	**B**
CHAMPAGNE BLANC DE BLANCS SIGNATURE NV, CHAMPAGNE DRAPPIER Champagne	*Amazing acidity well balanced in bed of sweet fruit, good complexity, delightful finish.*	£17.00	ABY	**B**

Wine	Tasting Notes	Price	Code	
J DE TELMONT BLANC DE BLANCS 1993, J DE TELMONT Champagne	*Soft mousse, great attractive buttery nose, full ripe fruit palate, good length and fresh acidity.*	£17.00	MWW	**B**
SAFEWAY ALBERT ETIENNE MILLÉSIME 1995, LANSON PÈRE ET FILS Champagne	*Lovely mousse, fresh clean nose followed by fresh peachy fruit palate with excellent acidity.*	£17.00	SAF	**B**
ANDRÉ SIMON CHAMPAGNE BRUT VINTAGE 1995, MARNE ET CHAMPAGNE DIFFUSION Champagne	*Very enjoyable mousse with attractive fresh fruit nose and fresh palate. Well balanced, good length.*	£17.90	GDS	**B**
WAITROSE BRUT VINTAGE 1990, DANIEL THIBAULT Champagne	*Rich aromas with high refreshing acidity, full bodied and long lingering finish. Exceptional quality.*	£18.00	WTS	**G**
CHAMPAGNE BRUT EDMOND ROUSSIN 1995, CHAMPAGNE MARIE STUART Champagne	*Herbal green apples on the nose and palate, elegant pleasant mousse, apple blossom finish.*	£18.00	LCC	**B**
CHAMPAGNE DEVAUX GRANDE RÉSERVE BRUT NV, CHAMPAGNE DEVAUX Champagne	*Toasted lemons on the nose, light coconut hints on a fruity palate, round full bodied mouthfeel.*	£18.00	DBY WCR VIW VIL	**B**
NICOLAS FEUILLATTE DEMI-SEC NV, NICOLAS FEUILLATTE Champagne	*Fresh grassy nose with honey and pear flavours, good balance and acidity. Stylish sparkly.*	£18.00	CNF	**B**
CHEURLIN DANGIN CUVÉE SPECIALE NV, CHEURLIN-DANGIN Champagne	*Very smooth sweet nose leads to excellent balance of fruits and acidity, nice length.*	£18.50	NEV	**B**

CHAMPAGNE CUVÉE VICTORY HENRI MANDOIS 1995, HENRI MANDOIS Champagne	*Lovely toasty green apples on the nose, some hints of peaches, flowers and apple blossom finish.*	£18.60	SHE	(B)
MHV LOUIS DE BELMANCE VINTAGE CHAMPAGNE 1995, CHAMPAGNE F BONNET Champagne	*Toasty characters on the nose, creamy pineapple palate, full bodied, very nice bitterness in strong finish.*	£18.90	MHV	(B)
LE BRUN DE NEUVILLE CUVÉE MILLÉSIMÉ 1991, LE BRUN DE NEUVILLE Champagne	*Fresh full nose, hints of walnuts on the palate, creamy nuts and fruity finish.*	£19.00	WAW	(S)
FLEUR DE CHAMPANGE BRUT 1ER CRU NV, DUVAL LEROY Champagne	*Delightful sweetness on the nose, fresh apple on the palate with excellent length, a true pleasure.*	£19.00	BDR	(B)
CHAMPAGNE DEMI SEC NV, PIPER-HEIDSIECK Champagne	*Honey citrus nose with crisp clean fruit palate with green apple finish and fine mousse.*	£19.60	WTS TOS BTH VIL FEN	(B)
CHAMPAGNE MANSARD BRUT 1992, CHAMPAGNE MANSARD Champagne	*Full bodied, lemony nose, very round palate with lovely mouthfeel, finishes with style.*	£20.00	FTH	(S)
CUVÉE SPECIALE CLUB BLANC DES BLANCS 1995, CHAMPAGNE A MARGAINE Champagne	*Attractive creamy apple on the nose, crisp citrus characters in good doses, delicious apple finish.*	£20.00	GGW	(B)
SAINSBURY'S GRAND CRU MILLENNIUM CHAMPAGNE 1995, BOIZEL Champagne	*Floral apple blossom nose, crisp green apple palate followed by sweet citrus, pleasant finish.*	£20.00	JSM	(B)

FRANCE • CHAMPAGNE • WHITE

Wine	Tasting Notes	Price	Stockists	
SOMERFIELD PRINCE WILLIAM MILLENNIUM CHAMPAGNE 1990, MARNE ET CHAMPAGNE Champagne	*Biscuity, delicious nose followed by a good round fruity palate with a very clean lemony finish.*	**£20.00**	SMF	B
CHAMPAGNE DEVAUX CUVÉE MILLÉSIMÉE 1995, CHAMPAGNE DEVAUX Champagne	*Honey and citrus aroma lead to expansive creamy palate, great mousse and lemony round finish.*	**£20.40**	DBY WCR VIL	B
BEAUMONT DES CRAYÈRES NOSTALGIE 1992, BEAUMONT DES CRAYÈRES Champagne	*Good mousse, lovely lemon and apple nose, creamy biscuit palate, very fresh acidity on finish.*	**£20.50**	TAN	B
PANNIER BRUT 1995, CHAMPAGNE PANNIER Champagne	*Savoury bread nose followed by juicy fruits on the palate, complex, seductive mouthfeel, good length.*	**£20.70**	MAD	S
LANSON IVORY LABEL NV, LANSON PÈRE ET FILS Champagne	*A yeasty nose with crushed grape and lemon palate, wonderful acidity and mousse.*	**£21.00**	SAF N&P	B
CHAMPAGNE DEUTZ BRUT CLASSIC NV, CHAMPAGNE DEUTZ Champagne	*Lovely floral nose followed by soft creamy fruit palate, very good weight and depth on finish.*	**£21.60**	ODD BWC JSS HDS CTC	B
CHAMPAGNE MAILLY GRAND CRU CUVÉE LES ECHANSONS VINTAGE 1988, MAILLY GRAND CRU Champagne	*Attractive and clean, fresh toasty aroma, balanced fruit and acidity, strong fresh pleasant acidity on finish.*	**£21.90**	ALI	S
CANARD-DUCHENE VINTAGE 1991, CANARD-DUCHENE Champagne	*Gentle floral creamy nose, rich attractive ripeness of fruit on the palate, fresh citrus finish.*	**£22.00**	BBO BNK NRW FQU FEN WES CTC	S

CHAMPAGNE MERCIER VINTAGE 1995, CHAMPAGNE MERCIER Champagne	*Very upfront good mousse, lovely pears and apples on the palate, full bodied.*	£22.00	MHU FQU VIL	(S)
GRAND CRU CUVÉE EXCELLENCE NV, CHAMPAGNE JEAN-LOUIS MALARD Champagne	*Rich fruit well integrated, clear, round characters with good length and lovely mousse in the mouth.*	£22.00	PEC	(B)
H BLIN & CO VINTAGE BRUT 1995, H BLIN & CO Champagne	*Good depth of flavour, good biscuity fruits on the palate preceded by lovely citrus aroma.*	£22.50	ODD JBF	(S)
ROYALE RÉSERVE BRUT PHILIPPONAT NV, CHAMPAGE PHILIPPONAT Champagne	*Some caramel overtones on the nose and palate, very pleasant integration of acidity. Good length.*	£22.50	ENO	(B)
CHAMPAGNE MANSARD CUVÉE 2000 1995, CHAMPAGNE MANSARD Champagne	*Fresh, clean crisp acidity and honeyed middle palate, excellent ripe fruit, long delicate floral finish.*	£23.00	FTH	(S)
NICOLAS FEUILLATTE BRUT 1ER CRU 1992, NICOLAS FEUILLATTE Champagne	*Crème brûlée nose followed by soft complex palate, tropical peachy fruit, excellent finish.*	£23.00	CNF	(S)
BESSERAT DE BELLEFON CUVÉE DES MOINES BRUT NV, BESSERAT DE BELLEFON Champagne	*Excellent fresh nose slipping into a fruity palate with nice high acidity and smooth finish.*	£23.00	MCD	(B)
CHARLES HEIDSIECK BRUT RÉSERVE MIS EN CAVE 1996 NV, CHARLES HEIDSIECK Champagne	*Clean fresh fruit nose, delicious ripe palate with refreshing acidity and very good length.*	£23.00	Widely Available	(B)

MOËT & CHANDON BRUT IMPERIAL NV, MOËT & CHANDON Champagne	*Nutty fruit nose invites to taste elegant fruit characters with good depth, excellent balance and complexity.*	£23.20	Widely Available	S
CHARLES HEIDSIECK BRUT RÉSERVE MIS EN CAVE 1995, CHARLES HEIDSIECK Champagne	*Pleasant toasty lemon on the nose, apple blossom with fine acidity on the palate. Nice maturity and fresh balance.*	£23.50	Widely Available	G
CHAMPAGNE A MARGAINE CUVÉE SPECIALE CLUB BLANC DES BLANCS 1989, CHAMPAGNE A MARGAINE Champagne	*Ripe sweet complex nose, soft creamy citrus fruit on the palate, full bodied, memorable experience.*	£23.50	GGW	S
JACQUART MOSAIQUE MILLÉSIMÉ 1992, CHAMPAGNE JACQUART Champagne	*Huge firm ripe fruit nose, nutty characters and good acidity on the palate, lovely finish.*	£23.50	MWW	S
R DE RUINART CHAMPAGNE NV, CHAMPAGNE RUINART Champagne	*Very good ripe fruit on the nose and palate with balancing citrus, good complexity, lovely finish.*	£23.50	QRW MAD FQU BTH WCR	B
FLEURY CHAMPAGNE BRUT 1993, FLEURY Champagne	*Soft creamy and lovely complexity, floral honey blossom nose, rich melon palate, delicate style.*	£23.90	WTS VRT	G
VEUVE CLICQUOT WHITE LABEL DEMI-SEC NV, VEUVE CLICQUOT Champagne	*Creamy mousse with wonderful bouquet and ripe fruit flavours, long sweet finish. Enchanting wine.*	£24.10	Widely Available	B
CHAMPAGNE DEVAUX CUVÉE D NV, CHAMPAGNE DEVAUX Champagne	*Very attractive nutty nose followed by delicious hints of pineapple on the palate, very good balance.*	£24.20	VIL	S

CUVÉE ROYALE VINTAGE 1995, CHAMPAGNE JOSEPH PERRIER Champagne	*Delicious nose leads to rich mousse, apples and pears on the palate with very nice length.*	£24.20	GRT CAM BLS ESL CVR	**B**
TAITTINGER BRUT RÉSERVE NV, CHAMPAGNE TAITTINGER Champagne	*Lovely mousse, an explosion of good fruit in the mouth, great balance, good length.*	£24.50	Widely Available	**B**
VEUVE CLICQUOT YELLOW LABEL BRUT NV, VEUVE CLICQUOT Champagne	*Very smooth fruit nose, apple blossom and nutty characters on the palate. Excellent acidity and length.*	£24.70	Widely Available	**S**
CHAMPAGNE PIERREL CUVÉE TRADITION VINTAGE 1995, PIERREL Champagne	*Crisp green apple and pears on the nose invite you to taste lemony ripe fruit.*	£25.00	FCC	**S**
GRAND BRUT MILLÉSIMÉ 1991, CHAMPAGNE JEAN-LOUIS MALARD Champagne	*Fresh berries on the nose, lovely mousse texture, delicious fruits on the palate. Great finish.*	£25.00	PEC	**B**
NICOLAS FEUILLATTE BRUT 1ER CRU BLANC DE BLANCS 1995, NICOLAS FEUILLATTE Champagne	*Rich appley nose continues in a mouse of apples and well integrated acidity. Round mouthfeel.*	£25.00	CNF	**B**
CHAMPAGNE DRAPPIER GRANDE SENDRÉE 1990, CHAMPAGNE DRAPPIER Champagne	*Rich full nose, smooth citrus fruit palate, lovely mousse, pleasant rich appley finish.*	£25.40	DBY N&P CST POR	**B**
TAITTINGER DEMI SEC NV, CHAMPAGNE TAITTINGER Champagne	*A enticing crisp nose with fine bubbles fusing with rich yeast notes and ripe full palate.*	£25.80	CFT	**B**

EGERIE DE PANNIER 1995, CHAMPAGNE PANNIER Champagne	*Honeyed fruit nose, upfront style and lovely refreshing acidity on the palate, creamy pineapple finish.*	£26.00	MAD	B
JACQUART BLANC DE BLANCS 1995, CHAMPAGNE JACQUART Champagne	*Ripe appley nose followed by clean crisp acidity on the palate, fresh ripe fruit finish.*	£26.00	PAT	B
VINTAGE PIPER-HEIDSIECK 1995, PIPER-HEIDSIECK Champagne	*Elegant inviting pineapple citrus aromas, clean pleasant fruity flavours, delicious extended finish.*	£26.00	WTS FQU	B
CHARLES HEIDSIECK BRUT RÉSERVE MIS EN CAVE 1993, CHARLES HEIDSIECK Champagne	*Excellent quality wine with attractive pineapple aroma and very pleasant full bodied fruity palate.*	£26.60	BDR ODD WTS CPW FQU FEN	S
CHAMPAGNE PERRIER JOUËT 1995, PERRIER-JOUËT Champagne	*Toasty fresh fruit creamy aroma, clean light fruit, soft mousse, citrus characters and fresh finish.*	£26.70	ODD RAV	B
NICOLAS FEUILLATTE BRUT 1ER CRU CUVÉE SPECIALE 1995, NICOLAS FEUILLATTE Champagne	*Very attractive subtle lemon and apple aroma, clean fresh ripe fruit palate, delicious extended finish.*	£28.00	CNF	G
NICOLAS FEUILLATTE BRUT 1ER CRU CUVÉE SPECIALE 1994, NICOLAS FEUILLATTE Champagne	*Lots of bubbles, youthful vegetal fruity aroma, pleasant flowery lemons on the palate, zesty finish.*	£28.00	CNF	S
LE REFLET DU MILLÉNAIRE PHILIPPONAT NV, CHAMPAGE PHILIPPONAT Champagne	*Obvious fresh nose, nuts and fresh fruit on the palate, full round mouthfeel. Good balance.*	£28.00	ENO	B

POMMERY BRUT VINTAGE 1992, CHAMPAGNE POMMERY Champagne	*Large bubbles in a light appealing fresh apply fruit scented wine, with delicious ripe fruit flavours.*	£28.00	TOS FQU	B
LANSON BRUT MILLÉSIME 1994, LANSON PÈRE ET FILS	*Very creamy ripe fruit on the nose with clean balanced mousse fruity palate, fresh acidity.*	£28.60	WTS WCR N&P	G
MOËT & CHANDON BRUT IMPERIAL VINTAGE 1993, MOËT & CHANDON Champagne	*Light complex floral fruit aroma followed by soft toasty fruit and well integrated acidity.*	£28.80	Widely Available	S
CHAMPAGNE MUMM CUVÉE LIMITÉE 1990, GH MUMM & CIE Champagne	*Some butter on the nose followed by creamy mature fruits, excellent integration with good acidity.*	£29.30	ODD RAV	S
CANARD-DUCHENE CHARLES VII BLANC DE NOIRS NV, CANARD-DUCHENE Champagne	*Creamy vanilla nose, complex flavours with creamy biscuity fruits on the palate. Very good length.*	£29.30	FEN CTC	B
R DE RUINART CHAMPAGNE 1995, CHAMPAGNE RUINART Champagne	*Creamy smooth fruit aroma followed by soft balanced fruit, clean palate with good length.*	£30.00	QRW	S
RÉSERVE MILLÉSIMÉ BRUT PHILIPPONAT 1991, CHAMPAGE PHILIPPONAT Champagne	*Soft toasty fruit on the nose leads to lemon green apple palate with fresh long finish.*	£30.50	ENO	S
CANARD-DUCHENE CHARLES VII GRANDE CUVÉE NV, CANARD-DUCHENE Champagne	*Sweet pleasant and inviting nose, soft ripe fruit palate, good citrus intervention, nicely balanced.*	£30.60	BBO JAG NRW FQU GHL CFT CTC	B

FRANCE • CHAMPAGNE • WHITE

CHARLES DE CAZANOVE CUVÉE PRESTIGE STRADIVARIUS 1990, CHARLES DE CAZANOVE Champagne	*Good intense champagne with appealing stylish nose, very sweet, full round palate with elegant finish.*	£33.00	WRW	(S)
TAITTINGER VINTAGE BRUT 1995, CHAMPAGNE TAITTINGER Champagne	*Delicious wholemeal biscuity nose, pineapple and strawberries with good acidity on the palate. Excellent finish.*	£34.20	MWW MAD QWW CTC	(S)
VEUVE CLICQUOT RICH RÉSERVE 1993, VEUVE CLICQUOT Champagne	*Polished honey and lemon nose with well balanced full fruit flavours. Mature vivid champagne.*	£34.40	Widely Available	(B)
POL ROGER BRUT VINTAGE 1993, POL ROGER Champagne	*Attractive smooth fruit aromas, round rich fabulous palate of sweet peaches and hints of lemon.*	£34.50	Widely Available	(G)
TAITTINGER VINTAGE BRUT 1992, CHAMPAGNE TAITTINGER Champagne	*Rich and complex nose followed by well balanced toasty juicy fruit palate. Good sophisticated finish.*	£35.20	Widely Available	(G)
VEUVE CLICQUOT VINTAGE RÉSERVE 1993, VEUVE CLICQUOT Champagne	*Some butter biscuits on the nose, lovely effect of lemon hints on the juicy fruit palate.*	£35.40	Widely Available	(S)
GRAND BLANC BRUT PHILIPPONAT 1991, CHAMPAGE PHILIPPONAT Champagne	*Very creamy biscuity nose followed by sweet well balanced creamy palate, delightful long acidity on finish.*	£41.50	ENO	(S)
BOLLINGER GRANDE ANNÉE 1990, BOLLINGER Champagne	*Appealing aromas of strawberry and caramel, delicious palate of creamy ripe fruit, delightful ripe finish.*	£43.50	Widely Available	(B)

LA GRANDE CUVÉE NOMINÉE DE JACQUART 1990, CHAMPAGNE JACQUART Champagne	*Very stylish nose leads to excellent combination of acidity and sweet fruits, with beautiful extended finish.*	£45.00	PAT	**S**
NICOLAS FEUILLATTE GRAND CUVÉE PALMES D'OR 1992, NICOLAS FEUILLATTE Champagne	*Wholemeal toasty ripe fruit on the nose and palate, delicious mature fruit with good support of acidity.*	£45.00	CNF	**B**
CHARLES HEIDSIECK RÉSERVE CHARLIE MIS EN CAVE 1990, CHARLES HEIDSIECK Champagne	*Lemons, peaches and apple blossom on the nose and palate good enough to get a glass now!*	£50.00	MAX	**G**
LANSON NOBLE CUVÉE 1988, LANSON Champagne	*Smooth beginning through the nose to find a full bodied palate with delicious apple and nuts.*	£50.20	WTS FQU CST	**G**
POMMERY LOUISE BLANC 1990, CHAMPAGNE POMMERY Champagne	*Pleasant ripe fruits on the nose lead to melon and pecab palate with refreshing acidity.*	£52.20	HVN FQU CST	**B**
CHAMPAGNE DEUTZ CUVÉE WILLIAM 1990, CHAMPAGNE DEUTZ Champagne	*Exceptional quality wine with flower hint on nose and beautiful mouthfeel of apple blossom.*	£55.00	BWC CTC	**G**
LANSON NOBLE CUVÉE 1989, LANSON PÈRE ET FILS Champagne	*Cantalope melon nose gives an invitation to a well balanced fruity palate with toasty tropical finish.*	£59.00	ODD FQU UNS	**S**
VEUVE CLICQUOT LA GRANDE DAME 1993, VEUVE CLICQUOT Champagne	*Toasty nose with hint of blackcurrant, palate full of flavour, hints of cherry, extended refreshing finish.*	£62.00	Widely Available	**S**

FRANCE • CHAMPAGNE • WHITE

LANSON BLANC DE BLANCS 1994, LANSON PÈRE ET FILS Champagne	*Very seductive aroma of apple blossom, lemon, peach and apples on the palate, fulfilling finish.*	£62.00	MCD	(B)
DOM PÉRIGNON 1992, MOËT & CHANDON Champagne	*Mouth watering soft sweet aromas, lovely ripe fruit with apple hint, gorgeous long finish.*	£65.80	Widely Available	(S)
TAITTINGER COMTES DE CHAMPAGNE BLANC DE BLANCS BRUT 1993, CHAMPAGNE TAITTINGER Champagne	*Delightful, complex nose followed by great balance of sweet green fruit and refreshing acidity and luxurious finish.*	£66.20	DBY CTC	(S)
CHAMPAGE PHILIPPONAT CUVÉE CLOS DES GOISSES BRUT 1990, CHAMPAGE PHILIPPONAT Champagne	*Very attractive appley juicy nose leads to pleasurable palate of tropical ripe fruit and great acidity.*	£69.80	ENO	(S)
TAITTINGER COMTES DE CHAMPAGNE BLANC DE BLANCS BRUT 1990, CHAMPAGNE TAITTINGER Champagne	*Close to the impossible perfection, esquisitely delicious nose effect leads to dream palate of elegant fruit mix.*	£74.80	Widely Available	(G)
POL ROGER SIR WINSTON CHURCHILL CUVÉE 1990, POL ROGER Champagne	*Sophistication to the extreme in a palate full of creamy and refreshing first class fruit.*	£74.90	Widely Available	(G)
CHARLES HEIDSIECK CHAMPAGNE CHARLIE 1985, CHARLES HEIDSIECK Champagne	*Delicate acidity on the nose, fresh ripe fruit on the palate, beautiful fresh long finish.*	£76.00	MAX	(G)
CHARLES HEIDSIECK BLANC DE BLANCS (OENOTHEQUE) 1982, CHARLES HEIDSIECK Champagne	*Gorgeous generous fruity nose invites to taste great acidity and ripe fruit palate with lovely finish.*	£90.00	CTC WTS	(G) TROPHY WINE

LANGUEDOC • FORTIFIED

DOM BRIAL MUSCAT DE RIVESALTES 1999, CAVE DES VIGNERONS DE BAIXAS Languedoc-Roussillon	*Pale greenish hints, wet sweet appley nose, big sweet dry apricot flavours. Enjoyable long finish.*	£4.20	SAF	Ⓑ
MUSCAT DE FRONTIGNAN NV, FRONTIGNAN CO-OPERATIVE Languedoc-Roussillon	*Clean light gold colour, high alcohol well integrated in slightly bitter palate, strong sweet aftertaste.*	£4.80	GRT SMF	Ⓑ
MUSCAT DE RIVESALTES 1998, DOMANIE CAZES Languedoc-Roussillon	*Lots of raisin on the nose, apricot kernels and attractive sweet flavours, good balance and acidity.*	£11.00	BLU DBY CTC	Ⓑ

LANGUEDOC • RED

VENAISON DU ROI 1999, CAVES DE LANDIRAS Languedoc-Roussillon	*Interesting soft fruit on the palate of warm sun-shine and spice, with balanced acidity and tannins.*	£3.00	GCF	Ⓑ
CHENET CABERNET SYRAH 1999, GRANDS CHAIS DE FRANCE Languedoc-Roussillon	*Delicate currants nose, confected jammy fruit, nice balance on the palate, good smokey finish.*	£4.00	BNK BGN TMW	Ⓑ
DANIEL BESSIÈRE COLLECTION CÔTES DU ROUSSILLON 1998, DANIEL BESSIÈRE Languedoc-Roussillon	*Attractive chocolate nose with black fruit and cedar wood complimenting this wine with style.*	£4.00	DLA	Ⓑ

FRANCE • LANGUEDOC • RED

RESERVE ST MARC SHIRAZ 1999, FONCALIEU Languedoc-Roussillon	*Fresh aromas, pleasant fruit with some tar and tobacco flavours, well integrated oak, lingering finish.*	£4.00	JSM	B
SOMERFIELD FITOU NV, MONT TAUCH Languedoc-Roussillon	*Rosemary and bramble aroma with pepper and plum preserve with savoury characteristics and a long finish.*	£4.00	SMF	B
TERRASSES D'AZUR CABERNET SAUVIGNON 1999, CASTEL FRÈRES Languedoc-Roussillon	*Good berry fruits and balanced blackcurrant palate, firm tannins and balancing acidity, lovely finish.*	£4.00	VIL	B
MARKS & SPENCER GOLD LABEL SYRAH 1999, PAUL SAPIN Languedoc-Roussillon	*Fragrant violet and rose petal nose, sweet red berry flavours on the palate, good acidity.*	£4.20	M&S	S
DOMAINE DE CONTENSON MERLOT 1998, VAL D'ORBIEU Languedoc-Roussillon	*Lively and youthful, very pleasant easy drinking lots of fruit of palate, long warm finish.*	£4.50	SAF	B
FITOU 1998, MONT TAUCH Languedoc-Roussillon	*Black cherries nose with hot spicy chocolate plum fruit character on this well structured wine.*	£4.50	THI UNS TAN	B
TERRASSES D'AZUR MERLOT 1999, CASTEL FRÈRES Languedoc-Roussillon	*Cassis, mint and blackberry nose, smooth ripe plum fruit crumble on the palate.*	£4.50	JSM	B
CHÂTEAU GIBALAUX-BONNET AC MINERVOIS 1998, CHÂTEAU GIBALAUX-BONNET Languedoc-Roussillon	*Deep chocolate and leather nose with lush spicy blackcurrant palate with a firm tail.*	£4.80	ALZ	S

Wine	Notes	Price	Stockist	
DOMAINE LA TOUR BOISÉE 1998, JEAN-LOUIS POUDOU Languedoc-Roussillon	*Rich bramble nose fusing with black juicy cherries and soft tannins. Well balanced stylish wine.*	£5.00	WAW	(G)
TESCO FITOU RESERVE BARON DE LA TOUR 1998, MONT TAUCH Languedoc-Roussillon	*Ripe plums and green peppers with moderate tannins and black berry and cherry palate. Good concentration.*	£5.00	TOS	(S)
CORBIÈRES HAUT ST GEORGES ROUGE 1998, VINS DE PRESTIGE Languedoc-Roussillon	*White pepper and currant nose with concentrated rich chocolate and berries with a clean finish.*	£5.00	THI	(B)
LA BAUME DOMAINE CABERNET SAUVIGNON 1998, BRL HARDY Languedoc-Roussillon	*Cherry bubblegum aromas lead to soft round palate, delicate balance, vibrant finish of fruit and tannins.*	£5.00	JSM WCR FEN	(B)
LES JAMELLES MOURVÈDRE 1998, BADET CLEMENT Languedoc-Roussillon	*Nice ripe fruit with spicy complexity blending with soft red cherries on a good backbone.*	£5.00	CAM BLU	(B)
PLAN DE BRUS 1998, SOUTHCORP FRANCE Languedoc-Roussillon	*Slightly cherry nose with a subtle fruit character on the palate and a firm tannin finish.*	£5.00	TOS	(B)
ROBERT SKALLI MINERVOIS 1998, SKALLI Languedoc-Roussillon	*Peppery, juicy fruit nose, ripe and attractive layers with gentle summer fruits and balanced acidity.*	£5.00	CAX	(B)
VIN DE PAYS D'OC CABERNET FRANC 1999, MAUREL VEDEAU Languedoc-Roussillon	*Nice ripe berries on the nose, smooth fruit flavours with strong tannin and long finish.*	£5.00	THI	(B)

FRANCE • LANGUEDOC • RED

VIN DE PAYS D'OC MERLOT OAK AGED 1998, MAUREL-VEDEAU Languedoc-Roussillon	*Plump mulberry and forest leaf nose with cool juicy plums and a pleasing finish.*	£5.00	THI	(B)
DOMAINE DES LAURIERS 1997, DOMAINE DES LAURIERS Languedoc-Roussillon	*Attractive fruit and herb nose, tannic structure with generous spicy raspberry fruit and classy balance.*	£5.50	SAF	(S)
DOMAINE BUADELLE 1999, DOMAINE BUADELLE Languedoc-Roussillon	*Dark black fruit nose with bags of blackcurrant and cherry flavours with gripping tannins.*	£5.50	BDR	(B)
FITOU CHÂTEAU LESPIGNE 1998, FREDERIC ROGER VIGNOBLES Languedoc-Roussillon	*Displays good character on both the nose and palate particularly with its well weighted tannins.*	£5.50	BGL	(B)
CHÂTEAU PECH-LATT CORBIÈRES 1999, CHÂTEAU PECH-LATT Languedoc-Roussillon	*Luscious raspberry with spiciness, soft ripe strawberry and berryfruit palate through till the end.*	£5.70	WTS LVF H&H	(S)
FOX WOOD CABERNET 1998, MICHAEL GOUNDREY Languedoc-Roussillon	*Herbaceous nose with chocolate and warm sweet berry fruit giving depth and great character.*	£5.80	MAD BNK POR	(B)
CHÂTEAU CLOVIS 1998, J&E FAUSSIÉ Languedoc-Roussillon	*Good intense style wine with ripe berries blending with firm tannins and with a polished backbone.*	£5.90	DLA RHV	(B)
CORBIERES CHÂTEAU LA DOMEQUE CUVEE SIGNE 1998, FREDERIC ROGER VIGNOBLES Languedoc-Roussillon	*Spice with hints of plum and cherry, warm centre with good concentration and drying tannins.*	£5.90	BGL	(B)

UTTER BASTARD SYRAH 1999, DOMAINES DU SOLEIL Languedoc-Roussillon	*Slight cherry nose with hints of plums, palate is broad with spice flavours and a lovely tannin tail. Anything but.*	**£5.90**	GYW FQU OWC	(B)
XV DU PRESIDENT 1999, DIRECT WINES Languedoc-Roussillon	*Attractively structured with herby ripe black fruit, firm tannins with concentration and pleasant fruit aroma.*	**£5.90**	BDR	(B)
DOMAINE LA TOUR BOISEE CUVEE MARIE-CLAUDE 1998, JEAN-LOUIS POUDOU Languedoc-Roussillon	*Pepper and plum nose integrating with rich dark smokey black fruit balanced by tannins and acidity.*	**£6.00**	WAW	(S)
QUE SERA BARREL AGED SYRAH 1999, LES VINS MAS-APLIN Languedoc-Roussillon	*Cracked pepper and all-spice offer an enticing start, good oak meets fine acidity, finishes warmly.*	**£6.00**	SWS	(S)
ABBOTTS CIRRUS 1998, ABBOTTS Languedoc-Roussillon	*Oak and some earthy characters on the nose, palate has spice and a slightly green character.*	**£6.00**	GYW	(B)
CHÂTEAU BONHOME PRESTIGE 1999, CHÂTEAU BONHOME Languedoc-Roussillon	*Leathery nose meshing with red cherries and pepper with soft tannins and acidity, nice finish.*	**£6.00**	OHI	(B)
CHÂTEAU CALBET SYRAH GRENACHE CABARDES 1999, LES VINS MAS-APLIN Languedoc-Roussillon	*Nose closed at present but palate displays good fruit character and lovely powdery tannins.*	**£6.00**	SWS	(B)
DOMAINE DE LA VISTOULE CABERNET SAUVIGNON 1998, BARTON & GUESTIER Languedoc-Roussillon	*Vegetal fruit nose, ripe blackcurrant and spicy palate, adequate acidity and very good tannins.*	**£6.00**	ODD	(B)

DOMAINES VIRGINIE GOLD LABEL RÉSERVE SYRAH 1998, DOMAINES VIRGINIE Languedoc-Roussillon	*Elegant aroma of red fruit flows to the palate with complexity, attractive wine with big future.*	£6.00	M&S	B
LE GRAND VERDIER 1998, SOUTHCORP FRANCE Languedoc-Roussillon	*Nicely perfumed nose that prepares you for the concentrated, juicy and very fruity flavours.*	£6.00	ODD	B
CHÂTEAU GIBALAUX-BONNET MINERVOIS AC 1997, CHÂTEAU GIBALAUX-BONNET Languedoc-Roussillon	*Quality fruit, palate has balance which although is tannic is still in harmony with the fruit.*	£6.00	ALZ	B
VINUS DU CHÂTEAU PAUL MAS COTEAUX DU LANGUEDOC 1999, LES VINS MAS-APLIN Languedoc-Roussillon	*Nose has some plums and cherry, good lift without too much oak, creamy fruit, needs time.*	£6.00	SWS	B
LES CABRETTES 1998, LES MAÎTRES VIGNERONS DE TAUTAVEL Languedoc-Roussillon	*Rich damson and oak on nose with black berry compote palate with a nice dry finish.*	£6.20	BDR	B
COLLECTION PRIVÉE ROUGE CHATEAU DE PENNAUTIER 1998, VIGNERONS LORGERIL Languedoc-Roussillon	*Wonderful herbal aroma with full ripe plum and berry palate with some greenness, short clean finish.*	£6.40	PBA DBY	B
LA CUVÉE MYTHIQUE 1998, VAL D'ORBIEU Languedoc-Roussillon	*Chocolate liquorice nose with deep plum and black currant jam with good tannins and acidity.*	£6.60	MWW WTS VDO CWS SAF ESL	B
CHÂTEAU PLANÉZES CÔTES DU ROUSSILLON VILLAGES 1998, LES VIGERNONS DE RASIGUÈRES Languedoc-Roussillon	*Lovely evolving aromas of cassis and other dark berry fruit with vegetal and oaky undertones*	£7.00	M&S VIC	G

Wine	Description	Price	Codes	
CHÂTEAU DE L'AMARINE CUVÉE DES BERNIS ROUGE 1998, CHÂTEAU DE L'AMARINE Languedoc-Roussillon	*Smokey, toasty notes over a lovely ripe fruity background. Impressive power and concentration.*	£7.00	PBA DBY JSS AMW BOO	(S)
CHÂTEAU CAZAL-VIEL CUVÉE DES FÉES 1998, CHÂTEAU CAZAL-VIEL Languedoc-Roussillon	*Herby berry fruit aromas fusing with black berries and plums giving good style and gripping tannins.*	£7.00	WTS	(B)
ABBOTTS BOREAS 1998, ABBOTTS Languedoc-Roussillon	*A wine displaying loads of promise, still very firm and needs time to display its full potential.*	£8.00	GYW	(B)
GRANDE CUVÉE 1998, CHÂTEAU DE LANCYRE Languedoc-Roussillon	*Curranty nose with spiciness on an intense style wine with black fruits and nice tannins.*	£8.00	BGL	(B)
TÊTE CUVÉE VIELLES VIGNES SYRAH 1997, FREDERIC ROGER VIGNOBLES Languedoc-Roussillon	*Youthful, dusty and powerful fruit aroma, slightly green but not tannic, very easy drinking.*	£8.90	BGL	(B)
LES HAUTS DE FORCA REAL CÔTES DU ROUSSILLON VILLAGES 1998, DOMAINE FORCA REAL Languedoc-Roussillon	*Earthy, mushroomy nose tannic, red fruits, spicy oak and liquorice flavours create a pleasant lingering finish.*	£9.30	PBA WES	(S)
CHÂTEAU MOURQUES DU GRÈS CAPITELLES DES MOURGUES 1998, FRANCOIS COLLARD Languedoc-Roussillon	*Fat, smokey, spiced nose, dominant syrah character that offers ripe, smokey bacon fruit and tobacco palate.*	£10.00	JNW	(S)
DOMAINE DE LA BAUME ESTATE RED 1998, BRL HARDY Languedoc-Roussillon	*Spicy vanilla and blackberry nose rich fruit wrapped in tannins, drying at the end with good acidity.*	£10.00	HBR	(S)

FRANCE • LANGUEDOC • RED

ELIXIR 1999, CHÂTEAU LA CONDAMINE BERTRAND Languedoc-Roussillon	*Good richness on nose, powerful black current, cherry and pleasant chocolate fruit, not overly sweet.*	£10.00	EUW	**S**
CHÂTEAU CAPENDU CUVÉE EUGÉNIE 1997, ALAIN GRIGNON Languedoc-Roussillon	*Spicy full fruit nose with pepper hints mingling with rich berries and fine tannins.*	£10.00	WTS	**B**
CÔTES DU ROUSSILLON LA CHANCE 1998, JEAN LUC COLOMBO Languedoc-Roussillon	*Intense nose of ripe jammy fruit, sweet oak with a slight medicinal touch and a clean finish.*	£10.00	JLW	**B**
LE JUGE DOMAINE CAPION 1997, DOMAINE DES ESPIERS Languedoc-Roussillon	*Spicy bacon nose, very dry but developing fruit flavours, berby and earthy palate.*	£11.50	BBR AMW	**S**
DOMAINE CAPION LE JUGE 1996, DOMAINE CAPION Languedoc-Roussillon	*Sweaty saddle and peppered nose, full black fruit flavours, lightly earthy, concentrated and vibrant fruit.*	£11.60	BBR NYW AMW BOO	**G**
DOMAINE CAPION LE JUJE SELECTION DU CARDINAL 1997, DOMAINE CAPION Languedoc-Roussillon	*Concentrated earthy fruit aromas, massive on the palate, refreshing style, lovely silky finish.*	£12.10	JNW DBY AMW BOO	**S**
CHÂTEAU PUECH-HAUT TÊTE DE CUVÉE 1997, GERARD BRU Languedoc-Roussillon	*Smokey and peppery nose, solid ripe fruit structure, intensity of leather and chocolate flavours.*	£13.80	HDS	**B**
LE PREMIER BUMMOIS MOURVÈDRE 1999, CHÂTEAU DU CHAT NOIR Languedoc-Roussillon	*Smokey, chocolatey nose rushes excitedly into nutty juvenile mourvèdre palate with "brilliant" never ending finish.*	£13.80	Available Widely	**B**

LANGUEDOC • WHITE

LA CITÉ CHARDONNAY VIN DE PAYS D'OC 1999, FONCALIEU Languedoc-Roussillon	*Ripe fruit aromas, great acidity on the palate well integrated to juicy fruit flavours. Elegant finish.*	£4.00	WTS	(S)
TERRASSES D'AZUR SAUVIGNON BLANC 1999, CASTEL FRÈRES Languedoc-Roussillon	*Very floral, tropical fruit aromas, excellent acidity and a soft apple tart palate with lovely length.*	£4.00	VIL	(S)
LES MARIONETTES MARSANNE 1999, TERROIR CLUB Languedoc-Roussillon	*Lifted strawberry and champagne nose, soft full round palate with leesy characters and good length.*	£4.00	SMF	(B)
TERRET CHARDONNAY DOMAINE SAINTE MADELEINE 1998, MARUREL VEDEAU Languedoc-Roussillon	*Flirty appley nose followed by delicious fruit flavours and a good acidity in a full, round mouthfeel.*	£4.20	AVB WES CTC	(B)
RESERVE ST MARC SAUVIGNON BLANC 1999, FONCALIEU Languedoc-Roussillon	*Intense freshly cut grass and gooseberry nose, subtle palate with high acidity and fresh citrus flavours.*	£4.30	JSM	(B)
GOUTS ET COULEURS CHARDONNAY VIOGNIER 1999, LES DOMAINES DE FONTCAUDE Languedoc-Roussillon	*Brilliant toasty fruit nose followed by crème caramel palate with good acidity and mouthfeel.*	£4.50	WST	(B)
LA POULE BLANCHE 1999, SACHA LICHINE INTERNATIONAL Languedoc-Roussillon	*Pronounced aromas of fruit, complex palate with fresh acidity and nice weight. Well balanced with a lingering finish.*	£4.50	DWL	(B)

LES MAZRIONNETTES CHARDONNAY VIOGNIER 1999, TERROIR CLUB Languedoc-Roussillon	*Tropical fruit aromas with ripe fruit hints, instantly approachable delicious tropical rich fruit flavours.*	£4.50	BGL	B
DOMAINE CAUDE-VAL CHARDONNAY 1999, DOMAINE PAUL MAS Languedoc-Roussillon	*Fresh bubbly appetising aromas, good fruit body, a well structured wine with a sweet fresh finish.*	£5.00	SWS	B
JAMES HERRICK CHARDONNAY 1999, JAMES HERRICK Languedoc-Roussillon	*Apple blossom nose, good acidity and structure with some weight and a crisp apple finish.*	£5.00	Widely Available	B
LA BAUME DOMAINE CHARDONNAY 1999, BRL HARDY Languedoc-Roussillon	*Light apple fruit nose, ripe fruit in round palate with a balancing acidity and an interesting creamy finish.*	£5.00	JSM ODD WCR FEN	B
DOMAINES VIRGINIE GOLD LABEL RÉSERVE CHARDONNAY 1999, DOMAINES VIRGINIE Languedoc-Roussillon	*Banana and pineapple aroma with peach and citrus palate with soft acid and a short finish.*	£6.00	M&S	B
LA BASTIDE D'ARAGON CHARDONNAY 1999, VIGNOBLES LORGEIL Languedoc-Roussillon	*Interesting peas, asparagus and melon aromas, nice balance of good acidity and a pleasant sweetness.*	£6.20	BDR	B
DOMAINE LAMARGUE CHARDONNAY VdP D'OC 1999, CHÂTEAU LAMARGUE Languedoc-Roussillon	*Floral and exotic fruit nose and palate, full bodied seductive structure with lots of flavour.*	£10.00	ALI	B
MAS DE DAUMAS GASSAC 1998, AIMÉ GUIBERT Languedoc-Roussillon	*Intense pawpaw and lemon nose with ripe tropical fruits, balanced acidity and a lovely moderate length.*	£18.00	Widely Available	B

LOIRE • RED

CHINON DOMAINE DE LA DILIGENCE 1998, COULY-DUTHEIL Loire	*Light fruit nose, medium depth of palate, good firm tannins, raspberry fruit and a long finish.*	£7.00	WCR	(S)
BOURGUEIL VIEILLES VIGNES 1998, PIERRE CASLOT Loire	*Fruity nose with pencil shaving notes, strawberry fruit on the palate with a long pleasant finish.*	£7.10	3DW	(B)
CHÂTEAU DE LA GRILLE 1997, LAURENT GOSSET Loire	*Delightful rich structure, good dry tannins on the palate with plenty of fruit on the finish.*	£7.50	MKV	(S)
CHÂTEAU DE LA GRILLE 1996, LAURENT GOSSET Loire	*Restrained but inviting aroma, some oak and raspberry fruit nose and palate, with a good balancing acidity.*	£7.50	MKV	(B)
SAUMUR-CHAMPIGNY LES 3 JEAN 1998, JEAN-LUC & JEAN-ALBERT MARY Loire	*A delightful nose on this wine, green tannins and red fruit, good balance and a lively finish.*	£8.30	3DW	(B)

LOIRE • WHITE

MHV MUSCADET SÉVRE ET MAINE SUR LIE 1999, JEAN BEAUQUIN Loire	*Charming and crisp citrusy aromas, good acidity on a limey fruit palate, and a clean fresh finish.*	£3.50	MHV	(B)

Wine	Tasting Note	Price	Code	
CUVÉE KIWI CHARDONNAY 1999, LACHETEAU Loire	*Apples and straw aromas with balanced warm mouthfeel of tropical fruit and a good clean finish.*	£4.00	WST	B
LOUISE D'ESTRÉE VOUVRAY 1999, VINIVAL Loire	*Bright and breezy nose, more intensity on the palate of full ripe fruit with a slight earthiness.*	£4.00	NTD	B
ANJOU BLANC 1998, DOMAINE DE SALVERT Loire	*Simple but well balanced, light notes of lychee and greengages, ends with a zingy finish.*	£4.80	3DW	B
MHV VOUVRAY 1999, DOMINIQUE BAUD Loire	*Full bodied tropical fruit with citrus and pineapple notes on this well made wine.*	£4.90	MHV BNK	B
TOURAINE SAUVIGNON 1999, DOMAINE DE L'AUMONIER Loire	*Clean, fresh grapefruit and green pea aromas, well balanced herbal fruit palate with balancing crisp acidity.*	£5.00	FCA	B
CHÂTEAU DU COING DE SAINT FIACRE 1998, VÉRONIQUE GÜNTHER-CHÉREAU Loire	*Lovely floral nose, very crisp acidity well integrated in strong juicy fruit with a lively finish.*	£5.50	WTH	B
VOUVRAY DEMI SEC CUVÉE GASTON DORLÉANS 1999, DOMAINE BOURILLON DORLÉANS Loire	*Dried figs and young bright fruit on the nose, with richness of palate, and a long scented finish.*	£5.60	TOS	B
CHÂTEAU DU COING COMTE DE ST HUBERT 1998, VGC Loire	*Green apples on the nose, soft round fruits on the palate with a very refreshing finish.*	£6.00	DLA	B

VOUVRAY DEMI SEC 1998, DOMAINE BOURILLON DORLÉANS Loire	*Green baked stuffed apples on the nose with good acidity and fruit on the palate.*	£6.00	MWW	**B**
DOMAINE DE CRAY MONTLOUIS SEC 1997, CHAPELLE DE CRAY Loire	*Intense nose, melon and honey on the layered palate with a clear quality finish.*	£6.20	PBA DBY NRW NYW WRK BOO WES	**B**
MHV POUILLY-FUME DOMAINE DES VALLEES 1999, MICHEL BAILLY Loire	*Green, bright, fruit nose precedes a palate of nice fresh gooseberry, supported by zippy acidity.*	£7.40	MHV	**B**
SANCERRE FOUASSIER PÈRE & FILS 1999, FOUASSIER PÈRE & FILS Loire	*Rich aromas reveal good rich fruit, fine complexity, lingering long acidity and structure.*	£8.00	JSM WTS SMF	**B**
VOUVRAY SEC 1998, DIDIER CHAMPALOU Loire	*Refreshingly elegant aromas, light honeyed citrus and green apple palate with a far reaching finish.*	£8.20	GRT COM CTC	**B**
HENRI BOURGEOIS 1999, HENRI BOURGEOIS Loire	*Good passionfruit aromas follow through onto the palate with minerally undertones, medium acidity and a long finish.*	£9.00	CAM	**B**
LES BARONNES 1999, HENRI BOURGEOIS Loire	*Intense gun metal nose, precedes a forward palate of green, citrus fruits with herbal undertones.*	£9.00	CAM	**B**
MENETOU-SALON CLOS DES BLANCHAIS 1999, DOMAINE HENRY PELLE Loire	*Intense perfumed, peardrops nose, precedes a well balanced lolly sweet, crisp palate with a good length.*	£9.00	ODD PBA DBY BOO H&H NYW JSS	**B**

FRANCE • LOIRE • WHITE

SANCERRE BONNES BOUCHES 1999, HENRI BOURGEOIS Loire	*Soft, fragrant herbaceous aromas, lively palate of nettles and gooseberry fruit with a long zingy acidity.*	£9.00	SAF	**B**
VOUVRAY TRIS DE GRAINS NOBLES 1995, DOMAINE BOURILLON DORLEANS Loire	*An interesting subtle nose presents this pleasant light and zesty well balanced wine.*	£9.20	JSM THI	**S**
VOUVRAY MARC BRÉDIF 1998, MARC BRÉDIF Loire	*Light pear fruit nose, slightly spicy, ripe rounded body leading to a clean dry finish.*	£9.40	JAG VIL TMW PIM FEN CTC	**B**
DOMAINE MICHEL THOMAS SANCERRE 1999, DOMAINE MICHEL THOMAS Loire	*Sweet peardrops, leafy, spicy aromas, elegant palate of pineapple fruit, good zippy acidity and nice length.*	£10.00	BDR	**S**
SANCERRE LES ROCHES 1998, DOMAINE VACHERON Loire	*Classy aromas of elderflower and pebbles, good fruit acid balance with a crisp dramatic finish.*	£10.10	ADN MWW DBY FRW	**B**
SANCERRE COMTE LAFOND GRANDE CUVEE BLANC 1996, DE LADOUCETTE Loire	*Honey, stewed apple nose, with spicy undertones give way to asparagus and limes, wonderful balance.*	£17.70	CTC	**B**

OTHER • RED

SOMERFIELD SYRAH VdP 1999, LES VIGNERONS ARDECHOIS Ardeche	*Violet and pepper nose, complimentary drying tannins which are pleasantly bold in the mouth.*	£3.00	SMF	**B**

EVOLUTION DU SERRET OAK AGED CABERNET SAUVIGNON NV, UVICA Ardeche	*Warm summer fruit aromas, nice balance of acidity and red fruits on the palate, good length.*	£6.00	BDR	(B)
LAITHWAITE GARAGE RED NV, DIRECT WINES CASTILLON	*Lovely intense sweet and dried fruit wrapped up in a fine structure of succulent acidity and tannin.*	£9.00	BDR	(S)

OTHER • SPARKLING

MHV SPARKLING CHARDONNAY BRUT NV, LOUIS BOUILLOT	*Clean, light and fresh with soft mousse, sweet apples on nose and palate, with a very stylish finish.*	£5.00	MHV BNK	(B)

OTHER • WHITE

ESPRIT DE COMBELLE CHARDONNAY 1998, UVICA Ardeche	*Ripe fruit nose, sweet green fruit on the palate with good integration of oak, and a balanced finish.*	£6.00	BDR	(B)

PROVENCE • RED

CUVÉE COLUMELLE 1998, DOMAINE RICHEAUME Provence	*A firm fruit driven wine with dry chalky tannins that intensify the rich, complex flavours.*	£10.30	VER YAP	(S)

FRANCE • PROVENCE • RED

Château de Pibarnon 1996, Château de Pibarnon Provence	*Intense smokey, black pepper, stewed strawberry and cherry aromas with attractive spiced dark fruit flavours.*	£13.70	DBY JNW	G
Château de Pibarnon 1997, Château de Pibarnon Provence	*Spicy leather, meaty and savoury nose. The palate is rich, with great acidity and firm tannins.*	£13.80	JNW	G
Château de Pibarnon 1998, Château de Pibarnon Provence	*Big, juicy and herbaceous wine with fine tannins that gives the palate its smoothness and elegance.*	£14.80	JNW	G
Terra d'Or 1997, M Chapoutier Provence	*Elegant, rich and ripe complexity, fine depth of fruit, tobacco flavoured aromas, this wine shows promise.*	£30.00	MZC	S

PROVENCE • WHITE

Domaine la Rosière Chardonnay 1998, Liotaud Provence	*Very attractive melon and honeysuckle aromas, extraordinary balance of acidity and juicy fruit flavours.*	£6.00	WIN	B

RHÔNE • FORTIFIED

Cuvée Les Trois Forts Muscat de Beaumes de Venise 1999, Domaine de Coyeux Rhone	*Pale golden colour, rich flavours with hints of honeyed grapiness. Good acidity and balance of finish.*	£10.70	AVB	B

RHÔNE • RED

CÔTES DU RHÔNE 1999, PRINCES DE FRANCE/BOTTLE GREEN Rhône	*A youthful wine offering subtle aromas on the nose and a palate which is concentrated and well structured.*	£3.10	TOS	B
LE PECHER CÔTES DU VENTOUX NV, PRINCES DE FRANCE Rhône	*A pleasant ripe berry fruit wine with a hint of spiciness, depth and firm tannin finish.*	£3.50	NTD	B
CÔTES DU RHÔNE ROUGE 1999, LOUIS MOUSSET Rhône	*Restrained nose aided by a spicy and juicy palate which shows lovely concentration and rounded structure.*	£4.40	STG	B
CROZES HERMITAGE 1999, JP SELLES Rhône	*Inviting ripe berry flavours offer a softer touch and combine nicely with the dry, fine tannins.*	£5.00	SMF	B
PERRIN LA VIEILLE FERME 1998, DOMAINES PERRIN Rhône	*Violets, plum and cherry allow for a full expression of fruit, tannin grip provides persistent length.*	£5.10	TOS ESL HST	B
CÔTES DU RHÔNE VILLAGES 1999, RASTEAU Rhône	*A wine of substance and depth, with a finesse that shows itself at such a young age.*	£5.50	TOS N&P	B
DOMAINE DE L'ENCLOS 1998, ANDRÉ BRUNEL Rhône	*Well defined meat and spice characters flow nicely towards a slightly green yet clean finish.*	£5.80	AVB DBY TRO CTC	B

FRANCE • RHÔNE • RED

CÔTES DU RHÔNE VILLAGES VINSOBRES 1998, DOMAINE PUY DU MAUPUS Rhône	*Soft, velvety dark fruits provide tremendous mouthfeel whilst the tannin and acidity complete this wine.*	£6.00	SAF	(S)
COMTE DE CASPARIN 1998, DOMAINES PERRIN Rhône	*Attractive fruit quality that shows sweet up front fruit character and firm tannins and acidity.*	£6.00	SKW	(B)
SINGLE BARREL CÔTES DU RHÔNE 1998, PRINCES DE FRANCE Rhône	*Concentrated nose and palate, firm tannins that form a fine marriage with the lovely balanced fruit.*	£6.00	BGL	(B)
VACQUEYRAS SAINT HENRI 1998, DOMAINE SAINT HENRI Rhône	*Pleasant raspberry and blueberry fruit flavours are well evident on the palate. A good medium bodied style.*	£6.10	CTC	(B)
CÔTES DU RHÔNE VALVIGNEYRE 1998, ALAIN PARET Rhône	*Ripe, warm fruit nose with leafy fruit flavours, crunchy acidity and firm drying tannins.*	£6.20	MAD BNK BOO RHV	(B)
CÔTES DU RHÔNE 1994, ANDRÉ VIGNAL DOMAINE ST GEORGES Rhône	*Spiced berries and caramel oak nose, firm tannins and maturing fruit flavours abound on the finish.*	£6.30	CPW	(B)
CÔTES DU RHÔNE TERROIR DU TRIAS 1998, LES VIGNERONS DES BEAUMES DE VENISE Rhône	*Sweet fruit, toasty oak nose and good intensity of fruit flavour that provides a lingering finish.*	£6.50	THI	(B)
CROZES HERMITAGE LES NOBLES RIVES 1999, CAVE DE TAIN L'HERMITAGE Rhône	*Lively cherries and black pepper aroma, fresh palate with up front fruit and balanced tannins.*	£7.00	Widely Available	(B)

PERRIN LA TOUR DU PRÉVÔT CÉPAGE SYRAH 1998, DOMAINES PERRIN Rhône	*Delicate cherry on the nose leads into youthful, fresh black fruit and spice characters with firm tannins.*	£7.00	MIS	B
CÔTES DU RHÔNE 1999, DOMAINE BRUSSET Rhône	*Medium bodied with rich quality fruit flavour and fine but gripping t annins. Intense and bold.*	£7.10	V&C DBY NYW CTC	B
VACQUEYRAS PERRIN 1998, DOMAINES PERRIN Rhône	*Distinct earthy nose, round and juicy flavours with a dusting of dry tannins provide superior structure.*	£7.50	MIS	G
S5 ROUX-LAITHWAITE 1998, CHUSCLAN Rhône	*Old fashioned style with powerful, warming, rich flavours and aromas with a great finish.*	£7.50	BDR	B
CHÂTEAUNEUF-DU-PAPE LES CELLIER DES PRINCES 1998, LES CELLIER DES PRINCES Rhône	*Perfumed lift, nice and bright with farmy complexity very approachable now, get into it!*	£7.80	PEC	S
CROZES HERMITAGE 1998, DOMAINE DE MURINAIS Rhône	*Stylish nose displaying an honest, well structured palate, with a very approachable fruit tannin backbone.*	£7.90	OWL	S
CÔTES DU RHÔNE CAIRANNE 1999, DOMAINE BRUSSET Rhône	*Stewed plum nose and big palate weight. The oak influences some rhubarb and whiskey flavours.*	£8.00	NYW EDC HVW CTC	B
CROZES HERMITAGE 1998, DOMAINE DES ENTREFAUX Rhône	*Deep smokey, plum fruit and spice on the nose carries over to a complex palate.*	£8.10	CPW TAN CPW ESL TAN	B

LA PETITE RUCHE 1998, M CHAPOUTIER Rhône	*Lifted fruit character with a spicy, herbal nose and savoury palate, finely balanced, drying finish.*	£8.90	Widely Available	B
ST JOSEPH CUVÉE MEDAILLE D'OR 1997, CAVE DE SAINT-DÉSIRAT Rhône	*Smoke, damsons and tobacco on the nose with rich, spicy, silky palate, almost gamey finish.*	£9.00	WTS	B
CHÂTEAUNEUF-DU-PAPE LE DEVERS 1998, GAEC CLOS SAINT JEAN Rhône	*Warm spice, earthy, chocolate flavours displaying persistent length. Tannins show a fine and firm texture.*	£9.50	ABY	B
CROZES HERMITAGE LES MEYSONNIERS 1998, M CHAPOUTIER Rhône	*Lovely spicy complex nose with nicely balanced spicy oak finish, pleasant traditional style.*	£9.80	ODD QRW DBY TAN N&P FEN	B
ST JOSEPH LES LARMES DU PÈRE 1998, ALAIN PARET Rhône	*Red fruits and leather nose, lovely tannic grip moulds the palate into a finely tuned wine.*	£9.90	MAD AMW RHV	S
CROZES-HERMITAGE CHÂTEAU CURSON 1997, ETIENNE POCHON Rhône	*Pronounced redcurrant and plum nose, rich, creamy and ripe, soft tannins on the deep palate.*	£9.90	J&B NYW	B
VACQUEYRAS MONTIRIUS 1999, ERIC SAUREL Rhône	*Rustic cherry, earthy, leathery aromas are the hallmarks of this densely flavoured, complex wine.*	£10.00	BGL	S
CLOS VACQUEYRAS MONTIRIUS 1999, ERIC SAUREL Rhône	*Violets, plum and dark cherries fill the nose and prepares the palate for a similar experience.*	£10.00	BGL	B

CÔTES DU RHÔNE VILLAGES 1998, DOMAINE DE LA JANASSE Rhône	*A fruit driven style that is soft, juicy and holds a certain elegance about it.*	£10.20	N&P HVW CTC	(S)
CROZES-HERMITAGE CLOS ST GEORGE 1997, DELAS FRÈRES Rhône	*Textured smokey bacon and black fruit, full concentration of fruit flavours and a spicy finish.*	£10.50	BWC	(B)
CROZES HERMITAGE 1999, DOMAINE COMBIER Rhône	*Quite intense tarmac and chocolate nose, full ripe peppery palate, nicely rounded and shows persistence.*	£10.50	CTC	(B)
SAINT JOSEPH FRANCOIS DE TOURON 1997, DELAS FRÈRES Rhône	*Confident rich nose, soft flavours on the palate consisting of black fruits and an earthy character.*	£10.50	BWC	(B)
DOMAINE DE LA MAVETTE 1997, GAEC LAMBERT Rhône	*Signs of maturity on the nose and a palate that is dominated by cracked black pepper.*	£10.70	BDR	(B)
GIGONDAS TRADITION 1998, DOMAINE BRUSSET Rhône	*Subtle aromas on the nose, the palate is delicate and complex with firm tannins and acidity.*	£11.60	BLU NYW CTC	(B)
CHÂTEAUNEUF DU PAPE LA SOLITUDE 1998, LANCON Rhône	*Advanced mushroom, farmyard nose and good, traditional fruit flavours that are well concentrated.*	£11.80	SMF AVB DBY	(B)
CHÂTEAU REDORTIER BEAUMES DE VENISE CUVÉE PRESTIGE 1998, DE MENTHON Rhône	*Fresh blackberry nose, bright fruit driven palate that is very clean and instantly appealing.*	£12.00	WIN	(B)

Châteauneuf-du-Pape 1998, Domaine de l'Arnesque Rhône	*Signs of ageing complexity with nice roundness, structure and balance. Sharp, slightly green, spicy finish.*	£12.00	NTD	B
Côtes du Rhône Villages Les Hauts du Village 1995, Rasteau Rhône	*Fruit and peppery aromas, signs of bottle age but still showing plenty of stimulating complexity.*	£12.00	EUW	B
Les Cailloux Grenache 1997, André Brunel Rhône	*Blackberry nose, soft cherry, fruit driven palate and a spicy finish, a good easy drinking style.*	£12.70	AVB CTC	B
Gigondas Domaine des Bosquets 1998, Sylvette Brechet Rhône	*Sweaty saddle and floral hints on the nose, delicate palate of mulberries and subtle oak.*	£12.80	POL	B
St Joseph 420 Nuits 1998, Alain Paret Rhône	*Luscious plum fruit, smokey, spicy blackcurrants and cigar box aromas that lead to gamey sweet flavours.*	£13.00	WSG	S
Gigondas Montirrius 1999, Eric Saurel Rhône	*Lifted strawberry jam aromas, full red berry fruit flavours and drying tannin finish.*	£13.00	BGL	B
Châteauneuf du Pape Laurus 1998, Gabriel Meffre Rhône	*Nice honest wine, delicately fruity on the palate with good tannin structure and length.*	£15.00	GYW	B
Hermitage Le Pied de la Côte 1997, Paul Jaboulet Aîné Rhône	*Inviting complex sweet fruit and oak aroma compliments the unique and pleasant citrus flavours.*	£17.80	ADN WTS DBY N&P VIL	B

CÔTE RÔTIE 1998, DOMAINE BOUCHAREY Rhône	*Unbelievably complex nose with an orange peel viognier lift and a toasty, meaty, elegant palate.*	£17.90	BDR	**G** TROPHY WINE
CHÂTEAUNEUF-DU-PAPE CHAUPIN 1998, DOMAINE DE LA JANASSE Rhône	*Light spicy fruit flavours with good dry texture and evolving well on the palate.*	£19.30	NYW EDC N&P	**B**
CÔTE ROTIE LA VIAILLÈRE 1995, JOEL CHAMPET Rhône	*Traditional style offering an elaborate mix of complexity and maturity with great depth and balanced acidity.*	£20.00	J&B YAP	**G**
HERMITAGE MARQUISE DE LA TOURETTE 1997, DELAS FRÈRES Rhône	*Earthy, new leather and gamey aromas, softer style, no need to sit back on this wine.*	£22.00	BWC CFT RHV	**B**
CÔTE-ROTIE SEIGNEUR DE MAUGIRON 1997, DELAS FRÈRES Rhône	*Ripe and elegant nose with massive fruit depth akin to dried fruits, dark cherry and blackcurrant.*	£23.00	BWC	**G**
CÔTE RÔTIE LES JUMELLES 1997, PAUL JABOULET AÎNÉ Rhône	*Classic chocolate and cherry richness that provides a clean, modern and attractive style of wine.*	£24.30	ADN ODF WTS DBY TAN N&P VIL	**B**

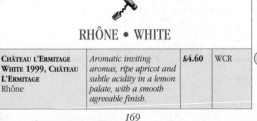

RHÔNE • WHITE

CHÂTEAU L'ERMITAGE WHITE 1999, CHÂTEAU L'ERMITAGE Rhône	*Aromatic inviting aromas, ripe apricot and subtle acidity in a lemon palate, with a smooth agreeable finish.*	£4.60	WCR	**S**

SOUTH WEST • RED

CHÂTEAU BELLEVUE LA FORÊT AOC ROUGE 1998, CHÂTEAU BELLEVUE LA FORÊT South West	*Caramel and bramble aroma with a wild raspberry and youthful palate, give it time to develop.*	**£5.00**	THI	B
CUVÉE 44 1998, LES VIGNERONS DE BUZET South West	*Deep ink colour, intense aromas of blackcurrant, ripe fruit and spice, soft on the palate.*	**£5.00**	THI TOS	B
PIGASSOU NV, DIRECT WINES South West	*Good black fruits on the nose with a soft black plum palate and fine tannins.*	**£5.20**	BDR	S
CHÂTEAU LES FONTENELLES 1999, South West	*Supple berry fruits on the palate, light weight with dry well structured tannins.*	**£5.60**	BDR	B
NOBLESSE DE SERENAC 1998, LABASTIDE DE LEVIS South West	*A wonderfully textured wine of soft plum fruit with soft tannins and good depth.*	**£5.70**	BDR	B
BERGERAC RÉSERVE DE CHÂTEAU GRINOU 1997, CUISSET South West	*Rich full cherry and plum on the palate, sweet ripeness, very drinkable, easy wine.*	**£5.90**	ALZ	S
CROIX DU MAYNE 1998, CVGSO South West	*A rich dark berry fruit nose, a hint of oak blending with soft tannins and blackberries.*	**£6.00**	BGL	S

DOMAINE DE SAINT HILAIRE LA SERPENTINE 1998, DOMAINE DE SAINT HILAIRE South West	*Deep and meaningful, this palate of fresh blackberries and vanilla, still in its youthful mood.*	£7.00	GRT CPW	(S)
PLÉNITUDE MADIRAN 1996, PRODUCTEURS PLAIMONT South West	*Great chocolatey nose with smokiness and intense jammy plums and berries, firm tannin finish.*	£7.00	HWL	(B)

SOUTH WEST • SWEET

MONBAZILLAC CUVEE PRESTIGE 1998, CHÂTEAU THEULET South West	*An uplifting peachy nose, stewed apples and custard dance on the tongue with a satisfying honey finish.*	£7.50	SGL	(B)
PACHERENC ST ALBERT 1998, PRODUCTEURS PLAIMONT South West	*Attractive lime peel aroma, smooth structure, lovely balance and integration of sweetness, good acidity.*	£9.50	ESL BOO	(B)
DOMAINE LÉONCE CUISSET 1996, PASCAL CUISSET South West	*Tantalising mushroom nose with well balanced tropical flavours and a smattering of lemon and honey.*	£10.00	JSM	(B)
SAUSSIGNAC CHÂTEAU GRINOU 1997, CUISSET GUY South West	*Mild greengages flirt with the nose of this intense yet not overpowering floral wine.*	£10.00	ALZ	(B)
CHÂTEAU LE PAYRAL CUVÉE MARIE JEANNE SAUSSIGNAC 1997, CHÂTEAU LE PAYRAL South West	*Soft honeyed nose, with fruity and buttery acidity leading to good length and a clean finish.*	£12.20	CTC	(B)

FRANCE • SOUTH WEST • SWEET

SAUSSIGNAC COUP DE COEUR 1997, CHÂTEAU RICHARD South West	*Amber nectar; wonderful colour, intense fruity marmalade taste and great equilibrium of acidity and length.*	£13.00	VRT	(S)
CLOS D'YVIGNE 1996, PATRICIA ATKINSON South West	*An invitation of citrus and honey fragrance which bursts into ripe fruity flavours on the tongue.*	£17.00	J&B	(S)

SOUTH WEST • WHITE

DOMAINE DE BOUSCAU 1999, CAVES DE LANDIRAS South West	*Clean floral green fruit aromas, rich tropical fruit, excellent balance, lively and fresh finish.*	£4.00	GCF	(S)
DOMAINE DE MONTAUBÉRON CÉPAGE MARSANNE 1999, PHILLIPE DE BERTIER South West	*Lifted lemon and lime aromas, very balanced with a long warm mouthfeel and lovely acidity.*	£4.00	MIS	(B)
DOMAINE DE PELLEHAUT 1999, PETER A SICHEL South West	*Good fruit concentration on the nose, palate has lovely acidity and hints of asparagus.*	£4.00	BTH	(B)
JURANÇON SEC CHANT DES VIGNES 1999, HENRI RAMONTEU DOMAINE CAUHAPE South West	*Salady on the nose, ripe spring fruits, well balanced with a full bodied structure, and a lovely gooseberry finish.*	£8.50	RAV WES CTC	(S)
MANSENG-PREMIÈRES GRIVES 1998, CHÂTEAU DU TARIQUET South West	*Soft honeyed nose with lime and orange, round rich palate, good length and a lingering sweet finish.*	£8.50	THI	(B)

GERMANY

Britain stills knows that Germany with its quality and price factor contiues to be a good buy. The quality wine regions such as Mosel-Saar-Ruwer produce some of the finest refreshing white wines with delicate fruit flavours, ready for any occasion. Such exquisite wines have been shown this year, that two Riesling trophies have been awarded, one to the tradionalist with an Auslese and one to the modernist with a dry style. Confused by German wine labels - remember, he who asks is a fool for five minutes, but he who does not ask, remains a fool forever.

GERMANY • SWEET

RIESLING EISWEIN 1998, WEINGUT VON SCHLEINITZ Mosel-Saar-Ruwer	*Excellent fruit driven style showing good complexity and refined length and character on the finish.*	£22.00	BBO	(B)
BERNKASTELER LAY RIESLING EISWEIN 1998, DR LOOSEN Mosel-Saar-Ruwer	*This exudes pure riesling, with an excellent balance, it is intense with a superbly long finish.*	£50.00	MAD	(S)

GERMANY • WHITE

RIESLING SELECTION 1998, WINZERVEREIN RUPPERTSBERG Pfalz	*Refreshing racey acidity on this elegant and floral palate, delicate finish with length of finish.*	£5.30	RSN	(S)
GRAACHER HIMMELREICH RIESLING SPATLESE 1997, ADOLF HUESGEN Mosel-Saar-Ruwer	*Pleasant floral nose, off-dry, medium bodied, red apples and citrus, wonderful intense finish.*	£5.50	JSM CWS	(S)

GERMANY • WHITE

SERRIGER VOGELSANG RIESLING AUSLESE 1989, PETER KIESGEN WEINKOMMISSION Mosel-Saar-Ruwer	*Rich fruit flavours on the palate, good balanced acidity with long lingering finish.*	£6.00	MWW	**S**
DEINHARD RIESLING PINOT BLANC 1998, DEINHARD Baden	*Fresh pears and lime nose followed by very pleasant acidity in a fruity palate and very cleansing finish.*	£6.20	AVB RNS CTC	**B**
JOHANNISBERGER KLAUS RIESLING SPÄTLESE 1990, SCHLOSS SCHONBORN Rheingau	*Straightforward lime and floral nose, giving a balanced light bodied honeyed citrus palate, lingering conclusion.*	£7.60	BDR WTS	**B**
D No1 RIESLING PINOT BLANC 1998, DEINHARD Baden	*Green fruit nose, some hints of baked apple on the palate, subtle acidity and length.*	£8.10	AVB CTC	**B**
WACHENHEIMER GOLDBACHEL RIESLING KABINETT TRORKEN 1998, JL WOLF Pfalz	*Warm ripe fruit of late harvest style, ripe strawberries on the palate, showing good complexity.*	£8.60	WCS	**S**
AUSLESE TROCKEN RUPPERTSBERG HOHEBERG 1998, WINZERVEREIN RUPPERTSBERG Pfalz	*Excellent ripe apples and lemons complex palate, a nice refreshing clean wine, subtle finish completes this pleasure.*	£9.00	RSN	**B**
JOHANNISBERGER MITTELHOLLE RIESLING KABINETT 1997, GH VON MUMM Rheingau	*Long lingering fruit complexity on the palate, good acidity and length with finesse.*	£9.20	AVB CTC	**B**
SCHLOSS JOHANNISBERGER RIESLING KABINETT RED SEAL 1998, SCHLOSS JOHANNISBERG Rheingau	*A stunningly refreshing wine ,spicy floral nose with hints of herbs, honeyed peaches on the palate.*	£10.80	WES	**G**

FORSTER KIRCHENSTUCK RIESLING SPÄTLESE 1997, VON BUHL Pfalz	*Crisp and characterful wine with subtle tropical fruit on the clean well made palate.*	£10.80	ODD	**S**
RUDESHEIMER BERG ROTTLAND RIESLING SPÄTLESE 1998, GH VON MUMM Rheingau	*Subtle spicy nose with peardrop confection on the palate, culminating in a broad sweet finish.*	£11.60	AVB CTC	**B**
VON BLAUEM SCHIEFER 1998, HEYMAN LOWENSTEIN Mosel-Saar-Ruwer	*Spritz on the entry, with lovely ripe apple palate, off dry with big body and finish.*	£11.90	M&V NYW	**S**
FORSTER PECHSTEIN RIESLING SPÄTLESE TROCKEN 1998, JL WOLF Pfalz	*Enticingly spicy and aromatic nose with grapefruit tartness on the palate, complex finishing notes.*	£13.30	NYW	**G** TROPHY WINE
WEHLENER SONNENUHR RIESLING AUSLESE 1990, ERNEST LOOSEN Mosel-Saar-Ruwer	*A classic example of rich aged Riesling, showing intense sweetness with acid balance. Wonderful viscosity.*	£16.20	WTS MAD JNW	**S**
SCHARZHOFBERGER RIESLING SPÄTLESE 1996, EGON MULLER Mosel-Saar-Ruwer	*Delicious mineral and slate on the wine with balanced acidity and a luscious zesty citrus finish. Just lingers.*	£17.30	NYW J&B	**G**
BRAUNEBERGER JUFFER SONNENUHR RIESLING AUSLESE 1997, FRITZ HAAG Mosel-Saar-Ruwer	*Green apple laden nose with herbaceous under- tones, a sweet succulent fruit palate.that conti- nue to the end.*	£18.50	J&B	**G** TROPHY WINE
BRAUNEBERGER JUFFER SONNENUHR RIESLING AUSLESE FUDER 6 1997, FRITZ HAAG Mosel-Saar-Ruwer	*Ripe silky summer fruit nose with wonderful ner- vous acidity showing bal- ance and lovely length..*	£18.50	J&B	**B**

| **WINNINGER UHLEN RIESLING 1997, HEYMAN LOWENSTEIN** Mosel-Saar-Ruwer | *Slightly unripe character, with attractive nose of spices and butter, interesting long finish.* | £19.80 | M&V | (B) |

GREECE

A s a mountainous country with difficult yet precious vineyard space they have excelled themselves to develop their wine industry to produce these wines of international appeal. Whether on the idyllic islands or the mainland, both red and white wines have been awarded great accolades, bringing together the noble grape varieties and the ancient and indigenous such as the Agiorgitiko grape into wines of world class appeal and quality. Not to forget the countries reputation for its sweet dessert wines which still shine.

GREECE • RED

TSANTALI AGIORGITIKO 1998, EVANGELOS TSANTALIS Peloponnese	*Attractive spicy berry nose with cassis fruit palate balanced with acidity, good simple style wine.*	**£5.00**	ODD	(B)
ST GEORGE MEGAS 1997, SKOURAS Peloponnese	*A pleasant meaty nose with mixed dried fruit leading to balanced tannins and acidity.*	**£6.40**	WCR	(B)
SPIROPOULOS PORFYROS 1998, SPIROPOULOS Peloponnese	*Charming floral cherry nose with strawberry and plum palate, good acidity and nice tannins.*	**£6.60**	ODD VRT	(B)
HATZIMICHALIS MERLOT 1998, HATZIMICHALIS Central Greece	*Intense aroma, juicy rich damsons and cassis fruits on the palate, pleasant lingering finish.*	**£6.80**	GWC	(S)
LAFAZANDIS NEMEA 1997, LAFAZANDIS Peloponnese	*Wonderful undergrowth nose with warm plums and black cherry fruit with chocolate, weighty body.*	**£7.00**	GWC	(B)

GREECE • RED

OENARI NEMEA 1997, AS PARPAROUSSIS Peloponnese	*Warm spicy eucalyptus nose combining with red juicy berry flavour, good tannins and nice finish.*	£7.00	YOD	**B**
NEMEA GRANDE CUVÉE 1997, SKOURAS Peloponnese	*Mature ripe fruit nose with balanced berry fruit and plums with solid tannins and acid.*	£8.00	GWC	**B**
SEMELI NEMEA 1998, SEMELI WINERY Attica	*Dry red fruit spicy nose with stylish black berries and firm tannins, complex backbone.*	£8.00	HDS	**B**
OLD VINES ESTATE NEMEA 1996, A&G PAPAIOANNOU Peloponnese	*Wonderful full red fruit nose blending with lush berries and damsons, well styled wine.*	£11.00	YOD	**B**
AMETHYSTOS CAVA 1996, DOMAINE CONSTANTIN LAZARIDI Macedonia	*Rich fruity spice nose, complex, full bodied, fruity palate, lots of enjoyable tannins on finish.*	£15.00	ODF	**S**
CHÂTEAU SEMELI 1997, SEMELI WINERY Attica	*Herbaceous notes combining with warm raspberry and plum jam flowing with supple tannins, great length.*	£15.00	HDS	**B**

GREECE • WHITE

CHÂTEAU JULIA OAKED CHARDONNAY 1999, DOMAINE CONSTANTIN LAZARIDI Adriani	*Fragrant nose with some oak, green tropical fruit flavours balanced with good acid, lovely finish.*	£8.00	ODD	**B**

ITALY

Up and coming regions from the south have shown themselves to be producers of inivation and quality, previously questionable varities such as Primitivo have rocketed to the status of Red Wine of the Year and other top trophies. They have once again excelled themselves as the country with the most diverse wines in the world. Yet more competition appears for the top notch "Super" rated wines and greater value and quality appears on the high street. Italy has true maverick style!

ITALY • FORTIFIED

VINELLI BIANCO, CDC WINES & SPIRITS	*Beautiful dark brown colour, rich nuts and red fruit on nose and palate, with a drying finish.*	£2.30	DWI	**B**
MHV BARONA ROSSO VERMOUTH, WINE SERVICES EUROPE	*Bright brown colour, appealing strawberry on nose, sweet fruits blended with nuts. Long pleasing finish.*	£3.10	MHV BNK	**B**
RALLO CREMVO MARSALA, RALLO Sicily	*Mocha coffee nose, orange marmalade, concentrated nutty toffee on the palate. Satisfying long finish.*	£4.00	GSJ	**S**
MARSALA SUPERIORE GARIBALDI DOLCE, PELLEGRINO Sicily	*Golden brown colour, shortbread orange nuts on nose, sappy, sweet peel, Brazil nuts, and a warm aftertaste.*	£6.00	WTS AVB GHL TRO CTC	**S**
TERRE ARSE MARSALA VERGINE, CANTINE FLORIO Sicily	*Bright gold, toasty ginger nuts on the nose, beautiful sweet and acid palate, with a long deep finish.*	£10.40	WCS CTC	**S**

MARTINGANA MOSCATO PASSITO DI PANTELLERIA 1996, SALVATORE MURANA Pantelleria	*Rich yellow colour, rich concentrated grape nose, sweet toffee caramel and good acidity. Great finish.*	**£15.30**	NYW CTC	**S**

ITALY • PIEDMONT

CALISSANO BARBERA 1998, CA' BIANCA Piedmont	*Large wine full of strawberries and good acidity, full bodied and a dry finish.*	**£5.00**	BWL	**B**
ARALDICA BARBERA ALASIA 1998, ARALDICA Piedmont	*Enticing cherry fruit nose, soft, sweet and developed palate leading to good acidity and length.*	**£6.00**	CTC	**B**
DOLCETTO D'ALBA BRICCO DI VERGNE 1998, BENI DI BATASIOLO Piedmont	*Dolcetto, the little sweet one, in this case produces a dry finishing fruity wine of complexity.*	**£6.20**	MON	**B**
DOLCETTO D'ALBA CRU VIGNA DI SAGRIN 1999, VILLA LANATA Piedmont	*Superb complex intense nose, bold bitter fruit flavours, long firm tannin finish, good structure.*	**£6.20**	JMC CTC	**B**
BARBERA D'ALBA SOVRANA 1997, BENI DI BATASIOLO Piedmont	*Palate full of soft ripe fruit and smooth tannins, on an earthy smokey nose.*	**£7.60**	MON	**B**
BARBERA D'ASTI DOC 1998, CASCINA CASTLE'T Piedmont	*Clean medium light style, great balance of berry fruit and acidity, good firm structure.*	**£8.00**	JMC	**B**

RIVE ALASIA 1998, ALASIA Piedmont	*Smooth fruit and oak nose, with hints of chocolate, very appealing, what a finish!*	£9.70	V&C NYW CTC	(G)
LITINA BARBERA D'ASTI DOC SUPERIORE 1997, CASCINA CASTLE'T Piedmont	*Excellent sour cherry nose, more red berries on the palate, restrained but attractive style.*	£10.00	ALI	(B)
NEBBIOLO D'ALBA MARNE BRUNE 1998, FONTANAFREDDA Piedmont	*Rich and opulent style, classic tar and roses on the nose, fine balance of acidity and tannins.*	£10.00	ENO	(B)
BARBERA D'ALBA 1997, VIBERTI VINEYARDS Piedmont	*Spicy liquorice and black fruit fuse to give a dry soft ripe plummy character.*	£10.40	VRT	(B)
BARBERA D'ASTI LA LUNA EI FALO' 1997, TERRE DA VINO Piedmont	*Powerful sweet nose, new oak well integrated with ripe lingering plums, has a big future.*	£10.80	VIN DBY	(G)
BARBARESCO 1997, BENI DI BATASIOLO Piedmont	*Light savoury taste and texture, subtle prunes on the palate, a very pleasant experience*	£11.80	MON	(B)
BARBERA D'ALBA 1998, ALDO VAJRA Piedmont	*Juicy cherries and plums on the palate, leading seductively to a soft dry finish.*	£12.20	BEN HST VIL CTC	(B)
DOLCETTO D'ALBA SANTO STEFANO 1998, GIUSEPPE MASCARELLO Piedmont	*Tar and roses on the nose of a fruit driven wine with long reverberating finish*	£12.20	CTC	(B)

ITALY • PIEDMONT

DOLCETTO D'ALBA COSTE E FOSSATI 1999, ALDO VAJRA Piedmont	*Young and fiesty style, rich spiced berries on the palate, marshmallows on the lengthy ending.*	£13.10	BEN CTC	**S**
BARBARESCO D'ALBA PAPAGENA 1997, FONTANAFREDDA Piedmont	*Warm baked fruit on the nose in this smooth medium bodied wine with good tannin structure.*	£14.00	ENO	**B**
LA MALORA 1997, TERRE DA VINO Piedmont	*Rich fruitcake nose with good acidity, held up all the way through with luscious fruit.*	£14.00	VIN	**B**
BAROLO 1993, F GIORDANO Piedmont	*Classic style for lovers of rich intense fruit with a long lingering supple finish.*	£15.20	DBY HVW	**S**
POLICALPO MONFERRATO ROSSO DOC 1997, CASCINA CASTLE'T Piedmont	*Deep, dark and youthful, very rich Christmas pudding, fruit in abundance, good acidity and length.*	£15.50	ALI	**S**
DOLCETTO D'ALBA BRICCO 1998, GIUSEPPE MASCARELLO Piedmont	*Liquorice nose, youthful bright palate of upfront fruit, pleasing acidity for future inviting delight.*	£16.00	ENO	**B**
BARBERA D'ALBA CODANA 1997, GIUSEPPE MASCARELLO Piedmont	*Rich earthy nose with hints of tobacco, pronounced cherry fruit flavours, good balance and length.*	£18.00	ENO	**B**
BAROLO DI SERRALUNGA D'ALBA 1996, FONTANAFREDDA Piedmont	*Ruby red warm fruit, lingering acidity, gamey and earthy character, good weight and length.*	£19.20	GRO CTC	**B**

PARUSSO BRICCO ROVELLA LANGHE ROSSO 1996, PARUSSO Piedmont	*Spiced fruit pudding nose, fantastic complexity, black fruit and refined oak combine to give a firm end.*	£19.50	ENO	(B)
VIGNASERRA 1997, ROBERTO VOERZIO Piedmont	*A rich complex wine of berry fruits, mingling to give firm tannins and good acidity.*	£20.40	V&C HST CTC	(B)
MONPRA' 1997, CONTERNO FANTINO Piedmont	*Rich butter shortbread and cherry conserve nose, complex ripe palate with long intense finish.*	£21.70	CTC	(B)
BAROLO CORDERO DI MONTEZEMOLO 1996, MONFALLETTO Piedmont	*A classic style from this famous region, full of Italian promise and rose cottage aromas.*	£23.00	WTS	(S)
PIN 1997, LA SPINETTA Piedmont	*A rich complex successful marriage of succulent fruit and well balanced acidity, a true maverick.*	£25.40	V&C NYW HST CTC	(S)
BAROLO SAN PIETRO 1996, MARZIANO & ENRICO ABBONA Piedmont	*Classic tar and roses, good fruit concentration, persistent tannin and acidity on alluring finish.*	£25.60	FLW AMW	(B)
BAROLO CRU LA CORDA DELLA BRICCOLINA 1995, BENI DI BATASIOLO Piedmont	*Mature nose and an integrated palate, black bramble fruits, dry mouth with good balance.*	£26.60	MON	(S)
BAROLO ENRICO VI 1996, CORDERO DI MONTEZEMOLO Piedmont	*A rich mellow red berry fruit palate with good tannin structure and long lingering finish.*	£29.20	HST	(S)

ITALY • PIEDMONT

BARBERA D'ALBA RISERVA POZZO DELL'ANNUNZIATA 1997, ROBERTO VOERZIO Piedmont	*Extraordinary dark colour, young black fruit nose, with morello cherries, blackcurrant and chocolate warm finish.*	£35.00	ENO	Ⓢ
BAROLO CEREQUIO 1996, ROBERTO VOERZIO Piedmont	*Delicious concentration of both nose and palate, full bodied lasting tannic structure with good acidity.*	£52.70	CTC	Ⓢ

ITALY • RED • OTHER

BIFERNO 1998, CARLO BOTTER Molise	*Nice ripe fruit on the nose of this simple, but well made wine, soft easy finish.*	£3.50	BGL	Ⓑ
DI CAPRIO PUGLIA RED 1999, GIACOBAZZI Puglia	*Vibrant strawberry nose, light fruity palate, with good length of plum fruit and clean finish.*	£3.50	PLB	Ⓑ
MHV FIRRIATO SICILIAN RED 1998, FIRRIATO Sicily	*Rich cherry fruit nose, gentle and attractive with well balanced warm characters on the finish.*	£3.70	MHV	Ⓢ
BARBERA COLLI TORTONESI 1998, CARLO BOTTER Piemonte	*Some funky complexity, big plum fruit, rich fruit and a spicy powerful finish lingering onwards.*	£4.00	BGL	Ⓢ
DI CAPRIO PRIMITIVO 1999, GIACOBAZZI Puglia	*Sweet full nose, concentrated fruit with good acidity on this easy drinking everyday wine.*	£4.00	PLB	Ⓑ

SERINA PRIMITIVO 1999, CALATRASI Puglia	*Deeply herbaceous, dark and plummy, with rich fruit follow through, sweet ripe finish to the end.*	£4.00	BWL SAF	**B**
TERRALE PRIMITIVO 1999, CALATRASI Sicily	*Complex palate with massive cherry fruit flavours and liquorice with a fine tannin structure.*	£4.00	BWL	**B**
CASA CALATRASI TU CARIGNAN MOURVÈDRE 1999, CALATRASI Puglia	*Damsons with a touch of coffee, spicy black cherry palate with a good structured backbone.*	£4.30	BWL	**S**
SAINSBURY'S COPERTINO RISERVA 1996, CANTINA SOCIALE COOPERATIVE Apulia	*Luscious plums and dark cherries on nose, subtle fruit on palate with signs of chocolate.*	£4.30	JSM	**S**
LA BROCCA PUGLIA ROSSO 1999, BASILIUM Puglia	*Berry and herbaceous nose with warm fleshy fruit palate, good acidity and tannin structure.*	£4.30	AVB CTC	**B**
IL PRIMITIVO DEL SALENTO 1999, DONSLLI VINI Apulia	*Plummy gamey nose with high but balanced acidity, well expressed fruit, firm fruit tannins.*	£4.50	M&M	**B**
MHV CABERNET SAUVIGNON GRAVE DEL FRIULI 1999, BIDOLI VINI SNC Friuli	*Intense youthful berry nose, great extracts of fruit with good tannin and acid combination.*	£4.60	MHV	**B**
MONTEPULCIANO D'ABRUZZO CHIARO DI LUNA 1999, MGM MONDO DEL VINO Abruzzo	*Delicious blueberry pancake aromas, fantastic fruit on palate and elegant finish on this charming wine.*	£4.80	WST	**S**

CANALETTO MONTEPULCIANO D'ABRUZZO 1998, CASA GIRELLI Trentino	*Smooth and medium bodied wine, ripe soft summer fruits, with a pleasing lingering finish.*	£4.80	N&P JSS PIM WCS	**B**
CA MONTINI MERLOT CABERNET 1998, CA MONTINI Umbria	*Smooth black fruits on the generous palate with style, and elegant long minty finish.*	£4.90	GSJ	**S**
LA BROCCA PRIMITIVO PUGLIA 1999, BASILIUM Puglia	*Vibrant blackcurrant on the nose, juicy baked fruits on the palate and gripping tannins.*	£4.90	AVB CTC	**B**
LEVERANO VIGNA DEL SARACENO 1997, CONTI ZECCA Puglia	*Rich ripe characterful structure, great fruit driven palate, with a spiced lengthy finish.*	£5.00	EHL	**S**
TRE UVE 1998, MGM MONDO DEL VINO Abruzzo	*Toffee and black bramble fruit preserves on nose, easy drinking but definite confident style.*	£5.00	ODD	**S**
VIGNA ALTA ME 1999, BASILICATA Basilicata	*Rich sweet intense berry fruit, balanced acidity and firm tannins on the finish, good structure.*	£5.00	WTS	**S**
L'ARCO CABERNET FRANC 1998, CABERT S&A Friuli-Venezia Giulia	*Warm inviting tarry nose, lots of tannins, well balanced full bodied structure with lovely finish.*	£5.00	JSM EHL TOS	**B**
RIPAROSSO MONTEPULCIANO D'ABRUZZO 1998, AZ AG DINO ILLUMINATI Abruzzo	*Big bunches of fruit flavours, let this wine speak and show itself to be an attractive wine.*	£5.00	SMF	**B**

VILLA SANDI CABERNET SAUVIGNON 1998, VILLA SANDI Veneto	*Soft summer fruit nose, hints of liquorice, well structured, soft tannins in long finish.*	**£5.00**	GSJ	**B**
SANGIOVESE 1998, CALATRASI Puglia	*Lovely blossom and cherry fruit nose, good rich mouthfeel, finish of firm tannins and violets.*	**£5.20**	BWL	**S**
STRAVENTO NERO D'AVOLA 1999, DIRECT WINES Sicily	*Mellow fruit on the initial palate developing into more intensity and pepper on the finish.*	**£5.20**	BDR	**B**
CANALETTO PRIMITIVO D'PUGLIA 1998, CASA GIRELLI Puglia	*Dense and complex, plenty of plummy fruit with tobacco spice and a long pleasant finish.*	**£5.50**	VIL	**S**
SANGIOVESE DI PUGLIA 1999, PROMESSA Puglia	*Smooth attractive nose with pepper and plums, good depth and balance, with great finish.*	**£5.50**	Widely Available	**B**
VALPOLICELLA CLASSICO SUPERIORE LE BINE 1998, GIUSEPPE CAMPAGNOLA Veneto	*Leather and black pepper on the nose, powerful berry fruit on palate, good mouthfeel.*	**£5.50**	EUW	**B**
VERETO SALICE SALENTINO 1997, AGRICOLE VALLONE Puglia	*Good rich colour, full in the mouth with baked fruit, powerful and rich, stewed prune finish.*	**£5.60**	Widely Available	**B**
POTENZA PRIMITIVO 1999, DIRECT WINES Puglia	*Rich toasty dark fruit, complex and slightly Burgundian in style, very long pleasing finish.*	**£5.70**	BDR	**S**

ITALY • RED • OTHER

MANDRAROSSA NERO D'AVOLA 1999, MANDRAROSSA Sicily	*Ample soft red fruits on the mouth with firm tannins, slightly confected on the finish.*	£5.70	V&C CTC	(B)
SALENTO ROSSO VALLE CUPA 1997, APOLLONIO Puglia	*Very full bodied and long lingering wine full of mellow toasty rich damson notes.*	£5.80	ALL	(S)
PORTA ITALICA MERLOT CABERNET BASILICATA 1999, BASILIUM Basilicata	*Light redcurrants on the nose, good round fruit with pepper notes and firm tannic finish.*	£5.80	AVB CTC	(B)
MONTEPULCIANO D'ABRUZZO TRALCETTO 1998, CICCIO ZACCAGNINI Abruzzi	*A nose of fresh bramble fruits infused with vanilla oak and a long fruity finish.*	£5.90	AIL	(B)
SANTI VALPOLICELLA CLASSICO 1997, SANTI Veneto	*Attractive mulberry nose with light body and long clean fruit on the palate, soft finish.*	£5.90	GDS N&P	(B)
PRIMITIVO DI PUGLIA 1999, A MANO Puglia	*Initial sweetness, gorgeous juicy cassis nose, creamy coffee finish, a true delight to enjoy.*	£6.00	Widely Available	(G) WINE OF THE YEAR
PRIMITIVO DI PUGLIA 1999, GI SPA Puglia	*Progressive and inivative techniques have rocketed this variety to the spotlight, a spicey complex southern delight.*	£6.00	VEX	(G)
TRE UVE ULTIMA 1998, MGM MONDO DEL VINO Abruzzo	*Affluent and luscious berry fruit showing stunningly well on this excellent classic Italian style.*	£6.00	ODD TOS	(G)

POLLO DEL RUSPO SANGIOVESE 1998, BARBI Orvieto	*Very soft rounded hints of savoury fruit on the nose, clean raspberry flavours to finish.*	£6.00	PLB	(S)
ALBERELLO IGT ROSSO DEL SALENTO 1998, FELLINE Puglia	*Sweet damsons and floral hints on the nose, rounded and balanced palate, with firm tannins.*	£6.00	ODD GHC	(B)
CIRO CLASSICO ROSSO 1998, LIBRANDI Calabria	*Delicious crème brulée nose, palate carried by abundant fruit, mature light dry elegant finish.*	£6.00	V&C CAM VIL CTC	(B)
TERRE DI GINESTRA NERO D'AVOLA 1998, CALATRASI Sicily	*Traditional old world style wine showing warm rustic characteristics, good weight of fruit on the finish.*	£6.00	BWL	(B)
VALPOLICELLA VALPANTENA VIA NOVA 1999, VALPANTENA Veneto	*Clean fruit in the mouth, raspberries and vanilla, good simple finish, light and refreshing.*	£6.00	ENO	(B)
VINICOLA CANTELE CARAMIA NEGROAMARO 1998, AZIENDA VINICOLA CANTELE Puglia	*Ample fruits on the rich and rugged palate, baked spiced fruit flavours to the far reaching conclusion.*	£6.00	IWS	(B)
SALICE SALENTINO RISERVA 1997, TAURINO Puglia	*Attractive warm spicy fruit nose, soft and dry, cherries and caramel, finishing in a satisfying sweetness.*	£6.10	MWW AVB SAF WCR CTC	(S)
TERRAZZE DELLA LUNA TEROLDEGO ROTALIANO 1998, CA' VIT Trentino	*Juicy sweet palate of fresh cherries and sweet supple tannins, medium body with lingering finish.*	£6.20	HDS GRO	(B)

TORRE DEL FALCO IGT PUGLIA ROSSO 1998, TORREVENTO Puglia	*Lovely plummy aromas lead to delicious jammy round palate, very good weight, sweet soft finish.*	£6.30	ALI	(B)
AGLIANICO DEL VULTURE I PORTOLI 1997, BASILLIUM-CONTRADA PIPOLI Basilicata	*Plenty of good rich fruit layers, well made with stewed spiced prunes on the finish.*	£6.50	MWW	(S)
LA TENUTA BELTRAME CABERNET FRANC 1998, CHRISTIAN BELTRAME Friuli-Venezia Giulia	*Deep purple colour, excellent ripe fruit with plenty of length and well integrated tannins to finish.*	£6.50	GRT	(S)
LA TENUTA BELTRAME MERLOT 1997, CHRISTIAN BELTRAME Friuli-Venezia Giulia	*Hints of herbs with delightful blackcurrant flavours checked by good acidity, fine tannins and stylish length.*	£6.50	GRT	(S)
MEDORO SANGIOVESE DELLE MARCHE 1998, UMANI RONCHI Marche	*Succulent and generous on the palate, a classy wine with much to say on the finish.*	£6.50	CTC	(B)
COPERTINO RISERVA 1997, COPERTINO Apulia	*Deep red appealing wine with good complexity and balance, mature rich warm fruit finish.*	£6.70	V&C DBY WCR GRO HVW POR CTC	(B)
VALPANTENA VALPOLICELLA CLASSICO LE VIGNE 1999, VALPANTENA Veneto	*Velvety rich raspberry palate, full and austere with long ripples of flavours on the finish.*	£6.70	BEL CTC	(B)
ZENATO MERLOT DELLE VENEZIE 1997, ZENATO Veneto	*Outstanding cracked blackpepper and blackcurrant nose, together with deep concentrated fruit coulis palate.*	£7.00	EUW	(S)

COSTERA CANNONAU DI SARDEGNA 1997, ARGIOLAS Sardinia	*Mixed fruit preserves on the nose, juicy plums and liquorice palate with a dry finish*	£7.00	BLS	**B**
TARUSO RIPASSATO 1998, ARCADIA VINI Veneto	*Attractive bitter cherry on the nose, intense fruit with supple tannins, sound soft dry finish.*	£7.00	TOS	**B**
ROSSO CONERO VIGNETO SAN LORENZO 1997, UMANI RONCHI Marche	*Intense cedar and bitter cherry nose, raspberries and lusciously smooth mouthfeel, with solid lingering finish.*	£7.10	V&C CAM JNW WCR CFT VIL CTC	**B**
CAPPELLACCIO AGLIANICO 1997, RIVERA Apulia	*Rich deep velvety tones with a summer pudding array of fruits, delivers southern Italian warmth and spice.*	£7.20	MON	**B**
MARA VALPOLICELLA CLASSICO SUPERIORE VINO DA RIPASSO 1997, CESARI Veneto	*Mature ripe luscious cherries coming through with soft supple tannins and rounded concentration on the finish.*	£7.20	AFI JSS	**B**
MONTEPULCIANO D'ABRUZZO JORIO 1998, UMANI RONCHI Marche	*Deep raspberry nose, lovely mouthfeel, hints of damson fruit from this well structured experience.*	£7.20	V&C CAM JNW VIL CTC	**B**
PORTILE PRIMITIVO DEL TARANTINO MASSERIA PEPE 1998, PERVINI Puglia	*Medium bodied style, bramble and minty palate, tannins and creamy oakiness with a dry finish.*	£7.30	PBA BOO	**B**
CAPPELLO DI PRETE ROSSO DEL SALENTO 1996, FRANCESCO CANDIDO Apulia	*Dark fruits and caramel on the nose, delicious big fruity palate with true Italian style.*	£7.40	CPW GRO CTC	**S**

Wine	Description	Price	Codes	
LA SEGRETA ROSSO 1999, PLANETA Sicily	*Ripe cherry jam nose, good weight of fruit on the palate, pleasing tannin structure.*	£7.50	BDR V&C CPW DBY GRO HVW CTC	S
REFOSCO DOC VALENTINO PALADIN 1999, PALADIN Veneto	*Deep and delicious, an array of rich berry fruits, laden down with flavour and structure.*	£7.50	AFI	G
SEDARA ROSSO 1998, DONNAFUGATA Sicily	*Showing development on the nose, ripe blackcurrant mouthfeel and a stylish serious finish with gripping tannins.*	£7.50	VIN	S
VALPOLICELLA SUPERIORE RIPASSO LE VIGNE 1998, VALPANTENA Veneto	*Warm berry fruit nose, with luxuriously deep palate, held through with good acidity and tannins.*	£7.90	V&C CTC	S
CANNONAU DI SARDEGNA RISERVA 1997, SELLA & MOSCA Sardinia	*Rich and spicy warm mouthfeel, powerful fruit finish lingers on through good acidity and tannins.*	£7.90	V&C RAV	B
SAN MARCO MERACO 1999, CANTINE SAN MARCO Lazio	*Attractive bite of bitter cherry fruit on nose and palate, good grip of lively fruit acidity.*	£8.00	MHV	S
RIPASSO VALPOLICELLA CLASSICO SUPERIORE 1997, TOMMASI VITICOLTORI Veneto	*Velvety luxurious wine on nose and palate, with tell tale signs of sundried fruits and sunshine.*	£8.00	L&T	B
VERSATO MERLOT IGT VENETO 1998, SANTA MARGHERITA Veneto	*A cedar nose with blackcurrant pastille on a youthful complex palate with a lovely finish.*	£8.20	ALI	B

PRIMITIVO DI MANDURIA DOC 1998, FELLINE Puglia	*Classic dry palate, starting soft and smokey then fruits of the forest in abundance.*	£8.50	ODD DBY BEN	(S)
CAPITEL SAN ROCCO ROSSO VINO DI RIPASSO 1997, TEDESCHI Veneto	*Slightly sweet upfront style, bitter dry finish with powerful rich berry fruits flavours on the finish.*	£8.60	MWW WCR POR COM CTC	(B)
CADENZA SANGIOVESE DEL UMBRIA 1999, MGM MONDO DEL VINO Abruzzo	*Well integrated fruit on the nose with milk chocolate on the palate, good depth and length.*	£8.70	WST	(S)
OTTOMARZO VALPOLICELLA CLASSICO SUPERIORE GROLA 1998, OTTOMARZO Veneto	*Warm fruits and spice on the nose, vanilla oak and ripe red fruit palate.*	£8.70	VRT	(B)
ZENATO VALPOLICELLA RIPASSA ZENATO 1996, ZENATO Veneto	*Warm sunshine on the palate of ripe soft fruit with a forward and appealing huge finish.*	£8.80	FQU CPW HST	(S)
CIRO CLASSICO RISERVA DUCA SAN FELICE 1997, LIBRANDI Calabria	*Immense depth and character to this wine, big ripe fruit palate with long austere finish.*	£9.00	VIL HVW CTC	(S)
REGIANO BARRIQUE 1996, PERLAGE Veneto	*Pungent nose of stewed fruits, blackcurrant crumble palate, appetising acidity creates a long lingering finish.*	£9.00	VER	(B)
IL FALCONE RISERVA CASTEL DEL MONTE 1997, RIVERA Apulia	*A big number of a wine with numerous dimensions, from spiced fruits to caramel.*	£9.30	MON	(S)

ITALY • RED • OTHER

CASTELLO GUERRIERI ROSSO 1995, GUERRIERI RIZZARDI Veneto	*Bursting with mature ripe fruit berries, good balance of stylish red fruit all the way through.*	£9.50	HBJ	(G)
IMMENSUM ROSSO DEL SALENTO 1998, FRANCESCO CANDIDO Apulia	*Powerful fruit driven wine with currants and well structured tannins leading to a cleansing finish.*	£9.50	CTC	(B)
TORNAMAGNO VDT 1996, COLONNARA Marche	*Velvety rich mouthfeel on this charming smooth wine with good acidity and length to finish.*	£9.50	ALI	(B)
PRIMITIVO DI MANDURIE TERRE DI DONPEPPE 1996, CANTINA DEL LOCOROTONDO Puglia	*Blackfruit and mint on the nose, Bramble fruit and smokey, dry on the palate.*	£9.60	ALI	(B)
DUNICO PRIMITIVO DI MANDURIA MASSERIA PEPE 1998, PERVINI Puglia	*Delightful cherry fruit ripeness and tannins on a medium bodied wine, cinnamon and aged fruit structure.*	£10.00	PBA	(S)
INFERI 1996, AZIENDA MARRAMIERO Abruzzi	*Rich and powerful in aroma and palate, long bursting fruit, with a bold finish.*	£10.50	ODD	(S)
LAUDATO DI MALBECH IGT VENETO ORIENTALE 1996, SANTA MARGHERITA Veneto	*Oaky cherry pie nose leading black fruit and plums on palate, full mouthfilling with wonderful structure.*	£10.50	ALI	(S)
SASSELLA LE TENSE 1996, NINO NEGRI Lombardy	*Rounded with a wealth of mature fruit on the palate, a blockbuster of classic Italian style.*	£10.50	CTC	(B)

VALPOLICELLA VALPANTENA SUPERIORE RIPASSO VIA NOVA 1998, VALPANTENA Veneto	*Dark cherry and chocolate powerful palate, balanced ripe fruit, firm fruit tannins and good acidity.*	£10.60	ENO	(S)
SAN CLEMENTE MONTEPULCIANO D'ABRUZZO 1997, CICCIO ZACCAGNINI Abruzzi	*Rich and spicy nose, with raspberries and cherries on the palate, good acidity and length.*	£11.00	AIL	(B)
ZANNA 1997, ILLUMINATI Abruzzi	*Finesse and elegance sum up this truly satisfying wine, with sweet plum and cherry finish.*	£11.10	AVB	(G)
ROSSO GRAVELLO 1996, LIBRANDI Calabria	*Off dry, deep luscious fruit with enhanced richness of dried fruits, Christmas cake nose, great balance.*	£11.60	CAM CTC	(S)
DUCA DI ARAGONA ROSSO DEL SALENTO 1994, FRANCESCO CANDIDO Apulia	*Soft berry plum nose, smokey and spice with a dry firm structured finish, showing maturity.*	£11.60	CPW CTC	(B)
LA GROLA 1997, ALLEGRINI Veneto	*Leafy rich nose, giving generously on the palate, with layers of intense fruit and lingering finish.*	£11.70	V&C DBY BEN HST POR CTC	(S)
ALLEGRINI PALAZZO DELLA TORRE 1997, ALLEGRINI Veneto	*Complex and concentrated on approach, dark morello cherry palate, lovely balanced finish tempting you further.*	£11.70	Widely Available	(S)
AMARONE DELLA VALPOLICELLA CLASSICO DOMINI VENETI NEGRAR 1994, NEGRAR Veneto	*Coffee bean and rich fruit aromas, followed by hefty fruit on the long powerful palate.*	£11.70	CTC	(S)

ANGHELI 1998, DONNAFUGATA Sicily	*Tarry nose, developed and concentrated on palate, big robust fruit all the way to the end.*	£12.00	VIN	**B**
LIANO SANGIOVESE CABERNET SAUVINGON EMILIA IGT 1997, UMBERTO CESARI Emilia Romagna	*Rich ripe berry and chocolate concentration, Christmas pudding in a glass, big and powerful.*	£12.50	ALI	**S**
VALLAROM PINOT NERO TRENTINO DOC 1997, VALLAROM Trentino	*Restrained vegetal nose gives way to an intense loganberry fruit palate with a green tannic structure.*	£12.70	ALI	**B**
AMARONE VALPOLICELLA 1995, BOSCAINI PAOLO & FIGLI Veneto	*Youthful plummy nose, with strawberries and cherries on the palate, firm structure and length.*	£13.00	SMF	**B**
COLLE PICCHIONI ROSSO 1997, PAOLA DI MAURO Latium	*Soft spiced berry and vanilla character and easily approached wine with backbone and long length.*	£13.50	WIN	**B**
ROSSO LA FABRISERIA 1998, TEDESCHI Veneto	*Deep mahogany fruit on the nose, luscious rich fruits and mint, enjoying a long lingering finish.*	£13.70	AVB NYW CTC	**S**
AMARONE DELLA VALPOLICELLA CLASSICO LE VIGNE 1996, VALPANTENA Veneto	*Delightful mouthfeel, ripe plums and cherry leading to a finish of cloves and redcurrant fruits.*	£13.70	CTC	**B**
AMARONE CLASSICO 1996, TEDESCHI Veneto	*Very rich ripe fruit style, warming on the palate, spicy and powerful with rich persistent fruit.*	£14.00	MWW AVB BNK GHL POR CTC	**B**

TANCREDI 1998, DONNAFUGATA Sicily	*Rich cassis nose, inviting and juicy berryfruit structure showing some age, lengthy finish.*	£14.00	VIN	(B)
CUMARO ROSSO CONERO 1997, UMANI RONCHI Marche	*Silk and velvet on approach, rich aromas, excellent structure of rich fruit with fine tannic structure.*	£14.50	Widely Available	(S)
AMARONE DELLA VALPOLICELLA CLASSICO DOC FROSTED BOTTLE 1997, CESARI Veneto	*Medium intensity nose, with ripe damson plum palate, filling the palate to its capacity.*	£14.50	AFI	(B)
AMARONE CLASSICO 1995, VIGNETI DI JAGO Veneto	*A young and upfront nose, palate of gorgeous fruit preserve with morello cherry finish.*	£14.90	GSJ	(S)
KOREM ISOLA DEI NURAGHI 1998, ARGIOLAS Sardinia	*Dense black cherry nose with ripe red fruits on the palate, medium body and well made.*	£15.00	CWS	(S)
CAPITEL RECIOTO CLASSICO MONTE FONTANA 1996, TEDESCHI Veneto	*A warm inky character on the nose, with baskets of summer fruits, intense but easy style.*	£15.80	BDR AVB MWW QWW NYW COM CTC	(G)
CA' D'ARCHI CABERNET SAUVIGNON ALTO ADIGE DOC 1997, SANTA MARGHERITA Veneto	*Fresh picked strawberries, minty, juicy cassis flavours layered onto the palate and nose. Fruit driven style.*	£15.80	ALI	(B)
AMARONE DELLA VALPOLICELLA CLASSICO 1995, TOMMASI VITICOLTORI Veneto	*Perfumed nose of plums and baked cherries, chunky ripe baked fruit on the palate, excellent acidity.*	£16.00	ADN	(S)

ITALY • RED • OTHER

ILLUMINATI LUMEN 1997, ILLUMINATI Abruzzi	*Deep dark but not mysterious, this wine with true backbone will please and delight.*	£16.70	AVB	(S)
AMARONE CLASSICO VIA NOVA 1997, VALPANTENA Veneto	*Vibrant crushed plum nose with silky ripe red fruits on palate, stylish finish.*	£16.80	ENO	(B)
TAURASI DOCG 1996, FEUDI DI SAN GREGORIO Campania	*Warm spicy fruits on the nose, harmonious and elegant sweet fruit on palate, blueberry jam finish.*	£16.90	RAV FRW	(B)
VALPOLICELLA AMARONE CLASSICO 1997, OTTOMARZO Veneto	*Rich smokey nose leads you temptingly into bitter chocolate and fruit pastilles, smooth and seductive.*	£17.00	VRT	(S)
SCIRI CERASUOLO DI VITTORIA DOC 1997, COS Sardinia	*Deep red, highly flavoured sour cherry nose, soft palate of sweet ripe juicy fruits.*	£17.00	ALI	(S)
AMARONE DELLA VALPOLICELLA 1996, SANTI Veneto	*Big fruity nose, high acidity and long toasty finish, nice and rounded with cherry tannins.*	£17.00	GIL	(B)
AMARONE CLASSICO 1995, BRIGALDARA Veneto	*Sharp bitter cherry nose, rich succulent plums integrated with intense chocolate, long complex finish.*	£17.10	V&C VIN DBY BTH BEL	(G)
GRATICCIAIA 1994, AGRICOLE VALLONE Puglia	*Sweet fruity palate, rich and chocolatey, showing age and plums on the finish.*	£18.30	NRW PBA HDS WRK AMW GRO BOO	(B)

TAURASI PIANO DI MONTEVERGINE DOCG RISERVA 1995, FEUDI DI SAN GREGORIO Campania	*Simnel cake and spicy fruit aromas, giving good concentration on palate, to compliment hearty cuisine.*	**£18.50**	ALI	(B)
AMARONE DELLA VALPOLICELLA RISERVA IL BOSCO 1995, CESARI Veneto	*An intense plummy elegant entry, chewy and sharp cherry tannins leading you on further.*	**£19.40**	AFI	(B)
TERRE BRUNE 1996, SANTADI Sardinia	*Ripe dark plum nose with soft juicy strawberry palate leading to finely grained tannins.*	**£19.50**	V&C VIL GRO HVW CTC	(B)
AMARONE CLASSICO DELLA VALPOLICELLA 1995, CORTEFORTE Veneto	*Warm ripe style, very apealing spicy complex stylish wine, cassis on the lengthy finish.*	**£20.70**	DBY BEN CTC	(S)
VAIO ARMARON AMARONE CLASSICO 1995, MASI Veneto	*Fruit compote aromas and high acidity with great fruit on the palate, going to whole way.*	**£21.00**	DBY	(B)
CAPITEL AMARONE CLASSICO MONTI OLMI 1996, TEDESCHI Veneto	*A mouthful of fruit preserves leading on to a leaner oaked style, ripe finish.*	**£21.20**	MWW AVB POR	(B)
PELAGO 1997, UMANI RONCHI Marche	*Lovely smokey cherries and plum lingering with cinnamon and herbs on a well structured palate.*	**£21.30**	V&C DBY JNW HST VIL GRO	(B)
AMARONE DELLA VALPOLICELLA CLASSICO CATERINA ZARDINI 1997, GIUSEPPE CAMPAGNOLA Veneto	*A melange of sweet raspberry and blackcurrant rich fruit palate, maraschino cherries on a luscious end.*	**£22.50**	EUW	(G)

ITALY • RED • OTHER

AMARONE DELLA VALPOLICELLA DOC 1995, CORTE SANT'ALDA Veneto	*Massive soft palate, rich deep cherry and velvet mouthfeel, sweet and spicy long lasting finish.*	£24.20	BEN	(B)
AMARONE DELLA VALPOLICELLA CLASSICO 1996, ALLEGRINI Veneto	*Fantastic round rich fruit, well balanced on the palate, with great acidity to age well.*	£24.80	Widely Available	(B)
LA POJA 1996, ALLEGRINI Veneto	*Luxurious and deep wine, style for a cosy night in front of a roaring open fire.*	£27.20	CAM DBY NYW BEN HST	(G)
SERPICO IGT 1997, FEUDI DI SAN GREGORIO Campania	*Spiced berry aroma, very young dark cherries and chocolate palate, fantastic structure and persistent finish.*	£29.00	ALI	(S)
AMARONE DELLA VALPOLICELLA CLASSICO RISERVA SERGIO ZENATO 1993, ZENATO Veneto	*Full bodied assertive wine, rich velvety fruit, giving complex bitter sweet far reaching conclusion.*	£30.80	WTS FQU HST	(G)
MILLE E UNA NOTTE ROSSO 1996, DONNAFUGATA Sicily	*Juicy red berry character, has a certain elegance, aromatic and powerful on the finish.*	£35.00	VIN	(S)

ITALY • SPARKLING

SAFEWAY ASTI DOLCE NV, PERLINO Piedmont	*Enticing perfumed nose with sweet zingy apple flavours with well balanced acidity and nicely developed.*	£4.00	SAF	(B)

MOSCATO D'ASTI 1999, BENI DI BATASIOLO Piedmont	*Intense lush grapey nose with lots of mousse and a mellow burnt apple finish.*	£4.80	MON	(B)
SOMERFIELD ASTI SPUMANTE NV, PERLINO Piedmont	*Slight complex nose with a wonderful sweet palate with fine bubbles, good acidity. Delicious style.*	£5.00	SMF	(B)
ASTI SPUMANTE DOCG 1999, VALLEBELBO Piedmont	*Crispy green apple nose with fresh clean palate, smooth mousse and wonderful lingering length.*	£6.60	RAV	(B)
SPUMANTE METODO CLASSICO DOSAGE ZERO 1992, BENI DI BATASIOLO Piedmont	*Biscuity nose followed by crisp clean ripe fruits, great acidity, balanced structure, clean finish.*	£7.00	MON	(B)
MOSCATO D'ASTI LA MORANDINA 1999, LA MORANDINA Piedmont	*A young vibrant zesty apple nose with fine bubbles and cloying apples and pears flavours.*	£10.00	WIN	(S)

ITALY • SWEET

PASSITO VERDICCHIO DEI CASTELLI DI JESI TORDIRUTA 1997, TERRE CORTESI MONCARO Marches	*Rich fresh fruit and honey aromas, very good acidity, great toasted hints on a marvellous lengthy finish.*	£4.50	EUW	(G)
MOSCATO DI PANTELLERIA NV, RALLO Pantelleria	*Open complex marmalade and apricot aroma, lovely sweetness well balanced in nice acidity dominance.*	£8.00	CTC	(B)

PASSITO DI PANTELLERIA MARE D'AMBRA NV, RALLO	*Marmalade and orange peel aromas, complex balanced sweetness and nutty fruit cake flavours.*	£11.00	CTC	**S**
MOSCATEL TARDÍ 1997, BENI DI BATASIOLO Piedmont	*Young and vivacious, clean and fruity to the nose, with a stunning underlying grapefruit twist.*	£15.50	MON	**B**

ITALY • TUSCANY

MHV CHIANTI DOCG 1999, GESTIONI PICCINI Tuscany	*Light aromatic nose, boiled sweets and ripe fruit on the palate, high lengthy acidity*	£4.00	MHV	**B**
SANGIOVESE DI TOSCANA CASA VINICOLA CECCHI 1999, CASA VINICOLA CECCHI Tuscany	*Bitter cherry nose followed up by good fresh fruit on the palate, easy drinking wine style.*	£4.00	JSM WTS TOS	**B**
CONTI SERRISTORI CHIANTI 1998, GRUPPO ITALIANO VINI Tuscany	*Dried fruit layers, peardrops and warm berry flavours, firm tannins and upholding acidity to the finish.*	£4.40	M&M	**B**
CECCHI CHIANTI 1999, CASA VINICOLA CECCHI Tuscany	*Berry fruits and vanilla on the nose, light bodied style, ending soft, sweet and attractively.*	£4.80	ADN	**B**
ROSSO TOSCANO 1997, CANTINE BONACCHI Tuscany	*Medium full depth, quite youthful, pleasing berry characters, lively acidity and a spicy finish.*	£5.30	M&S SAF	**S**

LE LAME ROSSO DI MONTEPULCIANO 1998, POLIZIANO DI FREDERICO CARLETTI Tuscany	*Round juicy fruits of jammy character, well structured and complex wine to the end.*	£5.30	ENO	(B)
CHIANTI 1999, TENUTA SAN VITO Chianti	*Cherries and cedar on the nose, simple juicy fruit style and a clean finish.*	£6.00	BGL	(B)
CHIANTI CLASSICO ISASSI 1997, MELINI Tuscany	*Warm stewed red fruits, with cigar box aromas, sweet ripe fruit giving a balanced finish.*	£6.50	GIL	(B)
CHIANTI COLLI FIORENTINI 1998, LANCIOLA Tuscany	*Soft appealing aromas on the palate of cherries and red fruits, tight acidity and long finish.*	£6.50	WAW	(B)
CANTINE LEONARDO CHIANTI 1999, CANTINE LEONARDO Tuscany	*Inky ruby red, restrained nose, dried fruit and spice, with rich juicy cherry and plum.*	£6.60	Widely Available	(B)
RENZO MASI CHIANTI RISERVA 1997, MASI RENZO Tuscany	*Intense sour plums and cherries on the nose, ripe chunky fruit on the lingering warm finish.*	£6.80	BDR	(G)
CHIANTI SAN VITO ORGANIC 1998, SAN VITO Tuscany	*Upfront cherry nose with minty notes, toasty and of medium weight, ageing smokey plummy fruit.*	£6.80	SAF JSS	(B)
TENUTA SAN VITO FIOR DI SELVA 1997, TENUTA SAN VITO Chianti	*Full plummy ripe nose, good structure on palate, soft and big with attractive finish.*	£7.00	BGL	(B)

TEUZZO CHIANTI CLASSICO 1998, CASA VINICOLA CECCHI Tuscany	*Sweet cherry fruit, some plums and greengages on the palate, dry bitter finish, easy drinking.*	£7.00	JSM	(B)
CHIANTI CETAMURA 1998, COLTIBUONO Tuscany	*Aromatic almond cherry nose, pleasant bitter berry fruit palate, leading to a dry finish.*	£7.10	AVB QWW CTC	(B)
CHIANTI CLASSICO LA SALA 1998, BARONTI LAURA Tuscany	*Morello cherries on the nose and palate, good leathery grip to the long finish.*	£8.30	AIL	(S)
CHIANTI CLASSICO DOCG BLUE LABEL 1997, LAMOLE DI LAMOLE Tuscany	*Rich cherry and fine chocolate truffle aromas on the palate, with long lingering ripe fruit finish.*	£8.50	ALI	(S)
CAPEZZANA BARCO REALE DI CARMIGNANO 1998, TENUTA D'CAPEZZANA Tuscany	*Luscious berries on the nose, inviting soft cherry and raspberry palate, great balancing acidity.*	£8.90	JNW HST	(B)
CHIANTI CLASSICO RISERVA 1995, MELINI Tuscany	*Typical aged rich velvety wine with succulent fruit flavours, producing a wine with wide appeal.*	£9.00	GIL	(S)
CHIANTI RISERVA NERISSO 1995, GIOVANNI PUIATTI Tuscany	*Mature soft vanilla nose, dark savoury perfume, weighty rich red fruits, hints of bitter cherry.*	£9.00	ENO	(S)
SUMMIT SANGIOVESE DI MAREMMA 1998, CECCHI Tuscany	*Cherries and oak successfully married together to give a medium bodied fruity appealing style.*	£9.00	WTS	(B)

CHIANTI RUFINA 1998, FATTORIA SELVAPIANA Tuscany	*Loganberries and chocolate, with hints of herbs, moving on to a refined and complex clean finish.*	£9.20	Widely Available	**B**
TERRE DI GALATRONA 1997, FATTORIA PETROLO Tuscany	*Fairly deep garnet colour, warm aromas, stewed mixed fruit, layered in stages to give an interesting finish.*	£9.40	BEN HST	**B**
CHIANTI CLASSICO 1998, CARPINETO Tuscany	*Lean and green fruit on the palate opening up on the finish to promise for the future.*	£9.60	BDR AVB CTC	**B**
CHIANTI CLASSICO ROBERTO STUCCHI 1998, COLTIBUONO Tuscany	*Deep reddish purple attraction, good cherry fruit nose, lighter sweeter style of good length.*	£9.60	AVB CTC	**B**
ROSSO DI MONTEPULCIANO 1999, POLIZIANO Tuscany	*Dark and austere, quite green fruit, but giving some cherry fruit on the palate, needs time.*	£9.70	V&C BEL BBO CAM NYW GRO CTC	**B**
CHIANTI CLASSICO RISERVA 1995, MACHIAVELLI Tuscany	*Slightly sour nose, leading to a fruit driven palate, with fleshy ripe cherries on the finish.*	£10.00	GIL	**S**
NITTARDI CHIANTI CALSSICO 1997, NITTARDI Tuscany	*Rich and powerful nose, high in tannins with good fruit, with hints of herbaceousness.*	£10.00	CKB	**B**
CASALE FALCHINI PARETAIO 1997, CASALE-FALCHINI Tuscany	*Cassis and bramble fruit nose, open and leafy with richness of finish, stylishly well made.*	£10.30	RHV	**S**

CHIANTI CLASSICO DOCG RISERVA 1996, VISTARENNI Tuscany	*Notes of berry fruits on the palate, good tight tannins, needs to accompany rich world dishes.*	£10.50	ALI	(S)
CHIANTI CLASSICO RISERVA DOCG MASSOVECCHIO 1995, MELINI Tuscany	*Rich dark extracted cherry fruit with coffee, on a full palate and a complex lingering finish.*	£10.70	MON	(B)
'E' 1998, CENNATOIO Tuscany	*Rose aromas on nose, good depth of fruit on the palate, subtle acidity and medium body.*	£10.80	V&V	(S)
CHIANTI CLASSICO DOCG RISERVA 1996, LAMOLE DI LAMOLE Tuscany	*Full of modern fruit on nose, vibrant sweet cherry fruit, with bitter cherry tannins on the finish.*	£10.90	ALI	(B)
CHIANTI CLASSICO RISERVA ROCCA GUICCIARDA 1997, BARONE RICASOLI Tuscany	*Elegant and characterful, full of complex fruit layers on the palate, with a long and attractive ending.*	£11.00	CTC	(S)
TORRE A DESTRA 1997, CASTELLO DELLA PANERETTA Tuscany	*Spices and game on this medium weight wine, complex palate, altogether a rather pleasant experience.*	£11.00	VIN	(S)
CHIANTI CLASSICO RISERVA 1995, GUANIERI Tuscany	*Mature bitter cherry nose, lots of fruit balanced well with acidity and a lingering finish.*	£11.00	WAW	(B)
CLASSICA AVIGNONESI VINO NOBILE DI MONTEPULCIANO 1997, AVIGNONESI Tuscany	*Medium bodied, warm fruit aromas, classic Italian character and charm, giving a long lingering finish.*	£11.00	WTS EUW	(B)

DUCALE CHIANTI CLASSICO RISERVA DOCG 1997, RUFFINO Tuscany	*Fresh juicy berries on the nose, ripe yet elegant palate with a genteel elegant finish.*	£11.40	ALI RAV	(B)
TERRINE 1997, CASTELLO DELLA PANERETTA Tuscany	*A summit of ripe fruit character, caramelised and intense warming palate, with an excellent lingering conclusion.*	£12.00	VIN	(S)
ROSSO DI MONTALCINO 1998, CASTELLO BANFI Tuscany	*Crimson depth, palate of sweet chewy crunchy black and red berry fruit, with a good mouthfeel.*	£12.00	V&C VIN	(B)
CHIANTI CLASSICO RISERVA 1996, CARPINETO Tuscany	*Very delicate fruit aromas, nice and round on the palate with subtle oak coming through.*	£12.20	AVB CTC	(S)
CHIANTI CLASSICO RISERVA LA SALA 1996, BARONTI LAURA Tuscany	*Rich spicy full aroma, ripe black cherry and leather with green banana tannins and a structured palate.*	£12.20	AIL	(S)
CHIANTI RUFINA FORNACE RISERVA 1996, FATTORIA SELVAPIANA Tuscany	*Forceful style both on the nose and palate, giving fruit of nearly ripe character.*	£12.20	TOS WSO HDS	(B)
CHIANTI SAN ZIO 1998, CANTINE LEONARDO Tuscany	*Wonderful and rich, bags of rounded fruit, soft tannins and plenty of character, a memorable wine.*	£12.40	V&C NRW GHL	(G)
VINO NOBILE DI MONTEPULCIANO 1997, CARPINETO Tuscany	*Attractive rich bramble fruit, good firm flavours of raspberry lingering along to the finish.*	£12.70	AVB	(S)

Wine	Tasting Note	Price	Stockist	
CODIROSSO IGT TOSCANA 1997, VISTARENNI Tuscany	*Nice nose of fresh fruit and spice, a touch of liquorice on the palate, may take time to soften.*	£13.00	ALI	B
IL ROCCOLO DOC ROSSO DI MONTALCINO 1998, OLIVETO Tuscany	*Slightly herbaceous nose, giving red berry fruits on the palate, great structure, will age.*	£13.20	ODD	S
CHIANTI CLASSICO RISERVA 1997, VITICCIO Tuscany	*Very intense with hints of ageing, subtle fruit on the palate, long with a good balance.*	£13.30	V&V	S
CHIANTI CLASSICO 1998, CASTELLO DI FONTERUTOLI Tuscany	*Good well balanced ripe bramble fruits on both nose and palate, fine tannins and a dry finish.*	£13.70	Widely Available	S
SAN IPPOLITO 1998, CANTINE LEONARDO Tuscany	*Refined aroma of red berries following onto the palate with true depth and length.*	£14.40	NRW GHL BEN CTC	B
POLIZIANO VINO NOBILE DI MONTEPULCIANO 1997, POLIZIANO Tuscany	*Rich bitter cherry nose, clean style with good weight and a lingering finish full of fruit.*	£14.50	V&C BBO CAM DBY NYW EDC CTC	S
CHIANTI CLASSICO RISERVA 1995, FATTORIA DI RIETINE Tuscany	*Good nose on this fruity full bodied wine, rich developed style, still has ageing potential.*	£14.60	FLW	B
CHIANTI CLASSICO RISERVA 1996, ANTINORI Tuscany	*Deep red, vegetal notes on the nose, blackcurrant fruit, showing age, classic pleasing style.*	£14.60	WTS V&C BNK DIC COM	B

FARNITO CABERNET SAUVIGNON DI TOSCANA 1996, CARPINETO Tuscany	*Full minty chocolate aromas elegantly leading to fresh cassis flavours, great mouthfeel and length.*	**£14.60**	BDR AVB CTC	(B)
TAVERNELLE 1996, CASTELLO BANFI Tuscany	*Smokey warm cassis nose balancing with ripe blackcurrant flavours with tons of tannins. Enjoyable.*	**£16.50**	VIN HST	(S)
LAMAIONE 1996, FRESCOBALDI Tuscany	*Hot blackcurrant nose with vibrant beefy fruit flavours, powerful tannins with good length. A stunner.*	**£18.00**	ODD	(S)
VINO NOBILE DI MONTEPULCIANO 1995, TENUTA VALDIPIATA Tuscany	*Rounded rich fruit, mature and fleshy cherries, good acidity and balance, with gripping tannins.*	**£18.10**	FLW	(S)
CHIANTI CLASSICO RISERVA O'LEANDRO 1996, CENNATOIO Tuscany	*Good evolved nose, touch of age on this intense palate of cherries and plums.*	**£18.50**	V&V	(S)
CHIANTI CLASSICO RISERVA 1997, CASTELLO DI FONTERUTOLI Tuscany	*Aromatic warm red berry fruits, well integrated with plums and damsons on the lingering palate.*	**£18.70**	Widely Available	(S)
CHIANTI CLASSICO RISERVA 1997, CASTELLO DELLA PANERETTA Tuscany	*Blockbuster style nose, deep fruity and herba-ceous palate, warming finish with pleasing length and acidity.*	**£19.00**	V&C VIN BEL	(G)
VILLA CAFAGGIO SAN MARTINO 1997, CASA GIRELLI Tuscany	*Well balanced with excellent flavour of plums and damsons, good finish, this wine will go far.*	**£19.20**	BDR JSS VIL	(S)

BRUNELLO DI MONTALCINO DOCG 1995, CASANOVA DI NERI Tuscany	*Rich orange peel and ripe cherry flavours give way to delight, maturing nicely with leathery overtones.*	**£19.50**	WTS	(B)
CASTELLO DI BROLIO CHIANTI CLASSICO 1997, CASTELLO DI BROLIO Tuscany	*Sweet ripe and elegant, a wealth of fruit layers, following through to a complex long finish.*	**£21.00**	NYW CTC	(B)
TORRIONE 1997, FATTORIA PETROLO Tuscany	*Classic and elegant this Tuscan delight has ripe fruit and a rounded long lingering finish.*	**£21.20**	HST	(S)
LE STANZE 1997, POLIZIANO Tuscany	*Rich complex cassis nose with sweet ripe warm fruit flavour ending on gripping tannins and a structured end.*	**£21.50**	CTC	(B)
BRUNELLO DI MONTALCINO 1994, CANTINA NARDI Tuscany	*Mature stylish nose of raspberry and cherry, well balanced, soft but with excellent structure.*	**£22.00**	BBO	(S)
CABREO IL BORGO IGT 1997, RUFFINO Tuscany	*Bitter cherries on the nose, of this impressive full styled wine with a definite backbone.*	**£22.50**	JMC FRW	(B)
ETRUSCO 1996, CENNATOIO Tuscany	*Complex, light perfumed nose, creamy fruit on the palate, firm tannic structure and a powerful finish.*	**£23.50**	V&V	(B)
CHIANTI CLASSICO RISERVA VIGNA DEL SORBO 1997, TENUTA FONTODI Tuscany	*Medium weight of elegant fruit and good balance, some oak and tar showing through.*	**£23.70**	V&C BEN VIL CTC	(B)

ROMITORIO DI SANTEDAME IGT TOSCANA 1996, RUFFINO Tuscany	*Lovely balance on the palate with great fruit concentration and texture, long spectacular velvety finish.*	£25.00	ALI	(G)
MONTESODI 1997, FRESCOBALDI Tuscany	*Subtle blackberry fruit with spice and vanilla, with a warming finish on this huge fruit driven wine.*	£25.00	MZC	(B)
BRUNELLO DI MONTALCINO 1995, CANTINA DI MONTALCINO Tuscany	*Soft tannins with considerable depth of fruit of red berries and good acidity and length.*	£26.00	LIB	(B)
ARCIBALDO 1996, CENNATOIO Tuscany	*Intense colour, fruit compote on nose, very open ripe fruit, with medium body and a lovely firm finish.*	£26.80	V&V	(S)
SUMMUS 1997, CASTELLO BANFI Tuscany	*Lovely rich tarry cherry nose, well balanced berries on the palate with excellent length.*	£27.00	VIN HST	(S)
FLACCIANELLO DELLA PIEVE 1997, TENUTA FONTODI Tuscany	*Solid spiced fruit structure, red berry finish, long lingering style showing great potential for its future.*	£28.50	V&C DBY NYW BEN HST CTC	(G) TROPHY WINE
SIEPI, ROSSO DI TOSCANA 1997, CASTELLO DI FONTERUTOLI Tuscany	*Luscious rich bed of berry fruits, with herbs and figs, with gripping plum fruit ripe tannins.*	£30.30	V&C JNW HST VIL CTC	(G)
EXCELSUS 1997, CASTELLO BANFI Tuscany	*A meaty vanilla nose with structured leathery fruit palate, good acid, ripe tannins and lovely length.*	£35.00	VIN	(S)

BRUNELLO DI MONTALCINO TENUTA NUOVA 1994, CASANOVA DI NERI Tuscany	*Good development shown on the nose, moving into a basket of plums and damsons.*	**£35.00**	WTS EUW HST	**B**

ITALY • WHITE

PINOT GRIGIO 1999, LA VIS Trentino	*Great soft oily texture, slight spritz, delicate and fresh with honeysuckle and pears, moderate length.*	**£4.00**	ASD	**S**
D'ISTINTO CATTARATO CHARDONNAY 1998, BRL HARDY Sicily	*Subtle grassy nose, with citrus fruit rich warm sunshine body and a good long lingering finish.*	**£4.00**	Widely Available	**B**
VILLA SANDI CHARDONNAY 1999, VILLA SANDI	*Bubble gummy aromas, very attractive and just asking you to drink it, taste its melon freshness.*	**£4.50**	GSJ	**S**
BRIGHT BROTHERS GREGANICO CHARDONNAY 1998, CANTINE SETTESOLI Sicily	*Good scented nose, characterful peachy style on the palate and a pleasant marzipan finish.*	**£4.50**	SMF	**B**
TRULLI CHARDONNAY 1999, AZIENDA VINICOLA CANTELE Puglia	*Refreshing oak and citrus nose, pleasant oak, peaches and pears on the palate, beautiful length.*	**£4.60**	ODD CWS SAF	**S** WINE OF THE YEAR
COSTALUPO 1999, ILLUMINATI Abruzzi	*Floral aromas on a palate of apples and pears, good acidity and finesse with a mineral finish.*	**£4.70**	AVB	**B**

SOAVE SUPERIORE 1999, FASOLI GINO Veneto	*Subtle cider apple nose, fuller fruit flavours on the finish with a balanced acidity.*	£4.90	VRT TOS	(B)
BRIGHT BROTHERS SICILIAN BARREL FERMENTED CHARDONNAY 1998, CANTINE SETTESOLI Sicily	*Spicy tropical fruits with vanilla on the nose integrating on a complex palate combined with a soft acidity.*	£5.00	SMF	(S)
LE VELE VERDICCHIO DEI CASTELLI DI JESI DOC CLASSICO 1999, TERRE CORTESI MONCARO Marche	*Restrained nose with warm rounded ripe fruit on the fruit driven palate and a long and dry finish.*	£5.00	EUW	(B)
MARC XERO CHARDONNAY 1999, AZIENDA VINICOLA CANTELE Puglia	*Soft tropical fruit with buttery oak hints on a soothing palate and a crisp cool finish.*	£5.00	TOS CWS	(B)
SAFEWAY ORGANIC SOAVE 1999, FASOLI GINO Veneto	*Good light floral notes on the nose, hints of ripe fruits on finish, clean and refreshing.*	£5.00	SAF	(B)
TERRE DI GINESTRA CATARRATTO 1999, CALATRASI Sicily	*Fruit driven aromas, citrus and oak with a clean long slightly tropical and complex finish.*	£5.20	BWL CTC	(S)
FRASCATI SUPERIORE 1999, FONTANA CANDIDA Latium	*Complex citrus fruit and mineral palate, clean refreshing and easy drinking, with a classy lingering finish.*	£5.20	MWW CVR NYW VIL HVW CTC	(B)
GRECO BASILICATA 1999, BASILIUM Basilicata	*Powerful citrus characters on nose, with bananas and peardrops on a zingy tasteful finish.*	£5.30	AVB	(B)

I MESI CHARDONNAY TRENTINO 1998, CASA GIRELLI Trentino	*Soft fruit nose, peaches and vanilla notes well integrated with a fresh acidity and bright finish.*	£5.70	GDS VIL	B
CARAMIA CHARDONNAY 1999, AZIENDA VINICOLA CANTELE Puglia	*Fragrant pineapple nose leading to refreshing citrus flavours, good acidity and a clean crisp finish.*	£6.00	IWS	B
CASALE FALCHINI VIGNA A SOLTAIO 1999, CASALE FALCHINI Tuscany	*A simple lively wine with a citrus fruit nose and palate, with a long characterful finish.*	£6.00	RHV	B
VIGNA NOVALI VERDICCHIO DEI CASTELLI DI JESI CLASSICO RESERVE 1997, TERRE CORTESI MONCARO Marche	*Aromatic fruit nose with a hint of rich honey and cloves, giving a pleasing finish.*	£6.50	EUW	B
VERDE DI CA' RUPTAE VERDICCHIO DEI CASTELLI DI JESI CLASSICO 1999, TERRE CORTESI MONCARO Marche	*Smooth rich and yummy, good prerequisites for this well structured wine of good fruit driven force.*	£6.90	EUW	B
ANTHILIA BIANCO 1999, DONNAFUGATA Sicily	*Grass and smoke on the nose, lots of attractive fruit, and a very appealing finish. Powerful.*	£7.00	VIN	S
FALANGHINA SANNIO BENEVANTANO DOC 1999, FEUDI DI SAN GREGORIO Campania	*Exotic aromas on the nose with a pleasant fruity dry palate, medium bodied and smooth.*	£7.20	ODD	S
GAVI DI GAVI CASCINA LA TOLEDANA 1999, VILLA LANATA Piedmont	*Crisp apple aromas on the nose, clean and pleasant palate, and a good delicate lasting finish.*	£7.30	CTC	B

VERDICCHIO CLASSICO SUPERIORE CASAL DI SERRA 1998, UMANI RONCHI Marche	*Apricot and honey rich gelati, on a well rounded fruit palate, good acidity and fair length.*	£7.30	Widely Available	(B)
FUNTANALIRAS VERMENTINO DI GALLURA 1999, CANTINA DEL VERMENTINO Sardinia	*Crisp and clean fruit driven palate, with good acidity and balanced lingering finish.*	£7.40	AVB	(S)
PINOT GRIGIO COLLIO CLASSICA 1999, LIVON Friuli	*Lovely sweet honeysuckle nose, fresh apple and pear fruit palate with a good crisp finish.*	£7.50	EUW	(S)
COLLIO PINOT GRIGIO DOC 1998, ATTEMS Friuli	*Fresh elegant citrus nose, light and clean palate with well balanced fruit giving a sophisticated finish.*	£7.80	RAV	(B)
CA' DEI FRATI LUGANA 1999, CA' DEI FRATI Veneto	*Exquisite nose on an alluring palate of freshly picked ripe apples and cantaloupe melon.*	£7.90	Widely Available	(B)
PINOT GRIGIO ISONZO 1999, I FEUDI DI ROMANS Veneto	*Beautiful sweetpea aroma, elegant floral notes on palate, and a rich array of apricots and peaches.*	£8.00	V&C	(G)
PODIUM VERDICCHIO DEI CASTELLI DI JESI CLASSICO SUPERIORE 1998, GAROFOLI Marche	*Full bodied wine of citrus and dried fruit character and length with good acidity and a lingering finish.*	£8.10	AVB CTC	(B)
MONTEORO VERMENTINO DI GALLURA DOC 1998, SELLA & MOSCA Sardinia	*Crisp and rich fruit flavours on this well made wine with individual grape character, creamy finish.*	£9.00	ALI	(B)

ITALY • WHITE

GRECO DI TUFO DOC 1999, FEUDI DI SAN GREGORIO Campania	*Full, rich and ripe for the picking, up front character and a grassy elegant finish.*	£9.10	V&C RAV JMC	(S)
SERRA FIORESE VERDICCHIO DEI CASTELLI DI JESI CLASSICO SUPERIORE 1997, GAROFOLI Marche	*Earthy lemon aromas with buttery flavours of green apples and tropical fruits on a nice finish.*	£9.20	AVB CTC	(B)
GAVI DI GAVI MASSERIA DEI CARMELITANI 1999, TERRE DA VAINO Piedmont	*Captivating delicate aromas on a fabulously alluring wine, pineapples and peach on the finish.*	£9.30	VIN DBY	(G)
LE VAGLIE VERDICCHIO DEI CASTELLI DI JESI CLASSICO 1998, SANTA BARBERA Marches	*Floral and grapey on the nose with good structure and clean fruits on the palate.*	£9.50	VIN GHL	(S)
AMEDEO BIANCO DI CUSTOZA 1998, CAVALCHINA Veneto	*Intense fruit nose of greengage and peaches, sharp quince on the palate and a powerful finish.*	£10.00	VIN	(B)
COLLE GAIO FRASCATI SUPERIORE DOC 1997, COLLI DI CATONE Lazio	*Greengage and peach on the nose with clean palate and minerals on the cleansing finish.*	£10.00	RAV	(B)
CUTIZZI GRECO DI TUFO VIGNA TARDIVA DOC 1998, FEUDI DI SAN GREGORIO Campania	*Rich ripe greengage on the nose, palate of honeyed peaches with a soft lengthy finish.*	£10.00	ALI	(B)
FIANO DI AVELLINO DOC 1999, FEUDI DI SAN GREGORIO Campania	*Heavy tropical nose, ripe sweet flavours on the palate with good a mouthfilling feel.*	£10.00	ALI	(B)

CAPUTO VIGNOLA GRECO DI TUFO 1999, CAPUTO Campania	*Grapey aromas, on a light floral palate, with honeydew melon on the very attractive finish.*	£10.30	AFI	(B)
BROLETTINO LUGANA 1998, CA' DEI FRATI Veneto	*Nutty and hay nose with creamy fleshy pineapple citrus fruits elegantly balanced and long finish.*	£10.70	V&C BLU DBY NYW BEN HST CTC	(S)
LE BUSCHE 1998, UMANI RONCHI Marches	*Attractive herbal leafy nose followed by fresh, complex, rich leesy palate, and a very decent length.*	£11.00	JNW VIL CTC	(S)
VITTORIO PUIATTI PINOT GRIGIO COLLIO 1999, VITTORIO PUIATTI Friuli	*Sophisticated and elegant aromas, spritz and spice on the lively dry fresh palate, excellent fruit.*	£11.50	TOS	(B)
LUGANA RISERVA SERGIO ZENATO 1997, AZIENDA VINICOLA ZENATO Veneto	*Soft mellow and nicely balanced apple fruit and pleasing acidity, with a gingerbread and vanilla finish.*	£12.00	EUW	(S)
VERNACCIA DI SAN GIMIGNANO RISERVA 1997, PANIZZI Tuscany	*Characterful nose on a wine of medium full body, with delicious essence of Tuscany.*	£12.10	CTC	(B)
BIANCO DI GIANNI BIANCO DI TOSCANA 1997, PANIZZI Tuscany	*Fresh and crisp with amazing length of complex fruit flavours and a clean finish.*	£12.40	CTC	(B)
JERMANN RIESLING RENANO AFIX 1998, JERMANN Friuli	*Green freshly picked fruit on the nose, clean and spritzy on the tongue, a delightful glass.*	£13.20	VIL WCS CTC	(B)

JERMANN PINOT BIANCO 1998, JERMANN Friuli	*Impressive weight of palate, with succulent pear and melon, well balanced and an elegant finish.*	£13.90	V&C HST VIL WCS CTC	**S**
CRU SANCT VALENTIN CHARDONNAY 1997, SAN MICHELE APPIANO Alto Adige	*Attractive intense fresh fruit nose with a delightful blend of ripe fruits and acidity on the palate.*	£14.00	EUW	**B**
SANCT VALENTIN SAUVIGNON CRU SANCT VALENTIN 1998, SAN MICHELE APPIANO Alto Adige	*Lovely subtle sauvignon nose, rich gooseberry, white fruit and passion fruit palate.*	£14.00	EUW	**B**
BRAIDE MATE CHARDONNAY COLLIO 1997, LIVON Friuli	*Good fine fruit nose, good grip of acidity well combined with ripe fruit and toasty touch.*	£14.50	EUW	**B**
JERMANN CAPO MARTINO 1997, JERMANN Friuli	*Complex peach fruit and nut nose with a mouthful of integrated summer fruits with an appealing length.*	£22.80	NYW VIL WCS CTC	**G**

NORTH AMERICA

This year like so many before, the boutique wineries have collected the majority of the Gold medals. Also a Trophy for the wine that has made its name in this land of the much revired Californian lifestyle, the delicous and robust Zinfandel. Washington State has shown itself to be a state that is now starting to compete on the World market with great strength and success. Over two thirds of the wines entered have been judged to be of a standard deservable of a medal.

CALIFORNIA • CABERNET

VALLEY OAKS CABERNET SAUVIGNON 1997, FETZER California	*Lovely rich raspberry nose followed by beautifully balanced fruit and oak, with complex, good length.*	£7.00	JSM ODD WTS CWS FQU WCR	S
TURNING LEAF VINTNER'S COLLECTION CABERNET SAUVIGNON 1995, ERNEST & JULIO GALLO California	*Interesting appeal of fruits on nose, cherry tannins on the palate and full of lively acidity.*	£7.20	WCR	B
SONOMA COUNTY CABERNET SAUVIGNON 1996, ERNEST & JULIO GALLO California	*Rich touch of ripe fruit on the nose, well made wine with tones of delicious black fruit.*	£8.00	Widely available	S
BONTERRA CABERNET SAUVIGNON 1997, BONTERRA California	*Light style with sherbet on the nose, good structure and balanced acidity, successfully combined to finish smoothly.*	£8.90	JSM ODD WTS TOS FQU VRT BTH	B
VINTNER'S RESERVE CABERNET SAUVIGNON 1997, KENDALL-JACKSON California	*Mocha, prune nose with leafy hint, ripe black fruit in smooth palate, good tannic support.*	£9.90	DBY G&M	B

QUATRO CABERNET SAUVIGNON 1997, CECCHETTI SEBASTIANI California	*Upfront and confident, classic blackcurrant aromas and palate, with hints of mint and leave.on the finish.*	£10.00	VNO	(B)
DRY CREEK VALLEY CABERNET SAUVIGNON 1994, ERNEST & JULIO GALLO California	*Good tropical new world aromas with ripe summer fruit flavours integrated with soft tannins.*	£12.70	JMC	(B)
DRY CREEK VINEYARD PRIVATE COLLECTION CABERNET SAUVIGNON 1995, FETZER California	*Ripe plum nose with spiciness developing into elegant structured palate and lengthy tail.*	£15.30	TOS UNS	(B)
DRY CREEK VINEYARD CABERNET SAUVIGNON 1997, DRY CREEK VINEYARD California	*Aromatic spicy vanilla nose with fresh crushed raspberry flavours mingling with gripping tannins and good length.*	£16.00	ALI	(B)
STONEGATE CABERNET SAUVIGNON 1996, STONEGATE California	*Complex and brooding, delicious rich blackcurrant dense style, great tannin structure and depth.*	£16.00	POU	(B)
ST FRANCIS CABERNET SAUVIGNON RESERVE 1996, ST FRANCIS California	*Minty plum nose leading to a smooth full bodied fruit coulis palate with mouth coating tannins.*	£16.90	MAD QWW POR	(S)
BUCKEYE CABERNET SAUVIGNON 1997, KENDALL-JACKSON California	*Smokey leathery nose with soft blackcurrants and strawberries, lovely mouthfeel and green tannins.*	£17.00	G&M	(B)
FIRESTONE RESERVE 1996, FIRESTONE California	*Black cherries and spice on soft supple palate, full of mouth coating tannins and attractive finish.*	£18.00	MCT	(B)

ALEXANDER RESERVE CABERNET SAUVIGNON 1997, GEYSER PEAK California	*Leathery damson nose with baked summer pudding flavours with solid tannins, lovely silky tail.*	**£20.00**	MAX	(S)
HILLTOP CABERNET SAUVIGNON SINGLE VINEYARD 1996, J LOHR California	*Leather and black cherry nose leading to stewed plums and hints of chocolate at the finale.*	**£21.00**	HST BEL	(B)
DRY CREEK VINEYARD CABERNET SAUVIGNON RESERVE 1997, DRY CREEK VINEYARD California	*Ripe juicy cherries with a bitter edge and mintiness with solid tannins on finish.*	**£23.60**	ALI	(B)
CAIN FIVE 1995, CAIN CELLARS California	*Fleshy fruit nose with well integrated oak in juicy plum flavour, excellent length. Terrific structure!*	**£29.00**	J&B	(G)
NORTHERN SONOMA CABERNET SAUVIGNON 1994, ERNEST & JULIO GALLO California	*Rich spicy tobacco nose with crushed black fruit and pepper palate, full bodied and long tail.*	**£30.00**	E&J	(S)
NORTHERN SONOMA CABERNET SAUVIGNON 1996, ERNEST & JULIO GALLO California	*Fresh leafy mineral nose, great blackcurrants and earthy spice palate, beautiful length, complex tail.*	**£33.30**	JMC WCR	(G)
BV GEORGES DE LATOUR CABERNET SAUVIGNON 1996, BV WINERY California	*Rich nose of ripe fruit, touch of oak finishing with great length and balance. Absolutely delicious.*	**£34.00**	POR	(G)
OPUS ONE 1996, BARON PHILIPPE DE ROTHSCHILD & MONDAVI California	*Rich elegant Bordelais nose with crushed cassis cascading with mocha and velvety tannins into infinity.*	**£90.00**	HVN UNS FRI VIL	(G)

CALIFORNIA • CHARDONNAY

STOWELLS OF CHELSEA CHARDONNAY NV, MATTHEW CLARK California	*Fragrant ripe fruit aroma, buttery edges on lemon and pear palate with a nice easy finish.*	£4.10	WCR MHV	**B**
HAYWOOD CHARDONNAY 1998, PETER HAYWOOD California	*Crisp peach aromas with vanilla hint, good tropical fruit and vanilla flavours, with lovely length.*	£6.00	HOT	**B**
SUNDIAL CHARDONNAY 1999, FETZER California	*Ripe fruits and pleasant wood on the nose and palate with lovely acidity and round mouthfeel.*	£6.50	MWW ODD FQU WCR	**B**
CANYON ROAD CHARDONNAY 1999, CANYON ROAD California	*Pleasant aromatic ripe fruit perfume followed by excellent balance of acidity in a floral fruit palate.*	£6.90	ODD CVR JMC	**B**
JEKEL VINEYARDS CHARDONNAY 1998, JEKEL California	*Vanilla and fresh fruits on the nose, ripe pears and pineapples notes on the palate.*	£7.50	FQU	**B**
BV COASTAL CHARDONNAY 1997, BV WINERY California	*Perfumed sweet oak nose, good balance of citrus notes, with good acidity and tannins on the palate.*	£8.00	PFC	**B**
CONCANNON CHARDONNAY 1997, CONCANNON California	*Ripe tropical fruit on the nose and palate, creamy texture with refreshing acidity and a lovely fruit finish.*	£8.00	AWS	**B**

SONOMA COUNTY CHARDONNAY 1998, ERNEST & JULIO GALLO California	*Well balanced lovely fresh fruit flavours with tones of figs and a long oak finish.*	£8.00	JMC WCR	**B**
GEYSER PEAK SONOMA COUNTY CHARDONNAY 1998, GEYSER PEAK California	*Melon with soft oak aroma, full rich palate of peaches and pineapples with a powerful finish.*	£9.00	JMC	**B**
CYPRESS CHARDONNAY 1998, J LOHR California	*Clean, light and fresh almond fragrances, elegant creamy bed of spicy fruits with a delightful finish.*	£9.20	CTC	**S**
R H PHILLIPS TOASTED HEAD CHARDONNAY 1998, RH PHILLIPS California	*Ripe tropical fruit nose followed by a delicious clean toasty fruit palate, excellent acidity and good length.*	£9.20	JWW JSS POR COM	**S**
BERINGER CHARDONNAY 1998, BERINGER California	*Full fruit nose followed by a tropical palate in a gentle style wine with good depth and length.*	£9.30	ODD BWC DBY	**S**
KENDALL-JACKSON VINTNER'S RESERVE CHARDONNAY 1998, KENDALL-JACKSON California	*Strong complex aroma invites you to taste melons and lime on the palate, with well balanced fresh acidity.*	£9.80	DBY JSS G&M	**B**
STEFANI VINEYARD CHARDONNAY 1997, ERNEST & JULIO GALLO California	*Soft fruit nose, stronger on the palate with good a combination of oak and acidity.*	£11.40	MWW JMC WCR	**B**
WILD HORSE CENTRAL COAST CHARDONNAY 1997, WILD HORSE California	*Creamy vanilla wooded nose, spicy ripe fruit on the palate, with good balance and a fresh oak finish.*	£11.50	EUW	**S**

RIVERSTONE CHARDONNAY MONTEREY 1998, J LOHR California	*Slightly earthy wood on the nose, melon, vanilla and banana notes with a good proportion of oak.*	£11.60	DBY VIL CTC	(S)
BYRON SANTA MARIA CHARDONNAY 1996, ROBERT MONDAVI California	*Pears and apples on the nose, fresh fruit with great acidity and a smooth long finish.*	£12.00	VIL	(B)
WENTE HERMAN RESERVE CHARDONNAY 1997, WENTE California	*Gently buttery nose and palate with easy fresh fruit, decent acidity and an elegant finish.*	£12.00	PNA	(B)
LAGUNA RANCH CHARDONNAY 1997, ERNEST & JULIO GALLO California	*Pronounced nose, strong oak and fresh fruits in balance with the acidity, and a pleasant nutty finish.*	£12.00	JMC	(B)
KENDALL-JACKSON CAMELOT CHARDONNAY 1998, KENDALL-JACKSON California	*Nutty boneyed nose, lovely crisp acidity well integrated to round mouthfeel with a gorgeous fresh finish.*	£12.70	G&M	(B)
SEBASTIANI SONOMA COUNTY CHARDONNAY 1998, SEBASTIANI California	*Soft lightly oaked nose, ripe broad tropical notes on the palate with a wonderful intense refreshing finish.*	£13.00	PLB	(G)
ACACIA CHARDONNAY 1995, ACACIA California	*Fruity slightly nutty nose, warm mouthfeel with a palate full of spicy oak and a definite finish.*	£13.00	WTS	(S)
FETZER VINEYARDS PRIVATE COLLECTION CHARDONNAY 1998, FETZER California	*Sweet pineapple and woody nose, clean fresh ripe fruit with a good balance of acidity and oak.*	£13.00	BRF	(B)

ST SUPERY NAPA VALLEY CHARDONNAY 1998, ST SUPERY California	*Intense fruits in soft oak balanced with creamy apples finishing in vanilla and peach with a full mouthfeel.*	**£13.10**	NRW CTC	**B**
CLOS DU VAL CHARDONNAY 1998, CLOS DU VAL California	*Fruit toasty oak, creamy melon and tropical fruit blended with excellent acidity, an elegant and refreshing finish.*	**£14.10**	AVB CPW	**B**
ST FRANCIS CHARDONNAY RESERVE 1997, ST FRANCIS California	*Soft pear nose followed by fresh acidity and good oak in a full round palate, with an extended finish.*	**£14.80**	MAD QWW	**B**
CLOS LA CHANCE NAPA VALLEY CHARDONNAY 1997, CLOS LA CHANCE California	*Rich baked biscuits and a nutty nose followed by a full round fruity palate with a wonderful oak presence.*	**£14.90**	ODD BBR	**G**
MARIMAR TORRES CHARDONNAY 1998, MARRIMAR TORRES California	*Pungent citrus nose, good acidity with balanced oak and fruit, excellent length and a pleasant finish.*	**£15.70**	BLS POR	**B**
KENT RASMUSSEN CHARDONNAY 1997, KENT RASMUSSEN California	*Nutty and toasty notes on the nose and palate with a huge structure and very pleasant depth.*	**£17.10**	ODD BBR	**B**
CHÂTEAU POTELLE MT VEEDER CHARDONNAY 1995, BRUNO CLAIR California	*Brilliant buttery nose, grand round fruit palate which is full of refreshing acidity, a lovely extended finish.*	**£18.00**	WBR J&B	**S**
EHLERS GROVE CHARDONNAY 1997, EHLERS GROVE California	*Big spicy oak, good tasteful fruit on the palate and a toasty biscuit finish with good length.*	**£18.00**	THI	**B**

ARROYO VISTA CHARDONNAY SINGLE VINEYARD 1997, J LOHR California	*Pronounced fruity nose, good weight on the palate with a pleasant touch of sweetness and spicy oak.*	£19.00	HST BEL	Ⓢ

CALIFORNIA • FORTIFIED

ELYSIUM BLACK MUSCAT, QUADY California	*Bright brilliant red colour, honeyed strawberry aromas, with rich berries and texture and a lovely warm finish.*	£7.00	Widely Available	Ⓑ
ESSENSIA QUADY , QUADY California	*Rich grapey honeyed nose, well integrated acidity in fruity flavours, luscious and good honeyed clear finish.*	£7.10	Widely Available	Ⓑ
QUADY STARBOARD BATCH 88, QUADY California	*Stunning orange aromas, with creme caramel notes on this quite warming starboard with long finish.*	£9.50	JSM HVN AVB GHL JNW WCR CTC	Ⓢ
VYA EXTRA DRY VERMOUTH, QUADY California	*Brilliant appealing nose followed by light sweet flavours, good acidity and very pleasant long caramel finish.*	£12.00	AVB NRW CEB GHL WRW	Ⓑ
VYA SWEET VERMOUTH, QUADY California	*Herbal ginger sweet nose, with a touch of bitterness in a well balanced creamy texture. Lovely clean finish.*	£13.00	AVB NRW GHL	Ⓑ

Pinpoint who sells the wine you wish to buy by turning to the stockist codes. If you know the name of the wine you want to buy, use the alphabetical index. If the price is your motivation, refer to the invaluable price guide index; red and white wines under £5, sparkling wines under £12 and champagne under £16. Happy hunting!

CALIFORNIA • PINOT NOIR

SUTTER HOME PINOT NOIR 1997, SUTTER HOME California	*Powerful, farmyard, savoury nose, a big, gutsy berry fruit palate, giving a broad mouthfeel.*	**£5.30**	Widely Available	**B**
REDWOOD TRAIL RESERVE PINOT NOIR 1998, SEAGRAM CHÂTEAU & ESTATE California	*Pleasant gentle straw-berry nose with chocolate undertones, good fruit and sweet oak on the finish.*	**£6.50**	MAD CWS WCR CST	**B**
ESTANCIA PINOT NOIR 1998, ESTANCIA California	*Overt, cranberry and farmyard aromas follow through onto a powerful flesh palate, nice balance and good length.*	**£9.00**	GSJ	**S**
KENDALL-JACKSON VINTNER'S RESERVE PINOT NOIR 1998, KENDALL-JACKSON California	*Subtle, savoury nose with hints of smokiness. Fruit driven jammy palate, with oaky hints that dominate the finish.*	**£9.80**	DBY JSS G&M	**S**
ESTANCIA PINOT NOIR PINNACLES 1998, ESTANCIA California	*Elegant pinot aromas with vegetal undercurrents flow onto a rich, long fruit palate revealing fine acidity.*	**£10.00**	MCT	**S**
FETZER BARREL SELECT PINOT NOIR 1998, FETZER California	*Text book New World pinot, big fruit palate with subtle oakiness under-neath. Full bodied jammy finish.*	**£10.00**	ODD TOS	**S**
BUENA VISTA CARNEROS PINOT NOIR 1996, BUENA VISTA California	*Lifted loganberry nose with vegetal bints yield to a good intense fruit palate with a tannic finish.*	**£12.50**	HOT	**B**

CÔTE DE CARNEROS 1996, CARNEROS CREEK California	*Spicy aromas of farmyard character with redcurrant fruit on the palate and good lingering length.*	**£12.50**	WGA	(B)
WILD HORSE CENTRAL COAST PINOT NOIR 1997, WILD HORSE California	*Sweet cherry fruit nose, with big sweet berries on the palate and nice intensity with some good soft tannins.*	**£13.50**	EUW	(B)
BYRON SANTA MARIA PINOT NOIR 1997, ROBERT MONDAVI California	*Complex pinot nose, soft cooked orange marmalade fruit, raised acidity that persists to the end.*	**£14.00**	MZC	(B)
SANTA MARIA PINOT NOIR 1998, AU BON CLIMAT California	*Raspberry and blackberry aromas with slight vegetal undertones, well balanced palate with good acidity and green tannins.*	**£15.20**	BLU DBY NYW HST GRO	(S)
SAINTSBURY CARNEROS PINOT NOIR 1997, SAINTSBURY California	*Clean nose with meaty, cherry and oaky aromas, medium weight with cherry and bramble fruit.*	**£16.20**	Widely Available	(S)
SANTA MARIA VALLEY PINOT NOIR 1997, FOXEN California	*Ripe summer fruit, oaky hints, up front delicate ripe fruit palate with firm tannins and moderate acidity.*	**£16.50**	MWW	(B)
CALERA PINOT NOIR 1997, CALERA California	*Developed, green notes on the nose give way to good fruit and a fine tannin palate.*	**£17.20**	WTS CPW	(B)
CUVAISON PINOT NOIR 1998, CUVAISON California	*Rich ripe chocolate with herbal hints on the nose, sweet and long fruit palate with good depth.*	**£17.70**	CPW TAN CFT AMW	(B)

CRICHTON HALL CARNEROS PINOT NOIR 1997, CRICHTON HALL California	*Confident and bold herbaceous, green nose. Rounded plummy, toasty characters on the palate with a subtle finish.*	£18.00	WBR	(B)
KENT RASMUSSEN PINOT NOIR 1997, KENT RASMUSSEN California	*Ripe strawberry and cherry aromas, jammy berry fruit palate, fine grained tannins with an impressive finish.*	£18.50	ODD BBR FWM	(S)
MARIMAR TORRES PINOT NOIR 1998, MARIMAR TORRES California	*Brambly, slightly peppery nose, that gives way to a lean palate with round acidity and woody edges.*	£19.10	ESL NYW POR	(B)
BUENA VISTA CARNEROS PINOT NOIR GRAND RESERVE 1995, BUENA VISTA California	*Evolved, tar and meaty aromas, ripe gripping fruit palate, subtly integrated oak. Beautifully balanced firm structure.*	£24.50	HOT	(G)
THE FAMOUS GATE DOMAINE CARNEROS PINOT NOIR 1998, CHAMPAGNE TAITTINGER California	*Aromas of an equestrian saddle, succulent and rich summer fruit pudding, with a velvet smooth mouthfeel.*	£24.60	MAD DBY VIL POR	(G)

CALIFORNIA • RED • OTHER

CALIFORNIA MOUNTAIN SYRAH 1998, CALIFORNIA DIRECT California	*Very fresh, concentrated raspberry nose, good balance of fruit tannin and acid, with a rolling finish.*	£4.50	ALD	(B)
CALIFORNIA MOUNTAIN GRENACHE CABERNET 1999, CALIFORNIA DIRECT California	*Open black cherry and pepper aroma, lighter style with traces of sweetness and controlled acids.*	£4.70	ALD	(B)

STONYBROOK MERLOT 1998, STONYBROOK California	*Healthy dense palate, good backbone on fresh ripe fruit flavours, good lasting finish.*	£4.80	JSM BRF BTH	B
ASDA ARIUS SYRAH 1998, CALIFORNIA DIRECT California	*Good clean, minty nose, excellent harmony on palate, refined red and black fruit flavour.*	£5.00	ASD	S
DELICATO SYRAH 1998, DELICATO California	*Young, minty ripe fruit nose, very smooth with spice and cinnamon on a generous palate.*	£6.00	CPD	S
IRONSTONE SHIRAZ 1997, KAUTZ IRONSTONE California	*Light fruit, clove and spice nose, warm, soft, exotically spiced and developed palate, consistent balance.*	£6.00	JSM MWW HWL SAF	S
CALIFORNIA OLD VINE ESTATES CARIGNANE 1998, CALIFORNIA DIRECT California	*Strawberry floral nose with red lush berries and a hint of spice, soft tannins and acid.*	£6.00	CDL TOS	B
HAYWOOD MERLOT 1997, PETER HAYWOOD California	*Soft supple and brimming over with black berry fruits which hold out to the finale.*	£6.00	HOT	B
SONOMA COUNTY MERLOT 1998, CANYON ROAD California	*Ripe fresh berry notes, well balanced with good fruit and cinnamon flavours. Lush tannins on tail.*	£7.00	ODD JMC	S
FETZER SYRAH 1997, FETZER California	*Powerful nose, good depth of flavour and follow through, fresh acidity is perfectly balanced, subtle oak.*	£7.50	ODD	S

OTHER • RED • CALIFORNIA • N. AMERICA

CONCANNON PETIT SIRAH 1997, CONCANNON California	*Elegant nose with fresh, ripe peaches and citrus. Deep, dense, brooding ripe fruit and toasty oak flavours.*	£8.00	AWS	(S)
QUARTO MERLOT 1997, CECCHETTI SEBASTIANI CELLAR California	*Fresh berry fruit aromas with plummy fruit, silky tannins and fresh acidity coming through.*	£8.00	VNO WBR	(S)
MONTEVINA SANGIOVESE 1997, MONTEVINA California	*Rather fresh style with raspberries and strawberries, light bodied with good acidity, herbaceous and cherry finish.*	£8.00	V&C PRG VIL CTC	(B)
MONTEVINA BARBERA 1996, MONTEVINA California	*Balsamic and herbs on the entrance, cherries and sun dried tomatoes on the palate.*	£8.10	V&C PRG ESL VIL CTC	(S)
BONNY DOON BIG HOUSE RED 1998, BONNY DOON California	*As the name suggests this is a big style wine. Rich, intense, full of complex flavours. You would break out of jail for it.*	£8.10	Widely Available	(B)
BONTERRA MERLOT 1997, BONTERRA California	*Brambles and oak with some leatheriness, bursting hot plums and cherries with great balance.*	£8.20	WTS UNS	(S)
PARDUCCI PETITE SIRAH 1997, PARDUCCI California	*Rich spicy cinnamon fruit palate with high acid and big tannins and a very hot finish.*	£8.20	CVR	(B)
FETZER VINEYARDS BARREL SELECT MERLOT 1997, FETZER California	*A fresh leafy nose with lush berries, vanilla flavours, lots of finesse and ready for drinking.*	£9.00	MWW	(S)

IRONSTONE LIBRARY COLLECTION MERITAGE 1994, KAUTZ IRONSTONE California	*Warm spicy brambly nose with lively black cherries and mintiness. A lovely sassy number.*	£9.00	HWL	(B)
BONTERRA MERLOT 1998, BONTERRA California	*Minty cassis aromas, with juicy red fruit and cherry finish with fine tannic grip.*	£10.00	WTS	(S)
ESTANCIA MERLOT 1997, ESTANCIA California	*Fragrant nose with plump silky plums and mulberries with drying tannins and spice flavours.*	£10.00	MCT	(B)
FIRESTONE MERLOT 1997, FIRESTONE California	*Hot aromas of cinnamon and mulberries marrying on a palate of bursting juicy plums.*	£10.00	MCT	(B)
EHLERS GROVE DOLCETTO 1997, EHLERS GROVE California	*Luscious fruit compote on nose with cassis and mint holding the palate, married together perfectly.*	£11.50	THI	(S)
MONTERRA MERLOT 1998, SAN BERNABE California	*Ripe plum nose with hints of mintiness, gusty fruit palate ending with drying tannins.*	£11.50	BDR CPD	(S)
SANGIOVESE 1997, VINO NOCETO California	*Bright garnet colour, heavy toasted nose, very full palate of ripe berry fruits, luxurious rich finish.*	£11.70	ADN CPW CAM NYW CTC	(S)
HIDDEN CELLARS SYRAH 1997, HIDDEN CELLARS California	*Slightly volatile nose, good depth of flavour, starting to show signs of some ageing complexity.*	£12.00	PAT	(B)

BONTERRA SYRAH 1997, BONTERRA California	*Exotic fruits on the nose, sweet and juicy on the palate with subdued tannins.*	£12.10	ODD BRF VRT	(B)
RH PHILLIPS SYRAH 1997, RH PHILLIPS California	*A rich, spicy, ripe cherry nose with good follow through and a wonderful tannin tail.*	£12.80	JWW NRW GHL JSS POR	(B)
LA FAMIGLIA SANGIOVESE 1997, ROBERT MONDAVI California	*Earthy aromas of dark fruit and oak, giving ripe forward flavours and dry tannins.*	£13.00	MZC	(B)
ST FRANCIS MERLOT 1997, ST FRANCIS California	*Warm berry and plums cascading with spice, supple tannins, good acidity and lovely length.*	£13.00	HMA MAD QWW	(B)
CLOS DU BOIS MERLOT 1996, CLOS DU BOIS California	*Leafy cherry lifted nose with plum jam wrapped in supple tannins with velvety texture.*	£14.00	FQU	(B)
VOSS MERLOT 1997, VOSS California	*Plums and cedar aromas fusing with juicy mulberries and warm cinnamon with lovely length.*	£14.30	NEG HVW	(B)
FETZER PRIVATE COLLECTION MERLOT 1997, FETZER California	*Berry nose blending with chocolate hints, fine tannins on a palate bursting with fruit.*	£16.00	BRF	(B)
RENAISSANCE MERLOT UNFILTERED 1996, RENAISSANCE California	*Blackberry and hinting cinnamon nose with warm juicy plum coulis, with dry tannins and weighty length.*	£16.00	THW	(B)

LE CIGARE VOLANT 1997, BONNY DOON California	*Leafy, blackcurrant nose, mellow jammy fruit with perfectly balanced tannins that holds the wine together nicely.*	£16.20	Widely Available	**B**
CRICHTON HALL MERLOT 1997, CRICHTON HALL California	*Complex nose of warm red fruit with hints of vanilla and minty aromas with some pepperiness. Beautiful.*	£16.50	WBR	**S**
SILVERADO HILL MERLOT 1996, SILVERADO HILL California	*Plump ripe bramble fruit with an excellent balance of acidity and tannins on the finish.*	£16.50	WIN	**B**
BIEN NACIDO SYRAH 1997, QUPE California	*Big damson plum nose, some developed characters, tight, full pepper, spice, sweet black fruit flavours.*	£17.10	DBY NYW	**S**
ST FRANCIS MERLOT RESERVE 1996, ST FRANCIS California	*Chocolate cinnamon nose with fine structure and smooth tannins, lot of cherries and blackberries.*	£17.70	MAD QWW DBY	**G**
SONOMA COUNTY SHIRAZ 1997, GEYSER PEAK California	*Deep oak and black fruit nose, big tight tannins, very concentrated with super weight, needs time.*	£20.00	MAX	**G**
VOSS SHIRAZ 1996, VOSS California	*Sooty, dusty nose, luscious on the palate, quality fruit, pepper touches, jam flavours, creamy oak.*	£20.00	NEG	**B**
CLOS DU VAL MERLOT 1997, CLOS DU VAL California	*Gorgeous mulberry nose with a complex palate of blackcherry plum and silky with fine tannins.*	£20.80	AVB QWW CTC	**G**

OTHER • RED • CALIFORNIA • N. AMERICA

JADE MOUNTAIN SYRAH 1997, JADE MOUNTAIN California	*Cherry and raspberry on the nose with a nicely rounded palate. Has a bright future ahead.*	**£21.50**	DBY HST	(S)
HILLSIDE SELECT SYRAH 1997, QUPE California	*Rich Christmas cake fruit intensity, great attack of nice berry oak, ripe tannins, pleasant chocolate finish.*	**£27.50**	DBY NYW HST	(S)
CECCHETTI SEBASTIANI NAPA VALLEY MERLOT 1996, CECCHETTI SEBASTIANI CELLAR California	*Exotic red fruits with a touch of herb and earthy notes. Velvety and stylish with firm finish.*	**£30.00**	VNO QWW	(S)

CALIFORNIA • SPARKLING

J SCHRAM NAPA VALLEY 1992, SCHRAMSBERG California	*Inviting round melony nose, earthy characters on the palate, smooth ripe fruit, good length. Nice bubbles.*	**£31.00**	EUW	(S)

CALIFORNIA • WHITE • OTHER

CANYON ROAD SAUVIGNON BLANC 1999, CANYON ROAD California	*Lashings of tropical fruit salad aromas lead on to a ripe fruit palate with and biting acidity.*	**£6.90**	MAX CVR JMC	(B)
BONTERRA MUSCAT 1999, BONTERRA California	*Refreshing lemon undertones on this simple easy drinking style with lasting acidity and pleasing length.*	**£7.00**	JSM ODD WTS SAF	(B)

N. AMERICA • CALIFORNIA • WHITE • OTHER

CA' DEL SOLO MALVASIA BIANCA 1998, BONNY DOON California	Ripe peach and apple nose, big fresh lychee and gooseberry palate, with a biscuity finish.	£8.70	Widely Available	(B)
ANGELO D'ANGELO PINOT BIANCO 1997, MASO California	Deep yellow colour, rich wine with vanilla and cantaloupe melons on the palate long complex finish.	£9.00	POU	(B)
GEYSER PEAK SONOMA COUNTY SAUVIGNON BLANC 1999, GEYSER PEAK California	Butter and fresh gooseberry on the nose of concentrated fruit , soft minerally palate with a long lively finish.	£9.00	MAX	(B)
RENAISSANCE DRY RIESLING 1997, RENAISSANCE California	Succulent warm ripe fruit aromas, good balance and complexity, a long slightly aged finish	£10.00	THW	(S)
BONTERRA VIOGNIER 1998, BONTERRA California	Intense honey, lime nose with pronounced ripe summer fruits on the palate and long finish.	£10.30	ODD VRT	(B)
BONTERRA ROUSSANNE 1999, BONTERRA California	Spicy tropical fruit nose with fruit salad and cream characteristic and crisp dry acidity.	£10.70	ODD VRT	(S)
RH PHILLIPS VIOGNIER 1998, R H PHILLIPS California	Cut pineapple nose with crisp peardrop and tropical fruit with good alcohol and acidity.	£11.10	GRT JWW NRW GHL JSS POR	(B)
ST SUPERY NAPA VALLEY SAUVIGNON BLANC 1999, ST SUPERY California	Lifted fruit and bits of herbaceousness, lovely rich, tropical fruit palate with gripping acidity and good length.	£11.80	NRW HST GRO WRK CTC	(S)

DRY CREEK FUMÉ BLANC RESERVE 1998, DRY CREEK California	*Honeyed, ripe pineapple, floral aromas with a lean, simple fruit palate and reasonable length.*	**£12.90**	ALI	(B)
ROUSSANNE 1998, BONNY DOON California	*Lemon and lime with floral hints on the nose, soft floral lychee palate with subtle acidity.*	**£13.10**	FRI DBY UBC VIL POR	(B)
ROTHBERG VIOGNIER 1997, FOXEN California	*Subtle aromatic nose, very seductive fruity exture on the palate with toasty grapefruit notes.*	**£19.00**	ENO	(B)

CALIFORNIA • ZINFANDEL

PEPPERWOOD GROVE ZINFANDEL 1998, CECCHETTI SEBASTIANI CELLAR California	*Young fresh nose, medium bodied, an easy summer red, with good structure. Goes down a treat.*	**£6.10**	Widely Available	(S)
CANTERBURY ZINFANDEL 1998, EHLERS GROVE California	*Good cherry stone aromas, sweet black fruit palate with pleasing concentration, balance and length.*	**£6.50**	THI	(B)
TURNING LEAF VINTNER'S COLLECTION ZINFANDEL 1996, ERNEST & JULIO GALLO California	*Full ripe fruit with power and punch, lasting blackberry and vanilla on the palate.*	**£7.20**	BNK JMC WCR	(S)
FETZER BARREL SELECT ZINFANDEL 1997, FETZER California	*Brooding deep black fruit with a touch of spice, multi levelled with long persistent finish.*	**£9.00**	ODD TOS	(S)

TALUS ZINFANDEL 1997, TALUS California	*Herbaceous, warm fruits, a real mouthful of a wine, a hearty food accompaniment.*	**£9.00**	FQU	S
REDS PATRICK CAMPBELL 1998, LAUREL GLEN California	*An abundance of lively fruit leads to a robust palate of assertive structure and complexity.*	**£9.00**	CAM	B
LIVE OAK ROAD OLD BUSH VINE ZINFANDEL 1999, BEAR CREEK California	*A blackberry preserve aroma, youthful concentration of fruit which has a promising future ahead of itself.*	**£10.00**	M&S	S
BRAMBLEWOOD ZINFANDEL 1998, J LOHR California	*A sophisticated aroma of sweet raspberries and blackberries, lovely soft rounded palate with luscious finish.*	**£10.00**	ENO	B
GEYSER PEAK SONOMA COUNTY ZINFANDEL 1997, GEYSER PEAK California	*Big bold and assertive, handsome Californian ripe fruit characteristics, having a long dry savoury finish.*	**£10.00**	MAX JMC	B
SEGHESIO ZINFANDEL 1997, SEGHESIO California	*Plums and loganberries on the palate, nice earthy maturity and firm structure, lingering finish.*	**£10.20**	EOR WSO	B
RH PHILLIPS KEMPTON CLARKE LOPEZ RANCH ZINFANDEL 1998, RH PHILLIPS California	*Rich bramble jelly with vanilla, cherries and liquorice on the palate, firm but elegant structure.*	**£10.50**	JWW NRW	B
MOTHER CLONE ZINFANDEL 1997, PEDRONCELLI California	*A confident youthful nose, with bramble fruits on the satisfying palate with good balanced acidity.*	**£10.70**	JLW NYW HST	S

DRY CREEK ZINFANDEL HERITAGE CLONE 1997, DRY CREEK California	*An array of dark berry fruits on the nose giving lingering vanilla and cinnamon the finish.*	£12.30	ALI	(S)
CHIOTTI VINEYARD ZINFANDEL 1997, ERNEST & JULIO GALLO California	*Velvety ripe fruit, very modern obvious style full of bramble fruit, up front and immediately appealing.*	£12.50	MWW	(S)
GALLO FREI RANCH ZINFANDEL 1996, ERNEST & JULIO GALLO California	*Good colour and concentrated nose with a touch of oak, plenty of blackberries on the mouth.*	£12.70	MWW JMC	(B)
CLOS DU VAL ZINFANDEL 1998, CLOS DU VAL California	*Rich and classic, a real sports car of a wine, ready to impress and thrill.*	£12.90	AVB CTC	(B)
GALLO FREI RANCH ZINFANDEL 1997, ERNEST & JULIO GALLO California	*Rich baked forest berry fruits, on the nose and palate, a truly delicious experience.*	£13.00	Widely available	(B)
SEBASTIANI SONOMA CASK ZINFANDEL 1998, SEBASTIANI California	*Sweet fresh fruit on the nose, plentiful red berries an attractive strawberries and cream finish.*	£13.00	PLB	(B)
CALIFORNIA ZINFANDEL 1998, DE LOACH California	*Traditional velvety complex wine, lots of bramble fruits, holding even more pleasure in the future.*	£13.40	ESL HST GRO	(B)
THE ADVENTURES OF COMMANDER SINSKEY ZINFANDEL 1997, ROBERT SINSKEY California	*Damson and dark cherry fruits, giving a rush of flavours and good smooth mouthfeel. A swashbuckler.*	£14.00	WIN	(S)

N. AMERICA • CALIFORNIA • ZINFANDEL

FIFE ZINFANDEL REDHEAD VINEYARD 1997, FIFE California	*A goodblast of baked bramble fruits bringing together complex and bold tannins and acidity.*	£16.30	NYW AMW	S
MONTE ROSSO VINEYARD SONOMA VALLEY ZINFANDEL 1997, VILLA MT EDEN California	*A blockbuster of a nose throwing you into a symphony of sweet bramble and cranberry fruits.*	£17.80	NYW CTC	S
LYTTON SPRINGS ZINFANDEL 1998, RIDGE California	*Very suave drinking style, luscious ripe fruits and spice giving a long complex lingering finish.*	£19.70	Widely Available	S
RIDGE GEYSERVILLE 1997, RIDGE California	*Succulent fruits of the forest, with rich tar and spice, a complex and far reaching coffee finish.*	£20.00	Widely Available	G

TROPHY WINE

CANADA • FORTIFIED

FRAMBOISE, SOUTHBROOK FARM Ontario	*Creamy pale red, straw-berries and cherry coulis on the palate, very fruity and very charming finish.*	£7.20	WTS NYW	B

OREGON • WHITE

KING ESTATE PINOT GRIS 1996, KING ESTATE Oregon	*Tangy grapefruit and lychee nose with peach and tropical fruits on the smooth creamy palate.*	£11.00	THW	B

KING ESTATE CHARDONNAY 1997, KING ESTATE Oregon	*Strong ripe fruit and vanilla nose, full bodied generous fruit flavours with adequate oak, great finish.*	**£13.00**	THW	(S)

WASHINGTON STATE • RED

HOGUE CELLARS FRUIT-FORWARD CABERNET MERLOT 1997, HOGUE CELLARS Washington State	*Open ripe fruit nose with spicy jammy fruit notes with supple tannins and a nice short finish.*	**£9.20**	G&M	(B)
HOGUE CELLARS BARREL SELECT MERLOT 1997, HOGUE CELLARS Washington State	*Ripe cherry nose with spicy oak, balanced palate of cassis fruit and leather with balanced tannins.*	**£10.00**	THW	(B)
NEVADA COUNTY GRAND RESERVE SYRAH 1996, VILLA MT EDEN Washington State	*Ripe berry nose, soft plum, red berries and mint flavours, creamy oak and persistent flavours.*	**£15.00**	LIB	(S)
CANOE RIDGE MERLOT 1996, CHÂTEAU STE MICHELLE Washington State	*Attractive berry flavours with leather hints leading to a well structured style and lovely length.*	**£18.40**	NYW	(B)
CANOE RIDGE CABERNET SAUVIGNON 1996, CHÂTEAU STE MICHELLE Washington State	*Liquorice aromas with some smokiness on a ripe berry fruit palate with smooth tannins to end.*	**£20.00**	LIB	(B)
COL SOLARE 1996, COL SOLARE Washington State	*Cracked black pepper and mineral nose with ripe mulberries checked by spicy smooth tannins.*	**£51.90**	CTC	(B)

WASHINGTON STATE • WHITE

HOGUE CELLARS FRUIT FORWARD CHARDONNAY 1997, HOGUE CELLARS Washington State	*Citrus fruit nose, hints of coconut and a little oak are well blended in a palate of juicy fruit.*	**£8.00**	THW	B
COLUMBIA WYCKOFF CHARDONNAY 1996, COLUMBA Washington State	*Rich butterscotch nose and ripe yellow banana notes on a complex palate with wonderful acidity.*	**£13.00**	FTH	S
CANOE RIDGE CHARDONNAY 1997, CHÂTEAU STE MICHELLE Washington State	*Pleasant intensity of ripe peach fruit on the nose and palate with good length.*	**£15.10**	V&C NYW	B

NEW ZEALAND

This stunningly beautiful Land of the Long White Cloud has brought in yet more home produce to be very proud of. The classic white successes of Sauvignon Blanc and Chardonnay have been joined in this celebrity line up by the red wines mainly of Hawke's Bay and Wairarapa, on the warmer North Island. From good value everyday wines to fine estate bottled examples that have given birth to many of the leading flying winemakers of the world. This country goes from strength to strength.

NEW ZEALAND • CABERNET/MERLOT

CORBANS ESTATE MERLOT CABERNET SAUVIGNON 1999, CORBANS Hawke's Bay	*Balanced fruit and mint on the nose of this dry peppery wine, long lingering finish.*	£6.00	CAX	B
MHV WHITECLIFF NEW ZEALAND MERLOT 1999, SACRED HILL Hawke's Bay	*Cherries and plums show off here with style and length, with a finish of mint.*	£6.20	MHV BNK	B
SAINT CLAIR MERLOT 1999, SAINT CLAIR ESTATES Marlborough	*Lovely blackcurrant fruit driven nose with good structure and balanced, a nice round mouthful.*	£7.20	AVB BNK WCS	B
KEMBLEFIELD MERLOT 1998, KEMBLEFIELD ESTATE East Coast	*Blackcherry and tobacco nose mingling well with lovely savoury flavours and a medium length.*	£8.50	HBJ	B
MATUA VALLEY SMITH- DARTMOOR MERLOT 1998, MATUA VALLEY WINES Hawkes Bay	*Toasty notes with mulberry and cherry flavours giving good balance and mouth coating tannins.*	£8.80	TMW HDS	B

NEW ZEALAND • CABERNET/MERLOT

CJ PASK MERLOT 1998, CJ PASK East Coast	*Sweet ripe damson nose with meat and smokiness on warm blackcurrants with nice acidity and tannins.*	£9.00	ADN TAN G&M POR	**S**
COOPERS CREEK MERLOT RESERVE 1998, COOPERS CREEK VINEYARD East Coast	*Spicy, pepper nose with hints of tobacco fusing with currants and savoury flavours. Simply lovely.*	£9.00	EHL	**S**
DELEGAT'S RESERVE CABERNET SAUVIGNON 1998, DELEGAT'S WINE ESTATE East Coast	*Soft cedar with ripe currant nose leading to vanilla and ripe plums with gripping tannins.*	£9.00	MWW ODD SAF	**S**
DELEGAT'S RESERVE MERLOT 1998, DELEGAT'S WINE ESTATE East Coast	*Meaty and herbal nose with currant fruit and caramel ending with oaky savoury tannins.*	£9.00	DEL	**S**
MILLTON CABERNET MERLOT 1998, JAMES MILLTON Gisborne	*Fragrant and clean, full of black fruits, light bodied style with complexity and elegance.*	£9.00	BGL	**B**
MONTANA RESERVE MERLOT 1998, MONTANA WINES Marlborough	*Herbaceous minty palate of berries with cassis aromas with velvet richness on the finish.*	£9.10	ODD MAD BNK FQU ESL RAV VIL	**B**
TRINITY HILL HAWKES BAY TRINITY 1998, TRINITY HILL East Coast	*Cinnamon floral bouquet with black velvety cherry palate with richness and harmony. Just lovely.*	£9.50	MAD WSO PIM	**B**
CHURCH ROAD RESERVE CABERNET SAUVIGNON MERLOT 1996, MONTANA WINES East Coast	*Herbaceous bouquet with complex fruit character with some toastiness and good structure.*	£9.70	ODD WTS CPW FQU JSS VIL	**B**

TE MATA ESTATE CABERNET SAUVIGNON MERLOT 1998, TE MATA ESTATE East Coast	*Blackcherry and blackcurrant leaf aromas with plums and liquorice on the enjoyable finish.*	£9.80	FQU ESL TAN AMW WRW	**B**
ESK VALLEY MERLOT CABERNET SAUVIGNON 1998, ESK VALLEY Hawke's Bay	*Dark cherries with peppery notes leading to smooth texture and mouthfeel, grippy tannins to end.*	£9.90	MAD BLS WCR	**B**
SACRED HILL BASKET PRESS CABERNET SAUVIGNON 1998, SACRED HILL WINERY East Coast	*Lovely blackcurrant nose with some toastiness and spicy ripe red fruit on the palate.*	£10.00	JCK	**S**
NGATARAWA GLAZEBROOK MERLOT CABERNET 1998, NGATARAWA East Coast	*Herbaceous nose with coffee hints flowing into liquid chocolate and blackcherries on a warm finish.*	£10.90	NYW AMW BOO RHV	**G**
SAINT CLAIR RAPAURA RESERVE MERLOT 1998, SAINT CLAIR ESTATES Marlborough	*Sweet perfumed blackberries with integrated oak, soft ripe tannins and lovely acid. Just succulent.*	£11.00	AVB WCS CTC	**S**
VILLA MARIA RESERVE MERLOT CABERNET 1998, VILLA MARÍA ESTATE Hawke's Bay	*Soft black cherry nose balanced with oak spice berries, great balance and acidity. Drink me.*	£11.90	ODD MAD WCR	**S**
MATARIKI ANTHOLOGY 1998, MATARIKI WINES Hawke's Bay	*Fresh strawberry cherry nose blending with blackcurrants and firm acidity with a silky tannin backbone.*	£12.00	ODD BEL	**G**
CJ PASK RESERVE CABERNET SAUVIGNON 1998, CJ PASK East Coast	*Toasty vanilla nose integrated smoothly with spicy plums and prunes. Lovely long elegant finish.*	£12.00	ADN TAN	**S**

COOPERS CREEK RESERVE MERLOT CABERNET FRANC 1998, COOPERS CREEK VINEYARD East Coast	*Spicy vegetal nose with cedar and warm blackcurrant creaminess with soft silky tannins and lovely acid.*	£12.00	EHL	S
COOPERS CREEK RESERVE CABERNET SAUVIGNON 1998, COOPERS CREEK VINEYARD East Coast	*Alluring vanilla nose with juicy cassis flavours flowing with firm tannins and good acidity. Lovely balance.*	£12.00	EHL	B
CRAB FARM MERLOT 1998, CRAB FARM East Coast	*Greengages on the nose with a savoury blackcurrant palate, good tannins and elegant lengthy backbone.*	£12.30	HST BOO	S
ELSPETH CABERNET MERLOT 1998, MILLS REEF East Coast	*Sprig of mint nose with well blended chewy cassis and plum fruits with hint of chocolate.*	£13.00	FTH	S
CJ PASK RESERVE MERLOT 1998, CJ PASK East Coast	*Fresh milk chocolate covering ripe mulberries wonderfully rich and balanced with oak complexity. Astounding.*	£14.00	ADN TAN G&M POR	G TROPHY WINE
SILENI MERLOT CABERNETS 1998, SILENI ESTATES East Coast	*Herbaceous ripe red fruit aromas, succulent juicy plums and youngberries with great mouthfeel. Lovely oak.*	£14.00	BLU ESL WBR TRO	S
MATUA VALLEY ARARIMU MERLOT CABERNET SAUVIGNON 1998, MATUA VALLEY WINES Hawkes Bay	*Ripe blackcurrant fruit integrated with lovely oak, balanced acidity and green tannins. Just delicious.*	£14.50	JAG	B
ESK VALLEY RESERVE MERLOT MALBEC CABERNET 1997, ESK VALLEY Hawke's Bay	*Sweet floral tobacco nose with rich savoury redcurrant notes hint of spice. Rich and gorgeous.*	£14.90	MAD QWW DBY BLS JMC JSS	G

FORREST CORNERSTONE 1997, FORREST East Coast	*Smokey developed blackcurrant nose with ripe soft plums and damsons with some earthiness. Good balance.*	£15.00	HAS	(S)
KIM CRAWFORD TANE 1998, KIM CRAWFORD Hawkes Bay	*Sweet damson and vanilla, lovely ripe brambles with soft acidity and lots of fruit grip.*	£15.00	LIB	(B)
UNISON SELECTION 1997, UNISON VINEYARD Hawke's Bay	*Rich fruit and liquorice aromas, fruit driven solid and rich on the attractive palate.*	£16.00	WTS	(B)
UNISON SELECTION MERLOT 1998, UNISON VINEYARD East Coast	*Vanilla and mulberry aroma with mint and rich ripe fruit palate, lovely structure and drying tannins.*	£16.00	SKW	(B)
VILLA MARIA RESERVE CABERNET MERLOT 1996, VILLA MARIA ESTATE Hawke's Bay	*Cigar box nose with vanilla mixed with stewed prunes, smooth ripe tannins, very quaffable.*	£16.30	ODF MAD	(B)
BENFIELD & DELAMARE MERLOT CABERNET 1998, BENFIELD & DELAMARE Wairarapa	*Lifted plums, vanilla and gamey nose, subtle oak with cherries and minty palate, dry tannin finish.*	£17.70	DBY	(S)
UNISON MERLOT 1998, UNISON VINEYARD East Coast	*Lively palate leading to ripe funky berries hinting at liquorice, soft silky and lovely length.*	£19.00	SKW	(B)
KAZ CABERNET 1998, OKAHU ESTATE Northland	*Plum pastille and floral nose, minty damson flavour hinting at smokiness, good medium finish.*	£20.00	GGW	(S)

ALPHA DOMUS AVIATOR 1998, ALPHA DOMUS East Coast	*Youthful banana aromas leading to blueberries and generous tannins and length. A wine to keep.*	**£22.00**	NYW	(S)

NEW ZEALAND • CHARDONNAY

MARLBOROUGH GOLD CHARDONNAY 1999, MARLBOROUGH GOLD Marlborough	*Rich ripe fruit nose, delicious banana notes in a structure of juicy fruits, very agreeable acidity.*	**£5.20**	MWW	(B)
SEIFRIED ESTATES OLD COACH ROAD CHARDONNAY 1999, SEIFRIED ESTATES Nelson	*Tropical oak and sweet aroma, round and full bodied palate of buttery vanilla fruits, good length.*	**£5.70**	GDS RAV JCK	(G)
VIDAL ESTATE CHARDONNAY HAWKES BAY 1999, VIDAL ESTATE Hawke's Bay	*Very upfront style with smooth oakiness on nose, full creamy fruit palate, nice citrus finish and good length.*	**£5.70**	GSJ	(B)
DELEGAT'S HAWKES BAY CHARDONNAY 1998, DELEGAT'S WINE ESTATE East Coast	*Plenty of caramel on the nose and palate well mixed with fresh acidity. Lovely length.*	**£6.00**	DEL	(B)
TAPU BAY BARREL FERMENTED CHARDONNAY 1998, SEIFRIED ESTATE Nelson	*Big buttery smokey oak and creamy citrus fruit in levelled acidity with very long end.*	**£6.00**	WAV	(B)
TASMAN BAY CHARDONNAY 1999, SPENCER HILL ESTATE Marlborough	*Nice vanilla and oak invitation to taste lovely rich apples on the palate. Long fresh finish.*	**£6.50**	HAL	(B)

TAPU BAY BARREL FERMENTED CHARDONNAY RESERVE 1997, SEIFRIED Nelson	*Beautiful exotic fruit nose, tropical fruits on the palate, lovely oak presence, excellent acidity.*	£7.00	JCK	(G)
SAINT CLAIR CHARDONNAY 1999, SAINT CLAIR ESTATES Marlborough	*Nice soft fruit aromas with vanilla essence, deep juicy apricot flavours with very good length.*	£7.00	AVB WCS CTC	(B)
MILLS REEF RESERVE CHARDONNAY 1998, MILLS REEF East Coast	*Subtle toasty oak nose, great harmony and balance in a full bodied wine with beautiful style.*	£7.10	FTH DBY	(B)
VILLA MARIA PRIVATE BIN MARLBOROUGH CHARDONNAY 1999, VILLA MARIA ESTATE Marlborough	*Cigar toasty nose followed by beautiful strong vanilla characters in bed of ripe fruit flavours.*	£7.10	Widely Available	(B)
MILLTON GISBORNE VINEYARDS CHARDONNAY 1999, JAMES MILLTON Gisborne	*Excellent ripe peaches and melon aromas, great ripe fruit palate with tones of toffee and light oak.*	£7.20	BGL GRO	(B)
OYSTER BAY CHARDONNAY 1999, OYSTER BAY WINES Marlborough	*Appealing creamy nose, ripe fruit with toffee notes, very pleasant acidity on the finish.*	£7.20	Widely Available	(B)
WINEMAKERS COLLECTION BARRIQUE FERMENTED CHARDONNAY 1998, SEIFRIED ESTATE Nelson	*Lemon nose, well balanced rich fruit flavour with notes of vanilla and long finish.*	£7.60	WAV	(B)
ESK VALLEY CHARDONNAY 1999, ESK VALLEY Hawkes Bay	*Good ripe green fruit nose, excellent round spicy palate blended with ripe tropical fruit and well integrated acidity.*	£8.00	MAD QWW DBY WCR JSS POR	(S)

NEW ZEALAND • CHARDONNAY

MONTANA RESERVE MARLBOROUGH CHARDONNAY 1999, MONTANA WINES Marlborough	*Sweet spicy nose, with medium intense sweet tropical fruit palate, with good apple acidity.*	£8.00	Widely Available	B
MOUNT RILEY MARLBOROUGH CHARDONNAY 1999, MOUNT RILEY Marlborough	*Powerful exotic fruit nose, firm acidity harmonised with lovely juicy fruit flavours. Gorgeous length.*	£8.00	ALI	B
PARKWOOD EAST COAST OAK AGED CHARDONNAY 1999, VIDAL ESTATE East Coast	*Interesting pleasant fruit style with good proportion of oak, dry acidity and long finish.*	£8.00	BDR	B
MONTANA RESERVE GISBORNE CHARDONNAY 1999, MONTANA WINES Gisborne	*Warm, fruity oak with citrus characters for a rich mouth feel with nice finish.*	£8.30	ODD FQU ESL WCR VIL	B
GROVE MILL MARLBOROUGH CHARDONNAY 1998, GROVE MILL Marlborough	*Vanilla and fresh fruits, pear and pineapple flavours with lively oak presence and nice long finish.*	£8.40	BNK NRW NYW N&P HVW CTC	S
KEMBLEFIELD CHARDONNAY 1998, KEMBLEFIELD ESTATE East Coast	*Soft fruit definition on the nose, good integration of oak on the palate and smooth finish.*	£8.50	HBJ	B
OMAKA SPRINGS ESTATE CHARDONNAY 1999, OMAKA SPRINGS ESTATE Marlborough	*Subtle aroma, with delicate fruit and oak, having a long lingering finish and style.*	£8.80	BBO BNK	B
MATUA VALLEY JUDD ESTATE CHARDONNAY 1999, MATUA VALLEY WINES Gisborne	*Inviting floral aromas lead to honeyed rich fruit palate, well balanced wine with long delightful finish.*	£9.00	JAG	S

DE REDCLIFFE ESTATES CHARDONNAY 1997, DE REDCLIFFE ESTATE Waikato	*Green fresh nose and ripe fruit palate, very well balanced, great acidity and good length.*	£9.00	MAD UNS	B
GIBBSTON VALLEY GREEN STONE CHARDONNAY 1999, GIBBSTON VALLEY Central Otago	*Lovely fruit nose, delightful exotic fresh fruit on the palate with firm persistent juicy finish.*	£9.00	NWG	B
GIESEN RESERVE BARREL SELECTION CHARDONNAY 1998, GIESEN WINE ESTATES Marlborough	*Smooth delicious fruit nose leads to a fresh mixture of apples and honeyed oak on the palate.*	£9.20	OWC G&M	S
JACKSON ESTATE CHARDONNAY 1999, JACKSON ESTATE Marlborough	*Rich tropical nose, delicious apples, peaches and oak on the palate, good length and fresh finish.*	£9.40	Widely Available	S
KOURA BAY CHARDONNAY 1998, KOURA BAY Marlborough	*Rich well balanced oak fruity nose, lovely sweet fruit flavours with good, smooth length.*	£9.40	OWL	B
REDWOOD VALLEY CHARDONNAY 1999, HERMANN SEIFRIED Nelson	*Peaches and green apples on the palate of this full bodied wine with balanced acidity.*	£9.50	FNZ	B
TRINITY HILL HAWKES BAY CHARDONNAY 1999, TRINITY HILL East Coast	*Smooth presence of oak in a well structured combination of lemony flavours and balanced acid finish.*	£9.60	MAD PIM	B
CRAGGY RANGE CHARDONNAY 1999, CRAGGY RANGE Hawke's Bay	*Some pleasant oak on the nose leads to subtle juicy fruit palate with fresh tropical notes.*	£9.80	WTS DBY PBA JCK	B

CRAGGY RANGE MARLBOROUGH CHARDONNAY 1999, CRAGGY RANGE Marlborough	*Attractive nose leads to citrus and ripe grapefruit flavours with nuts and green apples.*	£10.00	CPR NRW DBY NYW BOO	S
CORBANS PRIVATE BIN CHARDONNAY 1997, CORBANS Gisborne	*Rich plump fruit and oak aromas invite you to taste great extraction of tropical ripe fruit.*	£10.00	CAX	B
WAIPARA WEST CHARDONNAY 1998, TUTTON SIENKO & HILL Waipara	*Nice oak on the nose and a palate full of peaches, citrus with juicy sweetness, mild acidity.*	£10.00	WAW	B
CJ PASK RESERVE CHARDONNAY 1999, CJ PASK East Coast	*Refreshing spicy fruit aromas, big sweet tones, balanced with fresh acidity, delightful fresh finish.*	£10.10	TAN ADN	B
ALPHA DOMUS CHARDONNAY 1999, ALPHA DOMUS East Coast	*Ripe fruits with a nice touch of sweetness, balanced acidity and tannins with pleasant extended finish.*	£10.20	NYW BEL	B
RENWICK ESTATE CHARDONNAY 1997, MONTANA WINES Marlborough	*Spicy fragrant nose and well combined toasted oak notes in a fruit palate, exotic great length.*	£10.60	ODD DBY VIL	B
RENWICK ESTATE CHARDONNAY 1998, MONTANA WINES Marlborough	*Fresh apples on the nose, full bodied and well balanced structure, with a good lasting finish.*	£10.70	ODD DBY TMW VIL	S
CHURCH ROAD RESERVE CHARDONNAY 1998, MONTANA WINES East Coast	*Interesting pronounced fruit on the nose and palate, well balanced structure with lemon hints.*	£11.00	ODD CPW FQU VIL	S

ISABEL ESTATE CHARDONNAY 1998, ISABEL ESTATE Marlborough	*Nice combination of lemon, honey toast and fruits with lovely buttery long finish.*	£11.30	Widely Available	(B)
PALLISER ESTATE CHARDONNAY 1998, PALLISER ESTATE WINES Martinborough	*Peaches and honey on the nose, full ripe fruit flavours, delicious wine with great enjoyable length. Complex.*	£11.30	ABY DBY HVW	(B)
MARTINBOROUGH VINEYARD CHARDONNAY 1998, MARTINBOROUGH VINEYARD Wairarapa	*Inviting ripe fruit aromas, creamy full palate and round warm mouthfeel, lovely fresh acidity and length. Quite serious.*	£11.40	ODD V&C DBY CEB JNW WRK PFT	(S)
VILLA MARIA RESERVE CHARDONNAY 1998, VILLA MARIA ESTATE Marlborough	*Citrus fruit nose of good balance, tropical fruit flavours with notes of vanilla, powerful finish.*	£11.70	ODD MAD	(B)
COOPERS CREEK WILD FERMENT CHARDONNAY 1998, COOPERS CREEK VINEYARD East Coast	*Light fruit nose, citrus flavours with good acidity and wood on the palate with pleasing finish.*	£12.00	EHL	(B)
TOHU GISBORNE RESERVE CHARDONNAY 1999, TOHU WINES Gisborne	*Attractive fruit nose lead to warm palate with cigar oak notes and citrus fruit flavour.*	£12.00	BDR JSS	(B)
BABICH IRONGATE CHARDONNAY 1996, BABICH WINES Hawkes Bay	*Subtle nose, good fruit with touch of young apples and medium oak, good length.*	£12.30	TAN	(B)
ESK VALLEY RESERVE CHARDONNAY 1997, ESK VALLEY Hawkes Bay	*Great citrus nose, pleasant fresh lime and lemon notes on juicy palate. Lovely finish.*	£12.80	DBY JMC	(B)

NEW ZEALAND • CHARDONNAY

CORBANS COTTAGE BLOCK CHARDONNAY 1997, CORBANS Marlborough	*Delicate honeysuckle and vanilla balanced to perfection with lots of complexity and a lush, creamy finish.*	£13.00	WTS	(G) TROPHY WINE
COOPERS CREEK SWAMP RESERVE CHARDONNAY 1998, COOPERS CREEK East Coast	*Subtle lime and lemon nose followed by balanced vanilla notes, medium acidity and lingering finish.*	£14.00	EHL NYW	(B)
HAWKES BLACK LABEL CHARDONNAY RESERVE 1996, MORTON ESTATE Hawkes Bay	*Big toasty oak with a pineapple nose and palate, stylish complexity, good acidity and fine finish.*	£14.00	BWC DBY	(B)
PIA 1998, KIM CRAWFORD East Coast	*Subtle caramel nose, well balanced palate with fruits and vanilla giving a long elegant finish.*	£15.00	LIB	(B)
TRINITY HILL GIMBLETT ROAD CHARDONNAY 1998, JOHN HANCOCK East Coast	*Lime and lemon fruits, very well balanced full bodied fresh flavours with delicate finish.*	£18.00	LPD	(B)
MUDDY WATER CHARDONNAY 1998, MUDDY WATER FINE WINE Waipara	*Pleasant rich delicious juicy sweet fruit, palate full of layered melon and pineapple, excellent acidity.*	£21.00	FNZ	(S)

NEW ZEALAND • PINOT NOIR

SHINGLE PEAK PINOT NOIR 1999, MATUA VALLEY WINES Marlborough	*Savoury Bolognese nose. The palate reveals eucalyptus, bramble and rhubarb fruit. Pleasant, simple wine.*	£7.00	JSM	(B)

CORBANS STONELEIGH VINEYARDS PINOT NOIR 1999, CORBANS Marlborough	*Curranty nose with beetroot undertones, leads onto a lean but flavoursome palate. Nice New World style.*	£8.00	OWC	(B)
VIDAL ESTATE PINOT NOIR 1998, VIDAL ESTATE Hawke's Bay	*Vanilla oak with fruity hints yield to a prune and plumy palate offering good length.*	£8.50	GSJ	(B)
FRAMINGHAM PINOT NOIR 1998, FRAMINGHAM Marlborough	*Powerful nose precedes a jammy fruit and vanilla essence palate that flows into a long finish.*	£9.80	QRW FQU	(B)
MONTANA RESERVE PINOT NOIR 1998, MONTANA WINES Marlborough	*Rich, liquorice, berry fruit nose, rounded, gutsy palate offering a good, long, persistent finish.*	£9.90	JSM ODD FQU VIL FEN	(S)
HUNTER'S PINOT NOIR 1998, HUNTER'S WINES Marlborough	*Gentle oaky aromas yield to a classic strawberry palate with nicely integrated oak and long tannic finish.*	£10.10	GRT CPW BNK DBY CEB CVR JCK	(B)
JACKSON ESTATE PINOT NOIR 1999, JACKSON ESTATE Marlborough	*Subtle loganberry aromas. Soft raspberry fruit over even softer oak with a touch of vanilla.*	£10.20	CPW DBY HDS POR AMW GRO	(B)
LAWSON'S DRY HILLS PINOT NOIR 1999, LAWSON'S DRY HILLS Marlborough	*Intense, liquorice and spicy style, powerful fruit palate with well structured tannins and a slight gaminess.*	£11.00	VDV	(S)
PALLISER ESTATE PINOT NOIR 1998, PALLISER ESTATE WINES Martinborough	*Sweet violet and rose aromas reveal wonderfully integrated palate of forest fruits and ripe sweet oak tannins.*	£12.00	ABY FQU DBY NYW VIL HVW	(B)

PEREGRINE PINOT NOIR 1999, PEREGRINE WINES Central Otago	*Elegant earthy tones on the nose of a rich youthful wine displaying lingering flavours.*	**£12.00**	BBR	B
SANDIHURST PREMIER PINOT NOIR 1998, SANDIHURST WINES Canterbury	*Creamy, vanilla nose, palate offers rich pinot fruit and soft ice cream. Beautifully balanced sweet but rich flavours.*	**£12.50**	HST	S
ISABEL ESTATE PINOT NOIR 1998, ISABEL ESTATE Marlborough	*Hints of coffee in evidence on the nose with raspberry ripe fruit and vanilla palate.*	**£12.70**	Widely Available	B
MARTINBOROUGH PINOT NOIR 1998, MARTINBOROUGH VINEYARD Wairarapa	*Lifted, red berry nose. Good tight structure, elevated acidity, nice gripping tannins, concentrated fruit, good length.*	**£13.20**	V&C CEB FQU DBY JNW NYW WRK	S
WAIPARA WEST PINOT NOIR 1999, TUTTON SIENKO & HILL Waipara	*Intense oaky nose with fruitiness underneath gives way to a light savoury cherry palate.*	**£14.00**	WAW	B
MUDDY WATER PINOT NOIR 1998, MUDDY WATER FINE WINES Waipara	*Fresh plumy nose with hints of forest fruits is confirmed on a well balanced palate.*	**£14.50**	WSO GHC	B
MOUNT EDWARD PINOT NOIR 1998, MOUNT EDWARD Central Otago	*Soft strawberry leaf nose, sound intense ripe fruit palate that flows into a bold finish.*	**£18.80**	BBR	B
MARTINBOROUGH PINOT NOIR RESERVE 1997, MARTINBOROUGH VINEYARD Marlborough	*Some vegetal nose showing big aged characters on the palate. Long and complex, nice gamey earthy character.*	**£22.10**	ODF ODD NYW	B

NEW ZEALAND • SAUVIGNON BLANC

ANAPI RIVER SAUVIGNON BLANC 1999, ST HELENA Marlborough	*Green bean aromas, palate of clean balanced creamy fruits, rich pleasant finish and good length.*	**£3.50**	WAV	(S)
CORBANS ESTATE SAUVIGNON BLANC 1999, CORBANS Marlborough	*Lovely pine and minty characters flow through to a rich tropical fruit and gooseberry palate.*	**£5.40**	JSM WES	(B)
ALPHA DOMUS SAUVIGNON BLANC 1999, ALPHA DOMUS East Coast	*Lifted gooseberry nose follows through to the palate offering good rich flavours, good acidity and medium length.*	**£5.70**	MKV	(S)
VIDAL ESTATE SAUVIGNON BLANC HAWKES BAY 1998, VIDAL ESTATE Hawke's Bay	*Lemon and grassy aromas. Good zippy ripe fruit palate, subtle acidity and dry lingering finish.*	**£5.70**	GSJ	(S)
NOBILO SAUVIGNON BLANC 1999, NOBILO VINTNERS Marlborough	*Grassy green, herbaceous aromas, concentrated fruit palate of green gooseberry flavours, zippy acidity. Well made.*	**£5.90**	DBY JMC WES	(S)
CORBANS STONELEIGH VINEYARDS SAUVIGNON BLANC 1999, CORBANS Marlborough	*Luscious gooseberry aromas precede a palate of nettles and asparagus. Wonderfully balanced acidity and good length.*	**£6.10**	WTS WCR OWC VIL WES	(B)
MARLBOROUGH SAUVIGNON BLANC 1999, WHITEHAVEN WINE COMPANY Marlborough	*Well defined asparagus nose, light oak on the palate, well balanced structure, persistent clean finish.*	**£6.40**	EOR CVR	(B)

NEW ZEALAND • SAUVIGNON BLANC

SEIFRIED ESTATES SAUVIGNON BLANC 1999, SEIFRIED ESTATES Nelson	*Upfront sauvignon nose, clean crisp fruit, good balancing acidity, lemon and tomato leaf on the tail.*	£6.60	GDS JCK	**B**
VILLA MARÍA PRIVATE BIN SAUVIGNON BLANC 1999, VILLA MARÍA ESTATE Marlborough	*Crisp and clean with an attractive grassy, lemony nose, good middle palate fruit and crisp long finish.*	£7.00	Widely Available	**B**
COLEFIELD VINEYARD SAUVIGNON BLANC 1999, MORTON ESTATE Hawkes Bay	*Fresh red pepper nose in harmony with ripe melony fruits giving it good style.*	£7.70	BWC DBY FEN	**S**
CLIFFORD BAY SAUVIGNON BLANC 1999, CLIFFORD BAY ESTATE Marlborough	*Elegant ripe asparagus and fresh fruit aromas precede rich ripe lime and honeysuckle fruit palate.*	£7.80	FRI	**S**
LAWSON'S DRY HILLS SAUVIGNON BLANC 1999, LAWSON'S DRY HILLS Marlborough	*Lifted kiwis, gooseberries and grassy aromas, complex palate, tropical fruit and lemon, good gripping acidity.*	£7.80	BWL TOS DBY NYW VDV AMW	**S**
GROVE MILL MARLBOROUGH SAUVIGNON BLANC 1999, GROVE MILL Marlborough	*Leafy green hints with creamy gooseberry fruit aromas, complex and vegetal, spices and oak on the finish.*	£7.80	Widely Available	**B**
FORREST ESTATE SAUVIGNON BLANC 1999, FORREST ESTATE Marlborough	*Classic asparagus and green canopy nose. Subtle sweetness on the palate and a good acidic finish.*	£7.90	DBY JNW NYW BEN WRK PFT	**B**
GIESEN MARLBOROUGH SAUVIGNON BLANC 1999, GIESEN ESTATE Marlborough	*Kiwi fruit and asparagus nose, lashings of tropical notes and good acidity with well structured finish.*	£8.00	OWC G&M	**S**

SAUVIGNON BLANC • NEW ZEALAND

KONRAD AND CONRAD SAUVIGNON BLANC 1999, KONRAD AND CONRAD Marlborough	*Spicy, tropical fruit nose leads into a fresh, grassy palate with good herbal lift and finish.*	**£8.00**	LAU	(B)
SELAKS DRYLANDS ESTATE SAUVIGNON BLANC 1999, SELAKS WINES Marlborough	*Ripe minerally earthy aromas with hints of pepper. Gooseberry, grapefruit and appley fruit, nice zingy acidity.*	**£8.10**	ODD WSO DBY	(S)
ESK VALLEY SAUVIGNON BLANC 1999, ESK VALLEY Hawkes Bay	*Floral, grassy and gooseberry aromas, subtle fruit palate, rich in oak with a medium length.*	**£8.10**	MAD DBY BLS JMC WCR	(B)
FRAMINGHAM SAUVIGNON BLANC 1999, FRAMINGHAM Marlborough	*Good green bean and capsicum nose, prominent tropical fruit and citrus flavours, hint of oak.*	**£8.20**	QRW	(B)
LEGRYS MARLBOROUGH SAUVIGNON BLANC 1999, MUD HOUSE WINE Marlborough	*Ripe, bright grassy herbal mineral nose, powerful gooseberry palate with racy acidity on the finish.*	**£8.20**	H&H NYW	(B)
CHURCH ROAD SAUVIGNON BLANC 1999, MONTANA WINES East Coast	*Subtle fruit aromas, tropical fruit salad on the palate with a zippy grapefruit acid finish.*	**£8.30**	ODD VIL	(B)
MONTANA RESERVE SAUVIGNON BLANC 1999, MONTANA WINES Marlborough	*Gooseberry, syrupy aromas with hints of saffron, sweet pineapple pineapples, zippy acidity and a moderate length.*	**£8.30**	Widely Available	(B)
MANSION HOUSE BAY SAUVIGNON BLANC 1999, MANSION HOUSE BAY Marlborough	*Lovely ripe gooseberries and hints of green beans on the palate, great acidity, a well balanced wine.*	**£8.70**	GRO CTC	(S)

NEW ZEALAND • SAUVIGNON BLANC

CRAGGY RANGE SAUVIGNON BLANC 1999, CRAGGY RANGE Marlborough	*Delicious floral aromas, clean ripe fruit, appealing oiliness with good balanced acidity and a long fresh finish.*	£8.80	Widely Available	(S)
CORBANS WINEMAKER'S SELECTION SAUVIGNON BLANC 1999, CORBANS Marlborough	*Freshly cut nettles and mineral nose, mouth watering acidity of gooseberry fruit. An elegant style.*	£9.00	DBY	(S)
RESERVE MARLBOROUGH SAUVIGNON BLANC 1999, COOPERS CREEK Marlborough	*Gooseberry and nettle aromas, racy palate of creamy fruit with zingy acidity and a lasting finish.*	£9.00	EHL	(B)
WAIPARA WEST SAUVIGNON BLANC 1999, TUTTON SIENKO & HILL Waipara	*Intense gooseberry fruit aromas, attacking herbaceous acidity and sweet mineral undertones, long fruit driven finish.*	£9.00	WAW	(B)
PALLISER ESTATE SAUVIGNON BLANC 1999, PALLISER ESTATE WINES Martinborough	*Lovely grassy herbaceous aromas, sweet gooseberry flavours with kiwi undertones, crisp acidity and good length.*	£9.20	ABY FQU DBY NYW HVW	(B)
ISABEL ESTATE SAUVIGNON BLANC 1999, ISABEL ESTATE Marlborough	*Ripe fruit, well balanced palate of fresh grassy and flint flavours, with zippy acidity and a long finish.*	£9.60	Widely Available	(S)
NEUDORF SAUVIGNON BLANC 1999, NEUDORF Marlborough	*Attractive tropical fruit aromas, are followed by a rich pineapple palate with subdued acidity.*	£9.70	WSO CAM DBY RHV	(B)
KAITUNA HILLS RESERVE SAUVIGNON BLANC 1999, MONTANA WINES Marlborough	*Green, grassy nose precedes a herbaceous palate with hints of vanilla, spice and gun metal.*	£10.00	M&S	(B)

SAUVIGNON BLANC • NEW ZEALAND

MATARIKI SAUVIGNON BLANC 1998, MATARIKI WINES Hawkes Bay	*Herbaceous aromas give way to a vanilla palate with lively acidity and subtle finish.*	£10.00	BEL	**B**
TORLESSE SAUVIGNON BLANC 1999, TORLESSE Marlborough	*Lemon and grassy characters follow through to a palate of sweet fruit prominence with zippy acidity.*	£10.00	BBR VDV	**B**
VILLA MARÍA CLIFFORD BAY RESERVE SAUVIGNON BLANC 1999, VILLA MARÍA ESTATE Clifford Bay	*Inviting flowers and gooseberry aromas lead to rich fruit palate with refreshing acidity and good length.*	£10.00	ODD MAD JMC	**B**
HUNTER'S SAUVIGNON BLANC 1999, HUNTER'S WINES Marlborough	*Lime zest and pineapple nose is followed by peachy flavours, gripping acidity and good length.*	£10.10	Widely Available	**B**
HUNTER'S OAK AGED SAUVIGNON BLANC 1998, HUNTER'S WINES Marlborough	*Delicate pineapple and peach nose with some butteriness combined with pleasing acidity and green apple characters.*	£10.60	DBY CVR TAN WRW JCK	**S**
MONTANA WINES BRANCOTT ESTATE SAUVIGNON BLANC 1999, MONTANA WINES Marlborough	*Sweet fruit with hints of green pea precede an elegant palate of grass and subtle acidity.*	£10.80	JSM ODD BNK DBY TMW VIL FEN	**S**
PEREGRINE SAUVIGNON BLANC 1999, PEREGRINE WINES Central Otago	*A powerful nose of herbs and aromatic spices leads on to a tight palate.*	£11.00	BBR	**S**

Pinpoint who sells the wine you wish to buy by turning to the stockist codes. If you know the name of the wine you want to buy, use the alphabetical index. If the price is your motivation, refer to the invaluable price guide index; red and white wines under £5, sparkling wines under £12 and champagne under £16. Happy hunting!

NEW ZEALAND • SPARKLING

LINDAUER SPECIAL RESERVE NV, MONTANA WINES	*Attractive berries on nose, light raspberries on the palate, stylish and well balanced with elegant finish.*	**£8.90**	Widely Available	B
DEUTZ MARLBOROUGH CUVÉE NV, MONTANA WINES Marlborough	*Plenty of refreshing bubbles, light attractive fruit nose, pleasant sweetness with clean acidity on the palate.*	**£11.40**	Widely Available	B
MIRU MIRU MARLBOROUGH BRUT 1997, HUNTER'S WINES Marlborough	*Oatmeal toasty aroma with some appealing fruit, toasty fruit palate with soft mousse, delicate finish.*	**£11.90**	Widely Available	B
DEUTZ BLANC DE BLANCS 1996, MONTANA WINES Marlborough	*Attractive ripe fruit aroma of creamy apples, soft fruit flavour with hint of peaches and melons.*	**£12.40**	ODD DBY VIL	S
DANIEL LE BRUN BRUT NV, CELLIER LE BRUN Marlborough	*Full ripe cantalope melon nose, a palate with hint of peaches and toasty overtones.*	**£12.80**	DBY HDS AMW BEL POR	B
PELORUS 1995, CLOUDY BAY Marlborough	*Clean attractive toasty nose, fresh flavours with hint of good acidity, soft mousse and reasonable length.*	**£15.00**	Widely Available	B
DANIEL LE BRUN BLANC DE BLANCS 1995, CELLIER LE BRUN Marlborough	*Very pleasant mousse, attractive stylish toasty biscuity aroma, subtle ripe fruit palate. Fresh appley finish.*	**£16.00**	HWL DBY HDS	S

NEW ZEALAND • SWEET

FORREST ESTATE BOTRYTISED SEMILLON SAUVIGNON 1999, FORREST ESTATE Marlborough	*Caramelised lemon and baked apple nose, the palate displays apples, pears with a rise of toffee.*	£12.00	HAS	B
REKA BOTRYTISED RIESLING 1999, KIM CRAWFORD Marlborough	*Lovely intense boneyed nose with peachy and citrus tones that melt into a fully rounded wine.*	£20.00	LIB	B

NEW ZEALAND • SYRAH

MATARIKI SYRAH 1998, MATARIKI WINES Hawkes Bay	*Lightly toasted oak and spicy mint aromas, soft, rich and rounded, full of black fruits.*	£15.00	PAT	S
TRINITY HILL GIMBLETT ROAD SYRAH 1998, JOHN HANCOCK East Coast	*Good depth and complexity, spiced damson and plum flavours compliment medium weight tannins.*	£18.00	LPD	B
KAZ SHIRAZ 1998, OKAHU ESTATE Northland	*The warm, savoury, meaty nose works in accordance with the red and plum fruit palate.*	£21.20	GGW	S

Pinpoint who sells the wine you wish to buy by turning to the stockist codes. If you know the name of the wine you want to buy, use the alphabetical index. If the price is your motivation, refer to the invaluable price guide index; red and white wines under £5, sparkling wines under £12 and champagne under £16. Happy hunting!

NEW ZEALAND • WHITE • OTHER

CORBANS WHITE LABEL CHARDONNAY CHENIN BLANC 1999, CORBANS Marlborough	*Very elegant chardonnay aromas, refreshing firm acidity supporting well ripe fruit flavours.*	**£4.50**	WTS	(B)
BABICH RIESLING 1999, BABICH WINES Malborough	*Persistent long spicy palate on this aromatic mouthfilling wine with a spritz on the tongue.*	**£7.00**	BNK	(S)
CHANCELLOR MT CASS WAIPARA RIESLING 1999, CHANCELLOR ESTATE Waipara	*Lychee and lemons on the nose with seductively powerful rich fruit finish on the palate.*	**£7.00**	GRT	(S)
WAIPARA RIESLING ESTATE BOTTLED 1998, CANTERBURY HOUSE Waipara	*Light bodied and fruit driven, refreshing mouthfeel, on a finish of complexity and style.*	**£7.00**	EUW	(S)
DE REDCLIFFE ESTATE MARLBOROUGH RIESLING 1998, DE REDCLIFFE ESTATE Marlborough	*Delicate perfumed aroma, huge honeyed tropical fruit flavours, long and excessive finish with good balance.*	**£7.20**	MAD	(S)
JACKSON ESTATE RIESLING 1999, JACKSON ESTATE Marlborough	*Peaches and melons on the nose of this luscious and zesty palate with clean balanced finish.*	**£7.30**	CPW BTH TAN HDS CST GRO POR	(B)
LAWSON'S DRY HILLS GEWÜRZTRAMINER 1999, LAWSON'S DRY HILLS Marlborough	*Powerful floral notes on the nose, followed quickly by tropical fruit complexity to the end.*	**£7.50**	BWL TOS DBY VDV AMW	(B)

OMAKA SPRINGS ESTATE RIESLING 1998, OMAKA SPRINGS Marlborough	*Delicate floral nose, spiced lemon and lime with herbaceous notes, light acidity finishing well.*	**£7.80**	BBO JAG HST JSS	**B**
SEIFRIED RIESLING 1998, SEIFRIED ESTATE Nelson	*Rich and complex with good varietal characteristics, long clean refreshing acidity and pose.*	**£7.80**	GDS	**B**
MILLTON OPOU RIESLING 1999, JAMES MILLTON Gisborne	*Rich honeyed floral aromas, persisting through to the palate, big and confident, powerful finish.*	**£8.00**	BGL	**B**
KIM CRAWFORD MARLBOROUGH DRY RIESLING 1999, KIM CRAWFORD Marlborough	*Elegant nose, well integrated style showing character of ripe limes and melon, forthright finishing acidity.*	**£8.20**	V&C NRW DBY NYW VIL WRK CTC	**S**
MONTANA RESERVE RIESLING 1999, MONTANA WINES Marlborough	*Excellent body and complexity with petroleum and apricots on the palate, a true mouthful.*	**£8.20**	ODD RAV VIL	**B**
PEREGRINE PINOT GRIS 1999, PEREGRINE WINES Central Otago	*Lovely nutty nose, citrussy, green fruit on the palate, soft lemony structure, deep enjoyable length.*	**£14.00**	BBR	**B**

Pinpoint who sells the wine you wish to buy by turning to the stockist codes. If you know the name of the wine you want to buy, use the alphabetical index. If the price is your motivation, refer to the invaluable price guide index; red and white wines under £5, sparkling wines under £12 and champagne under £16. Happy hunting!

OTHER COUNTRIES

English wines have come along way since the approval of the 'Quality Wine Scheme', thus proving themselves with an array of medals, still mostly white and sparkling. Other countries that produce wines in unconventional circumstances are Morocco, Cyprus, the Lebanon, Switzerland and Tunisia who have all joined the list of medal winning countries. All worthy to be proud of their wines and the progress that has been made in winemaking skills and the investment in technology and equipment. This goes to show how the world of wine and its standards are ever advancing.

OTHER COUNTRIES • CYPRUS

CABERNET SAUVIGNON 1999, SODAP BOTTLE GREEN	*Inviting herbaceous nose, lots of red fruit showing and a long sweet finish.*	£5.00	BGL	B

OTHER COUNTRIES • ENGLAND

DENBIES SURREY GOLD 1999, DENBIES WINE ESTATE Surrey	*Excellent youthful wine with good concentration, simple, clean and balanced, will still evolve further.*	£4.50	DBS	S
ASTLEY DRY RESERVE 1996, JANET BALDWIN & JONTY DANIELS Worcestershire	*Clean, very refreshing green fruit nose, intense grand vegetable flavours with rhubarb. Nice acidity.*	£5.00	AST	B
CHAPEL DOWN FLINT DRY BACCHUS 1998, CHAPEL DOWN WINES Southern Counties	*Clean intense ripe fruits in complex nose and palate with appley acidity in fine balance.*	£5.00	WTS	B

CHAPEL DOWN EPOCH V 1995, CHAPEL DOWN WINES Southern Counties	*Lively mousse, strong aromatic flower nose, soft palate with dry ripe flavour, good acidity.*	**£5.50**	EWC BTH	(B)
SHAWSGATE BACCHUS 1999, SHAWSGATE WINERY East Anglia	*Fresh clean nose, fruity and crisp with a hint of spice and elderflower and a youthful finish.*	**£6.00**	SHA	(B)
HIDDEN SPRING SUSSEX SUNSET ROSÉ 1999, HIDDEN SPRING VINEYARD East Sussex	*Very fragrant floral fruit on the nose, zesty, refreshing grapefruit and peas with some nice acidity.*	**£6.70**	EWC	(B)
DENBIES REDLANDS 1999, DENBIES WINE ESTATE Surrey	*A toasty black pepper nose followed by blackcurrant palate, good balance of tannins and acidity.*	**£8.00**	DBS	(B)
VALLEY VINEYARDS FUMÉ 1998, VALLEY VINEYARDS Thames Valley	*Subtle complexity of peaches with hints of aniseed and crisp citrus fruits supported by fresh acidity.*	**£8.50**	VVS	(S)
VALLEY VINEYARDS FUMÉ 1995, VALLEY VINEYARDS Thames Valley	*A nutty oak nose leads to rich tropical fruits with a hint of herbaceousness and lengthy finish.*	**£8.50**	VVS	(B)
CHAPEL DOWN VINTAGE BRUT 1995, CHAPEL DOWN WINES Southern Counties	*Warm ripe fruit aromas, dry juicy citrus flavours, light structure with well balanced fresh acidity.*	**£10.50**	CDO	(B)
VALLEY VINEYARDS ASCOT NV, VALLEY VINEYARDS Thames Valley	*Elegant citrus nose with crisp cool apples on the palate, a balanced stylish structure. A true pleasure in the mouth.*	**£11.00**	VVS	(S)

OTHER COUNTRIES • ENGLAND

BREAKY BOTTOM BRUT MILLENNIUM CUVÉE MAMAN MERCIER 1996, PETER HALL East Sussex	*Soft fruit nose, very clean, light, delicate ripe fruit on the palate, crisp dry clean finish.*	£13.20	EWC	**B**
CUVÉE MERRET BELGRAVIA NV, RIDGEVIEW ESTATE Sussex	*Delicious herby fruit nose followed by nice complex wine, excellent acidity and savoury fruit finish.*	£14.00	RVE	**S**
CUVÉE MERRET BLOOMSBURY 1996, RIDGEVIEW ESTATE Sussex	*Appealing soft fruit aromas, sweet green lime palate with toasty hint, well integrated high acidity.*	£14.00	RVE	**B**

OTHER COUNTRIES • LEBANON

HOCHAR PÈRE ET FILS 1997, CHÂTEAU MUSAR Bekaa Valley	*Spicy redcurrant nose with warm ripe plums and crushed pepper palate, very pleasant finish.*	£7.60	Widely Available	**B**

OTHER COUNTRIES • MEXICO

LA CETTO PETITE SIRAH 1997, LA CETTO Baja California	*Spicy peppery nose, green herbaceous tones, ripe blackberry fruit, fresh acidity, firm tannins. Great balance.*	£5.20	WTS AWS DBY TAN G&M	**S**

Pinpoint who sells the wine you wish to buy by turning to the stockist codes. If you know the name of the wine you want to buy, use the alphabetical index. If the price is your motivation, refer to the invaluable price guide index; red and white wines under £5, sparkling wines under £12 and champagne under £16. Happy hunting!

OTHER COUNTRIES • MOROCCO

DOMAINE RIAD JAMIL 1995, LES CELLIERS DE MEKNES Beni M'tir	*Strawberry vanilla nose blending with baked apple and red berry characteristics, finishing well.*	£6.00	BGL	(B)

OTHER COUNTRIES • SWITZERLAND

PETITE ARVINE 1997, RENÉ FAVRE & FILS Valais	*Creamy tropical fruits on the nose, palate of green apples and pineapples combined with good acidity.*	£15.20	FLW	(B)
PINOT NOIR 1997, RENÉ FAVRE & FILS Valais	*Green peppers and fruity aromas, palate reveals high tannins and red fruit with a coffee finish.*	£17.40	FLW	(B)

OTHER COUNTRIES • TUNISIA

TUNISIAN RED 1999, CALATRASI	*Dense herb and currant nose fusing with brooding fruit characters finishig with long tail.*	£4.00	BWL	(B)

Pinpoint who sells the wine you wish to buy by turning to the stockist codes. If you know the name of the wine you want to buy, use the alphabetical index. If the price is your motivation, refer to the invaluable price guide index; red and white wines under £5, sparkling wines under £12 and champagne under £16. Happy hunting!

PORTUGAL

The standards shown here by the port producers has followed the demand for Port, which has never been greater and world-wide shipments continue to break all previous records. Vintage Port remains very popular, the rapid turnover in declared vintages has granted this array of vintages ready and waiting to be enjoyed. An overwhelming number of still wines have come from these traditional Port houses and single varietal wines proving the keen skills of both vineyard managers and winemakers alike.

PORTUGAL • MADIERA

BLANDY'S DUKE OF CLARENCE, BLANDY'S Madeira	*Captivating nutty and spicy nose leads to a refreshing, marvellous orange peel mouthfeel, with incredible balance.*	**£9.80**	Widely Available	S
BLANDY'S HARVEST MALMSEY, BLANDY'S Madeira	*Aromatic buttery oranges on the nose lead to a very rich sweet round palate.*	**£12.30**	MAD WCS	B
BLANDY'S 5 YO VERDELHO, BLANDY'S Madeira	*Gorgeous full bodied slightly smoked rich creamy palate introduced by luxurious warm full aromas.*	**£12.50**	Widely Available	S
COSSART GORDON 5 YO MALMSEY, COSSART GORDON & CO Madeira	*Seductive citrus peel nose and palate with perfect integration of sweetness and nut characters. Lovely.*	**£13.10**	ADN MAD SEB CVR WBR HST CFT	S
COSSART GORDON 5 YO SERCIAL, COSSART GORDON & CO Madeira	*Excellent inviting sweet nuts on the nose followed by generous full bodied fruit cake flavours.*	**£13.30**	MAD BLU SEB HST CFT	B

HENRIQUES & HENRIQUES 10 YO VERDELHO, HENRIQUES & HENRIQUES Madeira	*Honeyed amber colour, very expressive full bodied dried fruit, nice balance with perfect sweetness.*	**£15.30**	Widely Available	(S)
HENRIQUES & HENRIQUES 10 YO BUAL, HENRIQUES & HENRIQUES Madeira	*Detectable pleasant orangy nose. Lovely nuts and dried fruits with a toasty finish and good length.*	**£15.30**	Widely Available	(B)
HENRIQUES & HENRIQUES 10 YO SERCIAL, HENRIQUES & HENRIQUES Madeira	*Attractive sweet figs on the nose, good rich tropical characters and elegant style. Well balanced tang.*	**£15.60**	Widely Available	(S)
HENRIQUES & HENRIQUES 10 YO MALMSEY, HENRIQUES & HENRIQUES Madeira	*Rich toffee caramelised nose, complex, excellent weight on the palate. Good intensity and very pleasant finish.*	**£15.90**	Widely Available	(B)
BLANDY'S 10 YO MALMSEY, BLANDY'S Madeira	*Deep amber colour, rich toffee characterised nose, very nice weight on the palate and excellent complexity.*	**£16.30**	Widely Available	(B)
COSSART GORDON 10 YO BUAL, COSSART GORDON & CO Madeira	*Intense honey structure on the nose, very sweet dried fruits and a savoury long finish.*	**£17.40**	MAD WSO HST TRO	(B)
HENRIQUES & HENRIQUES 15 YO MALMSEY, HENRIQUES & HENRIQUES Madeira	*Very deep orange cognac colour with soft burnt caramel on the palate and an elegant seductive finish.*	**£20.40**	Widely Available	(S)
HENRIQUES & HENRIQUES 15 YO SERCIAL, HENRIQUES & HENRIQUES Madeira	*Deep orangy gold colour, light and citrussy nose, clean elegant structure, full bodied with a walnutty finish.*	**£21.50**	MAD QWW DBY HDS BEL PFT	(B)

HENRIQUES & HENRIQUES 15 YO VERDELHO, HENRIQUES & HENRIQUES Madeira	*Burnt marmalade on the nose, soft structure, lovely citrus balances great sweetness, excellent walnutty length.*	**£21.70**	MAD QWW DBY N&P HDS BEL PFT	(G)
HENRIQUES & HENRIQUES 15 YO BUAL, HENRIQUES & HENRIQUES Madeira	*Deep tangerine preserve on the nose, clean fruit with good positive acidity, leaning towards an enjoyable length.*	**£22.10**	Widely Available	(B)
BLANDY'S 15 YO MALMSEY, BLANDY'S Madeira	*Great clear tawny, citrus peel aromas, stewed fruit with balanced acidity, and lovely sweet finish.*	**£24.30**	Widely Available	(S)

PORTUGAL • OTHER

MOSCATEL DE SETÚBAL 1991, JP VINHOS Terras do Sado	*Lovely cold tea nose, full palate of ripe fruit greatly blended in a delicate acidity.*	**£9.00**	EHL	(B)

PORTUGAL • PORT

OLD MASTER RUBY PORT NV, SMITH WOODHOUSE Douro	*Lush red fruit with some earthy complexity, good weight of sweet raisins on the lasting finish.*	**£5.60**	GSJ CTC	(S)
MHV REGIMENTAL TAWNY PORT, SILVA & COSENS Douro	*Seductive and sweet raisin, candied peel and dried fig notes with a medium sweet finish.*	**£6.00**	MHV	(S)

MHV REGIMENTAL RUBY PORT, SILVA & COSENS Douro	*Raisin sweetness on the palate of moderate body and good structure with a lingering fine finish.*	£6.00	MHV	(B)
CALEM FINE WHITE NV, CALEM Douro	*Honey, cinnamon, and orange peel character with caramel and old fashion toffee on the finish.*	£7.00	RNS UNS	(B)
SAFEWAY VINTAGE CHARACTER PORT, CALEM Douro	*Mocha and rich Christmas pudding on the nose and palate with a soft smooth finish of character.*	£7.00	SAF	(B)
SOMERFIELD NAVIGATORS LBV 1992, REAL COMPANHIA VELHA Douro	*Stunningly attractive dense fruit on the nose, showing the full effect on the palate.*	£7.50	SMF	(S)
SAFEWAY LBV 1995, SYMINGTON Douro	*Nose is fresh with a lift of fruit, slightly sweet cherry fruit lingering on the finish.*	£7.60	SAF	(S)
POCAS LBV 1994, POCAS Douro	*Medium intensity of aroma and body, delicate ripe fruit, fresh berries and dates and a long end.*	£8.50	HOT	(B)
CROFT LBV 1994, CROFT Douro	*Rich deep ripe plummy style, with a hint of vanilla on the long mouthwatering length.*	£9.00	CWS	(B)
SMITH WOODHOUSE LODGE RESERVE, SMITH WOODHOUSE & CO Douro	*Lovely rich deep fruit on the nose, blackberry and liquorice on the lasting palate.*	£9.30	ODD WCS	(B)

BERRY'S WELLINGTON PORT, QUINTA DO NOVAL Douro	*Interesting marzipan characters on both the nose and palate with nuts and spice on the finish.*	£9.50	BBR	B
FONSECA LBV 1995, FONSECA GUIMARAENS Douro	*Rich chocolate cherry liqueurs, with a powerful finish on a big characterful palate.*	£9.60	CTC CEB DBY BEN VIL	B
DOW'S LBV 1995, SILVA & COSENS Douro	*Luscious berry and dried fruit layers, unravel to give a long ringing finish with a punch.*	£10.00	JSM CWS JMC AMW G&M	S
SANDEMAN IMPERIAL TAWNY, SANDEMAN Douro	*Intense dried fig and caramel nose, vanilla and coffee on the palate through to the end.*	£10.00	SEA	S
CALEM COLHEITA 1990, AA CALEM & FILHO Douro	*Mature and confident with good soft fruit driven structure, with a very soft and complex finish.*	£10.00	PNA	B
CHURCHILL'S DRY WHITE PORT, CHURCHILL GRAHAM Douro	*Delicious caramel character on the nose, smooth full bodied palate, and a hazelnut finish.*	£10.00	Widely Available	B
DO VALE DA MINA LBV 1995, VAN ZELLER Douro	*Good Swiss chocolate characters, firm tannins with a sweet fruit finish. Very alluring.*	£10.00	BDR	B
SOMERFIELD 10 YO TAWNY, REAL COMPANHIA VELHA Douro	*Treacle and nuts with a touch of spice and a warming fine long finish.*	£10.00	SMF	B

WARRE'S OTIMA, **WARRE & CA** Douro	*Outstanding complexity of rich dried fruit on the nose, toffee and walnuts on a confident finish.*	**£10.20**	Widely Available	**S**
SAINSBURY 10 YO **TAWNY PORT,** **QUINTA DO NOVAL** Douro	*Attractive fruit nose of spices and ripe strawberries, with hazel nut complexity. Toffeed nutty and youthful.*	**£10.30**	JSM CTC	**B**
CHURCHILL'S LBV 1994, **CHURCHILL GRAHAM** Douro	*Warming mouth feel with an abundance of berry fruit flavours, rich and ripe to the end.*	**£10.60**	Widely Available	**B**
SAFEWAY 10 YO TAWNY **PORT, SYMINGTON** Douro	*Sweet fruit coulis aromas, matched on the palate with pleasant length and flavour.*	**£10.70**	SAF	**B**
GRAHAM'S LBV 1995, **W&J GRAHAM & CO** Douro	*Spicy pepper and bitter chocolate, fresh succulent blackberry juices with a finish of good tannins.*	**£10.80**	Widely Available	**B**
NOVAL TRADITIONAL **LBV 1994,** **QUINTA DO NOVAL** Douro	*Plump red berries on the palate, spicy aroma and soft and simplistic elegant finish.*	**£11.10**	BBO QWW NYW TMW FEN CTC	**B**
PORTO BARROS LBV **1994, BARROS ALMEIDA** Douro	*Florentines abound, dried fruit on the palate with chocolate and spice. Rich and comforting.*	**£11.20**	AVB	**S**
PORTO BARROS QUINTA **DONA MATILDE 1997,** **BARROS ALMEIDA** Douro	*A huge concentration of fruit on the palate hold this well made and structured wine together till the end.*	**£11.50**	AVB	**S**

WAITROSE 10 YO, SYMINGTON Douro	*Fruit and nuts abound with good intensity and structure and a sweet and long warming inish.*	£11.50	WTS	Ⓢ
TAYLOR'S LBV 1995, TAYLOR'S FLADGATE & YEATMAN Douro	*Wonderful soft rich fruit, with good depth and length. An easy drinking pleasurable style.*	£11.70	Widely Available	Ⓑ
QUINTA DO NOVAL COLHEITA 1982, QUINTA DO NOVAL Douro	*Elegance and maturity showing on the nose. Good sweet concentration plus a Dundee cake finish.*	£11.80	QWW CTC	Ⓢ
NIEPOORT LBV 1995, NIEPOORT VINHOS Douro	*Bursting ripe plum and damson nose, with assertive prune richness on the long palate.*	£12.00	Widely Available	Ⓢ
ANDRESEN LBV 1994, JH ANDRESEN Douro	*Crimson fruit with an intense aroma, cardamon and ginger on the palate, with integrated tannins.*	£12.30	PFT	Ⓢ
GRAHAM'S SIX GRAPES, W&J GRAHAM & Co Douro	*Rich and velvety, many layers of ripe black fruits and dried prunes, with a fantastic and simple finish.*	£12.30	Widely Available	Ⓢ
BURMESTER LBV 1995, JW BURMESTER Douro	*Long rich velvety mouthfeel with intense dried figs on the palate of medium length.*	£12.50	HBJ	Ⓢ
QUINTA DO CRASTO LBV 1994, QUINTA DO CRASTO Douro	*Handsome and luscious aromas, on a dark and vibrant fruit concentrated finish. Very memorable.*	£12.50	ADN ODD V&C NYW WCR CTC	Ⓢ

KOPKE 10 YO TAWNY, KOPKE Douro	*Brown smokey nose and very fruity with a medium finish, lasting until the small hours.*	£12.70	CTC	**B**
SMITH WOODHOUSE LBV 1990, SMITH WOODHOUSE & CO Douro	*Rounded balanced sweet fruit flavour, simple and straightforward with great structure and alluring finish.*	£12.80	ODD PIM	**B**
DOW'S CRUSTED PORT 1997, SILVA & COSENS Douro	*Rich and complex with earthy, meaty tones, layered with rich fruit flavours aplenty on the finish.*	£13.00	JEF	**S**
QUINTA DO SAGRADO 10 YO TAWNY, AA CALEM Douro	*Marmalade and cinnamon aromas with good fruit length and structure, with a sweet orange finish.*	£13.00	VDV	**S**
BURMESTER TEN YO TAWNY, JW BURMESTER Douro	*Typical orange and dried fruit character, with lots to say on this full sweet palate.*	£13.50	HBJ	**B**
CASAL DOS JORDOES VINTAGE CHARACTER NV, PINTO E CRUZ Douro	*Warm sweet red fruits on the nose and palate, ample fruit lingering on in the finish.*	£13.50	VRT	**B**
QUINTA DA ROEDA 1983, CROFT Douro	*Fabulous rich caramel aromas on this splendidly persistent fruit driven palate, well balanced and a lingering finish.*	£14.00	MWW J&B	**G**
MARTINEZ GASSIOT 10 YO TAWNY, MARTINEZ GASSIOT Douro	*Caramelised red fruit aromas, rich brandy soaked raisins on the palate, and good length.*	£14.00	AMW	**B**

FONSECA 10 YO TAWNY, **FONSECA GUIMARAENS** Douro	*Youthful and vibrant on the powerful nose, clean racy summer fruits, with great length and acidity.*	**£14.10**	CEB DBY NYW BEN UBC VIL GRO	**B**
QUINTA DO NOVAL 10 YO TAWNY, **QUINTA DO NOVAL** Douro	*Crisp acidity with deep complex fruit, a vigorous flavour with delicious soft fruit.*	**£14.40**	WTS BBO QWW WBR HVW FEN CTC	**S**
BERRY'S WILLIAM PICKERING PORT, **QUINTA DO NOVAL** Douro	*Nutty aromas, subtle but well balanced with lots of dried fruit on the palate.*	**£14.70**	BBR	**B**
CALEM 10 YO TAWNY NV, AA CALEM & FILHO Douro	*Deep sweet caramel nose, sticky toffee pudding flavours, with an excellent and balanced finish.*	**£14.70**	PNA UNS	**B**
10 YO TAWNY PORT, **QUINTA DO PORTAL** Douro	*Subtle caramel and slightly nutty nose, with a balanced mouthful of fruit palate, and a powerful lingering finish.*	**£14.90**	ESL	**B**
DOW'S TEN YO TAWNY, **SILVA & COSENS** Douro	*Soft caramel aromas, light style, ripe fruit with toffee and spice on the well balanced finish.*	**£15.00**	JMC	**B**
ROYAL OPORTO 10 YO TAWNY, **REAL COMPANHIA VELHA** Douro	*Pale delicate spicy nose, powerful palate, pleasurable length of fruit that goes on forever.*	**£15.00**	PLB	**B**
GRAHAM'S TEN YO TAWNY, W&J GRAHAM & CO Douro	*Rich syrupy nose, with rich orange spiciness, and a warming finish on this mouthwatering palate.*	**£15.10**	ADN RNS DBY JNW FEN	**B**

WARRE'S BOTTLE MATURED LBV 1990, WARRE & CA Douro	*Full heavy aromas on the nose, light style with ripe fruit berry characters on the palate.*	**£15.20**	NRW AMW FEN	**B**
WARRE'S BOTTLE MATURED LBV 1992, WARRE & CA Douro	*Amazing depth of ripe sweet fruit, complex and rounded, with a surge of spice on the finish.*	**£15.40**	JSM NRW DBY NYW AMW PIM POR	**G**
QUINTA DE TERRA FEITA 1987, TAYLOR'S FLADGATE & YEATMEN Douro	*Richly perfumed wine with strength and stamina, plentiful ripe fruit layers and acidity on the palate.*	**£16.00**	DBY BTH BEN WCR TMW BEL	**B**
QUINTA DO PASSADOURO LBV 1995, NIEPOORT VINHOS Douro	*Soft plum fruit aromas, big ripe blackfruit conserve, lovely mouthfeel and a lingering end.*	**£16.20**	V&C BBO CAM NRW BEN BEL	**B**
OSBORNE LBV 1995, OSBORNE Douro	*Rich nutty and smooth, with sweet balanced spiced fruit of walnut and prunes on the finish.*	**£17.00**	ODD	**B**
GUIMARAENS 1986, FONSECA GUIMARAENS Douro	*Wonderful rounded sweet blackcurrant aromas, full fruit with good tannin structure and complexity.*	**£17.70**	DBY CVR BTH BEN VIL	**G**
QUINTA DAS CARVALHA VINTAGE 1997, REAL COMPANHIA VELHA Douro	*Cashew nut and liquorice on the nose, with notes of cigar box and rich fruit cake.*	**£18.00**	PLB	**S**
QUINTA DO PANASCAL 1987, FONSECA GUIMARAENS Douro	*This palate has some soft hide leather tones, attractively held together with abundant fruit.*	**£18.20**	DBY TMW VIL	**B**

SMITH WOODHOUSE MADALENA 1988, SMITH WOODHOUSE Douro	*Silky palate with crushed berry flavours on the palate, well structured with a spicy finish.*	£19.00	ODD	**B**
BARROS VINTAGE 1997, BARROS ALMEIDA Douro	*Traditional plums and Cuban cigar box aromas, youthful and rich fruit palate, offers much more to come.*	£19.10	AVB	**G**
COCKBURN VINTAGE 1997, COCKBURN SMITHES Douro	*Dark and rich mocha flavours, intense sweet finish on a rather stylish conclusion.*	£20.00	WSG	**B**
DOW'S QUINTA DO BOMFIM 1987, SILVA & COSENS Douro	*Elegant and powerful fruit driven style with great complexity and sweet lingering finish.*	£20.40	NRW DBY BTH	**B**
WARRE'S QUINTA DA CAVADINHA 1987, WARRE & CA Douro	*Raspberries and chocolate on the nose, ripe luscious fruit palate with a well balanced tannic structure.*	£20.70	Widely Available	**S**
WARRE'S QUINTA DA CAVADINHA 1988, WARRE & CA Douro	*Rich smooth mouthfeel, signs of maturity and individual character, showing with fine style.*	£20.90	NRW DBY AMW	**S**
GRAHAM'S MALVEDOS 1988, W&J GRAHAM & CO Douro	*Deliciously good depth of ripe and dried cherries, damson fruit on the never ending balanced finish.*	£21.10	CWS BEL DBY WBR JNW JMC AMW	**G**
QUINTA DE VARGELLAS 1987, TAYLOR'S FLADGATE & YEATMAN Douro	*Exotic and rich, this palate has figs, damsons and raison fruit all fighting for dominance Lovely drinking!*	£21.10	Widely Available	**G** TROPHY WINE

Dow's Quinta do Bomfim 1988, Silva & Cosens Douro	*Spiced chocolates on the nose, with a plentiful palate of deep fruit flavours.*	£21.20	DBY NYW G&M	(B)
Graham's Malvedos 1987, W&J Graham & Co Douro	*Warm earthy aromas, with chocolate dipped red fruit berries on the smooth elegant palate.*	£21.80	Widely Available	(S)
Sandeman 20 YO Tawny, Sandeman Douro	*Dundee cake and chocolate aromas with rich old fashioned toffee married together on the finish.*	£22.70	RAV	(S)
Very Old Reserve 1972, Quinto de Santa Eufémia Douro	*Marvellous marzipan on the nose, with citrus and burnt toffee, married with good acidity and length.*	£23.00	PGA	(S)
Churchill's Agua Alta Single Quinta 1998, Churchill Graham Douro	*A velvety depth fills this wine to the maximum palate, with a luscious and dreamy long-lasting finish.*	£23.00	HDS	(B)
Calem Quinta da Foz 1987, AA Calem & Filho Douro	*A contemporary style, showing maturity and power, with good acidity and structure on the f inish.*	£23.30	PNA BNK UNS	(B)
Sandeman Vau Vintage 1997, Sandeman Douro	*Smooth vanilla, rich spices and berry fruit balance well to give a long and lingering finish*	£24.70	CST	(B)
Osborne Vintage 1997, Bodegas Osborne Douro	*A wine with serious backbone, with powerful dried fruit and nuts. Full of character and elegance.*	£25.00	HBJ	(G)

QUINTA NOVA DE NOSSA SENHORA DO CARMO 1997, JW BURMESTER Douro	*Extremely elegant wine with good tannic structure and balance, will mature well for many years.*	£25.00	HBJ	(G)
BURMESTER VINTAGE 1997, JW BURMESTER Douro	*Long smooth palate with an abundance of ripe juicy fruits, lingering on to the finish.*	£25.00	HBJ	(S)
DOW'S 20 YO TAWNY, SILVA & COSENS LTD Douro	*Exquisite wine with lovely nutty complexity, fruit driven good acidity and a lingering finish.*	£25.00	JMC	(B)
WARRE'S 20 YO TAWNY, WARRE & CA Douro	*Fresh and nutty, with a well balanced velvety palate and dry tannins on the pleasing finish.*	£25.30	OWC	(S)
GRAHAM'S 20 YO TAWNY, W&J GRAHAM & CO Douro	*Sweet caramel flavours and a persistent clean finish on this palate that says so much.*	£26.60	ESL DBY	(B)
ROEDA VINTAGE 1997, CROFT Douro	*Beautifully soft and juicy, a very refined and elegant wine of importance with good structure.*	£27.00	J&B	(S)
DELAFORCE VINTAGE PORT 1992, DELAFORCE PORT Douro	*Intense prune and blackfruit aromas, cherry and damson fruit palate, with a firm and dry tannic finish .*	£29.00	J&B	(B)
QUINTA DO SILVAL 1997, QUINTA DO NOVAL Douro	*Appealing and rich fruit layers, providing a well balanced wine of character and length.*	£32.00	PRG	(S)

QUINTA DO NOVAL 20 YO TAWNY, QUINTA DO NOVAL Douro	*Rich walnut aromas with a long lingering finish on the palate of a soft smooth mouthful.*	£32.30	PRG BBO TNI CTC	**B**
DOW'S 30 YO TAWNY, SILVA & COSENS LTD Douro	*Intense Toblerone and mocha complexity, rich mature and deep, a port to lose yourself in.*	£35.00	G&M	**G**
CALEM VINTAGE 1997, AA CALEM & FILHO Douro	*Fine and elegant structure to this wine of character and individuality, has a long life ahead.*	£36.00	PNA	**G**
QUINTA DE SANTA EUFÉMIA 30 YO TAWNY, QUINTO DE SANTA EUFÉMIA Douro	*Attractive rich aroma of dried fruit, aged style with good lengthy acidity and a fine structure.*	£37.00	PGA	**B**
QUINTA DO VESUVIO 1998, SILVA & COSENS LTD Douro	*Powerful and rich fruit palate, with mulled wine spices and a long luscious finish.*	£39.00	ADN	**S**
GRAHAM'S 30 YO, W&J GRAHAM & CO Douro	*Luscious rich complex palate of figs and dried fruits, sweet with a very clean finish.*	£46.70	DBY FEN	**G**
CROFT VINTAGE 1994, CROFT PORT Douro	*Palate of prunes and black fruits. Smoothly balanced with refined tannins. Finishes with elegant viscose length.*	£46.80	J&B G&M	**B**
QUINTA DO NOVAL 40 YO TAWNY, QUINTA DO NOVAL Douro	*Rich nutty complex aroma, with considerable length and depth on this mature refine palate.*	£53.70	BBR PRG BBO BNK CTC	**S**

WARRES VINTAGE PORT 1977, WARRES Douro	*Nutty marzipan nose, immediate upfront fruit delivering delicate and fine fruit of extraordinary length.*	£57.50	WTS GHL HDS	(S)
GRAHAM'S FORTY YO, W&J GRAHAM & CO Douro	*Extremely mature style with length and breath of sweet and sour notes. This is one to savour!*	£65.00	DBY FEN	(G)

PORTUGAL • RED

JP TINTO 1999, JP VINHOS Terras do Sado	*Fruitcake nose with spicy jammy full fleshy fruit, good balance and structured with drying tannins.*	£3.30	EHL	(B)
VINHA DA MONTE 1998, SOGRAPE	*Cinnamon and cloves on the nose with earthy tones and ripe plum fruit on the palate.*	£5.00	WTS	(S)
BRIGHT BROTHERS PALMELA 1999, BRIGHT BROTHERS Palmela	*Strawberry jam nose blending with raspberry and smokey flavours with a nice long length.*	£5.00	SAF	(B)
FIUZA CABERNET SAUVIGNON 1998, FIUZA & BRIGHT Ribatejo	*Very clean nose of ripe fruit followed by good acidity combined with a soft red fruit palate.*	£5.00	EHL	(B)
FIUZA MERLOT 1998, FIUZA & BRIGHT Ribatejo	*Concentrated, medium weighted red and black fruit berry palate, with pleasing tannins on the finish.*	£5.00	EHL	(B)

BELA FONTE JAEN 1998, DFJ VINHOS Beiras	*Deep berry nose with a spicy fruit conserve palate with firm tannins of lovely texture.*	£5.20	SAF DBY PFT BOO	B
ROMEIRA PALMELA 1998, CAVES VELHAS Palmela	*Vanilla and toffee nose with ripe soft plummy fruit with wonderful balance and tannins.*	£5.20	PGA	B
PEDRAS DO MONTE 1999, DFJ VINHOS Terras do Sado	*Caramel and hint of coffee on the nose with plummy and berry notes ending with clean tannins.*	£5.30	UNS DBY PFT BOO	S
ESPORAO MONTE VELHO 1999, ESPORAO Alentejo	*Enticing crushed red fruit nose with wild strawberries blending with firm tannins and a good length.*	£5.30	WBR NYW POR	B
VINHA DO MONTE 1998, SOGRAPE VINHOS DE PORTUGAL Alentejo	*Hot ripe berry nose blending with spice and some blackpepper, good firm tannins and length.*	£5.40	CTC	B
DUQUE DE VISEU RED 1997, SOGRAPE VINHOS DE PORTUGAL Dao	*Wonderful herbaceous nose with red fruits and vanilla flavours on this mature wine with a good backbone.*	£5.50	CWS CTC	B
VINHO TINTO ESPIGA 1999, QUINTA DO BOAVISTA Estremadura	*Youthful plum and damson nose with soft sour fruit flavours ending with big tannins.*	£5.50	ODD CTC	B
QUINTA DA BACALHOA 1997, JP VINHOS Terras do Sado	*Some mature fruit on the nose followed by lovely tannins and ripe fruits with a long finish.*	£5.60	EHL	B

PORTUGAL • RED

JP Garrafeira 1990, JP Vinhos Terras do Sado	*Austere plummy fruit nose with a medley of berries and plums with upfront tannins.*	£5.90	EHL	(S)
Bright Bros Douro Torcular 1999, Bright Bros Douro	*A floral violet nose fusing with jammy red berries and currants with wonderful round tannins.*	£6.00	EHL	(S)
Rocha do Monte 1999, DFJ Vinhos Terras do Sado	*Plum and cinnamon medley nose with soft ripe bramble and thickness to the palate.*	£6.00	BOO	(B)
Cataplana Negra Mole 1999, DFJ Vinhos Algarve	*Toffee caramel nose with lovely cherry fruit complexity and balanced tannins, hickory wood in the mouth.*	£6.10	CEB PFT BOO	(B)
Quinta Das Setencostas Tinto 1999, Quinta Do Boavista Estremadura	*Charming berries and plum nose with soft red berry palate with gripping tannins and a nice length.*	£6.30	ODD BOO	(B)
Palha-Canas Tinto 1999, Quinta Do Boavista Estremadura	*Youthful berry and damson nose with bittersweet fruits and firm and lovely tannins.*	£6.60	ODD UNS BOO	(B)
Bright Bros Douro TFN 1998, Bright Bros Douro	*Lush floral character on a rich palate of berries and ripe plums, good ageing potential.*	£6.70	TOS SAF	(B)
Quinta dos Roques 1997, Quinta dos Roques Dão	*Developed nose of berries and plums with a spicy brambly palate with good acidity, tannins and length.*	£6.80	DBY HVW PFT	(B)

FIUZA RESERVA CABERNET MERLOT 1998, FIUZA & BRIGHT Ribatejo	*Mature spicy nose, lovely complex palate of juicy red fruit with delightful tannins on finish.*	£7.00	EHL	(S)
PALMELA PARTICULAR 1998, CAVES ALIANÇA Palmela	*Dark brambly nose with wild mulberries and sweet blackberries with concentrated creaminess and a good balance.*	£7.00	Widely Available	(S)
QUINTA DO CRASTO DOURO RED 1999, QUINTA DO CRASTO Douro	*Fruity berry forward nose with plenty of fruit, tannins and acid balancing well on a good backbone.*	£7.00	ADN ODD V&C DBY CTC HVW	(B)
ROMEIRA PALMELA GARRAFEIRA 1996, CAVES VELHAS Palmela	*Sweet damson nose blending with ripe blueberries, pepper and vanilla flavours and drying tannins.*	£7.00	PGA	(B)
SOGRAPE RESERVA DOURO RED 1997, SOGRAPE VINHOS DE PORTUGAL Douro	*Lifted plums and damson aroma blending with jammy red fruits and gripping tannins to end.*	£7.30	SGL CTC	(B)
PORCA DE MURCA RESERVA 1998, REAL COMPANHIA VELHA Douro	*Dusty fruit with smokiness leading to lush plums and black berries and nice tannins.*	£7.50	PLB	(B)
QUINTA DE LA ROSA DOURO TINTO 1998, QUINTA DE LA ROSA Douro	*Intense red fruit nose with moody black cherries and jammy plum flavours with a lingering finish.*	£7.50	Widely Available	(B)
GRAND 'ARTE ALICANTE BOUSCHET 1999, DFJ VINHOS Estremadura	*Stewed apple and custard nose blending with raspberry, blackcurrants and vanilla coulis palate with a clean tail.*	£7.70	BOO	(B)

PORTUGAL • RED

Mà Partilha 1997, JP Vinhos Terras do Sado	*Vanilla and plum nose with some green leafiness and full fruit flavours with a toasty butteriness on finish.*	£7.80	EHL	**B**
Esporão Aragonés 1998, Esporao Alentejo	*Juicy blackberry nose with a drying palate of berries and damsons with good depth and spiciness.*	£8.00	UNS	**B**
Vila Santa 1998, Joao Ramos Alentejo	*Summer berry fruit aromas hints of chocolate with sweet juicy red berry palate with vanilla.*	£8.00	WTS	**B**
Calcos do Tanha 1997, Manuel Pinto Hespanhol Douro	*Spicy notes on a full bodied fruit palate, hints of smokiness and good structure.*	£8.20	DBY CFT	**B**
Cortes de Cima 1999, Cortes de Cima Alentejo	*Delicate perfumed nose with jammy damsons and berry palate. Finishing with sweet gripping tannins.*	£8.50	ODD HWL JNW BOO	**S**
Esporao Reserva 1996, Esporao Alentejo	*Stewed fruit and vanilla aroma with chewy brambles and balanced acidity, silky tannins and hot finish.*	£8.50	NYW POR	**B**
Grand 'Arte Touriga Francesa 1999, DFJ Vinhos Estremadura	*Lovely cassis aroma with big succulent spicy cinnamon and mulberry flavours pouring out with firm tannins.*	£8.50	JSM PFT BOO	**B**
Touriga Nacional Casa Santos Lima 1999, Quinta Do Boavista Estremadura	*Soft oaky nose with raspberry and cassis flavours, well structured style and a lengthy finish.*	£9.10	ODD NYW CTC	**S**

QUINTA DO CRASTO DOURO TINTA RORIZ 1997, QUINTA DO CRASTO Douro	*Good green fruit nose with full bodied fruit on the palate and firm tannins.*	£9.30	ADN ODD	B
QUINTA DOS ROQUES RESERVA 1997, QUINTA DOS ROQUES Dão	*Spicy red fruit nose with hot redcurrants and cherries lingering on a well balanced palate.*	£9.40	ESL DBY HVW PFT	B
QUINTA DO CRASTO DOURO RESERVA 1998, QUINTA DO CRASTO Douro	*Big sweet smokey nose with cool velvety plums and damsons leading to firm tannins and nice length.*	£9.50	ADN ODD CPW DBY CTC HVW	S
CORTES DE CIMA RESERVA 1998, CORTES DE CIMA Alentejo	*A full bodied wine of liquorice, pepper with bramble and mixed berry preserve. Will develop more.*	£9.70	ODD JNW	S
TOURIGA FRANCESA CASA SANTOS LIMA 1999, QUINTA DO BOAVISTA Estremadura	*Brooding damsons with complexity and structure, good firm tannins with a nice clean finish.*	£10.50	ENO	B
ARAGONEZ 1998, CORTES DE CIMA Alentejo	*Vibrant plum nose with vanilla and big juicy red fruits with full tannins. A wine to keep.*	£10.70	ODD HWL JNW	S
TOURIZ CASA SANTOS LIMA 1999, QUINTA DO BOAVISTA Estremadura	*Seductive nose of wild berries onto a raspberry palate with good structure and full tannins.*	£10.70	ODD NYW CTC	S
FUNDAGAO EUGENIO DE ALMEIDA CARTUXA 1996, FUNDAGAO EUGENIO DE ALMEIDA Alentejo	*Vegetal fig and plum on nose with brambles and red fruits on palate with a firm finish.*	£11.00	REY	B

QUINTA DO CARMO 1997, QUINTA DO CARMO Alentejo	*Mature wine of spices mingling with concentrated berries an damsons with slightly dry tannins and stylish length.*	£12.00	DBY TAN POR	B
QUINTA DA CORTEZIA TINTA RORIZ 1998, CAVES ALIANÇA Estremadura	*Wild mulberry nose combining a berries and vanilla palate, with soft tannins complimenting the finish.*	£12.70	MER PBA BOO	B
ROQUES ALFROCHEIRO PRETO 1997, QUINTA DOS ROQUES Dão	*Lifted spicy mixed fruit nose with a good concentration of ripe fruit, acid and tannins.*	£13.10	V&C DBY HST JSS PFT	S
ROQUES TOURIGA NACIONAL 1997, QUINTA DOS ROQUES Dão	*Warm, sweet nose with sweet red fruit and vanilla on a well structured stylish wine.*	£13.60	DBY JSS PFT	S
QUINTA DOS CARVALHAIS TOURIGA NACIONAL 1996, SOGRAPE VINHOS DE PORTUGAL Dao	*Dusty rose aroma with brambles and blueberry flavours infusing with firm tannins and good length.*	£13.60	NYW	B
MAIAS JAEN 1997, SOCIEDADE AGRICOLA FALDAS DA SERRA Dão	*Blueberry and apple aroma on a jammy berry conserve palate with wonderful length, balanced all round.*	£14.00	REY	S
QUINTA DO PORTAL 1997, TINTA RORIZ QUINTA DO PORTAL Douro	*Savoury nose incorporated with jammy ripe red summer fruits making an attractive style wine.*	£14.00	CHN	B
INCÓGNITO 1998, CORTES DE CIMA Alentejo	*Youthful but given time will bloom. It has the charisma, balance and style that shows promise.*	£15.40	ADN ODD JNW BOO	B

PORTUGAL • WHITE

GRAND 'ARTE ALVARINHO CHARDONNAY 1999, DFJ VINHOS Estremadura	*Delicate fruit on the nose, fresh crispy apples on the palate and a refreshing fruity finish.*	£6.90	PFT BOO	(B)
ESPORAO RESERVA 1998, ESPORAO Alentejo	*Gooseberry and honeysuckle nose with pineapple and papaya fruit character, balanced acidity and a nice finish.*	£8.00	ODD NYW	(B)

SOUTH AMERICA

This is where you can feel confident in being able to buy good value, fruity and intense wines for everyday drinking. In recent years progress has been made and up market wines have been made available in the UK. Stability in the basic wines has given the new range of wines a head start. Argentina in particular has moved away from the rustic styles of old, but kept its use of indigenous grape varities as her unique selling point. Wonder around the South American world.

ARGENTINA • RED

CO-OP ARGENTINE MALBEC 1999, LA RIOJANA La Rioja	*Lush and spicy, ripe berry fruit leading to full bodied plums and grippy tannins.*	£4.00	CWS	B
SAFEWAY ARGENTINIAN BONARDA 1999, LA RIOJANA La Rioja	*Herbaceous nose with juicy concentrated bramble fruit palate, good length and complexity.*	£4.00	SAF	B
SAFEWAY ARGENTINIAN SYRAH 1999, LA RIOJANA La Rioja	*Warm, spice and herb nose, ripe full palate, smooth tannins, and a good fresh fruit finish.*	£4.00	SAF	B
DUARTE MALBEC 1999, MARQUÉS DE MONISTROL Mendoza	*Flowery leather and raspberry nose followed by peppery juicy fruit and agreeably tannins on the palate.*	£4.40	A&A	B
ADISENO CABERNET SHIRAZ 1999, ORFILA Mendoza	*Good ripe fruit and tannins on the palate with some chocolate, nice coffee in a rich warm finish.*	£4.50	IWS	S

FAR FLUNG MALBEC 1999, LA AGRÍCOLA Mendoza	*Ripe black cherry nose balanced with ripe black fruits and spiciness, good balance and lovely finish.*	£4.50	ASD	Ⓢ
BRIGHT BROTHERS BARRICA MALBEC 1998, PEÑAFLOR San Juan	*Oaky liquorice nose with sweet fruit brambles, strawberry flavours with soft tannins and nice length.*	£4.50	EHL	Ⓑ
RIO DE PLATA MALBEC 1999, BODEGAS ETCHART Mendoza	*Enticing ripe cherry nose with wonderful cedary, earthy and peppery red fruit flavours with firm tannins.*	£4.50	RAV WCR	Ⓑ
SANTA ANA MALBEC 1997, SANTA ANA Mendoza	*Intense plummy nose with smokey jammy black fruit palate with a medium finish.*	£4.50	WAV	Ⓑ
SANTA JULIA SYRAH 1999, LA AGRÍCOLA Mendoza	*Cooked fruit aroma, earthy and cherry fruit character, interesting meaty flavoured mid palate.*	£4.50	THI	Ⓑ
BALBI MALBEC 1999, BALBI VINEYARDS Mendoza	*Young dense ripe red fruit with spicy damsons and firm tannins. A balanced wine.*	£4.70	ODD GYW SAF OWC	Ⓑ
ELSA BARBERA 1998, VALENTIN BIANCHI Mendoza	*Earthy nose with hints of Cuban cigars, chocolate coated cherries and strawberries, dry on the finish.*	£4.90	GRT	Ⓑ
SANTA JULIA CABERNET SAUVIGNON MALBEC 1999, SANTA JULIA Mendoza	*Lovely floral berry nose slides into a well balanced palate displaying character, a nice wine.*	£4.90	JSM THI	Ⓑ

VALLE DE VISTALBA BARBERA 1999, NIETO E SENETINER Mendoza	*Rich and tarry, sweet ripe nose, light menage of fruit on the palate, some interesting complexity.*	£4.90	Widely Available	(B)
VIÑAS DE MEDRANO BONARDA 1999, VIÑAS DE MEDRANO Mendoza	*Lifted fruit and peppery nose with plenty of blackberries and plums on the palate with firm tannins.*	£4.90	GDS VIW	(B)
ARGENTO MALBEC 1999, CATENA Mendoza	*Enticing tobacco nose well balanced with soft dark plums and berry flavours with good length.*	£5.00	JSM MWW TOS FQU WCR	(S)
BRIGHT BROTHERS BARRICA MALBEC 1999, CABERT S&A Mendoza	*Spirity red fruit nose fusing with strawberries and berry flavours, medium tannins and balanced acidity.*	£5.00	EHL	(S)
FINCA LAS MARIAS BARBERA 1999, NIETO E SENETINER Mendoza	*Fresh, fabulous and fruity, loads of damson fruit married well to give a long powerful wine.*	£5.00	CPR BOO	(S)
ADISENO SHIRAZ 1999, ORFILA Mendoza	*Strong coffee scente nose rich raspberry and chocolatey palate, quality fruit evident and a clean finish.*	£5.00	IWS	(B)
BRIGHT BROTHERS RESERVE CABERNET SAUVIGNON 1999, PEÑAFLOR San Juan	*Leather and pepper nose with bramble fruit coulis leading to a nice tannin structure.*	£5.00	EHL	(B)
BRIGHT BROTHERS RESERVE SHIRAZ 1999, PEÑAFLOR San Juan	*Good quality nose with whiffs of tobacco, soft silky palate and a long rolling, spicy finish.*	£5.00	TOS	(B)

FANTELLI MALBEC 1999, JESUS CARLOS FANTELLI Mendoza	*A wonderful blend of ripe plums and blackpepper flavours harmonising with soft tannins.*	£5.00	BGL	(B)
FANTELLI SYRAH 1999, JESUS CARLOS FANTELLI Mendoza	*Bramble fruit aroma, lovely berry flavours, slight green texture. Promising wine that will surely improve.*	£5.00	BGL	(B)
HORACIO NESMAN MALBEC 2000, HARACIO NESMAN San Juan	*Ripe rich fruit aroma with jammy plums and berry palate with a firm dry finish.*	£5.00	BXT	(B)
MAGDELANA RIVER MALBEC CABERNET 1999, AGRÍCOLA Mendoza	*Spicy prune aroma with ripe black cherry palate with soft tannins and nice finish.*	£5.00	UNS	(B)
MONSTER SPICY RED 1999, PEÑAFLOR San Juan	*Finely crafted wine, good lift of fruit character, broad berry fruit flavours and consistent length.*	£5.00	TOS	(B)
Y2K SHIRAZ 1999, PEÑAFLOR San Juan	*Pleasant eucalyptus and berry fruit on the nose that flows to the mouth with intensity.*	£5.00	SAF	(B)
VALLE DE VISTALBA MALBEC 1999, NIETO E SENETINER Mendoza	*Young exotic fruit nose with sweet cherries and plums, balanced acid and firm tannins.*	£5.10	Widely Available	(S)
LUIS CORREAS MALBEC 1999, LUIS CORREAS Mendoza	*Sweet fragrant nose with juicy fleshy fruit, hint of smokiness, good length and balance.*	£5.30	BOO	(S)

VILLA ATUEL SYRAH 1999, VILLA ATUEL Mendoza	*Soft appealing easy nose, pleasant ripe cherry fruit, good follow through of spice character.*	£5.30	Widely Available	(B)
COLECCIÓN MALBEC 1999, TORINO Salta	*Earthy vegetal nose with pepper and juicy plums balanced by dry tannins with good length.*	£5.40	CTC AVB	(S)
ELSA'S VINEYARD MALBEC 1997, VALENTIN BIANCHI Mendoza	*Meaty cassis nose with rich spicy plums and berries, good firm tannins, pleasing bitter chocolate finish.*	£5.50	GRT ODD JAG TMW	(B)
VALLE DE VISTALBA MERLOT 1999, NIETO E SENETINER Mendoza	*Rich supple bramble fruit with tobacco and luscious mocha on the bold finish.*	£5.60	Widely Available	(S)
J&F LURTON MALBEC RESERVA 1999, J&F LURTON Mendoza	*Big ripe fruits with hints of liquorice flavours in balance with tannins and acidity. Excellent wine.*	£6.00	J&F	(G)
DIEGO MURILLO FAMILY RESERVE MALBEC 1998, HUMBERTO CANALE Rio Negro	*Herby plummy nose with ripe succulent berry flavours, good structure and a long finish.*	£6.00	SAF	(S)
ETCHART CABERNET SAUVIGNON 1998, BODEGAS ETCHART Salta	*Lots of rich ripe fruits on nose and palate, expressive well balanced structure, sweet fresh finish.*	£6.00	TOS WCR	(S)
TERRAZAS ALTO MALBEC 1999, BODEGA TERRAZAS Mendoza	*Cooked summer fruit flavours balanced with liquorice and spice, firm tannins with a good backbone.*	£6.00	Widely Available	(S)

FINCA EL RETIRO TEMPRANILLO 1999, FINCA EL RETIRO Mendoza	*Lovely strawberries and cherries on nose and palate, fruity creamy finish with good length.*	**£6.00**	Widely Available	(B)
SANTA JULIA MALBEC RESERVA 1998, LA AGRÍCOLA Mendoza	*Lighter style warm summer red fruit aroma with a sweet sensation in this elegant wine.*	**£6.00**	UNS	(B)
SANTA JULIA TEMPRANILLO SELECTION 1999, LA AGRÍCOLA Mendoza	*Inviting, strong, warm nose, sweet berries and well integrated oak on nose and palate, great finish.*	**£6.00**	CAM UNS	(B)
FINCA EL RETIRO MALBEC 1999, FINCA EL RETIRO Mendoza	*Very blackcurranty nose blending with juicy ripe cassis fruit and liquorice ending with medium tannins.*	**£6.10**	Widely Available	(S)
TERRAZAS ALTO CABERNET SAUVIGNON 1999, BODEGA TERRAZAS Mendoza	*Attractive toasty leaves on the nose, cedar wood in the palate well balanced, finishes with lovely oak.*	**£6.10**	Widely Available	(S)
FINCA EL RETIRO CABERNET SAUVIGNON 1999, FINCA EL RETIRO Mendoza	*Appealing ripe fruit on the nose, lots of blackcurrants beautifully marinated in tannins, nice finish.*	**£6.10**	Widely Available	(B)
TRAPICHE CABERNET OAK CASK 1997, BODEGAS TRAPICHE Mendoza	*Elegant and classy damson nose, full palate of ripe fruit, nice portion of tannins, long finish.*	**£6.10**	DBY	(B)
NIETO E SENETINER RESERVE SYRAH 1999, NIETO E SENETINER Mendoza	*Earthy and rich raspberry aromas flow to a delectable berry and mint palate with chewy tannins.*	**£6.40**	PBA AMW WCS	(B)

BRIGHT BROTHERS BARRICA RESERVE SHIRAZ 1999, BRIGHT BROTHERS San Juan	*Subtle aromatics with slight lift, deliciously sweet and elegant fruit, good alcohol and length.*	£6.50	TOS	**B**
TERRAZAS ALTO CABERNET SAUVIGNON 1999, BODEGAS CHANDON Mendoza	*Rich compote of stewed red berries, with plummy rather sour young finish with bold tannins.*	£6.50	BBO VIL WCS FEN	**B**
FINCA FLICHMAN MALBEC RESERVA 1998, FINCA FLICHMAN Mendoza	*Lovely spicy summer fruits with soft texture of meaty plums and a balanced structure.*	£6.60	CTC	**B**
FINCA FLICHMAN SYRAH RESERVA 1997, FINCA FLICHMAN Mendoza	*Very deep, concentrated colour, clean nose and soft subtle fruit, dry and smokey finish.*	£6.60	CTC	**B**
BRIGHT BROTHERS BARRICA SHIRAZ 1998, PEÑAFLOR San Juan	*Complex aromas of sweet flavoured strawberry ice cream and brimming with delicate berry fruit flavours.*	£7.00	TOS	**S**
BRIGHT BROTHERS BARRICA CABERNET SAUVIGNON 1998, PEÑAFLOR San Juan	*Matured beautiful nose, well balanced, big taste of cabernet, soft fruit and rusty tannins on finish.*	£7.00	EHL	**B**
BRIGHT BROTHERS BARRICA CABERNET SAUVIGNON SHIRAZ 1998, PEÑAFLOR San Juan	*Gamey appetising nose, soft and round ripe blackcurrant fruit, light medium finish with good oak.*	£7.00	TOS	**B**
BRIGHT BROTHERS BARRICA CABERNET SHIRAZ 1999, PEÑAFLOR San Juan	*Powerful, well balanced rich wine, sweet fruit and oak on nose and palate, nice spicy finish.*	£7.00	TOS	**B**

BRIGHT BROTHERS BARRICA CABERNET SHIRAZ 1998, PEÑAFLOR San Juan	*Beautifully developed to matured style, elegant fruit on the nose, with real intrinsic fruit to taste.*	£7.00	EHL	**B**
FANTELLI RESERVE 1999, JESUS CARLOS FANTELLI Mendoza	*Smooth cassis on the nose, sweet strawberries and oak with hint of muskiness. Good length.*	£7.00	BGL	**B**
TERRAZAS RESERVA MALBEC 1997, BODEGA TERRAZAS Mendoza	*Vanilla aromas blending with a rich complex palate of ripe plums and blackcurrants with great depth.*	£7.50	CTC BBO QWW GHL EDC	**B**
LUIGI BOSCA MALBEC 1999, LUIGI BOSCA Mendoza	*Rich vanilla strawberry aromas with spicy red fruit and a touch of smokiness and elegant length.*	£7.60	ADN DBY HVW WRW	**B**
LUIGI BOSCA SYRAH 1999, LUIGI BOSCA Mendoza	*Intense pepper and wild herb nose, mid weight palate, stylish varietal characters, well balanced.*	£7.80	ADN DBY MAD HVW	**B**
ETCHART ARNALDO B RESERVA 1997, BODEGAS ETCHART Salta	*Spicy cedar on the nose with rich ripe fruit on a soft palate with good balance.*	£8.00	CAX	**S**
FAMILIA ZUCCARDI Q TEMPRANILLO 1999, LA AGRÍCOLA Mendoza	*Delightful violet aromas lead to well balanced, full bodied wine with sweet juicy fruit.*	£8.00	TOS THI FQU	**B**
NIETO E SENETINER RESERVE MALBEC 1999, NIETO E SENETINER Mendoza	*Bramble mint on the nose, masses of berry fruit on the palate with a touch of smokiness.*	£8.80	DBY PBA AMW	**S**

SOUTH AMERICA • ARGENTINA • RED

FAMILIA ZUCCARDI Q MALBEC 1998, LA AGRÍCOLA Mendoza	*Earthy spice aromas, big full sweet fruit and chocolate palate with a long ending.*	£9.00	THI	(S)
FAMILIA ZUCCARDI Q MALBEC 1999, LA AGRÍCOLA Mendoza	*Youthful wine with ripe juicy berry fruit and prune flavours combined with moderate tannins, medium length.*	£9.00	THI	(B)
PRIVADA 1998, BODEGA NORTON Mendoza	*Dense nose of red berries blending with cassis coulis, firm tannins and a good tail.*	£9.00	ODD TOS BWC FQU JNW	(B)
WEINERT MALBEC 1995, BODEGAS Y CAVAS DE WEINERT Mendoza	*Spicy aromas, full plummy palate with big mouthfeel and oak integrating well on the finish.*	£9.70	Widely Available	(S)
J&F LURTON CABERNET SAUVIGNON RESERVA 1999, J&F LURTON Mendoza	*Rich damson and fruit cake flavours with a hint of chocolate and spices. Long pleasant finish.*	£9.80	ESL CFT	(B)
BALBI BARBARO 1997, BODEGAS BALBI Mendoza	*Lovely complex earthy aromas on a rich full palate of red and black fruits. Drink now.*	£10.00	GYW SAF	(G)
LUIGI BOSCA MALBEC VERDOT 1995, LUIGI BOSCA Mendoza	*Black berry fruit nose with vibrant fleshy plums and berry flavours, developed length.*	£12.20	ADN DBY MAD	(G)
LUIGI BOSCA MALBEC VERDOT 1996, LUIGI BOSCA Mendoza	*Smokey nose with red black fruit conserve combined with vanilla, moderate tannins and elegant length.*	£12.70	ADN MAD PFT	(S)

BODEGAS COLOME 1997, BODEGAS COLOME Salta	*Dark damson and black fruit with green peppercorn integrating with sweet blackberries and spiciness.*	**£15.10**	ADN NYW TNI WRK PFT	**B**
TERRAZAS GRAN CABERNET SAUVIGNON 1997, BODEGAS CHANDON Mendoza	*Spicy red fruit nose with berries covered in velvety chocolate flavours and firm tannins. Well balanced.*	**£16.00**	CTC BBO VIL WCS	**S**
TERRAZAS GRAN MALBEC 1997, BODEGAS CHANDON Mendoza	*Lovely raspberries, spices and oak on nose, beautiful mixed red berries, raspberries and tannins on palate*	**£16.40**	CTC BBO WBR VIL WCS	**B**
CADUS MALBEC 1997, NIETO E SENETINER Mendoza	*Damson bramble nose with jammy berry fruits, drying tannins and smokiness, good length.*	**£17.40**	CPR NYW PBA HDS WCS	**B**
ALTO 1998, ALTA VISTA Mendoza	*Rich black damson and peppery nose with smooth tannins, good acidity and elegant backbone.*	**£25.00**	J&B	**S**

ARGENTINA • SPARKLING

CHANDON ARGENTINA NV, CHANDON ESTATES Mendoza	*Soft melony nose, good ripe fruit with appley characters, clean pleasant sweet finish.*	**£8.20**	Widely Available	**B**

Pinpoint who sells the wine you wish to buy by turning to the stockist codes. If you know the name of the wine you want to buy, use the alphabetical index. If the price is your motivation, refer to the invaluable price guide index; red and white wines under £5, sparkling wines under £12 and champagne under £16. Happy hunting!

ARGENTINA • WHITE

CABALLO DE PLATA TORRONTES 1999, LA RIOJANA La Rioja	Seductive fresh fruit nose, new dried fruit palate with good integration of acidity and good length.	£3.50	SAF	B
TESCO ARGENTINIAN TORRONTES 1999, LA RIOJANA La Rioja	Attractive delicate juicy fruit nose, well balanced acidity on the full bodied fruit palate.	£3.50	TOS	B
RIO DE PLATA TORRONTES 1999, BODEGAS ETCHART Mendoza	Open citrus fruit on the nose, complex structure, adequate acidity in good fruit, pleasant length.	£4.00	BNK RAV WES	B
SANTA ROSA ESTATE CHENIN BLANC TORRONTES 1999, SANTA ROSA ESTATE Mendoza	Bright fresh nose and good fruit complexity, produces a delicate herbaceous finish at the end.	£4.40	QWW	B
TERRAZAS ALTO CHARDONNAY 1999, BODEGA TERRAZAS Mendoza	Clean creamy nutty nose leads to well balanced charming fruit and oak, elegant extended finish.	£6.00	Widely Available	S
SANTA JULIA VIOGNIER RESERVA 1999, LA AGRÍCOLA Mendoza	Crisp tropical fruit salad nose incorporated into the palate with good balance and acidity.	£6.00	WTS	B
VIÑA AMALIA CHARDONNAY 1999, FINCA LA AMALIA Mendoza	Seductive vanilla and caramel on nose, smooth acidity on nice sweet palate with elegant long finish.	£7.70	ODD PAM	B

| **FAMILIA ZUCCARDI Q CHARDONNAY 1999, LA AGRICOLA** Mendoza | *Captivating intense tropical fruit on the nose followed by rich oak and pear flavours.* | £9.00 | THI | S |

SOUTH AMERICA • CHILE • CABERNET

ANTARES CABERNET SAUVIGNON 1999, VIÑA SANTA CAROLINA Maule Region	*Deep red orange colour, butter and fruit candies on palate, attractive smokey fruit on finish.*	£4.00	THW	B
CARTA VIEJA CABERNET SAUVIGNON 1999, CARTA VIEJA Maule Region	*Mints and flowers on the nose, good tannic structure, soft fruits and bold finish.*	£4.10	ODD WCR MHV	B
VALLE ANDINO CABERNET SAUVIGNON 1998, VIÑEDOS TERRANOBLE	*Smooth vegetal nose with tobacco hints, sweet attractive round palate, velvety structure, good tannins.*	£4.10	CTC	B
ASDA CHILEAN CABERNET RESERVE 1999, VIÑA CONO SUR Rapel Valley	*Much oriented cocoa nose, good sweet fruit with lovely balance, delicious elegant long finish.*	£5.00	WST	S
LOS ROBLES CABERNET SAUVIGNON 1999, VINOS LOS ROBLES Maule Region	*Blackcurrants and vegetal nose, delightful acidity and tannic texture, some pleasant oak on finish.*	£5.00	JSM	S
CALITERRA CABERNET SAUVIGNON 1999, CALITERRA Central Valley	*Mint and leather nose, strong blackcurrants with pepperiness and dry tannins, well structured.*	£5.00	MAD DBY FQU JMC DIC	B

SOUTH AMERICA • CHILE • CABERNET

SANTA CATALINA CABERNET SAUVIGNON 1999, BODEGA BELLAVISTA Maule Region	*Rich luscious cassis medium bodied wine with pleasant easy drinking finish and light tannic structure.*	**£5.00**	EHL	(B)
TESCO CHILEAN CABERNET SAUVIGNON RESERVE 1999, VALDIVIESO Maule Region	*Very rich plummy aromas, well structured middle palate, nice integration of acidity and a firm finish.*	**£5.00**	TOS	(B)
ISLA NEGRA CABERNET SAUVIGNON 1999, VIÑA CONO SUR Rapel Valley	*Sweet warm almondy nose, ripe fruit with pleasant balance of tannins and great tannic finish.*	**£5.10**	ODD WTS FQU COM	(S)
LUIS FELIPE EDWARDS CABERNET SAUVIGNON 1998, LUIS FELIPE EDWARDS Rapel Region	*Full grapey aroma, lots of ripe fruit flavours in good harmony with tannins. Elegant finish.*	**£5.30**	MWW CAM VIL	(B)
CASA LA JOYA CABERNET SAUVIGNON 1998, VIÑAS BISQUERTT Rapel Region	*Leafy fresh blackcurrant nose, ripe fruit with great integration of oak and tannins, delightful finish.*	**£5.50**	NYW CTC	(S)
CASAS DEL BOSQUE CABERNET SAUVIGNON 1999, CASAS DEL BOSQUE Rapel Region	*Very deep rich nose, clean minty palate with lots of fruit, warm well balanced structure.*	**£5.50**	THI	(B)
LAS CASAS DEL TOQUI CABERNET SAUVIGNON RESERVE 1998, LAS CASAS DEL TOQUI Rapel Region	*Pleasant cassis nose, well balanced blackcurrants in smooth palate, extended firm tannic finish.*	**£5.70**	CPR DBY NRW PBA	(B)
TRIO CABERNET 1998, CONCHA Y TORO Maipo Region	*Extracts of savoury red fruit, lovely clean chewy mouthfeel and firm tannins, beautiful acidity.*	**£5.80**	CWA DBY FQU	(S)

CABERNET • CHILE • SOUTH AMERICA

ERRÁZURIZ CABERNET SAUVIGNON 1999, ERRÁZURIZ ESTATES Aconcagua	*Wild red fruit nose, pepper hints and strawberries on the palate with succulent sweet medium finish.*	£5.90	Widely Available	(S)
LA RONCIERE RESERVE CABERNET SAUVIGNON 1999, LA RONCIERE Central Valley	*Leafy nose, very delicate woody fruit with high tannins and good acidity, plummy finish.*	£5.90	QWW	(S)
CONO SUR RESERVE CABERNET SAUVIGNON 1998, VIÑA CONO SUR Rapel Valley	*Lovely oak balancing full spicy red fruit on mid palate with medium acidity and gorgeous tannins.*	£6.00	ODD	(G)
BODEGA DE LA FAMILIA 1997, UNDURRAGA Rapel Region	*Pepper and spice and all things nice on this wine with plentiful blackcurrant fruit and finesse.*	£6.00	PLB	(S)
CASA SILVA CABERNET SAUVIGNON 1998, VIÑA CASA SILVA Rapel Region	*Closed leather, blackberry and damson aroma, lovely balance of ripe fruit and trace of sweetness.*	£6.00	DIC	(B)
CONO SUR RESERVE CABERNET SAUVIGNON 1999, VIÑA CONO SUR Rapel Valley	*Cedary blackberry nose with liquorice cherry jam balancing well with acid and tannins. Generous wine.*	£6.00	ODD WTS	(B)
WHITE LABEL CABERNET SAUVIGNON 1998, VIÑA CASABLANCA Rapel Region	*Seductive eucalyptus nose, warm red fruits on the palate with great oak and tannins. Excellent length.*	£6.10	Widely Available	(S)
CASTILLO DE MOLINA RESERVA CABERNET SAUVIGNON 1998, VIÑA SAN PEDRO Maule Region	*Blackberry leafy leather aroma, ripe fruit palate with well balanced sweetness and acidity and firm tannins.*	£6.20	SAF JMC	(B)

LUIS FELIPE EDWARDS CABERNET SAUVIGNON RESERVA 1997, LUIS FELIPE EDWARDS Rapel Region	*Huge mouth watering jammy nose, big tannins and sweet fruit on the palate, pleasant lingering finish.*	£6.30	MWW TOS CAM QWW VIL	(S)
LA PALMERÍA CABERNET SAUVIGNON RESERVE 1999, VIÑA LA ROSA Rapel Region	*Dark and young with baked fruitpie nose, good tannic structure with enduring acidity.*	£6.30	ODD WCR	(B)
VIÑA ALAMOSA CABERNET SAUVIGNON RESERVE 1998, VIÑA DE LAROSE Rapel Region	*Clear bright, intense nose, soft fruity palate with a good support of oak and acidity.*	£6.50	GRT	(B)
MONTGRAS CARMENERE RESERVA 1998, MONTGRAS Colchagua Valley	*Velvety fruit entrance declaring rich luscious bramble and red berry notes, firm but fair tannins.*	£6.60	JSM WTS DBY HVW	(B)
VALDIVIESO RESERVE CABERNET SAUVIGNON 1998, VALDIVIESO Maule Region	*Inviting spicy nose with minty new oak, ripe subtle tannin, lots of soft spicy black fruit.*	£7.10	JSM BWL DBY FQU NYW	(G)
CALITERRA CABERNET SAUVIGNON RESERVA 1997, CALITERRA Maipo Valley	*Smooth peppery nose, chocolate, plums and pepper in smooth ripe palate, extended pleasant finish.*	£7.10	FQU JMC DIC FEN	(S)
CALITERRA CABERNET SAUVIGNON RESERVA 1998, CALITERRA Maipo Valley	*Deep dark ruby, rich, ripe fruit, stewed plum and chocolate on the palate, balanced acidity.*	£7.30	MAD FQU	(B)
DALLAS CONTE CABERNET SAUVIGNON 1998, MILDARA BLASS & VIÑA SANTA CAROLINA Rapel Region	*Lifted rich cassis nose, full, complex palate of ripe blackcurrants finishing with persistent fruit flavour.*	£7.50	ODD WFB	(G)

CASA SILVA CABERNET RESERVA 1997, VIÑA CASA SILVA Rapel Region	*Blackberry violet aroma, full bodied neat balance, trace of ripe fruit with very good tannic presence.*	£7.50	DIC	(B)
DE GRAS CABERNET SAUVIGNON RESERVA 1998, DE GRAS Rapel Region	*Complex cherry nose leads to a palate of fresh blackcurrants, oak and cherries with balanced tannic integration.*	£7.50	DBY NYW JNW HVW GRO CTC	(B)
CASA LA JOYA GRAN RESERVA CABERNET SAUVIGNON 1998, VIÑAS BISQUERTT Rapel Region	*Fresh cassis nose leads to amazing fresh blackcurrant flavours, beautiful lengthy finish with gentle acidity.*	£7.70	MCT NYW CTC	(G)
PORTA RESERVE CABERNET 1999, VIÑA PORTA Aconcagua	*Cassis fruit with touch of herbs on nose, blackberries and good tannin on the palate.*	£7.90	BBO RAV HVW	(B)
CABO DE HORNOS CABERNET SAUVIGNON 1997, VIÑA SAN PEDRO Maule Region	*Attractive complex aroma, damsons, dark chocolate and green peppers on palate, all in gorgeous balance.*	£8.50	JSM	(G)
ERRÁZURIZ CABERNET SAUVIGNON RESERVA 1997, ERRÁZURIZ ESTATES Aconcagua	*Smooth attractive minty fruit nose, soft savoury juicy fruit palate with some pepper, lingering fruity finish.*	£8.70	Widely Available	(S)
PORTA SELECT RESERVE CABERNET 1998, VIÑA PORTA Aconcagua	*Massive attractive palate of round ripe tannin and fruits, delightful concentrated richness with long finish.*	£9.00	ODD	(G)
CALITERRA ARBOLEDA CABERNET SAUVIGNON 1998, CALITERRA Central Valley	*Light toast on blackcurrant leafy nose, simple sweet black fruit palate. Very easy to drink.*	£9.00	HMA	(B)

SOUTH AMERICA • CHILE • CABERNET

SANTA CAROLINA BARRICA SELECTION CABERNET 1998, VIÑA SANTA CAROLINA Maipo Region	*Dark blackcurrant nose, loaded with fruits of the forest and a long drying finish.*	£9.00	THW	**B**
CONO SUR 20 BARREL CABERNET SAUVIGNON 1998, VIÑA CONO SUR Rapel Valley	*Complex aromas of cherry wood, juicy black cherries bursting on the palate with some toastiness.*	£10.30	ODD WSO	**S**
CASA LAPOSTOLLE CABERNET SAUVIGNON CUVÉE ALEXANDRE 1998, CASA LAPOSTOLLE Rapel Region	*Herbaceous brambly fruit aromas lead to a palate of rich crushed blackcurrants with lots of depth and tannins.*	£11.40	Widely Available	**S**
CARMEN WINE MAKER'S RESERVE RED 1997, CARMEN VINEYARDS Maipo Region	*Green Spanish olive and cedar nose, lovely fruity flavours, fine dry tannins and a long tail.*	£13.00	CTC	**S**
GRAN ARAUCANO 1998, J&F LURTON Rapel Region	*Juicy jammy red fruits with hints of cigar box integrating with fine tannins and a savoury tail.*	£13.00	J&F	**B**
HOUSE OF MORANDÉ CABERNET SAUVIGNON 1997, VIÑA MORANDÉ Maipo Region	*Hints of smokiness, lovely strawberry and raspberry palate with firm tannins and a medium finish.*	£13.00	THI	**B**
ERRÁZURIZ DON MAXIMIANO FOUNDERS RESERVE 1997, ERRÁZURIZ ESTATES Aconcagua	*Ripe cassis aromas with rich spicy plums balancing with soft oak, a mature stylish wine.*	£16.70	TOS QWW FQU JMC DIC POR	**B**
ERRÁZURIZ DON MAXIMIANO FOUNDERS RESERVE 1998, ERRÁZURIZ ESTATES Aconcagua	*Herbaceous gamey nose leading to a well structured palate full of fine tannins and intense fruit.*	£18.20	MAD DBY FQU DIC POR	**G**

DE MARTINO RESERVA DE FAMILIA CABERNET SAUVIGNON 1997, DE MARTINO Maipo Region	*Herbaceous notes with bramble fruit coulis, hints of gamey flavours on fine tannins and good texture.*	£18.60	BLS ASH	(B)
MONTES ALPHA M 1997, MONTES Rapel Region	*Warm spicy hotcross bun aroma balancing graceful tannins and acid right to the finish. Magnificent wine.*	£28.40	Widely Available	(G)

CHILE • MERLOT

CASA DONOSO MERLOT 1999, AGRÍCOLA SALVE Maule Region	*Balanced juicy fruit on the forefront, stewed fruit aromas with dry gripping tannins.*	£5.00	UNS	(B)
CASA LA JOYA SELECTION MERLOT 1998, VIÑAS BISQUERTT Rapel Region	*Eucalyptus on the nose with good blackberry fruits on the finish, supported by firm tannins.*	£5.50	CTC	(B)
DUETO MERLOT 1999, VIÑA MORANDÉ Aconcagua	*Rich minty and ripe cassis nose, young violets and cracked pepper on the palate, powerful finish.*	£5.50	THI	(B)
PALO ALTO MERLOT 1998, AGUIRRE Limari Valley	*Concentrated decadent fruit driven palate, with body and tannins holding up to the end.*	£5.60	AVB QWW CEB TMW CTC	(B)
DE GRAS MERLOT 1999, DE GRAS Rapel Region	*Mint leaves and lush fruit preserve with sweet berries, well structured base of fine tannins.*	£5.70	V&C NYW JNW GRO CTC	(B)

SOUTH AMERICA • CHILE • MERLOT

VIÑA GRACIA MERLOT VARIETAL CURIOSO 1999, VIÑA GRACIA DE CHILE Maipo Region	*Sweet juicy ripe fruit and tobacco, good length and a nice touch of tannin.*	**£5.70**	WBR POR	(B)
TRIO MERLOT 1999, CONCHA Y TORO Rapel Region	*Raspberry coulis, rich and intense with bramble fruit on the long lingering palate.*	**£5.80**	DBY FQU	(S)
VIÑA CASA SILVA MERLOT 1999, VIÑA CASA SILVA Rapel Region	*Confidence and power exude from this rich fruit giving wine, complex and long dry finish.*	**£6.00**	DIC	(G)
SANTA INÉS MERLOT RESERVE 1999, SANTA INÉS Maipo Region	*Complex fruit characters on the elegantly oaked palate, rich berry fruit and a lasting finish.*	**£6.00**	FQU	(S)
PALO ALTO RESERVADO MERLOT 1998, AGUIRRE Limari Valley	*Subtle nose, with rich complex palate and smooth pleasurable mouthfeel, combining well on the finish.*	**£6.00**	CTC	(B)
SANTA CAROLINA MERLOT RESERVA 1998, VIÑA SANTA CAROLINA Rapel Region	*Concentrated red berry nose with soft cinnamon peppery palate with good tannins and long tail.*	**£6.00**	THW	(B)
CASAS DEL BOSQUE MERLOT 1999, CASAS DEL BOSQUE Aconcagua	*Cassis soaked icecream on the nose, well balanced with finesse and a lengthy finish.*	**£6.20**	THI WCR	(B)
CONO SUR MERLOT RESERVE 1999, VIÑA CONO SUR Rapel Valley	*Blackcurrant fruit and leafy complexity come from this warm fruit based delight with lasting finish.*	**£6.30**	ODD SAF	(S)

VIÑA LA ROSA LA PALMERÍA MERLOT RESERVE 1999, VIÑA LA ROSA Rapel Region	*Gamey raspberry nose, lots of velvety mocha cherries, finishes with green pepper and finesse.*	£6.70	ODD DIC	B
VERAMONTE MERLOT 1997, VERAMONTE Maipo Region	*Jammy floral nose with oaky cassis palate, tannins are well mannered with stylish class.*	£7.00	FQU	S
ARESTI RESERVE MERLOT 1999, ARESTI Central Valley	*Good fruity nose, intense berries with excellent balance and lingering length of good standing.*	£7.00	EUW	B
CALITERRA MERLOT RESERVA 1998, CALITERRA Central Valley	*Dense leafy cassis nose with soft cherry and plum fruit, lovely oakiness finishing with seamless length.*	£7.40	MAD DIC	S
CASA LAPOSTOLLE MERLOT 1998, CASA LAPOSTOLLE Maule Region	*Classy style of rich juicy blackberries with spicy hint, lovely silky tannins and beautiful length.*	£7.70	Widely Available	B
DE GRAS MERLOT RESERVA 1998, DE GRAS Rapel Region	*A powerful and individual wine, with luscious black fruit and mint on the endless finish.*	£7.80	V&C DBY NYW JNW HVW GRO CTC	B
CARMEN MERLOT RESERVE 1998, CARMEN VINEYARDS Maipo Region	*Smokey red fruit with slight herbaceous aromas, gentle ripe blackcurrant flavours and smooth tannins.*	£7.90	ODD WSO HST WCR HVW WRW CTC	G
UNDURRAGA MERLOT RESERVA 1999, UNDURRAGA Central Valley	*Bramble and spice nose with rich blackcurrant fruit, chocolatey flavours, well balanced young wine.*	£7.90	PLB	B

SOUTH AMERICA • CHILE • MERLOT

SINGLE VINEYARD RESERVE MERLOT 1998, VALDIVIESO Maule Region	*Rich, ripe palate with fresh cherries and liquorice on the finish, firm tannin structure.*	**£8.50**	MWW SAF NYW	**S**
CONO SUR 20 BARREL MERLOT 1999, VIÑA CONO SUR Rapel Valley	*An elegant and rich full bodied style with obvious berry fruit flavours and complex tannins.*	**£10.00**	ODD	**B**
PORTA RESERVE MERLOT 1999, VIÑA PORTA Aconcagua	*Huge sweet ripe black-fruits, and cassis on a peppery style palate finishing with smooth tannins.*	**£10.00**	BBO	**B**
NINQUEN 1997, MONTGRAS Rapel Region	*Perfumed liquorice fruit aromas with sweet vanilla and ripe plums, gripping tannins, a well balanced wine.*	**£11.40**	V&C NYW VIL HVW CTC	**S**
MONTEMAR MERLOT 1999, ARESTI Central Valley	*Plum pudding to start, some interesting earthiness leads to a fruit driven palate.*	**£13.00**	TOS	**B**
CASA LAPOSTOLLE MERLOT CUVÉE ALEXANDRE 1998, CASA LAPOSTOLLE Rapel Region	*Hot plum spicy aroma with juicy young berries and hints of cinnamon with a silky tail.*	**£13.10**	Widely Available	**B**

CHILE • RED • OTHER

VIÑA MORANDÉ SYRAH 1999, VIÑA MORANDÉ Maipo Region	*Vanilla nose with maturing fruit flavours cascading onto a bed of fine grained tannins.*	**£4.50**	SAF	**B**

OTHER • RED • CHILE • SOUTH AMERICA

35 SUR SAUVIGNON BLANC 2000, VIÑA SAN PEDRO Maule Region	*Rich fruits and herbal nose leads to delicious gooseberries on the palate with great crisp acidity.*	£4.90	JSM SAF JMC	(B)
VALDIVIESO CARIGNAN 1999, VALDIVIESO Maule Region	*Restrained cherry nose combined with ripe lush blackcurrant palate and balanced fruit, tannins and acid.*	£5.00	TOS	(S)
TERRARUM CARMANERE 1999, VIÑA MORANDÉ Maipo Region	*Tobacco and red fruit on nose with big lush berry and plum fruit palate with sharp minty finish.*	£5.00	THI	(B)
TERRAMATER ZINFANDEL SYRAH 1999, TERRAMATER Maipo Region	*Inky black colour, bramble fruit and spice married to give a successful sweet lingering finish.*	£5.20	JSM SAF HVW	(S)
CALITERRA SYRAH 1999, CALITERRA Rapel Region	*Inky, elderberry and savoury aromas lead to tempting ripe, confected berry fruit flavours.*	£5.50	TOS	(S)
JOSÉ CANEPA ZINFANDEL 1999, JOSÉ CANEPA Maipo Region	*Plum and black cherry on the nose, spicy full bodied complex fruit on the palate.*	£5.60	TOS TRO	(B)
CASABLANCA WHITE LABEL MALBEC 1999, VIÑA CASABLANCA Rapel Region	*Sweet berry fruit nose with pleasant plums and berry flavours with smooth tannins and clean finish.*	£6.00	MAD BLU NYW JNW GRO BOO	(B)
LAURA HARTWIG CARMENÈRE 1999, SANTA LAURA Colchagua Valley	*Wonderful full red berry nose, damson and cherry flavours with firm tannins and good tail.*	£6.00	PLB	(B)

SOUTH AMERICA • CHILE • RED • OTHER

Luis Felipe Edwards Old Vine Carmenère 1999, Luis Felipe Edwards Rapel Region	*Vanilla nose with minty overtones leading to chocolate, lush damsons and plums, good weight.*	£6.30	CAM VIL	**B**
Quatro 1999, MontGras Rapel Region	*Biscuity nose, cedar and berries on the palate, well balanced, rich fruits in long finish.*	£6.60	TOS WCR CTC	**B**
MontGras Malbec Reserva 1999, MontGras Rapel Region	*Bramble fruit nose with jammy damsons and wild strawberries with good acidity and backbone.*	£6.80	NYW CTC	**B**
MontGras Zinfandel Single Vineyard 1999, MontGras Rapel Region	*Succulent ripe bramble fruits, offering excellent structure and length, a pleasure and delight to savour.*	£7.00	JSM	**S**
MontGras Carmenère Reserva Montgras 1999, MontGras Rapel Region	*Red fruit nose with warm fruit flavours with lovely acidity and full tannins, spicy on finish.*	£7.00	JSM HVW CTC	**B**
Caliterra Arboleda Syrah 1999, Caliterra Central Valley	*Pleasant light and spicy nose that continues onto the palate with some chewy fruit character.*	£7.20	HMA TOS	**S**
Las Lomas Cot Rouge Reserva 1998, CAV Cauquenes Maule Region	*Attractive spicy nose with rich plum and berry flavours with oak notes on a warm finish.*	£7.30	G2W	**S**
De Gras Carmenère Reserva De Gras 1999, De Gras Rapel Region	*Herbaceous and perfumed nose leading to rich plum fruit and chocolate flavours with a elegant backbone.*	£7.40	V&C DBY NYW HVW CTC	**B**

CARMEN SYRAH RESERVE 1997, CARMEN VINEYARDS Maipo Region	*Well made and balanced wine with attractive oaky nose, subtle fruit and balanced acidity.*	**£8.10**	DBY HST CTC	**G**
CARMEN RESERVE PINOT NOIR 1998, CARMEN VINEYARDS Maule Region	*Rich, almost jammy nose and deep blackcurrant fruit palate flow onto a long, persistent peppery finish.*	**£8.10**	ODD TNI CTC	**S**
SINGLE VINEYARD RESERVE CABERNET FRANC 1998, VALDIVIESO Maule Region	*Lovely deep colour, green and earthy attractive aromas, quite ripe with good acidity. Nice oaky finish.*	**£9.00**	MWW BWL SAF NYW	**S**
SINGLE VINEYARD RESERVE MALBEC 1998, VALDIVIESO Maule Region	*Brambly nose with ripe juicy plums and cassis fruit flavours leading to a dry finish.*	**£9.00**	BWL NYW	**S**
CALITERRA ARBOLEDA CARMENÈRE 1999, CALITERRA Central Valley	*Subtle oak vegetal nose leading to black plummy fruit and chocolate flavours. Well balanced, good backbone.*	**£9.00**	HMA	**B**
VALDIVIESO RESERVE MALBEC 1996, VALDIVIESO Maule Region	*Rich jammy vegetal nose with complex gamey plum fruit flavours, a lovely well made wine.*	**£9.20**	JSM SAF TOS	**S**
VALDIVIESO RESERVE MALBEC 1998, VALDIVIESO Maule Region	*Sweet vanilla nose with spicy red fruit blending with fine tannins and good acidity.*	**£9.30**	SAF DBY	**B**
MONTES ALPHA SYRAH 1999, MONTES Maule Region	*Grilled bacon nose, slightly hidden fruit but showing some underlying quality that will develop in time.*	**£9.60**	QRW HDS AMW POR	**B**

SOUTH AMERICA • CHILE • RED • OTHER

ERRÁZURIZ PINOT NOIR RESERVA 1999, ERRÁZURIZ ESTATES Aconcagua	*Subtle, floral fruit aromas yield to a nice jammy fruit and earthy palate. Spicy, cherry finish.*	£9.80	ODD MAD DBY FEN	(S)
MONTGRAS CARMENERE RESERVA SINGLE VINEYARD 1999, MONTGRAS Rapel Region	*Confected sweet fruit nose with soft ripe plum fruit with minty background on full rounded palate.*	£9.90	ENO	(B)
ERRÁZURIZ SANGIOVESE RESERVA 1998, ERRÁZURIZ ESTATES Aconcagua	*Very herbal, minty aromatic nose, soft ripe balanced fruit, good rich morello cherry flavours.*	£10.00	MAD DBY	(S)
ERRÁZURIZ SANGIOVESE RESERVA 1999, ERRÁZURIZ ESTATES Aconcagua	*Youthful slightly bitter cherry aromas, clean light harmonious fruit on the palate and a dry finish.*	£10.00	MAD	(S)
SANTA RITA TRIPLE C 1997, SANTA RITA Maipo Region	*Stunningly fresh and fruity wine, with great fruit body and finesse, showing warm climate character.*	£11.00	MWW NYW	(G)
VERAMONTE PRIMUS 1998, VERAMONTE Aconcagua	*Herbal minty aromas with soft juicy cassis and damson palate with hints of oak and clean finish.*	£11.00	SKW BEL	(S)
ERRÁZURIZ SYRAH RESERVA 1998, ERRÁZURIZ ESTATES Aconcagua	*Good nutty nose, with lots of pepper, spice and red berries on a well structured finish.*	£11.80	MAD TOS SAF DIC POR	(B)
CABALLO LOCO NO 4 NV, VALDIVIESO Maule Region	*Rich cassis and vanilla nose with a compote of strawberries and red berries completed with a good length.*	£13.70	MWW DBY CPW FQU NYW HST	(S)

CHILE • WHITE

CO-OP LONG SLIM CHARDONNAY SEMILLON 1999, R&R WINES Central Valley	*Good aromatic ripe fruit continues on the palate, well harmonised structure with very nice acidity.*	£3.80	CWS	Ⓑ
CARTA VIEJA SAUVIGNON BLANC 1999, CARTA VIEJA Maule Region	*Smokey green beans on the nose, fine balance of sweet apples and acidity on the palate.*	£4.10	ODD MHV	Ⓑ
MISTY PEAK LIMARI VALLEY WHITE 1999, AGUIRRE Limari Valley	*Inviting floral nose, strong grapey palate with fresh acidity and appealing subtle lemony finish.*	£4.20	AVB WES CTC	Ⓑ
LA PALMERÍA SAUVIGNON BLANC 1999, VIÑA LA ROSA Rapel Region	*Bold asparagus and freshly cut grass abound, refreshing acidity and a lasting citrus finish.*	£4.50	HWL	Ⓑ
TIERRA ARENA SAUVIGNON BLANC 1999, AGUIRRE Limari Valley	*Green asparagus aroma with herbaceous undertones precedes a fresh fruity palate with refined acidity.*	£4.60	HOH AVB RNS QWW WES CTC	Ⓑ
CALITERRA SAUVIGNON BLANC 1999, CALITERRA Central Valley	*Clean, faintly herbaceous, oaky aromas offering a soft palate of light acidity and lingering citrus flavour.*	£4.80	MAD DBY WBR JMC DIC FEN	Ⓑ
LA PALMERÍA CHARDONNAY 1999, VIÑA LA ROSA Rapel Region	*Light fruit nose with some pleasant ripe fruit delicious on palate, attractive distinguished structure.*	£4.80	ODD WCR DIC	Ⓑ

SOUTH AMERICA • CHILE • WHITE

Cono Sur Viognier 1999, Viña Cono Sur Rapel Valley	*Spicy honey aroma, a well structured blend of fruit and high acidity, a pleasure on the palate.*	**£5.00**	MWW ODD	(S)
San Pedro 35 Sur Chardonnay 1999, Viña San Pedro Maule Region	*Creamy bananas and pineapples well balanced with fresh acidity. Good weight of fruit on palate.*	**£5.00**	SAF JMC	(B)
Carta Vieja Reserve Chardonnay 1998, Carta Vieja Maule Region	*Hot summer citrus nose with pineapple and peaches lingering with satiny acid on the tail.*	**£5.10**	ODD MHV	(B)
Isla Negra Chardonnay 1999, Viña Cono Sur Rapel Valley	*Light lemony nose, great balance of sweet fruit and acidity, soft elegant style with huge mouthfeel.*	**£5.10**	ODD COM	(B)
Veramonte Sauvignon 1999, Veramonte Casablanca	*Upfront, grassy style, good rounded structure, limes and tropical fruit, nice bite and good length.*	**£5.20**	CTC	(B)
Varietal Reposado Chardonnay 1999, Viña Gracia de Chile Bío Bío	*Rich buttery ripe fruit nose, subtle exotic creamy fruit flavours with exquisite long finish.*	**£5.40**	WBR	(B)
Casas del Bosque Chardonnay 1999, Casas del Bosque Aconcagua	*Nice light peachy aromas, soft vanilla in tropical fruit palate, round structure, good acidity on finish.*	**£5.50**	THI	(S)
La Pintora Chardonnay 1999, Concha y Toro Central Valley	*Gentle vanilla in buttery nose, round structure and full bodied fruit palate, light fresh mouthfeel.*	**£5.50**	TAV	(S)

LAS LOMAS SAUVIGNON BLANC 1999, CAV CAUQUENES Maule Region	*Warm, spicy, pale fruit aromas follow through to a heady palate with a touch of grassiness.*	£5.50	G2W	**B**
TRIO CHARDONNAY 1999, CONCHA Y TORO Aconcagua	*Pleasant nose of ripe fruit balanced with very good acidity, very charming finish.*	£5.90	DBY FQU VIL	**B**
SANTA ISABEL SAUVIGNON BLANC 1999, VIÑA CASABLANCA Aconcagua	*Intense and creamy ripe tropical fruit nose, round fruit palate, fresh acidity and long finish.*	£6.40	ODD MAD JNW	**B**
CASTILLO DE MOLINA RESERVA CHARDONNAY 1999, VIÑA SAN PEDRO Maule Region	*Attractive tropical toasty oak and ripe fruit aroma, buttery creamy fruit palate, smooth acidity.*	£6.50	JMC	**B**
ERRÁZURIZ CHARDONNAY 1998, ERRÁZURIZ ESTATES Aconcagua	*Tropical flavours in round palate with smooth oak, pleasant lasting finish makes you want some more.*	£6.50	Widely Available	**B**
PORTA CHARDONNAY 1999, VIÑA PORTA Rapel Region	*Fresh tropical fruit salad nose, ripe fruit palate, honeyed finish, good weight and long.*	£6.50	ODD BBO RAV HVW	**B**
OAK FERMENTED CHARDONNAY 1999, VIÑA TARAPACÁ Maule Region	*Very pronounced peachy nose, good weight on the palate, nice oak integration, balanced long finish.*	£6.70	BDR	**B**
UNDURRAGA CHARDONNAY RESERVA 1999, UNDURRAGA Central Valley	*Smooth appley nose, pleasant pears and peas on the palate ending with lovely acidity and beautiful length.*	£7.00	PLB	**S**

Wine	Tasting Notes	Price	Stockists	
CALITERRA CHARDONNAY RESERVA 1998, CALITERRA Aconcagua	*Toasty vanilla nose with some fruit showing through, pleasant, complex structure with fresh fruit finish.*	£7.20	MAD FQU JMC DIC	S
CALITERRA CHARDONNAY RESERVA 1997, CALITERRA Aconcagua	*Very strong melon aromas, attractive palate with lots of ripe fruit and great acid balance. Refreshing.*	£7.20	MAD FQU JMC FEN	B
DE GRAS CHARDONNAY RESERVA 1999, DE GRAS Rapel Region	*Intense green apples and floral notes on the nose and palate with determined acidity and a pleasant finish.*	£7.40	V&C JNW CTC	B
CASA SILVA CHARDONNAY RESERVA 1999, VIÑA CASA SILVA Rapel Region	*Crisp apples and pears on the nose, sweet apples and citrus with a long finish.*	£7.50	DIC	B
CHÂTEAU LOS BOLDOS CHARDONNAY VIEILLES VIGNES 1999, CHÂTEAU LOS BOLDOS Rapel Region	*Light fruit nose followed by balanced acidity and pleasant mouthfeel with pineapple hints. Very slurpy.*	£7.50	HBJ	B
ERRÁZURIZ CHARDONNAY RESERVA 1998, ERRÁZURIZ ESTATES Aconcagua	*Creamy citrus nose, pineapple flavours with notes of grapefruit and soft oak on the palate.*	£8.20	MAD TOS DBY WCR MHV DIC	B
VILLARD ESTATE CHARDONNAY PREMIUM RESERVE 1998, VILLARD ESTATE Maipo Region	*Attractive broad fruit nose, well integrated ripe fruit on the palate, delicious finish and good length.*	£8.20	ODD PBA RNS WRK	B
SANTA ISABEL BARREL FERMENTED CHARDONNAY 1998, VIÑA CASABLANCA Aconcagua	*Smokey nose, hints of bananas and apples over fine, well integrated oak with a pleasant finish.*	£8.30	ODD MAD DBY WSO JNW GRO POR	S

ERRÁZURIZ CHARDONNAY RESERVA 1997, ERRÁZURIZ ESTATES Aconcagua	*Buttery lemon nose, gorgeous flavour of pineapple with grapefruit and oak and a buttery finish.*	**£8.30**	Widely Available	**S**
CARMEN NATIVA CHARDONNAY 1998, CARMEN VINEYARDS Maipo Region	*Full bodied, complex structure, lime and vanilla notes with tropical fruits and green apple flavour.*	**£8.40**	ODD WTS TNI HVW WRW CTC	**B**
SANTA CAROLINA BARRICA SELECTION CHARDONNAY 1999, VIÑA SANTA CAROLINA Maipo Region	*Lovely melon nose with hint of guavas in a full palate of fresh apples and apricot.*	**£9.00**	THW	**S**
ERRÁZURIZ WILD FERMENT CHARDONNAY 1998, ERRÁZURIZ ESTATES Aconcagua	*Fresh buttery nose, good hints of peaches and oak for a lovely mouthfeel, good length.*	**£9.60**	ODD BBR MAD DBY JMC DIC	**B**
MONTES ALPHA CHARDONNAY 1998, MONTES Maule Region	*Rich inviting gooseberry nose with pleasant combination of nuts, apples, peaches and pears on the finish.*	**£9.80**	Widely Available	**S**
CASA LAPOSTOLLE CHARDONNAY CUVÉE ALEXANDRE 1997, CASA LAPOSTOLLE Aconcagua	*Seductive vanilla nose, fresh citrus fruit ripeness on paate giving warm mouthfeel, and a clean, lively finish.*	**£10.60**	Widely Available	**S**

Pinpoint who sells the wine you wish to buy by turning to the stockist codes. If you know the name of the wine you want to buy, use the alphabetical index. If the price is your motivation, refer to the invaluable price guide index; red and white wines under £5, sparkling wines under £12 and champagne under £16. Happy hunting!

URUGUAY • RED

CATAMAYOR MERLOT TANNAT 1999, BODEGAS CASTILLO VIEJO San Jose	*Soft creamy red summer fruit pudding, gentle rounded tannins, with depth and structure.*	**£5.00**	FTH	B
CASA LUNTRO 1997, J&F LURTON Montevideo	*Mellow plum aroma with toasty ripe wild strawberries and black cherries. Enjoyable to the last drop.*	**£6.00**	J&F	B
PISANO RPF TANNAT 1999, PISANO Progreso	*Chocolate liquorice nose with blackcurrant and plum enveloped in firm tannins and lovely finish.*	**£7.70**	WTS BNK HDS AMW PFT	B

SOUTH AFRICA

The Rainbow Nation has progressed with innovation and opportunity changing the face of the countries wine industry. Although Pinotage put South Africa on the international map, a meze of varietals are now available in medal winning quality, with the noble grapes constantly increasing in value and interest. The regions cooled by the ocean breezes are competing successfully and producing fine Pinot Noir. This diverse country is proactively addressing the demand for red wines with investment and commitment in scrubbing out lesser whites and replanting on a massive scale.

SOUTH AFRICA • PINOTAGE

AFRICAN LEGEND PINOTAGE 1999, SONOP Western Cape	*Subtle fruit nose with spicy blackcurrants on the palate leading to a soft tannin tail.*	**£5.00**	TOS UNS	B
TESCO BEYERS TRUTER PINOTAGE 1999, BEYERSKLOOF Stellenbosch	*Deep intense colour on a balanced palate of soft fruits, nice and very enjoyable.*	**£5.00**	TOS	B
KANONKOP KADETTE 1996, KANONKOP ESTATE Stellenbosch	*Deep cherry purple colour with aromas of ripe plums on a soft balanced palate.*	**£6.00**	SAF	B
FAIRVIEW PINOTAGE 1999, CHARLES BACK WINES Coastal	*Excellent smokey, plum aroma with well poised acid and tannins on a long finish.*	**£6.60**	ADN JSM GRT	B
MARTHINUS PINOTAGE 1999, BOVLEI Wellington	*Cigar box and cedar wood on the nose with soft bananas and stewed fruit, finishing with good length.*	**£6.80**	BDR	S

DUMISANI RESERVE PINOTAGE 1998, WINECORP	*Sweet herbaceous nose blending with a ripe spicy fruit palate and a dry finish.*	£7.00	PLB	Ⓑ
CO-OP THREE WORLDS PINOTAGE 1999, FAIRVIEW Coastal	*Green herbaceous nose, lovely peppery spicy fruit with youthful lightness to end.*	£7.00	CWS	Ⓑ
CLOS MALVERNE PINOTAGE 1999, CLOS MALVERNE Stellenbosch	*Lifted plums with earthy aromas on a soft jammy palate and a refreshing tail.*	£7.20	Widely Available	Ⓑ
DELHEIM PINOTAGE 1998, DELHEIM ESTATES Stellenbosch	*A flattering nose of fruity plum with a well oaked palate and a fine conclusion.*	£7.50	JWW JSS	Ⓑ
KERSFONTEIN BUSH VINE PINOTAGE 1998, SONOP Coastal	*Oaky cedar nose with a cherry, raspberry palate full of pepper and spice. Good drinking.*	£7.50	BDR	Ⓑ
CLOS MALVERNE PINOTAGE RESERVE 1998, CLOS MALVERNE Stellenbosch	*Fresh mushrooms lead to a full bodied gamey mouthful of ripe cherries. Nice and naughty.*	£8.00	CPR DBY PBA BOO	Ⓑ
CLOS MALVERNE BASKET PRESSED PINOTAGE 1999, CLOS MALVERNE Stellenbosch	*Purple hues leading to a full bodied palate of cherries and vanilla with spicy oak notes.*	£8.10	Widely Available	Ⓢ
STELLENZICHT PINOTAGE 1998, STELLENZICHT Stellenbosch	*Freshly turned earth mingles with spicy oak, a balanced palate of cleansing acid finishes well.*	£8.20	ODD CTC	Ⓑ

KWV CATHEDRAL CELLAR PINOTAGE 1997, KWV Paarl	*Exotic fruit smells on a sweet spicy plum and berry palate with a dash of coffee.*	£8.60	SAF DBY JMC G&M	(S)
SPICE ROUTE PINOTAGE 1999, CHARLES BACK WINES Swartland	*Aromas of violets and cherries lead to a palate of sweet fruit with tannins and acid supporting.*	£8.60	JSM CWS UNS	(S)
OLD ROAD PINOTAGE 1998, GRAHAM BECK Franschhoek	*Aromas of roses and plum tasting fruit, the firm tannins finish with a lasting impression.*	£9.00	BWL NYW CTC	(S)
CHAPMANS CHANCE PINOTAGE 1999, FLAGSTONE WINERY Coastal	*Complex cherry nose with chocolate and plum fruit, lovely balanced tannins and acidity.*	£9.00	BDR	(B)
FAIRVIEW AMOS PINOTAGE 1998, CHARLES BACK WINES Coastal	*Dense smokey bacon and coffee leads to a jammy berry, plum palate with a luscious ending.*	£9.00	GRT	(B)
MÔRESON SOLEIL DU MATIN PINOTAGE 1998, MÔRESON SOLEIL DU MATIN Western Cape	*Light earthy aroma with a soft cherry palate ending with a hint of eucalyptus.*	£10.20	BNK BLS GRO	(S)
L'AVENIR PINOTAGE 1998, L'AVENIR Stellenbosch	*Attractive clean lifted fruits on a finely grained tannin palate with good length.*	£10.20	CPR DBY NYW PBA HDS	(B)
DOUGLAS GREEN PINOTAGE 1998, DOUGLAS GREEN BELLINGHAM Western Cape	*Gorgeous oak nose with a good depth of spicy fruit flavour and soft tannins.*	£10.50	EHL	(B)

SOUTH AFRICA • PINOTAGE

SPICE ROUTE FLAGSHIP PINOTAGE 1998, CHARLES BACK WINES Swartland	*Toffee, caramel nose with lush sweet fruit and chocolate combining with a good tannin backbone.*	£12.00	WSO NYW	(B)
GRANGEHURST PINOTAGE 1997, GRANGEHURST Stellenbosch	*Cherry nose with plums and clove palate showing nice balance with a firm finish.*	£12.50	BWL DBY NYW CTC	(B)
DELHEIM VERA CRUZ PINOTAGE 1998, DELHEIM ESTATES Stellenbosch	*Deep plum and spice nose, rich full flavour with touch of cherry oak on the palate.*	£15.00	JWW	(B)
HIDDEN VALLEY PINOTAGE 1997, HIDDEN VALLEY Stellenbosch	*Plum, prune nose, fruity palate with a dash of spice integrating with balanced tannins.*	£15.70	JSM BWL NYW	(G)

SOUTH AFRICA • RED • OTHER

CULLINIAN VIEW CINSAULT 2000, CULLINIAN VIEW	*Sweaty dark fruit nose with fleshy plums and spiciness with lovely tannins, good finish.*	£3.70	GSJ	(B)
SOMERFIELD SOUTH AFRICAN CINSAULT RUBY CABERNET 1999, LOUWSHOEK-VOORSORG Worcester	*Crisp young red fruit with lovely spiciness with a jammy nose and good acidity balance.*	£4.00	SMF	(B)
LANDSKROON CINSAULT SHIRAZ 1999, LANDSKROON ESTATE Paarl	*Sweet spicy oak nose with zesty plums and blackcurrant with balanced acidity and tannins.*	£4.30	SAF	(B)

KUMALA CINSAULT PINOTAGE 1999, SONOP Western Ridge	*Smokey intense red currant flavours with good acidity, elegant tannins and lovely finish.*	**£4.60**	TOS FQU SAF BTH	(B)
TESCO SOUTH AFRICAN SHIRAZ CABERNET 1998, DOUGLAS GREEN BELLINGHAM Western Cape	*Attractive young, sweet fruit and lifted nose, mellow fruit flavours, showing depth, poise, astonishing length.*	**£5.00**	TOS	(B)
NEDERBURG EDELROOD 1997, NEDERBURG Western Cape	*Delicious mellow plums on the nose, straightforward ripe fruit and lovely wood, flavourful dry finish.*	**£5.80**	CAX	(B)
APOSTLES FALLS CABERNET SAUVIGNON 1998, STELLENBOSCH VINEYARDS Stellenbosch	*Mature leafy nose, toasty oak in lots of ripe fruits on the palate, long rich finish.*	**£6.00**	TOS SAF	(S)
PORCUPINE RIDGE MERLOT 1999, BOEKENHOUTSKLOOF ESTATE Paarl	*Plum pudding with vanilla custard, the fruit still waiting to come to the full, but promising.*	**£6.00**	ORB	(S)
FAIRVIEW MALBEC 1999, CHARLES BACK WINES Coastal	*Deep leathery raspberry aroma, earthy blackcurrant and rosemary palate with a wonderful mouthfeel. Excellent wine.*	**£6.30**	ADN SAF	(S)
KWV MERLOT 1998, KWV Western Cape	*Chocolate covered morello cherries, rich and luscious, with warm palate and fine tannic structure.*	**£6.30**	GDS UNS DBY JMC G&M	(S)
ROBERTSON CABERNET SAUVIGNON 1999, ROBERTSON WINERY Robertson	*Smokey, delicious jammy nose, upfront and youthful palate with pleasant support of acidity, gripping finish.*	**£6.50**	ABY	(B)

FAIRVIEW SHIRAZ 1998, CHARLES BACK WINES Coastal	*Clean palate with very young firm tannins, nice plummy, bramble fruit flavours, fine balance.*	£6.60	ADN GRT THEUNS	**B**
FAIRVIEW ZINFANDEL CINSAULT 1999, CHARLES BACK WINES Coastal	*Minty nose, soft cassis and plum characters, quite sweet long finish with enjoyable acidity and tannins.*	£6.60	ADN ODD	**B**
FAIRVIEW SHIRAZ MOURVÈDRE 1998, CHARLES BACK WINES Coastal	*Intense fruit and spice flavour slightly hidden by the weight of very fine tannins, brooding wine.*	£7.00	ODD	**S**
FAIRVIEW MERLOT 1998, CHARLES BACK WINES Coastal	*Aromatic fragrance offering plum and berry flavours on stylish tannins with all round style.*	£7.00	GRT MWW UNS	**B**
GRAHAM BECK SHIRAZ 1998, GRAHAM BECK Franschhoek	*Nose displaying spicy fruit, fresh berries, red currants and sweet jam, with a palate consisting of blackberry and spice.*	£7.20	BWL NYW CTC	**S**
CLOS MALVERNE CABERNET PINOTAGE 1998, CLOS MALVERNE Stellenbosch	*Lovely weight and structure, some baked leafy, minty characters, jammy palate with ripe tannins.*	£7.50	JSM CPR WSO DBY PBA BOO	**B**
VILLIERA CRU MONRO 1997, VILLIERA WINE ESTATE Paarl	*Rich raspberry aromas, ripe and smooth black fruits giving an easy drinking style, excellent structure.*	£7.70	FQU	**B**
LE BONHEUR PRIMA MERLOT 1997, LE BONHEUR Stellenbosch	*Rich and elegant style, ripe fruit in multiple layers and a fine complexity on the finish.*	£7.80	CTC	**B**

OTHER • RED • SOUTH AFRICA

RUST EN VREDE MERLOT 1998, RUST EN VREDE ESTATE Stellenbosch	*Fragrant perfume nose with liquid chocolate covering crushed plum flavours with silky tannins and tail.*	**£7.80**	JLW DBY CFT COM	**B**
CATHEDRAL CELLAR STELLENBOSCH CABERNET SAUVIGNON 1997, KWV Stellenbosch	*Attractive toasty nose, dominance of pleasant tannins in a bed of ripe fruits, good drying finish.*	**£8.00**	JMC	**S**
SPICE ROUTE CABERNET MERLOT 1999, CHARLES BACK WINES Swartland	*Sweet, spicy fruit full of chocolate covered plums, youthful and adventurous to the end.*	**£8.00**	JSM TOS CWS UNS BTH	**B**
VILLIERA MERLOT 1998, VILLIERA WINE ESTATE Paarl	*Bold and supple, rich berry fruits explode from this, well made fruit driven wine.*	**£8.10**	WTS FQU	**S**
OVERGAAUW MERLOT 1997, OVERGAAUW ESTATE Stellenbosch	*Hints of freshly brewed coffee and rich cassis bring this lovely well balanced wine together.*	**£8.10**	RNS JSS AMW PIM	**B**
FAIRVIEW CYRIL BACK SHIRAZ 1998, CHARLES BACK Paarl	*Brambly black fruits with slight vanilla lift, fresh and clean palate, attractive berry fruit, quality tannins.*	**£8.50**	GRT WTS	**S**
KUMALA RESERVE MERLOT 1999, MEERLUST Stellenbosch	*Ripe, sun warmed fruit characters of raspberry and blackcurrant coulis, good lengthy finish.*	**£8.50**	WST	**S**
KAAPZICHT MERLOT 1998, KAAPZICHT Stellenbosch	*Spicy cedar aromas mingling with mulberry and wild strawberry coulis, enjoyable to the end.*	**£8.60**	AMW	**B**

SOUTH AFRICA • RED • OTHER

SPICE ROUTE SHIRAZ 1999, CHARLES BACK WINES Swartland	*Earthy, animal tones on the nose, brooding palate, brilliant mouthfeel, very deep style wine.*	£8.80	JSM UNS	S
JORDAN MERLOT 1998, JORDAN ESTATE Stellenbosch	*Sleek, rich plum palate, touches of cloves and blackfruit on the fine lengthy finish.*	£8.80	BLU CPW WCR HVW WRW	B
DIEU DONNE MERLOT 1998, DIEU DONNE Franschhoek	*Savoury cedar nose with soft supple plums and softening tannins with a velvety finish.*	£9.00	PAT	S
KUMALA CABERNET SAUVIGNON RESERVE 1999, MEERLUST Stellenbosch	*Attractive herbaceous rich fruit nose and palate, soft to start then strong tannins on the finish.*	£9.00	TOS	B
BOSCHENDAL MERLOT 1996, BOSCHENDAL Paarl	*Velvety plums with roasted coffee blending with silky tannins ,great backbone. What a pleasure.*	£9.40	OWC WRK WCS CTC	B
BOSCHENDAL SHIRAZ 1997, BOSCHENDAL Paarl	*Nose driven by berries, mint and pepper, full attractive wine with good weight on the palate.*	£9.60	NYW OWC WRK CTC	S
CONSTANTIA UITSIG MERLOT 1998, CONSTANTIA UITSIG Constantia	*Fragrant violet nose on a spicy plum palate with mouth coating tannins. Silky full body.*	£9.60	CPR NRW FQU DBY PBA BOO	B
STEENBERG MERLOT 1998, STEENBERG Constantia	*A velvet palate of fragrant minty chocolate with upfront fresh bursting summer fruits and sillky tannins.*	£9.60	WTS WRK COM	B

DE TRAFFORD CABERNET SAUVIGNON 1998, DE TRAFFORD Stellenbosch	*Cloves and cinnamon on the nose, with rich blackcurrant palate and smooth fine finish.*	£9.70	BWL	(B)
DE TRAFFORD MERLOT 1998, DE TRAFFORD Stellenbosch	*Vibrant, buttery chocolate nose with soft supple plums and berries, leads to a lovely finish.*	£9.70	BWL	(B)
FAIRVIEW ESTATE SWEET RED SHIRAZ 1998, CHARLES BACK WINES Paarl	*A harmonious wine with sweetish ripe tannins, good concentrated berry fruit, long and complex.*	£9.70	GRT	(B)
SAXENBERG PRIVATE COLLECTION SHIRAZ 1997, SAXENBERG Stellenbosch	*Attractive berry and pepper nose, good ripe fruit and savoury elements, sustained and complex finish.*	£9.70	ODD BBR DBY	(B)
KLEIN CONSTANTIA CABERNET SAUVIGNON RESERVE 1997, KLEIN CONSTANTIA Constantia	*Very classy cranberry aromas, minty with inky complexity, has a super tannic grip.*	£10.00	MZC	(B)
THE RIDGE SHIRAZ 1998, GRAHAM BECK Robertson	*Mocha oak edge and vibrant nose of spicy fruit, with appealing sweet black fruit flavour.*	£10.70	BWL NYW CTC	(S)
VERDUN CABERNET SAUVIGNON 1997, VERDUN WINE ESTATE Stellenbosch	*Wonderful cedar and mixed spice nose, ripe plums and berry concentration on the palate, lovely balance.*	£11.20	BEL BOO	(B)
SPICE ROUTE FLAGSHIP SHIRAZ 1998, CHARLES BACK WINES Swartland	*Quality fruit, dense aromas and flavours of plums, coffee and vanilla, palate has long drying tannins.*	£11.70	WSO	(S)

SOUTH AFRICA • RED • OTHER•

PLAISIR DE MERLE CABERNET SAUVIGNON 1997, PLAISIR DE MERLE Western Cape	*Subtle oak and berry nose with boiled sweet and black fruit palate ending with a structured backbone.*	£11.70	SAF CVR UBC	**B**
WHALEHAVEN PINOT NOIR 1997, WHALEHAVEN WINES Walker Bay	*Strong vegetal aromas, slightly subtle middle palate, good tannin structure that flows into a long finish.*	£12.00	DBY AMW POR BOO	**B**
JORDAN COBBLERS HILL MERLOT 1997, JORDAN ESTATE Stellenbosch	*Macerated dark plums and cherries with chocolate and clove hints, lovely texture and structure.*	£12.20	GHL	**B**
GALPIN PEAK PINOT NOIR Tête de Cuvée 1997, BOUCHARD FINLAYSON Hermanus	*Concentrated red fruit and new oak aromas, very approachable palate revealing silky tannins and beautifully balanced finish.*	£13.00	BWL	**G** TROPHY WINE
GRANGEHURST CABERNET MERLOT 1997, GRANGEHURST Stellenbosch	*Mulberries and quiet coffee aromas mingling with dusty plums, balanced with textured tannins and acid.*	£13.20	BWL DBY CTC	**B**
FAIRVIEW CYRIL BACK ZINFANDEL 1997, CHARLES BACK WINES Coastal	*A monumental compote of summer fruit flavours, complex and dense structure with supple tannins.*	£13.50	ODF ODD	**G**
VEENWOUDEN MERLOT 1997, VEENWOUDEN Paarl	*Plump and rich on the palate, great structure and style, warm berry fruits abound on the finish.*	£14.30	QWW NYW HDS COM	**B**
VERDUN THERESA 1997, VERDUN WINE ESTATE Stellenbosch	*Hints of green pepper and roasted coffee mingling with mulberries and lovely oak tail. Superb.*	£14.90	AMW BEL BOO	**S**

MEERLUST RUBICON 1995, MEERLUST Stellenbosch	*Big currant nose with brambles and currants resounding on the palate with hints of oak.*	**£15.30**	BDR QRW DBY WBR GHC POR	(B)
RUST EN VREDE ESTATE WINE 1996, RUST EN VREDE ESTATE Stellenbosch	*Exotic aromas of black cherries and spice blending with gorgeous blackcurrants and cedar wood.*	**£15.90**	JLW	(S)
HAMILTON RUSSELL PINOT NOIR 1998, HAMILTON RUSSELL Walker Bay	*Toasty oak aromas yield to nice fruit tannin offering good structure and a full sophosticated finish.*	**£16.00**	Widely Available	(S)
MORGENHOF CABERNET SAUVIGNON RESERVE 1998, MORGENHOF ESTATE Stellenbosch	*Velvety mocha with a mineral core, rich minty sweet nose and fruit laden fleshy finish.*	**£17.00**	MKV	(S)

SOUTH AFRICA • SPARKLING

GRAHAM BECK BLANC DE BLANCS 1993, GRAHAM BECK Robertson	*Very pleasant nutty characters in fruity nose leads to excellent balanced palate of ripe fruit and acidity.*	**£9.20**	BWL NYW	(S)

SOUTH AFRICA • WHITE

MILLENNIUM EARLY RELEASE CHENIN BLANC 2000, KLEIN ALPHEN Western Cape	*The freshening winds of the Cape have helped to produce this clean young well balanced wine.*	**£3.50**	WST	(B)

SOUTH AFRICA • WHITE

Wine	Description	Price	Codes	
STOWELLS OF CHELSEA CHENIN BLANC NV, MATTHEW CLARK Coastal	*Good tropical fruits, still a traditional style of medium sweet finish of good length.*	£4.00	CWS WCR	(B)
GOEDVERWACHT ESTATE COLOMBARD 2000, GOEDVERWACHT ESTATE Robertson	*Strong passion fruit characters on the nose, very good acidity balanced with full bodied tropical palate.*	£5.00	SAF	(B)
PACIFIC WINES CAPE WHITE 1999, PACIFIC WINES Stellenbosch	*Subtle fruit nose, offering much more on the palate of apples and grapefruit, holds a dry finish.*	£5.00	UNS	(B)
VILLIERA GEWÜRZTRAMINER 1999, VILLIERA WINE ESTATE Paarl	*Very broad on both the nose and palate, draws together well with tropical fruits and spice.*	£5.50	WST	(B)
BON COURAGE CHARDONNAY PRESTIGE CUVÉE 1999, BON COURAGE ESTATE Robertson	*Rich buttery fruit nose, ripe pineapple on the palate, generous rich finish with wonderful acidity.*	£6.40	WBR	(B)
DE WETSHOT LESCA CHARDONNAY 1999, DE WETSHOT ESTATE Robertson	*Fresh grass, lime and lemon aromas, well balanced acidity and sweetness on the palate, long fruity finish.*	£6.50	JSM MWW BLS VIL	(B)
GRAHAM BECK CHARDONNAY 1999, GRAHAM BECK Robertson	*Amazing, captivating juicy fruit nose followed by great acidity in complex full bodied ripe fruit flavours.*	£6.60	BWL NYW CTC	(S)
BOSCHENDAL SAUVIGNON BLANC 1999, BOSCHENDAL Paarl	*Almost overpowering with its classic varietal aromas. Palate offers crisp lemon acidity and good rounded fruit balance.*	£7.00	QRW BBO WRK WCS CTC	(B)

GRANDE CUVÉE SAUVIGNON BLANC 1998, BOSCHENDAL Paarl	*A sweet nose with lean but ripe fruit palate, zippy citrus acidity and good length.*	£7.50	TOS BBO WCS CTC	B
LOUISVALE CHARDONNAY 1998, LOUISVALE WINES Stellenbosch	*Ripe grapefruit aromas, succulent cantaloupe melons with well integrated oak on the palate, big mouthfeel.*	£7.50	JWW	B
WARWICK ESTATE CHARDONNAY 1999, WARWICK ESTATE Stellenbosch	*Peaches and citrus fruits in a well balanced wine with good length and levelled acidity.*	£7.50	WTS CAM DBY NYW	B
VILLIERA CHARDONNAY 1999, VILLIERA WINE ESTATE Paarl	*Lemon butter aromas, touch of spice on the palate of fruit and minerals, an elegant finish.*	£7.70	FQU	S
GROOTE POST SAUVIGNON BLANC 1999, GROOTE POST Swartland	*Grassy aromas precede an upfront palate of peas and asparagus, good balancing acidity and persistent finish.*	£7.90	ESL	S
JORDAN BLANC FUME 1999, JORDAN ESTATE Stellenbosch	*Intense bell pepper nose with spicy citrus fruit character and vanilla in a stylish wine.*	£8.00	AUS	S
PAUL CLUVER SAUVIGNON BLANC 1999, PAUL CLUVER Elgin	*Lashings of grassy, gooseberry aromas, balanced palate of delicate pineapple and gooseberry, steely acidity and long finish.*	£8.00	VNF	S
NEDERBURG RESERVE CHARDONNAY 1999, NEDERBURG Western Cape	*Intense fruit and oak combination with a good touch of vanilla and an elegant finish.*	£8.00	CAX	B

SOUTH AFRICA • WHITE

FAIRVIEW VIOGNIER 1999, CHARLES BACK WINES Paarl	*Seductive floral nose with a lime and mango palate ending with balanced acidity and tannins.*	£8.20	ODF	**B**
GROOTE POST CHARDONNAY 1999, GROOTE POST Swartland	*Lovely inviting nose, hints of peaches well integrated with strong fresh acidity and vanilla flavours.*	£8.50	LOL	**S**
FAIRVIEW AKKERBOS CHARDONNAY 1999, CHARLES BACK WINES Coastal	*Light fruit aromas in a sweet buttery oak structured wine with notes of grapefruit.*	£8.50	ODD	**B**
JORDAN CHARDONNAY 1999, JORDAN Stellenbosch	*Lovely limes and melons on the nose, nutty creamy fruit palate with a mouth watering finish.*	£8.80	CPW UNS GHL WRW	**B**
JORDAN CHARDONNAY 1998, JORDAN Stellenbosch	*Elegant and graceful, citrus peel and hazelnut complexity, has subtle butterscotch on the finish.*	£8.90	Widely Available	**B**
BOSCHENDAL CHARDONNAY RESERVE 1998, BOSCHENDAL Paarl	*Subtle aromas of wood and pineapple followed by a rich round fruit palate with great length.*	£9.10	BBO NYW WCS CTC	**B**
PLAISIR DE MERLE CHARDONNAY 1999, PLAISIR DE MERLE Western Cape	*Interesting tropical nose, appealing well integrated ripe fruit and oak with smooth extended finish.*	£9.30	CVR	**S**
MISSION VALE CHARDONNAY 1998, BOUCHARD FINLAYSON Hermanus	*Layers of creaminess, tropical melon and peach flavours on this clean lingering finish.*	£9.50	CTC	**B**

FORT SIMON CHARDONNAY 1998, FORT SIMON Stellenbosch	*Buttery sweet aromas, nice attractive style with an oak touch and lots of ripe fruit flavours.*	£10.00	WCR	(S)
LINTON PARK CHARDONNAY 1998, LINTON PARK WINES Paarl	*Subtle fruit nose, well balanced and integrated acidity with dense citrus fruit on the palate.*	£10.30	BEL PFT	(B)
RUSTENBERG STELLENBOSCH CHARDONNAY 1999, RUSTENBERG Stellenbosch	*Charming tropical pear nose, well balanced nutty characters and acidity in a fruit full palate, great finish.*	£10.50	NYW HST FEN	(S)
STELLENZICHT SEMILLON RESERVE 1999, STELLENZICHT Stellenbosch	*Grassy aromatic nose with some developing complexity. Intense fruit, well balanced acidity, rich complex and oaky finish.*	£10.80	ODD AVB	(B)

SPAIN

S pain has provided us with a wide array of wine styles, from the traditional much loved Rioja's to the regions such as Aragon and Ribera del Duero, who are offering upfront fruit driven examples, made with New World winemaking techniques. Light and delicate wines such as Albariño have shown us a new wave in Spanish wine, such wines are in complete contrast to the rich reds found in Catalonia, full of tradition. Both approaches yield a diverse display of wines, reflecting the Spanish passion for the vine.

SPAIN • FORTIFIED

PORTMAN'S FINE RUBY, CDC WINES & SPIRITS	*Easter biscuit aroma, with a light palate of soft red fruits, easy and enjoyable.*	£3.50	DWI	(B)
FINEST AMONTILLADO, SÁNCHEZ ROMATE Jerez	*Warm roasted nuts showing good raisins with lovely freshness and a long finish.*	£4.40	TOS	(S)
MOSCATEL AÑEJO, DE MULLER	*Pale yellow colour, light fruit aromas lead to grapey very sweet flavour, lovely depth.*	£4.60	HST VIL	(B)
FINEST PALE AMONTILLADO, SÁNCHEZ ROMATE Jerez	*Raisins with honey and nuts flavour and aroma, very delightful savoury notes with generous length.*	£5.00	TOS	(S)
WAITROSE SOLERA JEREZANA AMONTILLADO SECCO, LUSTAU Jerez	*Nutty nose with full bodied dryness giving you a wonderful kickstart. Well structured with long finish.*	£5.50	WTS	(S)

WAITROSE SOLERA JEREZANA MANZANILLA, LUSTAU Jerez	*Pale gold hue with attractive nutty flor nose, a slight sweetness and a dry finish.*	**£5.50**	WTS	(B)
WAITROSE SOLERA JEREZANA DRY OLOROSO, LUSTAU Jerez	*Hot nutty toffee aromas with great red fruit and spiciness, ending shows dryness and good acidity.*	**£5.50**	WTS	(B)
WAITROSE SOLERA RICH CREAM, DIEGO ROMERO Jerez	*Warm nutty rich flavours with a bit of grip leading to a fresh tangy finish. Lovely structure.*	**£5.50**	WTS	(B)
REGENTE OLOROSSO SECCO, SÁNCHEZ ROMATE Jerez	*Lovely allspice with dried fruit characters, bursting with character, good acidity and lovely length.*	**£6.00**	EHL	(B)
DON PX VINO DULCE DE PASAS, BODEGAS TORO ALBALA Montilla-Moriles	*Butterscotch and raisin nose, fantastic on tongue with elegant style and lingering long tail.*	**£8.00**	POR	(S)
AMONTILLADO DEL PUERTO ALMACENISTA JOSÉ LUIS GONZÁLES OBREGÓN, LUSTAU Jerez	*Nutty treacle aromas with rich warm walnuts, full fruit, elegantly finishing peppered dry notes.*	**£8.70**	BDR GHL NYW BEN OWC	(S)
MANZANILLA AMONTILLADO ALMACENISTA MANUEL CUEVAS JURADO, EMILIO LUSTAU Jerez	*Dry raisin and nuttiness character with fresh acidity and a lovely smooth salty conclusion.*	**£8.90**	BDR GHL NYW BEN HST OWC	(S)
PALO CORTADO ALMACENISTA VIDES, LUSTAU Jerez	*Nutty orange marmalade flavours with a handful of green walnuts with lingering spicy finish.*	**£8.90**	GHL NYW BEN HST OWC AMW	(S)

AMONTILLADO DE JEREZ ALMACENISTA MIGUEL FONTADEZ FLORIDO, LUSTAU Jerez	*Bone dry raisins with velvety nuttiness and wild fig flavours and a salty conclusion.*	£8.90	M&V NYW BEN HST OWC	B
DON NUNO DRY OLOROSO, LUSTAU Jerez	*Orange peel aroma, lovely elegant old oak and tangy flavour with good acidity and light dry finish.*	£9.40	Widely Available	B
MANZANILLA PASADA ALMACENISTA MANUEL CUEVAS JURADO, LUSTAU Jerez	*Delicate nutty aroma with salted almonds, rich intensity with a nice delicious dry finish.*	£9.40	DBY GHL BTH BEN OWC PIM	B
DOS CORTADOS, BODEGAS WILLIAMS & HUMBERT SL Jerez	*Toffee nose with wonderful warm fruit waxy flavours, big mouthfeel and fantastic delicious fresh dry finish.*	£10.00	EHL DBY WBR NYW BEL	S
EMILIN MOSCATEL, EMILIO LUSTAU Jerez	*Floral aromatic toffee nose with lovely raisin flavours and a sniff of new oak, nice finish.*	£10.10	DBY GHL NYW BEN OWC WRK	B
BARBADILLO PRINCIPE AMONTILLADO, ANTONIO BARBADILLO Jerez	*Inviting caramel nose, palate showing elegance coming in waves of powerful fruit, utterly delicious.*	£10.20	JCP FRW BOO	S
BARBADILLO CUCO OLOROSO SECO, ANTONIO BARBADILLO Jerez	*Smokey syrup with wonderful creamy mouthfeel leading to saltiness and a good length.*	£10.50	FRW BOO	B
SAN EMILIO PEDRO XIMENEZ, LUSTAU Jerez	*True black treacle aroma with lovely burnt caramel with waves of raisiny flavours. Try it.*	£11.70	Widely Available	S

OLIVARES MONASTRELL DULCE 1998, BODEGAS OLIVARES La Manche	*Deep purple colour, strong fruity nose, very rich palate with tons of fruit. Long creamy finish.*	£14.50	MOR	(B)
BARBADILLO LA CILLA PEDRO XIMENEZ, ANTONIO BARBADILLO Jerez	*Rich molasses with caramelled sweet raisins poured over vanilla icecream with attractive layered finish.*	£15.00	JEF	(S)
SANDEMAN ROYAL CORREGIDOR, SANDEMAN Jerez	*Spicy smoked nut nose with robust dense fruits and rancio with wonderful stylish length.*	£15.00	SEA	(S)
SANDEMAN ROYAL AMBROSANTE, SANDEMAN Jerez	*Inviting toffee nose with lovely burnt caramel and raisin flavour with immense depth. Not cloying.*	£15.00	SEA	(B)
GONZÁLEZ BYASS APÓSTOLES, GONZÁLEZ BYASS Jerez	*Hot spicy hotcross buns just out of the oven aroma and flavours, great mouthfeel. Must have.*	£18.30	Widely Available	(G)
GONZÁLEZ BYASS MATUSALEM, GONZÁLEZ BYASS Jerez	*Nutty coffee nose with robust fruity saltiness and hints of chocolate, lovely balance and finish.*	£18.40	Widely Available	(S)
GONZÁLEZ BYASS NOÉ, GONZÁLEZ BYASS Jerez	*Exciting burned toffee nose with rich velvety nuts and spice flavours with a long tail.*	£20.50	ODF DBY VIL	(G)
GONZÁLEZ BYASS AMONTILLADO DEL DUQUE, GONZÁLEZ BYASS Jerez	*A complex walnutty nose with nice raisin and caramel richness, lovely, warm and long.*	£21.20	ODF BLU DBY VIW VIL	(B)

SPAIN • FORTIFIED

BARBADILLO OBISPO GASCON PALO CORTADO, ANTONIO BARBADILLO Jerez	*Warm toasted cinnamon meshing with caramelised oranges and nutmeg, wonderfully lingering finish. Very elegant.*	**£22.00**	JEF	G TROPHY WINE
OSBORNE PALO CORTADO ABOCADO SOLERA, BODEGAS OSBORNE Jerez	*Fresh yeasty croissant aroma layered with orangy citrus marmalade, wonderfully mouthfilling and handsome length.*	**£24.00**	HBJ	S
OSBORNE PEDRO XIMÉNEZ VIEJO, BODEGAS OSBORNE Jerez	*Liquid chocolate colour with treacle floral nose, bags of depth rather nicely done. Elegant style.*	**£28.00**	HBJ	S
SINGLE CASK PALO CORTADO BODEGA DE TONEL, EMILIO LUSTAU Jerez	*Spicy almonds and butter cake aroma with orange marmalade and salty bread. Rich powerful, hot finish.*	**£29.00**	M&V	G
SINGLE CASK AMONTILLADO BODEGA VIEJA, EMILIO LUSTAU Jerez	*Spicy raisins with full bodied caramel fruit flavours with complexity and great full length.*	**£30.50**	M&V HST OWC	B
SINGLE CASK OLOROSO BODEGA VIEJA, EMILIO LUSTAU Jerez	*Smokey, nutty orange nose with almonds and walnuts. Good acidity with spiciness to end.*	**£30.50**	M&V HST OWC	B

SPAIN • RED • OTHER

FUENTE DEL RITMO 1998, BODEGAS CENTRO ESPAÑOLAS La Mancha	*Mature berry nose with elegantly balanced savoury palate of mocha and curranty fruit. Good integration.*	**£4.00**	WST	B

PIEDEMONTE MERLOT TEMPRANILLO 1999, PIEDEMONTE Navarra	*Rich plummy fruit with cedar nose, nice and juicy, well balanced with good length.*	**£4.00**	TOS	(B)
SEÑORÍO DE CONDESTABLE CRIANZA 1996, SEÑORÍO DE CONDESTABLE La Manche	*Polished mocha, berry nose with a spicy red berry complex palate ending with dry tannins.*	**£4.10**	MER NRW JCP PBA AMW	(B)
VALDETÁN MACERACIÓN CARBÓNICA 1999, BODEGAS EMETERIO FERNÁNDEZ Cigales	*Rich delightful fruit, deep blackcurrants and spicy hints. Beautiful extended finish.*	**£4.30**	C&D	(G)
JAUME SERRA MERLOT 1998, JAUME SERRA Penedes	*Young refreshing style, some brooding black berry fruit still to emerge from the palate.*	**£5.00**	D&D	(B)
PIEDEMONTE MERLOT CABERNET 1999, BODEGAS PIEDEMONTE Navarra	*Quiet coffee and young berries leading to velvety tannins and good acidity with elegant finish.*	**£5.00**	ODD	(B)
TESCO HUGE JUICY RED 1999, SAN GREGORIO Aragón	*Lighter style, youthful fruit evident, concentrated tannins, ripe zingy red berry character, dusty oak.*	**£5.00**	TOS	(B)
MARQUÉS DE MONISTROL MERLOT 1997, MARQUÉS DE MONISTROL Penedés	*Grandma's plum jam on the nose, lovely minty fruit, young but confident on the finish.*	**£5.40**	CWS CAM TRO	(S)
PALACIO DE LA VEGA CABERNET TEMPRANILLO CRIANZA 1997, PALACIO DE LA VEGA Navarra	*Lovely mellow ripe fruit nose, good acidity and ripe smooth tannins on palate, nice length.*	**£5.90**	ODD JCP UBC JSS	(B)

CONCAVINS MERLOT 1998, CONCAVINS Tarragona	*Spanish sunbaked red ripe berry fruit cascading into velvety tannins and a smooth finish.*	£6.00	VIL	(S)
DOMINIO LOS PINOS CRIANZA 1998, MANUEL OLAECHEA Valencia	*Lovely cherry nose, soft pleasant acidity and good tannins support, round ripe fruit palate.*	£6.00	WTS	(B)
LAGRIMA VIRGEN 1999, TOSOS ECOLÓGICOS Aragón	*Fresh, slightly confected red and black fruit, good varietal character and clean finish.*	£6.50	VRT	(B)
SOTELO 1996, TELMO RODRÍGUEZ Navarra	*Inviting vanilla nose leads to palate of very mature red fruit, well balanced big fruity finish.*	£7.00	M&S	(S)
RAIMAT MERLOT 1996, RAIMAT Catalonia	*Spicy Spanish style of jammy plum and berry fruit, hints of spice and silky tannins to end.*	£7.70	FQU DBY HVW	(B)
JEAN LEON MERLOT 1997, MIGUEL TORRES Penedés	*Straightforward and clean fruit flavours, with medium bodied structure and a good lingering finish.*	£7.80	JSM RAV HVW	(B)
EL CHAPPARRAL OLD VINE GRENACHE 1998, BODEGAS Y VIÑEDOS Navarra	*Funky, earthy, peppery nose with a light to medium body weight and smooth, ripe, peppery palate.*	£8.50	HBJ	(B)
COSTERS DEL GRAVET CELLER DE CAPÇANES 1998, CELLER DE CAPGANES Navarra	*Blackcurrant and toasted oak on the nose and palate, firm tannins, good depth on palate.*	£8.70	MWW ODD DBY	(B)

PALACIO DE LA VEGA CABERNET SAUVIGNON RESERVA 1996, PALACIO DE LA VEGA Navarra	*Chocolatey aromas, soft ripe fruit, great tannins and acidity coming through on the lovely jammy finish.*	£9.00	ODD	(S)
MAS IGNENS FA 206 1998, ANP WINES Catalonia	*Smokey, tarry aromas lead to ripe black fruit flavours offering a smooth and spicy palate.*	£9.40	VRT	(S)
ROTLLAN I TORRA RESERVA 1995, ROTLLAN I TORRA Priorato	*Very deep and vibrant coloured wine with sweet ripe and spicy cherry and raspberry fruit.*	£9.40	MAD HDS GRO	(B)
CONCAVINS RESERVE CABERNET SAUVIGNON 1996, CONCAVINS Tarragona	*Warm summer fruit aroma with peppery oak integrating with brambles and blackcurrants. Just lovely.*	£10.00	VIL	(S)
ALBERT I NOYA CABERNET SAUVIGNON COL LECCIO 1998, ALBET I NOYA Penedés	*Menthol aromas followed by good rich round fruit flavours and lovely minty chocolate finish.*	£10.20	VRT	(S)
OLIVER CONTI NEGRE 1998, OLIVER CONTI Catalonia	*Wonderful closed fruit nose with crushed plums flavours, full bodied tannins with chewiness. Great.*	£10.50	MAD	(B)
VEGAVAL AVALON MERLOT RESERVA 1993, BODEGAS MIGUEL CALATAYUD Valdepeñas	*Smokey savoury nose leading to attractive berry fruits with warm tannins, full bodied and good length.*	£11.00	FTH	(S)
ALBERT I NOYA SYRAH COL LECCIO 1998, ALBET I NOYA Penedés	*Spicy and dusty nose, elegant fruit character of plums and berries leading to well balanced tannins.*	£11.00	VRT	(B)

Wine	Tasting Note	Price	Stockist	
DOMINIO DE VALDEPUSA SYRAH 1998, MARQUÉS DE GRIÑON Castilla-La Manche	*Ripe and lifted bouquet, supple fruit, savoury complexity, fine tannins and a pleasant finish.*	£12.00	ABU	**B**
DOMINIO DE VALDEPUSA PETIT VERDOT 1998, MARQUÉS DE GRIÑON Castilla-La Manche	*Youthful savoury nose with rich raspberry palate with massive tannins and nice drying finish.*	£12.30	NYW A&A	**B**
RAIMAT CABERNET SAUVIGNON RESERVA 1994, RAIMAT Catalonia	*Minty liquorice nose with complex youngberry, hint of spice, good mouthfeel and some length.*	£12.90	HVW	**B**
MONJARDÍN GRAN RESERVA CABERNET SAUVIGNON 1994, BODEGAS CASTILLO DE MONJARDÍN Navarra	*Warm minty oak nose with a mature palate of gentle plums and brambles, with lovely polished finish.*	£17.60	VIL	**B**
MAS LA PLANA 1995, MIGUEL TORRES Penedés	*Green olives and warm fruits on the nose with good oak and plum fruit coulis palate.*	£20.60	Widely Available	**B**
DOMINIO DE VALDEPUSA EMERITUS 1997, MARQUÉS DE GRIÑON Castilla-La Manche	*Sweet vanilla fruit nose with big juicy currants, sift tannins and a short tail.*	£27.50	A&A	**B**
CLOS DE L'OBAC 1997, COSTERS DEL SUVRANA Catalonia	*Soft fruit style, smokey nose and a palate that is sleek with firm fruit character.*	£32.00	DBY HST VIL POR	**G**

Pinpoint who sells the wine you wish to buy by turning to the stockist codes. If you know the name of the wine you want to buy, use the alphabetical index. If the price is your motivation, refer to the invaluable price guide index; red and white wines under £5, sparkling wines under £12 and champagne under £16. Happy hunting!

SPAIN • ROSÉ

GRAN FEUDO ROSÉ 1999, BODEGAS JULIAN CHIVITE Navarra	*Clean fresh bright pink, soft summer fruit aroma, crisp acidity, good length, delicious finish.*	£4.80	ODD WBR JSS WRW	(B)
ENATE ROSADO 1999, ENATE Somontano	*Clean freshly picked summer fruits on the nose and palate with remarkable acidity and gorgeous finish.*	£6.50	AVB GHL N&P	(S)
FAUSTINO Y ROSADO 1999, FAUSTINO Rioja Alavesa	*Plummy fruit and red berry aromas, notes of strawberries on the fruity palate, dry finish.*	£6.50	MAX UBC	(B)

SPAIN • SPARKLING

TESCO DEMI SEC CAVA NV, CASTELLBLANCH Penedès	*Big generous upfront fruit style with a light mousse on spritzy palate with crisp finish.*	£5.00	TOS	(B)
CAVA BRUT CODORNIU NV, CODORNIU Penedés	*Tropical toasty aromas followed by fruit flavour, full round palate, fresh, clean, lovely length.*	£6.40	SPR HVW	(B)
RAVENTOS I BLANC CAVA BRUT RESERVA NV, JOSEP MARIA RAVENTOS I BLANC Penedés	*Inviting appley nose, clean young fresh fruits on the palate, light toasty character, nice length.*	£10.00	WAW	(S)

SPAIN• SPARKLING

JAUME CODORNÍU NV, CODORNÍU Catalonia	*Lovely gentle crisp acidity, creamy texture, citrus apple palate, tropical hint, full mousse, elegant style.*	£20.00	CON	**B**

SPAIN • TEMPRANILLO

ALDEANUEVA AZABACHE NV, ALDEANUEVA Rioja	*Lovely seductive perfumed nose, good acidity incorporated with fruit flavours and firm tannins.*	£4.00	TOS	**B**
PALACIO DE LEÓN 1998, BODEGAS VINOS DE LEÓN Castilla y León	*Good depth, sweet fruit tannins and good acidity, smooth finish. Notes of chocolate and spice.*	£4.00	PEC	**B**
ESPIRAL TEMPRANILLO CABERNET 1999, BODEGA PIRINEOS Aragon	*Sweet cherry fruit on the nose and palate, juicy upfront lively texture, lots of charming tannins.*	£4.50	WTS	**S**
CO-OP RIOJA TINTO VIÑA GALA NV, BODEGAS MURIEL Rioja	*Delightful inviting aromas of bananas and grapefruit lead to warm round fruit palate with exquisite acidity.*	£4.50	CWS	**B**
VALDETÁN TINTO JOVEN 1998, BODEGAS EMETERIO FERNÁNDEZ Cigales	*Perfumed with dry figs and cherries. Well balanced palate with juicy ripe fruits, pleasant tannic finish.*	£4.80	DBY	**B**
BRIGHT BROTHERS OLD VINES TEMPRANILLO 1999, VINIBERIA Vinos de Madrid	*Very rich ripe fruit on the nose followed by delicious fruit with raspberry characters. Good balance*	£5.00	EHL	**B**

DAMA DE TORO 1998, BODEGAS FARINA Castilla y León	*Big full fruit nose. Lovely raspberry fruit in a full tannin palate with great raspberries on finish.*	**£5.00**	JSM	**B**
VIÑA ALBALI GRAN RESERVA 1993, FÉLIX SOLIS Valdepenas	*Fragrant floral pepper nose, creamy fruit vanilla flavours. Good balance and length. Simply delightful.*	**£6.00**	JSM BGN JMC BTH WCR	**S**
MAS COLLET CELLER DE CAPGANES 1998, CELLER DE CAPGANES Navarra	*Rich fruity nose, strong lovely buttery feeling in the mouth balanced with soft fruit. Good length.*	**£6.00**	MWW WSO DBY	**B**
SONSIERRA TINTO JOVEN 1999, BODEGAS SONSIERRA Rioja	*Intense dark cherry on the nose. Delicious fruits well balanced with tannin acidity. Pleasant finish.*	**£6.00**	L&S ESL VIL	**B**
CASTELL DEL REMEI GOTIM BRU 1997, CASTELL DEL REMEI Catalonia	*Earthy strawberries on the nose, lovely soft detectable tannins, great structure, complex pleasant wine.*	**£6.70**	MAD NYW HDS POR BOO	**B**
ESPIRAL TEMPRANILLO BARRIQUE 1999, BODEGA PIRINEOS Aragon	*Powerful creamy fruit on nose and palate with hints of buttered fresh carrots. Huge dry tannins.*	**£7.00**	IWS	**S**
TORO CRIANZA 1997, VIÑA BAJOZ Toro	*Warm caramel nose blending with succulent fruits and delightful soft tannins with good length.*	**£7.00**	BWL NYW	**S**
EDERRA CRIANZA 1997, BODEGAS BILBAINAS Rioja	*Fresh fruits in jammy nose. Soft ripe fruity in slightly almondy palate. Spicy finish.*	**£7.00**	CON	**B**

MARQUÉS DEL PUERTO RESERVA 1994, MARQUÉS DEL PUERTO Rioja	*Subtle wood nose, pleasant mouthful with lots of tannins and rich ripe fruit with nice length.*	£7.00	WAV	B
MIRALMONTE CRIANZA 1996, BODEGAS FRUTOS VILLAR Castilla y León	*Full deep fruity nose. Ripe with nice weight on the palate with pleasant tannins and acidity.*	£7.00	VIL	B
ENATE TEMPRANILLO CABERNET SAUVIGNON CRIANZA 1997, ENATE Somontano	*Rich raspberry aroma followed by an extremely pleasant complex structure full of fresh fruit.*	£7.20	AVB DBY GHL WCR CTC	B
CONDE DE VALDEMAR CRIANZA 1997, MARTÍNEZ BUJANDA Rioja	*Nice oak overtones, good fruit flavours, dusky tannins, lovely balance with good depth and good length.*	£7.40	FQU DBY TAN N&P JSS HVW COM	S
TORRE ORIA MARQUÉS DE REQUENA CRIANZA 1994, TORRE ORIA Levant	*Good gummy and mealy nose leads to delicious tarry chocolate vanilla palate with good length.*	£7.60	BDR	B
VEGAVAL GRAN RESERVA 1991, BODEGAS MIGUEL CALATAYUD Valdepeñas	*Chocolate nose and soft spicy wood. Lush red fruit palate leading to a strong finish.*	£7.90	NRW A&A WRW	B
VIÑA ALARDE RESERVA 1996, BERBERANA Rioja	*Deep, very traditional and seductive style of rich juicy black fruit, great length and cedar finish.*	£8.00	ABU	S
ALDOR CRIANZA 1998, VIÑEDOS Y BODEGAS VALBUENA DE DUERO Ribera del Duero	*Young fresh fruit on the nose, full well structured creamy palate with fine tannins.*	£8.10	V&V BNK	B

Wine	Description	Price	Codes	Award
ABADÍA RETUERTA RIVOLA 1998, **ABADÍA RETUERTA** Castilla y León	*Elegant oak and plum aromas invite you to taste a complex well structured wine with gorgeous tannins.*	£8.20	EUW NYW HST HVW	S
BARÓN DE LEY RESERVA 1996, **BARON DE LEY** Rioja	*Deep ripe sweet fruit on nose and palate with lovely structure and terrific tannic finish.*	£8.20	FQU HVW	S
TINTO AÑARES RESERVA 1996, **BODEGAS OLARRA** Rioja	*Sweet seductive aroma followed by extremely harmonised tannins and acidity blended with juicy fruit.*	£8.40	CPW RAV HST	B
ONDARRE RESERVA 1996, **ONDARRRE** Rioja	*Captivating cherries on nose lead to magnificent fruity mouthfeel with sensational acidity and tannins.*	£8.50	AVB QWW NYW WCR FEN CTC	G
VIÑA ALBERDI RESERVA 1994, **LA RIOJA ALTA** Rioja	*Great style wine with soft fruits and excellent flavour. Pleasant dusky oakiness and tobacco, long finish.*	£8.80	DBY VIL AMW POR	S
MARQUES DE REQUENA RESERVA 1994, **TORRE ORIA** Levant	*Strawberry vanilla aromas, very pleasant combination of ripe fruit and tannins with elegant finish.*	£9.00	BDR	S
CEREMONIA 1996, **GANDIA** Valencia	*Flowery ripe fruit in a delicious chocolatey fruit palate followed by lovely balanced tannins.*	£9.00	SAF	B
LAN GRAN RESERVA 1994, **BODEGAS LAN** Rioja	*Vanilla fruit nose, rich ripe fruit with lovely depth ending in dry tannic finish. Good length.*	£9.10	HVW	B

SPAIN • TEMPRANILLO

ARTADI VIÑAS DE GAIN RIOJA CRIANZA 1997, COSECHERAS ALAVES Rioja	*Attractive toasty nose leads to fruity flavour with good tannins and rich oak finish.*	£9.20	MWW ODD HST	**S**
CEREMONIA 1996, GANDIA Valencia	*Herbal hints on fruity nose lead to very smooth easy to drink fruits with great finish.*	£9.30	PIM	**B**
CONDE DE VALDEMAR RESERVA 1995, MARTÍNEZ BUJANDA Rioja	*Soft fruit nose, purple fruits on palate of berries and tannins, good balance, jammy long finish.*	£9.40	FQU DBY TAN N&P JSS HVW COM	**B**
LAN RESERVA 1996, BODEGAS LAN Rioja	*Plums, damson and some rhubarb on nose and palate, sophisticated unforgettable long finish. Go for it!*	£9.50	ABY	**G**
BODEGAS CORRAL RESERVA DON JACOBO 1995, BODEGAS CORRAL Rioja	*Light raspberry and strawberry fruits, vanilla overtones on nose and palate with balanced acidity and tannins.*	£9.60	CTC	**B**
MARQUES DE VITORIA GRAN RESERVA 1992, MARQUES DE VITORIA Rioja	*Beautiful ripe fruit aromas followed by well complemented warm rich ripe fruit palate and tannic length.*	£10.50	JSM	**B**
RIBERAL CRIANZA 1996, BODEGAS SANTA EULALIA Ribera del Duero	*Intense delightful nose with steamy aromas leads to smooth mouthfeel with long rich fruit finish.*	£10.50	L&S	**B**
CAMPILLO RESERVA 1995, BODEGAS CAMPILLO Rioja	*Subtle leathery notes in a very nice sweet and juicy palate of mashed cherries*	£11.00	TOS	**S**

BARON DE OÑA RESERVA 1995, TORRO DE OÑA Rioja	*Attractive soft smokey fruit aroma. Soft ripe fruit with some berries hints. Good length.*	£11.30	ESL AMW	(B)
MARQUÉS DE RISCAL RESERVA 1996, MARQUÉS DE RISCAL Rioja	*Very inviting concentration of white peppers in a bed of rich fruit with enjoyable tannin.*	£11.50	Widely Available	(G)
ARZUAGA CRIANZA 1997, BODEGAS ARZUAGA NAVARRO Ribera del Duero	*Soft definite oak on nose and palate, full bodied structure and spicy juicy finish.*	£11.50	OWL DBY JNW HVW	(B)
ABADÍA RETUERTA 1997, ABADÍA RETUERTA Castilla y León	*Opaque inviting mature nose. Vegetables and good ripe fruit, high acidity and tannins, full bodied.*	£12.10	FQU NYW HST HVW	(B)
TINTO RESERVA ESPECIAL 1995, MARQUÉS DE MURRIETA Rioja	*Very pleasant oak on nose invites to taste ripe fruit and supporting tannins with lovely finish.*	£13.70	Widely Available	(B)
VIÑA VICALANDA DE VIÑA POMAL RESERVA 1995, BODEGAS BILBAINAS Rioja	*Cedary oak and soft fruit on nose and palate with plenty of tannins and plumb hints.*	£14.00	ODD	(B)
GUELBENZU EVO 1998, BODEGAS GUELBENZU Navarra	*Lovely violets and black fruits in luscious structure with lots of tannin. Drying tannins on finish.*	£14.40	MAD DBY TAN OWC HDS BOO	(S)
RIBERAL RESERVA 1995, BODEGAS SANTA EULALIA Ribera del Duero	*Subtle nose of attractive oak. Round juicy deep palate. Very pleasant, well balanced with good length.*	£14.50	L&S	(B)

ALBERT I NOYA RESERVA MARTI 1996, ALBERT I NOYA Penedés	*Rich complex attractive nose leads to full fruity flavour with some oak notes and nice tannins.*	**£15.50**	VRT	**B**
CAMPILLO GRAN RESERVA 1992, BODEGAS CAMPILLO Rioja	*Very interesting chocolatey aromas with notes of butter lead to soft fruit palate with good length.*	**£15.50**	TOS	**B**
MAYOR DE ONDARRE RESERVA 1995, ONDARRE Rioja	*Sweet toasty nose followed by nice oaky palate and strong tannins well balanced with ripe fruit.*	**£16.30**	AVB QWW CTC	**S**
VIÑA LANCIANO RESERVA 1996, BODEGAS LAN Rioja	*Excellent full bodied structure with large smokey nose, dry tannins harmonising well with fruit and oak finish.*	**£17.10**	ABY	**G**
GRAN ALBINA RESERVA ESPECIAL 1996, BODEGAS RIOJANAS Rioja	*Fresh fruit subtle nose, firm tannins with concentrated fruit and good integration of oak on palate.*	**£17.20**	DBY	**B**
BODEGAS PALACIO RESERVA ESPECIAL 1995, BODEGAS PALACIO Rioja	*Excellent fruity nose, peppery hints in the mouth with wonderful late after taste with nice oak notes.*	**£17.70**	ODD OHI	**B**
BODEGAS CORRAL ALTOS DE CORRAL 1995, BODEGAS CORRAL Rioja	*Lifted vanilla nose, red fruit palate with notes of blackcurrants. Soft sustained finish. Well structured.*	**£17.90**	GSJ	**B**
VIÑA LANCIANO RESERVA 1995, BODEGAS LAN Rioja	*Gentle vanilla aromas, berry fruit characters in an intense well structured mouthful with very long finish.*	**£18.00**	ABY CEB	**B**

CASTELL DEL REMEI 1780 1997, CASTELL DEL REMEI Catalonia	*Some lovely dark fruit aromas, intense fruits and tannins with notes of plums and blackberries.*	**£19.10**	MAD NYW POR	(S)
MONTE VILLALOBÓN 1996, GRANDES BODEGAS Ribera del Duero	*Beautiful fruit nose, full bodied balanced oak and acidity, blackcurrant notes and nice tannins.*	**£22.00**	MOR	(S)
MARQUÉS DE RISCAL BARÓN DE CHIREL 1995, MARQUÉS DE RISCAL Rioja	*Very appealing purple wine with chocolatey nose and palate, and fine tannin balance.*	**£25.20**	MAD DBY	(B)
GUELBENZU LAUTUS 1996, BODEGAS GUELBENZU Navarra	*A very interesting spicy nose leads to a palate full of round fruits and great tannic finish.*	**£25.50**	MAD POR	(S)
DIVO 1999, BODEGAS RICARDO BENITO Vinos de Madrid	*Ripe raspberries on the nose, ripe sweet fruit palate with smokey characters, firm pleasant finish.*	**£35.00**	VXL	(B)
DOÑA BEATRIZ SAUVIGNON BLANC 1999, BODEGAS CERROSOL Rueda	*Intense honeyed gooseberry follows through to bright fruit oozing citrus complexities and good steely acidity.*	**£4.80**	PLB	(B)

SPAIN • WHITE

DURUIS BLANCO 1997, MARQUES DE GRIÑON Castilla y Lèon	*Ripe tinned asparagus aromas with green citrus fruit and delicate acidity with buttery finish.*	**£5.00**	ABU	(B)

SPAIN • WHITE

MARQUÉS DE RISCAL RUEDA 1999, MARQUÉS DE RISCAL Castilla y León	*Bright green hues in this full bodied wine with banana and peach notes and good weight.*	£6.70	V&C MAD BLU	B
CON CLASS SAUVIGNON BLANC 1999, CUEVAS DE CASTILLO Rueda	*Freshly cut lemon and lime aromas with a complex structure, subtle fruit and good length.*	£7.00	GRT MOR HDS	B
VILLAREI ALBARIÑO 1999, PAZO DE VILLAREI Rias Baixas	*Very pleasant soft, crisp, green apple aromas with melony hints, good fresh fruit on the palate.*	£7.90	MER DBY JMC WRK BOO	B
ALBARIÑO MORGADIO 1999, ADEGA MORGADIO Rías Baixas	*Delicate fresh crisp nose followed by fresh pears on round palate, good balancing acidity.*	£8.00	BSS	B
CHARDONNAY BARREL FERMENTED 1997, BODEGAS CASTILLO DE MONJARDÍN Navarra	*Lemon jelly aromas with cut melon flavour, hints of almond biscuits and honey on the finish.*	£8.10	VIL WRW POR	B
BIANCO RESERVA ESPECIAL 1995, MARQUÉS DE MURRIETA Rioja	*Lovely ripe fruit aromas with a spoonful of honey and a balanced mature lush palate.*	£8.80	ADN WBR BTH HST POR	B
RAIMAT CHARDONNAY SELECCÍON ESPECIAL 1998, RAIMAT Catalonia	*Great aromatic green fruit nose, some grapefruit on the palate with long fresh finish.*	£9.00	CON	B
LAGAR DE CERVERA 1999, LAGAR DE FORNELOS Rías Baixas	*Appley nose leads to citrus acidity that marries well with lovely ripe fruit on the palate.*	£9.30	JSM BLU CPW VIL AMW	B

MAS IGNENS FA 104 1999, ANP WINES Catalonia	*Spicy floral hints of vanilla onto full lush melon characteristics with lovely length and acidity.*	£9.40	VRT	B
JEAN LEON CHARDONNAY 1998, MIGUEL TORRES Penedés	*Subtle fresh perfumed nose, fruit tart on the palate with good oak support, big long finish.*	£9.70	RAV HVW	B
ALBARIÑO VALMINOR 1999, BODEGAS VALMINOR Rias Baixas	*Delicate green fruit nose, very smooth over the tongue, some real elegance on the long finish.*	£10.20	CTC	S
ENATE CHARDONNAY BARRIQUE FERMENTED 1998, ENATE Somontano	*Pleasant full round buttery palate with well integrated oak, refreshing acidity and nice length.*	£11.50	AVB DBY HST CTC	B

SPARKLING • £16 AND UNDER

Seaview Chardonnay Blanc de Blancs 1996	£ 8.80	G
MHV The House Brut Champagne NV	£ 14.50	G
Rosemount Estate Kirri Billi Brut 1997	£ 7.60	S
Seaview Chardonnay Blanc de Blancs 1995	£ 9.00	S
Graham Beck Blanc de Blancs 1993	£ 9.20	S
Moscato d'Asti La Morandina 1999	£ 10.00	S
Raventos I Blanc Cava Brut Reserva NV	£ 10.00	S
Valley Vineyards Ascot NV	£ 11.00	S
Deutz Blanc de Blanc 1996	£ 12.40	S
Midnight Cuvée NV	£ 12.70	S
Cuvée Merret Belgravia NV	£ 14.00	S
Sainsbury's Champagne Extra Dry NV	£ 14.00	S
Laurenti Père et Fils Grande Cuvée Brut NV	£ 15.00	S
Champagne Forget Brimont NV	£ 15.50	S
Le Brun de Neuville Cuvée Chardonnay NV	£ 16.00	S
Safeway Asti Dolce NV	£ 4.00	B
Moscato d'Asti 1999	£ 4.80	B
MHV Sparkling Chardonnay Brut NV	£ 5.00	B
Chapel Hill Sparkling Chardonnay NV	£ 5.00	B
Somerfield Asti Spumante NV	£ 5.00	B
Tesco Demi Sec Cava NV	£ 5.00	B
Chapel Down Epoch V 1995	£ 5.50	B
Sommerfield Australian Sparkling Brut NV	£ 5.70	B
Cava Brut Codorniu NV	£ 6.40	B
Seaview Brut NV	£ 6.60	B
Asti Spumante DOCG 1999	£ 6.60	B
Ice Crystal 1995	£ 7.00	B
Spumante Metodo Classico Dosage Zero 1992	£ 7.00	B
Chandon Argentina NV	£ 8.20	B
Cremant de Bourgogne Cave De Vire NV	£ 8.20	B
Pierre Larousse Blanc de Blancs Brut NV	£ 8.50	B
Yellowglen Pinot Noir Chardonnay NV	£ 8.70	B
Seaview Pinot Noir Chardonnay 1997	£ 8.80	B
Lindauer Special Réserve NV	£ 8.90	B
Seppelt Sparkling Shiraz 1995	£ 9.10	B
Yellowglen Vintage 1997	£ 10.50	B
Chapel Down Vintage Brut 1995	£ 10.50	B
Deutz Marlborough Cuvée NV	£ 11.40	B
Miru Miru Marlborough Brut 1997	£ 11.90	B

Green Point Vintage Brut 1996	£ 12.20	B
Green Point Rosé 1996	£ 12.70	B
Daniel Le Brun Brut NV NV	£ 12.80	B
Ashton Hills Salmon Brut 1995	£ 12.90	B
Breaky Bottom Brut Millennium Cuvée Maman Mercier 1996	£ 13.20	B
Champagne Drappier Carte d'Or Demi-Sec NV	£ 13.20	B
Cuvée Merret Bloomsbury 1996	£ 14.00	B
MHV Paul Langier Brut NV Champagne NV	£ 14.00	B
Jean de Praisac Brut Champagne 1996	£ 14.00	B
Seppelt Show Sparkling Shiraz 1990	£ 14.10	B
André Simon Champagne Brut NV NV	£ 14.10	B
Tesco Blanc De Blanc Champagne NV	£ 14.70	B
Cheurlin Dangin Carte d'Or NV	£ 15.00	B
Champagne Maison Lenique Cuvée de Réserve NV	£ 15.00	B
Bouche Père et Fils Cuvée Réserve Brut NV	£ 15.00	B
Jean Moutardier Brut NV Selection NV	£ 15.50	B
Bonnaire Blanc de Blanc NV	£ 15.70	B

WHITES • £6 AND UNDER

Passito Verdicchio dei Castelli di Jesi Tordiruta 1997	£ 4.50	G
Double Bay Chardonnay 1998	£ 6.00	G
Anapi River Sauvignon Blanc 1999	£ 3.50	S
Terrasses d'Azur Sauvignon Blanc 1999	£ 4.00	S
Domaine de Bouscau 1999	£ 4.00	S
La Cité Chardonnay Vin de Pays d'Oc 1999	£ 4.00	S
La Vis Pinot Grigio 1999	£ 4.00	S
MHV Australian Semillon NV	£ 4.20	S
Woolpunda Chardonnay 1998	£ 4.50	S
Denbies Surrey Gold 1999	£ 4.50	S
Villa Sandi Chardonnay 1999	£ 4.50	S
Castle Creek Semillon 1998	£ 4.60	S
Château l'Ermitage White 1999	£ 4.60	S
Trulli Chardonnay 1999	£ 4.60	S
Hardy's Nottage Hill Chardonnay 1999	£ 4.90	S
Jindalee Chardonnay 1998	£ 5.00	S
Cono Sur Viognier 1999	£ 5.00	S
Bright Brothers Sicilian Barrel Fermented Chardonnay 1998	£ 5.00	S
Terre di Ginestra Catarratto 1999	£ 5.20	S
Miranda Chardonnay 1999	£ 5.30	S
Riesling Selection 1998	£ 5.30	S
Miranda Chardonnay 1998	£ 5.40	S
Miranda Brothers Oak Aged Chardonnay 1999	£ 5.50	S
Casas del Bosque Chardonnay 1999	£ 5.50	S
La Pintora Chardonnay 1999	£ 5.50	S
Graacher Himmelreich Riesling Spatlese 1997	£ 5.50	S
Long Terrace Semillon Chardonnay 1999	£ 5.60	S
Kingston Estate Wildlife Chardonnay 1998	£ 5.70	S
Alpha Domus Sauvignon Blanc 1999	£ 5.70	S
Vidal Estate Sauvignon Blanc Hawkes Bay 1998	£ 5.70	S
Laithwaite Sauvignon Blanc 1999	£ 5.80	S
Nobilo Sauvignon Blanc 1999	£ 5.90	S
Terrazas Alto Chardonnay 1999	£ 6.00	S
E&C McLaren Vale Chardonnay 1999	£ 6.00	S
Serriger Vogelsang Riesling Auslese 1989	£ 6.00	S
Nikita Chardonnay Viognier 1999	£ 2.60	B
Copper Crossing Dry White Bulgarian Wine NV	£ 3.00	B
Tesco Argentinian Torrontes 1999	£ 3.50	B
Caballo de Plata Torrontes 1999	£ 3.50	B

Ballingal Semillon 1999	£ 3.50	B
Boyar Chardonnay 1999	£ 3.50	B
MHV Muscadet Sévre et Maine Sur Lie 1999	£ 3.50	B
Millennium Early Release Chenin Blanc 2000	£ 3.50	B
Co-Op Long Slim Chardonnay Semillon 1999	£ 3.80	B
Rio de Plata Torrontes 1999	£ 4.00	B
Riverhill Semillon Chardonnay 1999	£ 4.00	B
Ballingal Semillon Chardonnay 1999	£ 4.00	B
Les Marionettes Marsanne 1999	£ 4.00	B
Louise d'Estrée Vouvray 1999	£ 4.00	B
Domaine de Montaubéron Cépage Marsanne 1999	£ 4.00	B
Domaine de Pellehaut 1999	£ 4.00	B
Cuvée Kiwi Chardonnay 1999	£ 4.00	B
Spice Trail White 1999	£ 4.00	B
D'Istinto Cattarato Chardonnay 1998	£ 4.00	B
Stowells of Chelsea Chenin Blanc NV	£ 4.00	B
The Pioneers Raisined Muscat Miranda 1998	£ 4.10	B
Carta Vieja Sauvignon Blanc 1999	£ 4.10	B
Stowells of Chelsea Chardonnay Colombard NV	£ 4.10	B
Misty Peak Limari Valley White 1999	£ 4.20	B
Terret Chardonnay Domaine Sainte Madeleine 1998	£ 4.20	B
Parsons Brook Chardonnay 1999	£ 4.30	B
Reserve St Marc Sauvignon Blanc 1999	£ 4.30	B
Santa Rosa Estate Chenin Blanc Torrontes 1999	£ 4.40	B
Viña La Rosa La Palmería Sauvignon Blanc 1999	£ 4.50	B
La Poule Blanche 1999	£ 4.50	B
Château Chanteloup Bordeaux Blanc Sec 1999	£ 4.50	B
Les Mazrionnettes Chardonnay Viognier 1999	£ 4.50	B
Gouts et Couleurs Chardonnay Viognier 1999	£ 4.50	B
Bright Brothers Greganico Chardonnay 1998	£ 4.50	B
Corbans White Label Chardonnay Chenin Blanc 1999	£ 4.50	B
Hardys Stamp Riesling Gewürztraminer 1999	£ 4.60	B
Miranda Opal Ridge Semillon Chardonnay 1999	£ 4.60	B
Tierra Arena Sauvignon Blanc 1999	£ 4.60	B
Banrock Station Chardonnay 1999	£ 4.70	B
Penfolds Bin 202 Riesling 1999	£ 4.70	B
Sacred Hill Semillon Chardonnay 1999	£ 4.70	B
Caliterra Sauvignon Blanc 1999	£ 4.80	B
Viña La Rosa La Palmería Chardonnay 1999	£ 4.80	B
Anjou Blanc 1998	£ 4.80	B
Dona Beatriz Sauvignon Blanc 1999	£ 4.80	B
Colombard Deakin Estate 1999	£ 4.90	B
MHV Vouvray 1999	£ 4.90	B
Soave Superiore 1999	£ 4.90	B

Wynns Coonawarra Estate Riesling 1999	£ 5.00	B
Angove's Classic Reserve Chardonnay 1999	£ 5.00	B
Tesco Overtly Aromatic White NV	£ 5.00	B
Normans Unwooded Chardonnay 1999	£ 5.00	B
Safeway Australian Oaked Chardonnay 1999	£ 5.00	B
Andrew Peace Chardonnay 1999	£ 5.00	B
Normans Pendulum Chardonnay 1999	£ 5.00	B
San Pedro 35 Sur Chardonnay 1999	£ 5.00	B
Astley Dry Reserve 1996	£ 5.00	B
Chapel Down Flint Dry Bacchus 1998	£ 5.00	B
Baron de Lestac Blanc 1999	£ 5.00	B
La Baume Domaine Chardonnay 1999	£ 5.00	B
Pont Neuf Mâcon Blanc Villages 1998	£ 5.00	B
James Herrick Chardonnay 1999	£ 5.00	B
Domaine Caude-Val Chardonnay 1999	£ 5.00	B
Domaine de l'Aumonier Touraine Sauvignon 1999	£ 5.00	B
Marc Xero Chardonnay 1999	£ 5.00	B
Le Vele Verdicchio dei Castelli di Jesi DOC Classico 1999	£ 5.00	B
Safeway Organic Soave 1999	£ 5.00	B
Goedverwacht Estate Colombard 2000	£ 5.00	B
Pacific Wines Cape White 1999	£ 5.00	B
Lindemans Bin 65 Chardonnay 1999	£ 5.00	B
Duruis Blanco 1997	£ 5.00	B
New World South Eastern Australia Chardonnay 1999	£ 5.10	B
Jacob's Creek Chardonnay 1999	£ 5.10	B
Normans Lone Gum Chardonnay 1999	£ 5.10	B
Carta Vieja Reserve Chardonnay 1998	£ 5.10	B
Isla Negra Chardonnay 1999	£ 5.10	B
Veramonte Sauvignon 1999	£ 5.20	B
Frascati Superiore 1999	£ 5.20	B
Marlborough Gold Chardonnay 1999	£ 5.20	B
Rosemount Estate Semillon 1999	£ 5.30	B
Best's Victoria Colombard 1999	£ 5.30	B
Greco Basilicata 1999	£ 5.30	B
Mitchelton Thomas Mitchell Chardonnay 1999	£ 5.40	B
Andrew McPherson Chardonnay 1999	£ 5.40	B
Cranswick Estates Castle Creek Chardonnay 1999	£ 5.40	B
Varietal Reposado Chardonnay 1999	£ 5.40	B
Corbans Estate Sauvignon Blanc 1999	£ 5.40	B
Lennard's Crossing Semillon Sauvignon 1999	£ 5.50	B
Las Lomas Sauvignon Blanc 1999	£ 5.50	B
Château du Coing de Saint Fiacre 1998	£ 5.50	B
Tesco Petit Chablis 1999	£ 5.50	B
Villiera Gewürztraminer 1999	£ 5.50	B

Vouvray Demi Sec Cuvée Gaston Dorléans 1999	£ 5.60	B
Brown Brothers Dry Muscat 1999	£ 5.70	B
I Mesi Chardonnay Trentino 1998	£ 5.70	B
Vidal Estate Chardonnay Hawkes Bay 1999	£ 5.70	B
Peter Lehmann Semillon 1999	£ 5.80	B
Trio Chardonnay 1999	£ 5.90	B
Santa Julia Viognier Reserva 1999	£ 6.00	B
McGuigan Bin 6000 Verdelho 1999	£ 6.00	B
Wellwood Estate Sticky Botrytis Semillon 1997	£ 6.00	B
Willandra Chardonnay 1998	£ 6.00	B
Lindemans Limestone Coast Chardonnay 1998	£ 6.00	B
Mallee Point Chardonnay 1999	£ 6.00	B
Pewsey Vale Riesling 1997	£ 6.00	B
Tesco McLaren Vale Chardonnay 1998	£ 6.00	B
Barrington Estate Pencil Pines Semillon 1999	£ 6.00	B
Shawsgate Bacchus 1999	£ 6.00	B
Château du Coing Comte de St Hubert 1998	£ 6.00	B
Esprit de Combelle Chardonnay 1998	£ 6.00	B
Entre-Deux Mers Château Ducla Blanc 1999	£ 6.00	B
Vouvray Demi Sec Domaine Bourillon Dorléans 1998	£ 6.00	B
Domaine la Rosière Chardonnay 1998	£ 6.00	B
Domaines Virginie Gold Label Réserve Chardonnay 1999	£ 6.00	B
Gewürztraminer Gold Medal Ribeauville 1997	£ 6.00	B
Gewürztraminer Weingarten 1998	£ 6.00	B
Baron de Hoen Gewürztraminer Issu de Vieilles Vignes 1998	£ 6.00	B
Chablis 1er Cru 1997	£ 6.00	B
Tokay Pinot Gris Cave de Ribeauvillé 1997	£ 6.00	B
Hilltop Neszmely Chardonnay Virgin Vintage 1999	£ 6.00	B
Hilltop Neszmely Sauvignon Blanc Virgin Vintage 1999	£ 6.00	B
Caramia Chardonnay 1999	£ 6.00	B
Casale Falchini Vigna a Soltaio 1999	£ 6.00	B
Delegat's Hawkes Bay Chardonnay 1998	£ 6.00	B
Haywood Chardonnay 1998	£ 6.00	B

REDS • £6 AND UNDER

Valdetán Maceración Carbónica 1999	£ 4.30	G
Beaujolais la Bareille 1999	£ 5.00	G
Domaine la Tour Boisee 1998	£ 5.00	G
McGuigan Black Label Merlot 1999	£ 5.20	G
Boyar Lambol Merlot 1999	£ 3.70	S
MHV Firriato Sicialian Red 1998	£ 3.70	S
Suhindol Cabernet Merlot Reserve 1996	£ 4.00	S
Suhindol Merlot Reserve 1996	£ 4.00	S
Barbera Colli Tortonesi 1998	£ 4.00	S
Marks & Spencer Gold Label Syrah 1999	£ 4.20	S
Casa Calatrasi Tu Carignan Mouvedre 1999	£ 4.30	S
Sainsbury's Copertino Riserva 1996	£ 4.30	S
Adiseno Cabernet Shiraz 1999	£ 4.50	S
Far Flung Malbec 1999	£ 4.50	S
Domaine Boyar 1er Cuvée Cabernet Sauvignon 1999	£ 4.50	S
Domaine Boyar Premium Cuvée Merlot 1999	£ 4.50	S
Quinson Château de la Bruyère 1999	£ 4.50	S
Espiral Tempranillo Cabernet 1999	£ 4.50	S
Minervois AC Château Gibalaux-Bonnet 1998	£ 4.80	S
Montepulciano D'abruzzo Chiaro Di Luna 1999	£ 4.80	S
Ca Montini Merlot Cabernet 1998	£ 4.90	S
Argento Malbec 1999	£ 5.00	S
Bright Brothers Barrica Malbec 1999	£ 5.00	S
Finca Las Marias Barbera 1999	£ 5.00	S
Asda Chilean Cabernet Reserve 1999	£ 5.00	S
Los Robles Cabernet Sauvignon 1999	£ 5.00	S
Valdivieso Carignan 1999	£ 5.00	S
Tesco Fitou Reserve Baron de la Tour 1998	£ 5.00	S
Leverano Vigna del Saraceno 1997	£ 5.00	S
Tre Uve 1998	£ 5.00	S
Vigna Alta Me 1999	£ 5.00	S
Vinha da Monte 1998	£ 5.00	S
Asda Arius Syrah 1998	£ 5.00	S
Valle de Vistalba Malbec 1999	£ 5.10	S
Isla Negra Cabernet Sauvignon 1999	£ 5.10	S
McGuigan Black Label 1999	£ 5.20	S
Terramater Zinfandel Syrah 1999	£ 5.20	S
Pigassou NV	£ 5.20	S
Sangiovese Calatrasi 1998	£ 5.20	S
LA Cetto Petite Sirah 1997	£ 5.20	S
Luis Correas Malbec 1999	£ 5.30	S

Rosso Toscano 1997	£ 5.30	S
Pedras do Monte 1999	£ 5.30	S
Coleccion Malbec 1999	£ 5.40	S
Miranda Cabernet Shiraz 1999	£ 5.40	S
Marques de Monistrol Merlot 1997	£ 5.40	S
Caliterra Syrah 1999	£ 5.50	S
Casa La Joya Cabernet Sauvignon 1998	£ 5.50	S
Domaine des lauriers 1997	£ 5.50	S
Canaletto Primitivo d'Puglia 1998	£ 5.50	S
Valle de Vistalba Merlot 1999	£ 5.60	S
Château Pech-Latt AOC Corbieres 1999	£ 5.70	S
Potenza Primitivo 1999	£ 5.70	S
Trio Cabernet 1998	£ 5.80	S
Trio Merlot 1999	£ 5.80	S
Salento Rosso Valle Cupa 1997	£ 5.80	S
Errazuriz Cabernet Sauvignon 1999	£ 5.90	S
La Ronciere Reserve Cabernet Sauvignon 1999	£ 5.90	S
Bergerac Réserve de Château Grinou 1997	£ 5.90	S
JP Garrafeira 1990	£ 5.90	S
Somerfield Syrah VdP d'Oc 1999	£ 3.00	B
Venaison du Roi 1999	£ 3.00	B
Côte du Rhône 1999	£ 3.10	B
JP Tinto	£ 3.30	B
Le Pecher Côtes du Ventoux NV	£ 3.50	B
Biferno 1998	£ 3.50	B
Di Caprio Puglia Red 1999	£ 3.50	B
Szekszardi Bulls Blood 1998	£ 3.60	B
Cinsault Cullinian View 2000	£ 3.70	B
Segneurs d'Aiguilhe 1998	£ 3.80	B
Co-Op Argentine Malbec 1999	£ 4.00	B
Safeway Argentinian Bonarda 1999	£ 4.00	B
Safeway Argentinian Syrah 1999	£ 4.00	B
Co-Op Jacaranda Hill Shiraz 1999	£ 4.00	B
Sommerfield Australian Dry Red 1999	£ 4.00	B
Domaine Boyar Cabernet Sauvignon 1999	£ 4.00	B
Stambolovo Bulgarian Reserve Merlot 1994	£ 4.00	B
Antares Cabernet Sauvignon 1999	£ 4.00	B
Chenet Cabernet Syrah 1999	£ 4.00	B
Daniel Bessiere Collection Carignan Mourvèdre 1998	£ 4.00	B
Reserve St Marc Shiraz 1999	£ 4.00	B
Somerfield Fitou NV	£ 4.00	B
Terrasses d'Azur Cabernet Sauvignon 1999	£ 4.00	B
Hungarovin Bulls Blood 1997	£ 4.00	B
Di Caprio Primitivo 1999	£ 4.00	B
MHV Chianti 1999	£ 4.00	B
Sangiovese di Toscana Casa Vinicola Cecchi SRL 1999	£ 4.00	B
Serina Primitivo 1999	£ 4.00	B

Terrale Primitivo 1999	£4.00	B
Reserve Merlot 1999	£4.00	B
Somerfield South African Cinsault Ruby Cabernet 1999	£4.00	B
Aldeanueva Azabache NV	£4.00	B
Fuente Del Ritmo 1998	£4.00	B
Palacio De Leon 1998	£4.00	
Merlot Tempranillo 1999	£4.00	B
Tunisian Red 1999	£4.00	B
Banrock Station Shiraz Mataro 1999	£4.10	B
Carta Veja Cabernet Sauvignon 1999	£4.10	B
Valle Andino Cabernet Sauvignon 1998	£4.10	B
Señorío de Condestable Crianza 1996	£4.10	B
Tesco Australian Shiraz 1999	£4.30	B
MHV Henri La Fontaine Beaujolais 1999	£4.30	B
La Brocca Puglia Rosso 1999	£4.30	B
Landskroon Cinsaut Shiraz 1999	£4.30	B
Duarte Malbec 1999	£4.40	B
Côtes du Rhône Rouge 1999	£4.40	B
Conti Serristori Chianti 1998	£4.40	B
Bright Brothers Barrica Malbec 1998	£4.50	B
Rio de Plata Malbec 1999	£4.50	B
Santa Ana Malbec 1997	£4.50	B
Viña Morande Syrah 1999	£4.50	B
Domaine de Contenson Merlot 1998	£4.50	B
Fitou Mont Tauch 1998	£4.50	B
Terrasses d'Azur Merlot 1999	£4.50	B
Il Primitivo Del Salento 1999	£4.50	B
Co-op Rioja Tinto Viña Gala NV	£4.50	B
California Mountain Vineyard Syrah 1998	£4.50	B
Miranda Opal Ridge Shiraz Cabernet 1999	£4.60	B
MHV Cabernet Sauvignon Grave Del Friuli 1999	£4.60	B
Kumala Cinsault Pinotage 1999	£4.60	B
Balbi Malbec	£4.70	B
California Mountain Vineyards Grenache Cabernet 1999	£4.70	B
Canaletto Montepulciano d'Abruzzo 1998	£4.80	B
Casa Vinicola Cecchi SrL Chianti 1999	£4.80	B
Valdetán Tinto Joven 1998	£4.80	B
StonyBrook Vineyards Merlot 1988	£4.80	B
Elsa Barbera 1998	£4.90	B
Santa Julia Malbec Cabernet Sauvignon 1999	£4.90	B
Valle de Vistalba Barbera 1999	£4.90	B
Viñas de Medrano Bonarda 1999	£4.90	B
35 Sur Sauvignon Blanc 2000	£4.90	B
La Brocca PrimitivoPuglia 1999	£4.90	B
Adiseno Shiraz 1999	£5.00	B
Bright Brothers Reserve Cabernet Sauvignon 1999	£5.00	B
Bright Brothers Reserve Shiraz 1999	£5.00	B

Fantelli Malbec 1999	£5.00	B
Fantelli Syrah 1999	£5.00	B
Horacio Nesman Malbec 1999	£5.00	B
Magdelana River Malbec Cabernet 1999	£5.00	B
Monster Spicy Red 1999	£5.00	B
Y2K Shiraz 1999	£5.00	B
Jindalee Shiraz 1999	£5.00	B
MHV Nine Pines Estate Australian Shiraz 1998	£5.00	B
Woodvale Shiraz 1998	£5.00	B
Caliterra Cabernet Sauvignon 1999	£5.00	B
Casa Donoso Merlot 1999	£5.00	B
Santa Catalina Cabernet Sauvignon 1999	£5.00	B
Terrarum Carmanère 1999	£5.00	B
Tesco Chilean Cabernet Sauvignon Reserve 1999	£5.00	B
Sodap Bottle Green Cabernet Sauvignon 1999	£5.00	B
Château Bellevue la Forêt AOC Rouge 1998	£5.00	B
Corbières Haut St Georges Rouge 1998	£5.00	B
Crozes Hermitage Selles 1999	£5.00	B
Cuvée 44 1998	£5.00	B
La Baume Domaine Cabernet Sauvignon 1998	£5.00	B
Les Jamelles Mourvedre 1998	£5.00	B
Plan de Brus 1998	£5.00	B
Robert Skalli Minervois 1998	£5.00	B
Maurel VedeauVdP d'Oc Cabernet Franc 1999	£5.00	B
Maurel VedeauVdP d'Oc Merlot Oak Aged 1998	£5.00	B
Tsantali Agiorgitiko 1998	£5.00	B
Calissano Barbera 1998	£5.00	B
Cabernet Franc 1998	£5.00	B
Riparosso Montepulciano d'Abruzzo 1998	£5.00	B
Villa Sandi Cabernet Sauvignon 1998	£5.00	B
Bright Brothers Palmela 1999	£5.00	B
Cabernet Sauvignon 1998	£5.00	B
Fiuza Merlot 1998	£5.00	B
African Legend Pinotage 1999	£5.00	B
Tesco Beyers Truter Pinotage 1999	£5.00	B
Tesco South African Shiraz Cabernet 1998	£5.00	B
Bright Brothers Old Vines Tempranillo 1999	£5.00	B
Dama de Toro 1998	£5.00	B
Jaume Serra Merlot 1998	£5.00	B
Piedemonte Merlot Cabernet 1999	£5.00	B
Tesco Huge Juicy Red 1999	£5.00	B
Catamayor Merlot Tannat 1999	£5.00	B
Perrin La Vieille Ferme 1998	£5.10	B
MHV Henri La Fontaine Macon Rouge 1999	£5.20	B
Stravento Nero d'Avola 1999	£5.20	B
Bela Fonte Jaen 1998	£5.20	B
Romeira Palmela 1998	£5.20	B

Villa Atuel Syrah Villa Atuel 1999	£ 5.30	B
Luis Felipe Edwards Cabernet Sauvignon 1998	£ 5.30	B
Beaujolais Villages 1999	£ 5.30	B
Le Lame Rosso di Montepulciano 1998	£ 5.30	B
Esporao Monte Velho 1999	£ 5.30	B
Sutter Home Pinot Noir 1997	£ 5.30	B
Vinha do Monte 1998	£ 5.40	B
Elsa's Vineyard Malbec 1997	£ 5.50	B
Gosling Creek Shiraz 1998	£ 5.50	B
Casa La Joya Selection Merlot 1998	£ 5.50	B
Casas Del Bosque Cabernet Sauvignon 1999	£ 5.50	B
Dueto Merlot 1999	£ 5.50	B
Domaine Buadelle 1999	£ 5.50	B
Fitou Château Lespigne 1998	£ 5.50	B
Rasteau Côtes du Rhône Villages 1999	£ 5.50	B
Sangiovese Di Puglia Promessa 1999	£ 5.50	B
Valpolicella Classico Superiore Le Bine 1998	£ 5.50	B
Duque de Viseu Red 1997	£ 5.50	B
Vinho Tinto Espiga 1999	£ 5.50	B
José Canepa y Cia Zinfandel 1999	£ 5.60	B
Palo Alto Merlot 1998	£ 5.60	B
Château l'Estang 1998	£ 5.60	B
Château les Fontenelles 1999	£ 5.60	B
Vereto Salice Salentino 1997	£ 5.60	B
Quinta da Bacalhoa 1997	£ 5.60	B
Angove's Classic Reserve Shiraz 1998	£ 5.70	B
De Gras Merlot 1999	£ 5.70	B
Las Casas del Toqui Cabernet Sauvignon Reserve 1998	£ 5.70	B
Viña Gracia Merlot Varietal Curioso 1999	£ 5.70	B
Noblesse de Serenac 1998	£ 5.70	B
Tesco Red Burgundy 1998	£ 5.70	B
Mandrarossa Nero d'Avola 1999	£ 5.70	B
Sandford Estate Cabernet Sauvignon 1998	£ 5.80	B
Château Joinin 1997	£ 5.80	B
Domaine de l'Enclos 1998	£ 5.80	B
Fox Wood Cabernet 1998	£ 5.80	B
MHV Henri La Fontaine Beaujolais Villages 1999	£ 5.80	B
Porta Italica Merlot Cabernet Basilicata 1999	£ 5.80	B
Nederburg Edelrood 1997	£ 5.80	B
McGuigan Bin 2000 Shiraz 1999	£ 5.90	B
Château Clovis 1998	£ 5.90	B
Corbières Château La Domeque Cuvée Signe 1998	£ 5.90	B
Utter Bastard Syrah 1999	£ 5.90	B
XV du President 1999	£ 5.90	B
Montepulciano d'Abruzzo Tralcetto 1998	£ 5.90	B
Santi Valpolicella Classico 1997	£ 5.90	B
Palacio de la Vega Cabernet Tempranillo Crianza 1997	£ 5.90	B

GOLD MEDALS

Valdetán Maceración Carbónica 1999	£ 4.30	G
Passito Verdicchio dei Castelli di Jesi Tordiruta 1997	£ 4.50	G
Domaine la Tour Boisée 1998	£ 5.00	G
Beaujolais la Bareille 1999	£ 5.00	G
McGuigan Black Label Merlot 1999	£ 5.20	G
Seifried Estates Old Coach Road Chardonnay 1999	£ 5.70	G
J&F Lurton Malbec Reserva 1999	£ 6.00	G
Double Bay Chardonnay 1998	£ 6.00	G
Cono Sur Reserve Cabernet Sauvignon 1998	£ 6.00	G
Viña Casa Silva Merlot 1999	£ 6.00	G
Primitivo di Puglia 1999	£ 6.00	G
Tre Uve Ultima 1998	£ 6.00	G
Primitivo di Puglia 1999	£ 6.00	G
Renzo Masi Chianti Riserva 1997	£ 6.80	G
Château Planézes Côtes du Roussillon Villages 1998	£ 7.00	G
Tapu Bay Barrel Fermented Chardonnay Reserve 1997	£ 7.00	G
Valdivieso Reserve Cabernet Sauvignon 1998	£ 7.10	G
Rouge Homme Chardonnay 1999	£ 7.40	G
Dallas Conte Cabernet Sauvignon 1998	£ 7.50	G
Vacqueyras Perrin 1998	£ 7.50	G
Casa La Joya Gran Reserva Cabernet Sauvignon 1998	£ 7.70	G
Carmen Merlot Reserve 1998	£ 7.90	G
Seppelt DP63 Rutherglen Show Muscat	£ 8.00	G
Pinot Grigio Isonzo 1999	£ 8.00	G
Carmen Syrah Reserve 1997	£ 8.10	G
Knappstein Cabernet Merlot 1998	£ 8.20	G
Plantagenet Omrah Shiraz 1998	£ 8.20	G
Cabo de Hornos Cabernet Sauvignon 1997	£ 8.50	G
Ondarre Reserva 1996	£ 8.50	G
Seaview Chardonnay Blanc de Blancs 1996	£ 8.80	G
Evans & Tate Margaret River Shiraz 1999	£ 9.00	G
Porta Select Reserve Cabernet 1998	£ 9.00	G
Gavi di Gavi Masseria dei Carmelitani 1999	£ 9.30	G
Castello Guerrieri Rosso 1995	£ 9.50	G
Lan Reserva 1996	£ 9.50	G
Rive Alasia 1998	£ 9.70	G
Rothbury Brokenback Shiraz 1998	£ 9.80	G
Tim Adams Shiraz 1998	£ 9.80	G
Balbi Barbaro 1997	£ 10.00	G
Primo Estate Il Briconne 1998	£ 10.00	G

Weingut Münzenrieder Sämling Bouvier TBA 1997	£ 10.00	G
Château de la Nauve 1998	£ 10.00	G
Château Peychaud Misoneuve 1997	£ 10.00	G
Mt Ida Shiraz 1998	£ 10.70	G
Schloss Johannisberger Riesling Kabinet -Red Seal 1998	£ 10.80	G
Barbera d'Asti La Luna el Falo' 1997	£ 10.80	G
Ngatarawa Glazebrook Merlot Cabernet 1998	£ 10.90	G
Paul Conti Manjimup Shiraz 1997	£ 11.00	G
Santa Rita Triple C 1997	£ 11.00	G
Zanna 1997	£ 11.10	G
Wolf Blass Presidents Selection Shiraz 1996	£ 11.20	G
Marqués de Riscal Reserva 1996	£ 11.50	G
Miranda Family Reserve Chardonnay 1998	£ 11.60	G
Domaine Capion Le Juge 1996	£ 11.60	G
Riesling Wintzenheim Grand Cru 1997	£ 11.70	G
Chateau Reynella Shiraz 1997	£ 12.00	G
Matariki Anthology 1998	£ 12.00	G
Luigi Bosca Malbec Verdot 1995	£ 12.20	G
Chianti San Zio 1998	£ 12.40	G
Riesling Altenberg de Bergheim Grand Cru 1997	£ 13.00	G
Corbans Cottage Block Chardonnay 1997	£ 13.00	G
Galpin Peak Pinot Noir Tête de Cuvée 1997	£ 13.00	G
Sebastiani Sonoma County Chardonnay 1998	£ 13.00	G
Forster Pechstein Riesling Spätlese Trocken 1998	£ 13.30	G
Geoff Merrill Reserve Shiraz 1996	£ 13.50	G
Tokay Pinot Gris Furstentum Grand Cru 1998	£ 13.50	G
Fairview Cyril Back Zinfandel 1997	£ 13.50	G
Moulin-à-Vent Clos de Rochegres 1997	£ 13.70	G
Château de Pibarnon 1996	£ 13.70	G
Château de Pibarnon 1997	£ 13.80	G
Lindemans Pyrus 1997	£ 14.00	G
CJ Pask Reserve Merlot 1998	£ 14.00	G
Quinta da Roeda 1983	£ 14.00	G
MHV The House Brut Champagne NV	£ 14.50	G
Château de Pibarnon 1998	£ 14.80	G
Seppelt Great Western Shiraz 1997	£ 14.90	G
Esk Valley Reserve Merlot Malbec Cabernet 1997	£ 14.90	G
Clos La Chance Napa Valley Chardonnay 1997	£ 14.90	G
Annie's Lane Contour Vineyard Shiraz 1997	£ 15.00	G
Lenswood Knappstein Pinot Noir 1998	£ 15.00	G
Wirra Wirra The Angelus 1996	£ 15.10	G
Tatachilla Foundation Shiraz 1998	£ 15.20	G
Warre's Bottle Matured LBV 1992	£ 15.40	G
Hidden Valley Pinotage 1997	£ 15.70	G
Capitel Recioto Classico Monte Fontana 1996	£ 15.80	G
Riesling Sommerberg Grand Cru 1998	£ 16.00	G

Yering Station Reserve Pinot Noir 1998	£ 17.00	G
Tyrrell's Vat 8 Shiraz Cabernet 1997	£ 17.10	G
Amarone Classico 1995	£ 17.10	G
Viña Lanciano Reserva 1996	£ 17.10	G
Tokaji 5 Puttonyos 1994	£ 17.20	G
Scharzhofberger Riesling Spätlese 1996	£ 17.30	G
St Romain 1998	£ 17.60	G
Guimaraens 1986	£ 17.70	G
St Francis Merlot Reserve 1996	£ 17.70	G
Côte Rôtie 1998	£ 17.90	G
Steve Maglieiri Shiraz 1998	£ 18.00	G
Riesling Rangen de Thann Grand Cru No 10 1997	£ 18.00	G
Waitrose Brut Vintage 1990	£ 18.00	G
Errázuriz Don Maximiano Founders Reserve 1998	£ 18.20	G
González Byass Apóstoles	£ 18.30	G
Brauneberger Juffer Sonnenuhr Riesling Auslese 1997	£ 18.50	G
Mountadam Cabernet Sauvignon 1996	£ 18.90	G
Pinot Gris Heimbourg Grand Cru 1998	£ 19.00	G
Meursault 1997	£ 19.00	G
Chianti Classico Reserva 1997	£ 19.00	G
Barros Vintage 1997	£ 19.10	G
Peter Lehmann Stonewell Shiraz 1994	£ 20.00	G
Côte Rotie La Viaillère 1995	£ 20.00	G
Puligny Montrachet Claude Chonion 1997	£ 20.00	G
Sonoma County Shiraz 1997	£ 20.00	G
Ridge Geyserville 1997	£ 20.00	G
Yaldara Farms Shiraz 1998	£ 20.20	G
Stonewell Shiraz 1994	£ 20.20	G
Riesling Furstentum Grand Cru Vielles Vignes 1998	£ 20.30	G
González Byass Noé	£ 20.50	G
Clos du Val Merlot 1997	£ 20.80	G
Graham's Malvedos 1988	£ 21.10	G
Quinta de Vargellas 1987	£ 21.10	G
Henriques & Henriques 15 YO Verdelho	£ 21.70	G
Muskat Ottonel No 5 Zwischen Den Seen Beerenauslese 1997	£ 22.00	G
Barbadillo Obispo Gascon Palo Cortado	£ 22.00	G
Amarone Della Valpolicella Classico Caterina Zardini 1997	£ 22.50	G
Château Trottevieille 1996	£ 22.80	G
Jermann Capo Martino 1997	£ 22.80	G
Côte-Rotie Seigneur de Maugiron 1997	£ 23.00	G
Charles Heidsieck Brut Réserve Mis en Cave 1995	£ 23.50	G
Fleury Champagne Brut 1993	£ 23.90	G
Buena Vista Carneros Pinot Noir Grand Reserve 1995	£ 24.50	G
The Famous Gate Domaine Carneros Pinot Noir 1998	£ 24.60	G
Gewürztraminer Rangen de Thann Grand Cru SGN 1994	£ 25.00	G
Volnay 1er Cru Les Chevrets 1996	£ 25.00	G

Romitorio di Santedame IGT Toscana 1996	£ 25.00	G
Quinta Nova de Nossa Senhora do Carmo 1997	£ 25.00	G
Osborne 1997	£ 25.00	G
Elderton Command Shiraz 1996	£ 25.80	G
Allegrini La Poja 1996	£ 27.20	G
Nicolas Feuillatte Brut 1er Cru Cuvée Speciale 1995	£ 28.00	G
Nuits St George Les Vaucrains 1er Cru 1994	£ 28.20	G
Montes Alpha M 1997	£ 28.40	G
Flaccianello Della Pieve 1997	£ 28.50	G
Lanson Brut Millésime 1994	£ 28.60	G
Eileen Hardy Shiraz 1997	£ 28.70	G
Houghton Jack Mann 1996	£ 28.80	G
Single Cask Palo Cortado Bodega de Tonel	£ 29.00	G
Cain Five 1995	£ 29.00	G
E&E Black Pepper Shiraz 1997	£ 29.20	G
Rosemount Estate Balmoral Syrah 1997	£ 30.20	G
Siepi Rosso di Toscana 1997	£ 30.30	G
Amarone Della Valpolicella Classico Riserva Sergio Zenato 1993	£ 30.80	G
Moët & Chandon Brut Impérial Vintage Rosé 1993	£ 31.50	G
Clos de l'Obac 1997	£ 32.00	G
Grant Burge Meshach 1991	£ 32.20	G
Northern Sonoma Cabernet Sauvignon 1996	£ 33.30	G
BV Georges de Latour Cabernet Sauvignon 1996	£ 34.00	G
Pol Roger Brut Vintage 1993	£ 34.50	G
Vosne-Romanee 1997	£ 35.00	G
Dow's 30 YO	£ 35.00	G
Taittinger Vintage Brut 1992	£ 35.20	G
Corton Bressandes 1997	£ 35.20	G
Michael Shiraz 1997	£ 35.30	G
Penfolds Bin 707 Cabernet Sauvignon 1997	£ 35.90	G
Calem Vintage 1997	£ 36.00	G
Penfolds RWT Shiraz 1997	£ 36.10	G
Graham's 30 YO	£ 46.70	G
Charles Heidsieck Réserve Charlie Mis en Cave 1990	£ 50.00	G
Lanson Noble Cuvée 1988	£ 50.20	G
Champagne Deutz Cuvée William 1990	£ 55.00	G
Corton Charlemagne 1996	£ 55.00	G
Vieux Château Certan 1996	£ 59.60	G
Graham's Forty YO	£ 65.00	G
Refosco DOC Valentino Paladin 1999	£ 72.00	G
Taittinger Comtes de Champagne Blanc de Blancs Brut 1990	£ 74.80	G
Pol Roger Sir Winston Churchill Cuvée 1990	£ 74.90	G
Charles Heidsieck Champagne Charlie 1985	£ 76.00	G
Charles Heidsieck Blanc de Blancs (Oenotheque) 1982	£ 90.00	G
Opus One 1996	£ 90.00	G
Vieux Château Certan 1986	£ 96.70	G

SILVER MEDALS

Anapi River Sauvignon Blanc 1999	£ 3.50	S
Boyar Lambol Merlot 1999	£ 3.70	S
MHV Firriato Sicialian Red 1998	£ 3.70	S
Suhindol Cabernet Merlot Reserve 1996	£ 4.00	S
Suhindol Merlot Reserve 1996	£ 4.00	S
Terrasses d'Azur Sauvignon Blanc 1999	£ 4.00	S
Domaine de Bouscau 1999	£ 4.00	S
La Cité Chardonnay Vin de Pays d'Oc 1999	£ 4.00	S
La Vis Pinot Grigio 1999	£ 4.00	S
Barbera Colli Tortonesi 1998	£ 4.00	S
Rallo Cremvo Marsala	£ 4.00	S
MHV Australian Semillon NV	£ 4.20	S
Marks & Spencer Gold Label Syrah 1999	£ 4.20	S
Sainsbury's Copertino Riserva 1996	£ 4.30	S
Casa Calatrasi Tu Carignan Mourvèdre 1999	£ 4.30	S
Finest Amontillado	£ 4.40	S
Adiseno Cabernet Shiraz 1999	£ 4.50	S
Far Flung Malbec 1999	£ 4.50	S
Woolpunda Chardonnay 1998	£ 4.50	S
Domaine Boyar Premium Cuvée Cabernet Sauvignon 1999	£ 4.50	S
Domaine Boyar Premium Cuvée Merlot 1999	£ 4.50	S
Denbies Surrey Gold 1999	£ 4.50	S
Quinson Château de la Bruyère 1999	£ 4.50	S
Villa Sandi Chardonnay 1999	£ 4.50	S
Espiral Tempranillo Cabernet 1999	£ 4.50	S
Castle Creek Semillon 1998	£ 4.60	S
Château l'Ermitage White 1999	£ 4.60	S
Trulli Chardonnay 1999	£ 4.60	S
Minervois AC Château Gibalaux-Bonnet 1998	£ 4.80	S
Montepulciano D'abruzzo Chiaro di Luna 1999	£ 4.80	S
Hardy's Nottage Hill Chardonnay 1999	£ 4.90	S
Ca Montini Merlot Cabernet 1998	£ 4.90	S
Argento Malbec 1999	£ 5.00	S
Bright Brothers Barrica Malbec 1999	£ 5.00	S
Finca Las Marias Barbera 1999	£ 5.00	S
Jindalee Chardonnay 1998	£ 5.00	S
Valdivieso Carignan 1999	£ 5.00	S
Los Robles Cabernet Sauvignon 1999	£ 5.00	S
Asda Chilean Cabernet Reserve 1999	£ 5.00	S

SILVER MEDALS

Cono Sur Viognier 1999	£ 5.00	S
Tesco Fitou Reserve Baron de la Tour 1998	£ 5.00	S
Bright Brothers Sicilian Barrel Fermented Chardonnay 1998	£ 5.00	S
Leverano Vigna del Saraceno 1997	£ 5.00	S
Vigna Alta Me 1999	£ 5.00	S
Tre Uve 1998	£ 5.00	S
Vinha da Monte 1998	£ 5.00	S
Finest Pale Amontillado	£ 5.00	S
Asda Arius Syrah 1998	£ 5.00	S
Valle de Vistalba Malbec 1999	£ 5.10	S
Isla Negra Cabernet Sauvignon 1999	£ 5.10	S
McGuigan Black Label 1999	£ 5.20	S
Terramater Zinfandel Syrah 1999	£ 5.20	S
Pigassou NV	£ 5.20	S
Sangiovese Calatrasi 1998	£ 5.20	S
Terre di Ginestra Catarratto 1999	£ 5.20	S
LA Cetto Petite Sirah 1997	£ 5.20	S
Luis Correas Malbec 1999	£ 5.30	S
Miranda Chardonnay 1999	£ 5.30	S
Riesling Selection 1998	£ 5.30	S
Rosso Toscano 1997	£ 5.30	S
Pedras do Monte 1999	£ 5.30	S
Colección Malbec 1999	£ 5.40	S
Miranda Cabernet Shiraz 1999	£ 5.40	S
Miranda Chardonnay 1998	£ 5.40	S
Marqués de Monistrol Merlot 1997	£ 5.40	S
Miranda Brothers Oak Aged Chardonnay 1999	£ 5.50	S
Caliterra Syrah 1999	£ 5.50	S
Casas del Bosque Chardonnay 1999	£ 5.50	S
Casa La Joya Cabernet Sauvignon 1998	£ 5.50	S
La Pintora Chardonnay 1999	£ 5.50	S
Domaine des Lauriers 1997	£ 5.50	S
Graacher Himmelreich Riesling Spatlese 1997	£ 5.50	S
Canaletto Primitivo d'Puglia 1998	£ 5.50	S
Waitrose Solera Jerezana Amontillado Secco	£ 5.50	S
Valle de Vistalba Merlot 1999	£ 5.60	S
Long Terrace Semillon Chardonnay 1999	£ 5.60	S
Old Master Ruby Port NV	£ 5.60	S
Kingston Estate Wildlife Chardonnay 1998	£ 5.70	S
Château Pech-Latt AOC Corbières 1999	£ 5.70	S
Potenza Primitivo 1999	£ 5.70	S
Alpha Domus Sauvignon Blanc 1999	£ 5.70	S
Vidal Estate Sauvignon Blanc Hawkes Bay 1998	£ 5.70	S
Trio Merlot 1999	£ 5.80	S

Trio Cabernet 1998	£ 5.80	S
Laithwaite Sauvignon Blanc 1999	£ 5.80	S
Salento Rosso Valle Cupa 1997	£ 5.80	S
Errázuriz Cabernet Sauvignon 1999	£ 5.90	S
La Ronciere Reserve Cabernet Sauvignon 1999	£ 5.90	S
Bergerac Réserve de Château Grinou 1997	£ 5.90	S
Nobilo Sauvignon Blanc 1999	£ 5.90	S
JP Garrafeira 1990	£ 5.90	S
Etchart Cabernet Sauvignon 1998	£ 6.00	S
Terrazas Alto Malbec 1999	£ 6.00	S
Terrazas Alto Chardonnay 1999	£ 6.00	S
Diego Murillo Family Reserve Malbec 1998	£ 6.00	S
E&C McLaren Vale Chardonnay 1999	£ 6.00	S
Penfolds Magill Tawny	£ 6.00	S
Santa Inés Merlot Reserve 1999	£ 6.00	S
Bodega de La Familia 1997	£ 6.00	S
Que Sera Barrel Aged Syrah 1999	£ 6.00	S
Domaine la Tour Boisee Cuvee Marie-Claude 1998	£ 6.00	S
Domaine Puy du Maupas Côtes du Rhône 1998	£ 6.00	S
Croix du Mayne 1998	£ 6.00	S
Serriger Vogelsang Riesling Auslese 1989	£ 6.00	S
Pollo Del Ruspo Sangiovese 1998	£ 6.00	S
Marsala Superiore Garibaldi Dolce	£ 6.00	S
MHV Regimental Tawny Port	£ 6.00	S
Bright Bros Douro Torcular 1999	£ 6.00	S
Porcupine Ridge Merlot 1999	£ 6.00	S
Apostles Falls Cabernet Sauvignon 1998	£ 6.00	S
Viña Albali Gran Reserva 1993	£ 6.00	S
Concavins Merlot 1998	£ 6.00	S
Delicato Syrah 1998	£ 6.00	S
Ironstone Shiraz 1997	£ 6.00	S
Terrazas Alto Cabernet Sauvignon 1999	£ 6.10	S
Finca el Retiro Malbec 1999	£ 6.10	S
The Mill Chardonnay 1999	£ 6.10	S
Casablanca White Label Cabernet Sauvignon 1998	£ 6.10	S
Salice Salentino Riserva 1997	£ 6.10	S
Pepperwood Grove Zinfandel 1998	£ 6.10	S
Hanwood Cabernet Sauvignon 1997	£ 6.20	S
Rouge Homme Shiraz Cabernet 1998	£ 6.20	S
Seppelt Terrain Shiraz 1999	£ 6.20	S
Essington Shiraz 1999	£ 6.20	S
Bleasdale Malbec 1999	£ 6.20	S
Deen De Bortoli Vat 1 Durif 1998	£ 6.30	S
Deen De Bortoli Vat 8 Shiraz 1999	£ 6.30	S

SILVER MEDALS

Luis Felipe Edwards Cabernet Sauvignon Reserva 1997	£ 6.30	S
Cono Sur Merlot Reserve 1999	£ 6.30	S
Fairview Malbec 1999	£ 6.30	S
KWV Merlot 1998	£ 6.30	S
Wakefield Estate Riesling 1996	£ 6.40	S
Jacob's Creek Reserve Chardonnay 1998	£ 6.50	S
La Tenuta Beltrame Cabernet Franc 1998	£ 6.50	S
La Tenuta Beltrame Merlot 1997	£ 6.50	S
Aglianico del Vulture I Portoli 1997	£ 6.50	S
Enate Rosado 1999	£ 6.50	S
High Country Cabernet Sauvignon 1998	£ 6.60	S
Régnié 1999	£ 6.60	S
Graham Beck Chardonnay 1999	£ 6.60	S
Jacob's Creek Limited Release Shiraz Cabernet 1995	£ 6.80	S
Hatzimichalis Merlot 1998	£ 6.80	S
Marthinus Pinotage 1999	£ 6.80	S
Château Pevy-Saincrit 1997	£ 6.90	S
Bright Brothers Barrica Shiraz 1998	£ 7.00	S
Riddoch Estate Chardonnay 1998	£ 7.00	S
Wolf Blass South Australian Chardonnay 1999	£ 7.00	S
E&C McLaren Vale Cabernet Sauvignon 1998	£ 7.00	S
Primo Estate La Biondina 1999	£ 7.00	S
Botany Creek Black Seal 1998	£ 7.00	S
Stanton & Killeen Rutherglen Muscat	£ 7.00	S
Montgras Zinfandel Single Vineyard 1999	£ 7.00	S
Undurraga Chardonnay Reserva 1999	£ 7.00	S
Veramonte Merlot 1997	£ 7.00	S
Château de L'Amarine Cuvée des Bernis Rouge 1998	£ 7.00	S
Chinon Domaine de La Diligence 1998	£ 7.00	S
Chenas Château de Chenas 1999	£ 7.00	S
Domaine de Saint Hilaire La Serpentine 1998	£ 7.00	S
Zenato Merlot Delle Veneziie 1997	£ 7.00	S
Anthilia Bianco 1999	£ 7.00	S
Babich Riesling 1999	£ 7.00	S
Chancellor Mt Cass Waipara Riesling 1999	£ 7.00	S
Waipara Riesling Estate Bottled 1998	£ 7.00	S
Palmela Particular 1998	£ 7.00	S
Fiuza Reserva Cabernet Merlot 1998	£ 7.00	S
Fairview Shiraz Mourvèdre 1998	£ 7.00	S
Sotelo 1996	£ 7.00	S
Toro Crianza 1997	£ 7.00	S
Espiral Tempranillo Barrique 1999	£ 7.00	S
Sonoma County Merlot 1998	£ 7.00	S
Valley Oaks Cabernet Sauvignon 1997	£ 7.00	S

Caliterra Cabernet Sauvignon Reserva 1997	£ 7.10	S
Campbells Rutherglen Muscat	£ 7.20	S
Diamond Valley Chardonnay Blue Label 1998	£ 7.20	S
Yenda Vineyards Botrytis Semillon 1996	£ 7.20	S
Caliterra Arboleda Syrah 1999	£ 7.20	S
Caliterra Chardonnay Reserva 1998	£ 7.20	S
Moulin-à-Vent 1997	£ 7.20	S
Falanghina Sannio Benevantano DOC 1999	£ 7.20	S
De Redcliffe Estate Marlborough Riesling 1998	£ 7.20	S
Graham Beck Shiraz 1998	£ 7.20	S
Turning Leaf Vintner's Collection Zinfandel 1996	£ 7.20	S
Baileys Shiraz 1998	£ 7.30	S
Wyndham Estate Bin 555 Shiraz 1998	£ 7.30	S
Rosemount Estate Shiraz 1999	£ 7.30	S
Peter Lehmann Shiraz 1998	£ 7.30	S
d'Arry's Original Grenache Shiraz 1998	£ 7.30	S
Las Lomas Cot Rouge Reserva 1998	£ 7.30	S
Wakefield Estate Chardonnay 1998	£ 7.40	S
Caliterra Merlot Reserva 1998	£ 7.40	S
Cappello di Prete Rosso del Salento 1996	£ 7.40	S
Funtanaliras Vermintino di Gallura 1999	£ 7.40	S
Conde de Valdemar Crianza 1997	£ 7.40	S
Elderton Riesling 1999	£ 7.50	S
Stonyfell Metala Shiraz Cabernet Sauvignon 1998	£ 7.50	S
Jacob's Creek Limited Release Shiraz Cabernet 1996	£ 7.50	S
Chapel Hill Unwooded Chardonnay 1998	£ 7.50	S
Château de la Grille 1997	£ 7.50	S
La Segreta Rosso 1999	£ 7.50	S
Pinot Grigio Collio Classica 1999	£ 7.50	S
Sedara Rosso 1998	£ 7.50	S
Somerfield Navigators LBV Port 1992	£ 7.50	S
Fetzer Syrah 1997	£ 7.50	S
Rosemount Estate Kirri Billi Brut 1997	£ 7.60	S
Safeway LBV Port 1995	£ 7.60	S
Mitchelton Blackwood Park Riesling 1999	£ 7.70	S
Stonyfell Metala Shiraz Cabernet Sauvignon 1997	£ 7.70	S
Pirramimma Petit Verdot 1997	£ 7.70	S
Colefield Vineyard Sauvignon Blanc 1999	£ 7.70	S
Villiera Chardonnay 1999	£ 7.70	S
Tokay Pinot Gris Heimbourg Grand Cru 1998	£ 7.80	S
Châteauneuf-du-Pape Les Cellier des Princes 1998	£ 7.80	S
Lawson's Dry Hills Sauvignon Blanc 1999	£ 7.80	S
Clifford Bay Sauvignon Blanc 1999	£ 7.80	S
Basedow Chardonnay 1998	£ 7.90	S

SILVER MEDALS

Crozes Hermitage 1998	£ 7.90	S
Valpolicella Valpantena Superiore Ripasso Le Vigne 1998	£ 7.90	S
Groote Post Sauvignon Blanc 1999	£ 7.90	S
Etchart Arnaldo B Reserva 1997	£ 8.00	S
Three Valleys Cabernet Sauvignon 1998	£ 8.00	S
Jamiesons Run Merlot 1998	£ 8.00	S
Coldstream Hills Chardonnay 1997	£ 8.00	S
Seppelt Chalambar Shiraz 1997	£ 8.00	S
Andrew Garrett Martindale Hall 1998	£ 8.00	S
Yarra Glen Cabernet Sauvignon 1998	£ 8.00	S
Normans Old Vines Shiraz 1998	£ 8.00	S
Bleasdale Bremmer View Shiraz 1998	£ 8.00	S
Riesling Heimbourg Grand Cru 1996	£ 8.00	S
Chablis Vielles Vignes Tour de Roy 1998	£ 8.00	S
Ducla Permanence 1998	£ 8.00	S
Chablis André Simon 1999	£ 8.00	S
Château Mercier Cuvée Prestige 1997	£ 8.00	S
St Amour Guy Patissier 1999	£ 8.00	S
Chablis 1999	£ 8.00	S
Hilltop Neszmely Aszu 5 Puttonyos 1993	£ 8.00	S
San Marco Meraco 1999	£ 8.00	S
Esk Valley Chardonnay 1999	£ 8.00	S
Giesen Marlborough Sauvignon Blanc 1999	£ 8.00	S
Jordan Blanc Fume 1999	£ 8.00	S
Paul Cluver Sauvignon Blanc 1999	£ 8.00	S
KWV Cathedral Cellar Stellenbosch Cabernet Sauvignon 1997	£ 8.00	S
Don PX Vino Dulce de Pasas	£ 8.00	S
Viña Alarde Reserva 1996	£ 8.00	S
Quarto Merlot 1997	£ 8.00	S
Sonoma County Cabernet Sauvignon 1996	£ 8.00	S
Concannon Petit Sirah 1997	£ 8.00	S
Carmen Reserve Pinot Noir 1998	£ 8.10	S
Selaks Drylands Estate Sauvignon Blanc 1999	£ 8.10	S
Villiera Merlot 1998	£ 8.10	S
Clos Malverne Basket Pressed Pinotage 1999	£ 8.10	S
Montevina Barbera 1996	£ 8.10	S
Brown Brothers Cabernet Sauvignon 1998	£ 8.20	S
Windowrie Shiraz 1999	£ 8.20	S
Fleurie 1999	£ 8.20	S
Kim Crawford Marlborough Dry Riesling 1999	£ 8.20	S
Barón de ley Reserva 1996	£ 8.20	S
Abadia Retuerta Rivola 1998	£ 8.20	S
Bonterra Merlot 1997	£ 8.20	S
Peter Lehmann Cabernet Sauvignon 1998	£ 8.30	S

Errázuriz Chardonnay Reserva 1997	£ 8.30	S
Casablanca Santa Isabel Barrel Fermented Chardonnay 1998	£ 8.30	S
Chianti Classico la Sala 1998	£ 8.30	S
Brown Brothers Shiraz 1997	£ 8.40	S
Grove Mill Marlborough Chardonnay 1998	£ 8.40	S
Brown Brothers Family Reserve Riesling 1997	£ 8.50	S
Knappstein Shiraz 1997	£ 8.50	S
Normans Old Vines Grenache 1998	£ 8.50	S
Single Vineyard Reserve Merlot 1998	£ 8.50	S
Valley Vineyards Fumé 1998	£ 8.50	S
Jurancon Sec Chant des Vignes 1999	£ 8.50	S
Chianti Classico DOCG Blue Label 1997	£ 8.50	S
Primitivo di Manduria DOC 1998	£ 8.50	S
Cortes de Cima 1999	£ 8.50	S
Groote Post Chardonnay 1999	£ 8.50	S
Fairview Cyril Back Shiraz 1998	£ 8.50	S
Kumala Reserve Merlot 1999	£ 8.50	S
Elderton Golden Semillon 1997	£ 8.60	S
Lindemans Padthaway Shiraz 1997	£ 8.60	S
Riesling Wineck-Schlossberg Grand Cru 1997	£ 8.60	S
Chablis Les Vignerons de Chablis 1998	£ 8.60	S
Wachenheimer Goldbachel Riesling Kabinett Troken 1998	£ 8.60	S
Spice Route Pinotage 1999	£ 8.60	S
KWV Cathedral Cellar Pinotage 1997	£ 8.60	S
Nepenthe Unwooded Chardonnay 1999	£ 8.70	S
St Hallett Barossa Shiraz 1998	£ 8.70	S
Fernhill Estate Semillon 1998	£ 8.70	S
Errázuriz Cabernet Sauvignon Reserva 1997	£ 8.70	S
Cadenza Sangiovese del Umbria 1999	£ 8.70	S
Mansion House Bay Sauvignon Blanc 1999	£ 8.70	S
Amontillado del Puerto Almacenista	£ 8.70	S
Nieto e Senetiner Reserve Malbec 1999	£ 8.80	S
Best's Victoria Cabernet Sauvignon 1998	£ 8.80	S
Mount Pleasant Elizabeth Semillon 1994	£ 8.80	S
The Twenty Eight Road Mourvèdre 1998	£ 8.80	S
Zenato Valpolicella Ripassa Zenato 1996	£ 8.80	S
Craggy Range Sauvignon Blanc 1999	£ 8.80	S
Spice Route Shiraz 1999	£ 8.80	S
Viña Alberdi Reserva 1994	£ 8.80	S
Manzanilla Amontillado Almacenista Manuel Cuevas Jurado	£ 8.90	S
Palo Cortado Almacenista Vides	£ 8.90	S
Familia Zuccardi Q Malbec 1998	£ 9.00	S
Familia Zuccardi Q Chardonnay 1999	£ 9.00	S
Seaview Chardonnay Blanc de Blancs 1995	£ 9.00	S

SILVER MEDALS

Penfolds Bin 28 Shiraz 1997	£ 9.00	S
Yalumba Noble Pick Botrytis Viognier 1998	£ 9.00	S
Maglieri Shiraz 1998	£ 9.00	S
St Hallett Semillon Select 1998	£ 9.00	S
Single Vineyard Reserve Cabernet Franc 1998	£ 9.00	S
Single Vineyard Reserve Malbec 1998	£ 9.00	S
Santa Carolina Barrica Selection Chardonnay 1999	£ 9.00	S
Laithwaite Garage Red NV	£ 9.00	S
Château Reynon Rouge 1998	£ 9.00	S
Moulin-à-Vent C Flamy 1999	£ 9.00	S
Chianti Riserva Nerisso 1995	£ 9.00	S
Ciro Classico Riserva Duca San Felice 1997	£ 9.00	S
Chianti Classico Riserva 1995	£ 9.00	S
Delegat's Reserve Merlot 1998	£ 9.00	S
Delegat's Reserve Cabernet Sauvignon 1998	£ 9.00	S
Coopers Creek Merlot Reserve 1998	£ 9.00	S
Corbans Winemaker's Selection Sauvignon Blanc 1999	£ 9.00	S
Matua Valley Judd Estate Chardonnay 1999	£ 9.00	S
CJ Pask Merlot 1998	£ 9.00	S
Old Road Pinotage 1998	£ 9.00	S
Dieu Donne Merlot 1998	£ 9.00	S
Palacio de la Vega Cabernet Sauvignon Reserva 1996	£ 9.00	S
Marques de Requena Sauvignon 1994	£ 9.00	S
Fetzer Vineyards Barrel Select Zinfandel 1997	£ 9.00	S
Fetzer Vineyards Barrel Select Merlot 1997	£ 9.00	S
Estancia Pinot Noir 1998	£ 9.00	S
Talus Zinfandel 1997	£ 9.00	S
Chittering Estate Cabernet Merlot 1998	£ 9.10	S
Tatachilla Padthaway Cabernet Sauvignon 1998	£ 9.10	S
Mamre Brook Cabernet Sauvignon 1997	£ 9.10	S
Greco di Tufo DOC 1999	£ 9.10	S
Touriga Nacional Casa Santos Lima 1999	£ 9.10	S
Mclaren Vale Picture Series Grenache 1998	£ 9.20	S
Valdivieso Reserve Malbec 1996	£ 9.20	S
Vouvray Tris de Grains Nobles 1995	£ 9.20	S
Giesen Reserve Barrel Selection Chardonnay 1998	£ 9.20	S
Graham Beck Blanc de Blancs 1993	£ 9.20	S
Artadi Viñas de Gain Rioja Crianza 1997	£ 9.20	S
Cypress Chardonnay 1998	£ 9.20	S
R H Phillips Toasted Head Chardonnay 1998	£ 9.20	S
Campbells Bobbie Burns Rutherglen Shiraz 1998	£ 9.30	S
Chateau Reynella Chardonnay 1998	£ 9.30	S
Vasse Felix Semillon Sauvignon 1999	£ 9.30	S
Haselgrove Bentwing Wrattonbully Shiraz 1998	£ 9.30	S

Gewürztraminer Vieilles Vignes 1999	£ 9.30	S
Les Hauts de Forca Real Côtes du Roussillon Villages 1998	£ 9.30	S
Il Falcone Riserva Castel del Monte 1997	£ 9.30	S
Plaisir de Merle Chardonnay 1999	£ 9.30	S
Beringer Vineyards Chardonnay 1998	£ 9.30	S
Hut Block Cabernets 1998	£ 9.40	S
Bridgewater Mill Shiraz 1997	£ 9.40	S
Rosemount Estate Hill Of Gold Shiraz 1998	£ 9.40	S
d'Arenberg Noble Riesling 1998	£ 9.40	S
Nepenthe Sauvignon Blanc 1999	£ 9.40	S
Jackson Estate Chardonnay 1999	£ 9.40	S
Mas Ignens FA 206 1998	£ 9.40	S
Mamre Brook Shiraz 1998	£ 9.50	S
Penfolds Bin 128 Coonawarra Shiraz 1997	£ 9.50	S
Tim Adams Cabernet Sauvignon 1998	£ 9.50	S
Sandalford Shiraz 1997	£ 9.50	S
Château du Seuil Graves Blanc 1998	£ 9.50	S
Le Vaglie Verdicchio Dei Castelli di Jesi Classico 1998	£ 9.50	S
Quinta Do Crasto Douro Reserva 1998	£ 9.50	S
Quady Starboard Batch 88	£ 9.50	S
Rosemount Estate Orange Vineyard Cabernet Sauvignon 1997	£ 9.60	S
Isabel Estate Sauvignon Blanc 1999	£ 9.60	S
Boschendal Shiraz 1997	£ 9.60	S
Weinert Malbec 1995	£ 9.70	S
Devils Lair Fifth Leg Red 1998	£ 9.70	S
Charles Cimicky Daylight Chamber Grenache 1998	£ 9.70	S
Château Ludon-Pomies Agassac 1997	£ 9.70	S
Cortes de Cima Reserva 1998	£ 9.70	S
Anthony's Reserve Shiraz 1997	£ 9.80	S
Errázuriz Pinot Noir Reserva 1999	£ 9.80	S
Montes Alpha Chardonnay 1998	£ 9.80	S
Blandy's Duke Of Clarence	£ 9.80	S
Kendall-Jackson Vintner's Reserve Pinot Noir 1998	£ 9.80	S
St Joseph les Larmes du Père 1998	£ 9.90	S
Montana Reserve Pinot Noir 1998	£ 9.90	S
Riddoch Estate Shiraz 1998	£ 10.00	S
E&C Section 353 Shiraz 1997	£ 10.00	S
E&C Section 353 Chardonnay 1997	£ 10.00	S
Temple Bruer Cabernet Petit Verdot 1998	£ 10.00	S
Chapel Hill Shiraz 1998	£ 10.00	S
Mclaren Vale Picture Series Shiraz 1998	£ 10.00	S
Errázuriz Sangiovese Reserva 1998	£ 10.00	S
Errázuriz Sangiovese Reserva 1999	£ 10.00	S
Château Mourques du Grès Capitelles des Mourgues 1998	£ 10.00	S

SILVER MEDALS

Domaine de la Baume Estate Red 1998	£ 10.00	S
Domaine Michel Thomas Sancerre 1999	£ 10.00	S
La Grande Cuvée de Dourthe Margaux 1996	£ 10.00	S
Montirius Vacqueyras 1999	£ 10.00	S
Dunico Primitivo di Manduria Masseria Pepe 1998	£ 10.00	S
Chianti Classico Riserva 1995	£ 10.00	S
Craggy Range Marlborough Chardonnay 1999	£ 10.00	S
Sacred Hill Basket Press Cabernet Sauvignon 1998	£ 10.00	S
Dow's LBV 1995	£ 10.00	S
Sandeman Imperial Tawny	£ 10.00	S
Fort Simon Chardonnay 1998	£ 10.00	S
Raventos I Blanc Cava Brut Reserva NV	£ 10.00	S
Dos Cortados	£ 10.00	S
Concavins Reserve Cabernet Sauvignon 1996	£ 10.00	S
Fetzer Barrel Select Pinot Noir 1998	£ 10.00	S
Bonterra Vineyards Merlot 1998	£ 10.00	S
Live Oak Road Old Bush Vine Zinfandel 1999	£ 10.00	S
Estancia Pinot Noir Pinnacles 1998	£ 10.00	S
Renaissance Dry Riesling 1997	£ 10.00	S
Yalumba Barossa Growers Shiraz 1998	£ 10.10	S
Côtes du Rhône Village 1998	£ 10.20	S
Château la Clarière Laithwaite 1998	£ 10.20	S
Warre's Otima	£ 10.20	S
Môreson Soleil du Matin Pinotage 1998	£ 10.20	S
Albarino Valminor 1999	£ 10.20	S
Barbadillo Principe Amontillado	£ 10.20	S
Albert i Noya Cabernet Sauvignon Col Leccio 1998	£ 10.20	S
Leasingham Domaine Shiraz 1996	£ 10.30	S
Yering Station Pinot Noir 1998	£ 10.30	S
Cono Sur 20 Barrel Cabernet Sauvignon 1998	£ 10.30	S
Cuvée Columelle 1998	£ 10.30	S
Casale Falchini Paretaio 1997	£ 10.30	S
Terre Arse Marsala Vergine	£ 10.40	S
Pipers Brook Riesling 1998	£ 10.50	S
Fleurie Poncie 1999	£ 10.50	S
Chianti Classico DOCG Riserva 1996	£ 10.50	S
Laudato di Malbech IGT Veneto Orientale 1996	£ 10.50	S
Inferi 1996	£ 10.50	S
Rustenberg Stellenbosch Chardonnay 1999	£ 10.50	S
'I' Nebbiolo 1997	£ 10.60	S
Blue Pyrenees Estate Chardonnay 1998	£ 10.60	S
Casa Lapostolle Chardonnay Cuvée Alexandre 1997	£ 10.60	S
Valpolicella Valpantena Superiore Ripasso Via Nova 1998	£ 10.60	S
Hunter's Oak Aged Sauvignon Blanc 1998	£ 10.60	S

SILVER MEDALS		
Nostalgia Rare Tawny	£ 10.70	S
Brolettino Lugana 1998	£ 10.70	S
Renwick Estate Chardonnay 1998	£ 10.70	S
Touriz Casa Santos Lima 1999	£ 10.70	S
Aragonez 1998	£ 10.70	S
The Ridge Shiraz 1998	£ 10.70	S
Mother Clone Zinfandel 1997	£ 10.70	S
Bonterra Vineyards Roussanne 1999	£ 10.70	S
Grant Burge Old Vine Shiraz 1998	£ 10.80	S
Bethany Wines Shiraz 1997	£ 10.80	S
Forster Kirchenstuck Riesling Spätlese 1997	£ 10.80	S
'E' 1998	£ 10.80	S
Montana Wines Brancott Estate Sauvignon Blanc 1999	£ 10.80	S
Steve Hoff Barossa Shiraz 1998	£ 11.00	S
Veramonte Primus 1998	£ 11.00	S
Valley Vineyards Ascot NV	£ 11.00	S
Gewürztraminer Collection 1998	£ 11.00	S
Chianti Classico Riserva Rocca Guicciarda 1997	£ 11.00	S
Passito di Pantelleria Mare d'Ambra NV	£ 11.00	S
Torre a Destra 1997	£ 11.00	S
Lawson's Dry Hills Pinot Noir 1999	£ 11.00	S
Chruch Road Reserve Chardonnay 1998	£ 11.00	S
Peregrine Sauvignon Blanc 1999	£ 11.00	S
Saint Clair Rapaura Reserve Merlot 1998	£ 11.00	S
Vegaval Avalon Merlot Reserva 1993	£ 11.00	S
Campillo Reserva 1995	£ 11.00	S
Cranswick Botrytis Semillon 1996	£ 11.10	S
Beaune 1er Cru Les Avaux 1998	£ 11.20	S
Porto Barros LBV 1994	£ 11.20	S
Nepenthe Chardonnay 1998	£ 11.30	S
Simon Hackett Foggo Road Cabernet Sauvignon 1997	£ 11.40	S
Casa Lapostolle Cabernet Sauvignon Cuvée Alexandre 1998	£ 11.40	S
Ninquen 1997	£ 11.40	S
Martinborough Vineyard Chardonnay 1998	£ 11.40	S
Yarra Valley Chardonnay 1998	£ 11.50	S
Lake Breeze Bernoota 1998	£ 11.50	S
Brian Barry Cabernet Sauvignon 1998	£ 11.50	S
Le Juge Domaine Capion 1997	£ 11.50	S
Château la Freynelle Bordeaux Rouge Emotion 1998	£ 11.50	S
Porto Barros Quinta Dona Matilde 1997	£ 11.50	S
Waitrose 10 YO Tawny	£ 11.50	S
Monterra Merlot 1998	£ 11.50	S
Ehlers Grove Dolcetto 1997	£ 11.50	S
Wild Horse Chardonnay Central Coast 1997	£ 11.50	S

SILVER MEDALS

Wolf Blass Presidents Selection Cabernet Sauvignon 1996	£ 11.60	S
Rosso Gravello 1996	£ 11.60	S
Riverstone Chardonnay Monterey 1998	£ 11.60	S
Katnook Estate Cabernet Sauvignon 1998	£ 11.70	S
Simon Hackett Foggo Road Cabernet Sauvignon 1996	£ 11.70	S
Allegrini La Grola 1997	£ 11.70	S
Allegrini Palazzo della Torre 1997	£ 11.70	S
Amarone Classico Domini Veneti Negrar 1994	£ 11.70	S
Spice Route Flagship Shiraz 1998	£ 11.70	S
San Emilio Pedro Ximinez	£ 11.70	S
Sangiovese Vino Noceto 1997	£ 11.70	S
Gewürztraminer Hengst Grand Cru 1997	£ 11.80	S
Quinta do Noval Colheita 1982	£ 11.80	S
St Supery Napa Valley Sauvignon Blanc 1999	£ 11.80	S
Von Blauem Schiefer 1998	£ 11.90	S
Villa Maria Reserve Merlot Cabernet 1998	£ 11.90	S
Lugana Riserva Sergio Zenato 1997	£ 12.00	S
Terrine 1997	£ 12.00	S
Coopers Creek Reserve Merlot Cabernet Franc 1998	£ 12.00	S
CJ Pask Reserve Cabernet Sauvignon 1998	£ 12.00	S
Niepoort LBV 1995	£ 12.00	S
Plantagenet Pinot Noir 1998	£ 12.10	S
Domaine Capion Le Juje Selection du Cardinal 1997	£ 12.10	S
Maxwell Ellen Street Shiraz 1998	£ 12.20	S
Chianti Classico Riserva la Sala 1996	£ 12.20	S
Chianti Classico Riserva 1996	£ 12.20	S
Crab Farm Merlot 1998	£ 12.30	S
Graham's Six Grapes	£ 12.30	S
Andresen LBV 1994	£ 12.30	S
Dry Creek Zinfandel Heritage Clone 1997	£ 12.30	S
Kingston Reserve Shiraz 1997	£ 12.40	S
Kingston Reserve Petit Verdot 1997	£ 12.40	S
Deutz Blanc de Blanc 1996	£ 12.40	S
Liano Sangiovese Cabernet Sauvingon Emilia IGT 1997	£ 12.50	S
Sandihurst Premier Pinot Noir 1998	£ 12.50	S
Quinta do Crasto LBV 1994	£ 12.50	S
Blandy's 5 YO Verdelho	£ 12.50	S
Burmester LBV 1995	£ 12.50	S
Chiotti Vineyard Zinfandel 1997	£ 12.50	S
St Hallett Blackwell Shiraz 1996	£ 12.60	S
Luigi Bosca Malbec Verdot 1996	£ 12.70	S
Midnight Cuvée NV	£ 12.70	S
Vino Nobile di Montepulciano 1997	£ 12.70	S
Yarra Valley Shiraz 1998	£ 12.80	S

	SILVER MEDALS	
Rosemount Estate GSM 1998	£ 12.80	S
Old Adam Shiraz 1997	£ 12.80	S
Tatachilla Clarendon Vineyard Merlot 1998	£ 12.80	S
Hillstowe Mary's Hundred Shiraz 1998	£ 12.80	S
Red Hill Pinot Noir 1998	£ 13.00	S
Peacock Normans 1997	£ 13.00	S
Rossco's Shiraz 1998	£ 13.00	S
Carmen Wine Maker's Reserve Red 1997	£ 13.00	S
St Joseph 420 Nuits 1998	£ 13.00	S
Riesling Altenberg de Bergheim Grand Cru 1996	£ 13.00	S
Saussignac Coup de Coeur 1997	£ 13.00	S
Elspeth Cabernet Merlot 1998	£ 13.00	S
Quinta do Sagrado 10 YO Port	£ 13.00	S
Dow's Crusted Port 1997	£ 13.00	S
Columbia Wyckoff Chardonnay 1996	£ 13.00	S
King Estate Chardonnay 1997	£ 13.00	S
Acacia Chardonnay 1995	£ 13.00	S
Mountadam Chardonnay 1997	£ 13.10	S
Aldo Vajra Dolcetto d'Alba Coste e Fossati 1999	£ 13.10	S
Cossart Gordon 5 YO Malmsey	£ 13.10	S
Roques Alfrocheiro Preto 1997	£ 13.10	S
Penfolds Bin 389 Cabernet Shiraz 1997	£ 13.20	S
Gewürztraminer Steingrübler Grand Cru 1998	£ 13.20	S
Il Roccolo doc Rosso di Montalcino 1998	£ 13.20	S
Martinborough Vineyard Pinot Noir 1998	£ 13.20	S
Rosemount Estate Show Reserve Shiraz 1997	£ 13.30	S
Chianti Classico Riserva 1997	£ 13.30	S
Yarra Valley Cabernet Sauvignon 1995	£ 13.40	S
de Bortoli Noble One Semillon 1996	£ 13.50	S
Geoff Merrill Reserve Shiraz 1995	£ 13.50	S
Roques Touriga Nacional 1997	£ 13.60	S
Rosemount Estate Orange Vineyard Merlot 1998	£ 13.70	S
Plantagenet Shiraz 1997	£ 13.70	S
Caballo Loco No 4 NV	£ 13.70	S
Chianti Classico 1998	£ 13.70	S
Rosso La Fabriseria 1998	£ 13.70	S
Rosemount Estate Show Reserve Cabernet Sauvignon 1997	£ 13.80	S
Jermann Pinot Bianco 1998	£ 13.90	S
Yarra Valley Pinot Noir 1998	£ 14.00	S
McGuigan Personal Reserve Shiraz 1998	£ 14.00	S
Petaluma Chardonnay 1998	£ 14.00	S
Seppelt Dorrien Cabernet Sauvignon 1996	£ 14.00	S
Seppelt Drumborg Cabernet Sauvignon 1996	£ 14.00	S
David Wynn Patriach Shiraz 1997	£ 14.00	S

SILVER MEDALS

Cuvée Merret Belgravia NV	£ 14.00	S
Moulin-à-Vent Champ de Cour 1997	£ 14.00	S
Sainsbury's Champagne Extra Dry NV	£ 14.00	S
Sileni Merlot Cabernets 1998	£ 14.00	S
Maias Jaen 1997	£ 14.00	S
Zinfandel The Adventures of Commander Sinskey 1997	£ 14.00	S
H Series Mclaren Vale Shiraz 1998	£ 14.10	S
David Wynn Patriach Shiraz 1996	£ 14.20	S
Quinta do Noval 10 YO Tawny	£ 14.40	S
Guelbenzu Evo 1998	£ 14.40	S
Lindemans Limestone Ridge 1997	£ 14.50	S
Joanna Limestone Coast Cabernet Sauvignon 1998	£ 14.50	S
Poliziano Vino Nobile di Montepulciano 1997	£ 14.50	S
Cumaro Rosso Conero 1997	£ 14.50	S
Rosemount Estate Traditional 1998	£ 14.60	S
Devils Lair Chardonnay 1998	£ 14.60	S
d'Arenberg Ironstone Pressings GSM 1998	£ 14.70	S
Amarone Classico Vigneti di Jago 1995	£ 14.90	S
Verdun Theresa 1997	£ 14.90	S
Brown Brothers Pinot Noir 1997	£ 15.00	S
Brian Barry Merlot 1998	£ 15.00	S
Wirra Wirra RSW 1997	£ 15.00	S
Laurenti Père et Fils Grande Cuvée Brut NV	£ 15.00	S
Amethystos Cava 1996	£ 15.00	S
Korem Isola dei Nuraghi 1998	£ 15.00	S
Forrest Cornerstone 1997	£ 15.00	S
Barbadillo La Cilla Pedro Ximenez	£ 15.00	S
Sandeman Royal Corregidor	£ 15.00	S
Nevada County Grand Reserve Syrah 1996	£ 15.00	S
Saltram No1 Shiraz 1997	£ 15.10	S
Riesling Clos Hauserer 1998	£ 15.10	S
Charles Cimicky Signature Shiraz 1997	£ 15.20	S
Barolo 1993	£ 15.20	S
Santa María Pinot Noir 1998	£ 15.20	S
Tarrawarra Chardonnay 1998	£ 15.30	S
The Virgilius 1999	£ 15.30	S
Tokaji Aszu 5 Puttonyos 1992	£ 15.30	S
Martingana Moscato Passito Di Pantelleria 1996	£ 15.30	S
Henriques & Henriques 10 YO Verdelho	£ 15.30	S
Margaret River Cabernet Merlot 1997	£ 15.40	S
Jim Barry McCrae Wood Shiraz 1997	£ 15.50	S
Geoff Merrill Henley Shiraz 1996	£ 15.50	S
Champagne Forget Brimont NV	£ 15.50	S
Policalpo Monferrato Rosso DOC 1997	£ 15.50	S

SILVER MEDALS		
The Virgilius 1998	£ 15.60	S
Henriques & Henriques 10 YO Sercial	£ 15.60	S
Summerfield Shiraz 1997	£ 15.70	S
Penley Estate Cabernet Sauvignon Reserve 1994	£ 15.90	S
Rust en Vrede Estate Wine 1996	£ 15.90	S
Terrazas Gran Cabernet Sauvignon 1997	£ 16.00	S
Traminer Eiswein Elite 1999	£ 16.00	S
Le Brun de Neuville Cuvée Chardonnay NV	£ 16.00	S
Pannier Brut Sélection NV	£ 16.00	S
Gewürztraminer Altenbourg Grand Cru 1998	£ 16.00	S
Amarone della Valpolicella Classico 1995	£ 16.00	S
Daniel le Brun Blanc de Blancs 1995	£ 16.00	S
Hamilton Russell Pinot Noir 1998	£ 16.00	S
Château Poujeaux 1997	£ 16.10	S
Evans & Tate Shiraz 1998	£ 16.20	S
Wehlener Sonnenuhr Riesling Auslese 1990	£ 16.20	S
Saintsbury Carneros Pinot Noir 1997	£ 16.20	S
Tyrrell's Vat 47 Pinot Chardonnay 1999	£ 16.30	S
Mayor de Ondarre Reserva 1995	£ 16.30	S
Fife Zinfandel Redhead Vineyard 1997	£ 16.30	S
Summerfield Cabernet Sauvignon 1997	£ 16.50	S
Tavernelle 1996	£ 16.50	S
Crichton Hall Merlot 1997	£ 16.50	S
Illuminati Lumen 1997	£ 16.70	S
The Signature 1996	£ 16.90	S
St Francis Cabernet Sauvignon Reserve 1996	£ 16.90	S
Tim Adams The Aberfeldy 1998	£ 17.00	S
Champagne Blanc de Blancs 1er Cru NV	£ 17.00	S
Clos d'Yvigne 1996	£ 17.00	S
Meursault 1998	£ 17.00	S
Château L'Ancien 1998	£ 17.00	S
Safeway Albert Etienne Champagne Vintage 1993	£ 17.00	S
Sciri Cerasuolo di Vittoria DOC 1997	£ 17.00	S
Ottomarzo Valpolicella Amarone Classico 1997	£ 17.00	S
Morgenhof Cabernet Sauvignon Reserve 1998	£ 17.00	S
Bien Nacido Syrah 1997	£ 17.10	S
Joseph Moda Amarone 1998	£ 17.30	S
Elderton Shiraz 1997	£ 17.70	S
Benfield & Delamare Merlot Cabernet 1998	£ 17.70	S
d'Arenberg Dead Arm Shiraz 1998	£ 17.80	S
Monte Rosso Vineyard Sonoma Valley Zinfandel 1997	£ 17.80	S
Lamaione 1996	£ 18.00	S
Quinta das Carvalha Vintage 1997	£ 18.00	S
Château Potelle Mt Veeder Chardonnay 1995	£ 18.00	S

SILVER MEDALS

Mount Langi Ghiran Shiraz 1998	£ 18.10	S
Vino Nobile di Montepulciano 1995	£ 18.10	S
Leasingham Classic Clare Shiraz 1997	£ 18.20	S
Antique Tawny	£ 18.20	S
Champagne Devaux Rosé NV	£ 18.30	S
Leasingham Classic Clare Cabernet Sauvignon 1997	£ 18.40	S
González Byass Matusalem	£ 18.40	S
Dalwhinnie Estate Shiraz 1998	£ 18.50	S
Muskat No 1 Zwischen Den Seen Beerenauslese 1997	£ 18.50	S
Chianti Classico Riserva O'Leandro 1996	£ 18.50	S
Kent Rasmussen Pinot Noir 1997	£ 18.50	S
Chianti Classico Riserva 1997	£ 18.70	S
Le Brun de Neuville Cuvée Millésimé 1991	£ 19.00	S
Arroyo Vista Chardonnay Single Vineyard 1997	£ 19.00	S
Castell del Remei 1780 1997	£ 19.10	S
Villa Cafaggio San Martino 1997	£ 19.20	S
Charles Melton Nine Popes 1998	£ 19.40	S
Charles Melton Shiraz 1998	£ 19.40	S
Bouvier No 2 Bouvier Beerenauslese 1997	£ 19.50	S
Lytton Springs Zinfandel 1998	£ 19.70	S
Pommard 1er Cru Le Clos Blanc 1997	£ 20.00	S
Monthelie 1er Cru Sur la Velle 1997	£ 20.00	S
Champagne Mansard Brut 1992	£ 20.00	S
Kaz Cabernet 1998	£ 20.00	S
Alexander Reserve Cabernet Sauvignon 1997	£ 20.00	S
Henriques & Henriques 15 YO Malmsey	£ 20.40	S
Pannier Brut 1995	£ 20.70	S
Amarone Classico Della Valpolicella 1995	£ 20.70	S
Warre's Quinta da Cavadinha 1987	£ 20.70	S
Warre's Quinta da Cavadinha 1988	£ 20.90	S
Mitchelton Print Label Shiraz 1996	£ 21.00	S
Muddy Water Chardonnay 1998	£ 21.00	S
Vosne Romanee 1er Cru Les Suchots 1997	£ 21.20	S
Torrione 1997	£ 21.20	S
Kaz Shiraz 1998	£ 21.20	S
Scheurebe No 3 Zwischen Den Seen Beerenauslese 1997	£ 21.50	S
Charles de Cazanove Brut Rosé NV	£ 21.50	S
Jade Mountain Syrah 1997	£ 21.50	S
Graham's Malvedos 1987	£ 21.80	S
Champagne Mailly Grand Cru Cuvée les Echansons 1988	£ 21.90	S
Champagne Mercier Vintage 1995	£ 22.00	S
Canard Duchene Vintage 1991	£ 22.00	S
Gewürztraminer Furstentum Grand Cru SGN 1997	£ 22.00	S
Brunello di Montalcino 1994	£ 22.00	S

	SILVER MEDALS	
Alpha Domus Aviator 1998	£ 22.00	S
Monte Villalobón 1996	£ 22.00	S
Chablis Bougros Grand Cru 1998	£ 22.30	S
Chambolle Musigny 1997	£ 22.40	S
H Blin & Co Vintage Brut 1995	£ 22.50	S
Meursault 1997	£ 22.70	S
Sandeman 20 YO	£ 22.70	S
Champagne Mansard Cuvée 2000 1995	£ 23.00	S
Nicolas Feuillatte Brut 1er Cru 1992	£ 23.00	S
Barolo Cordero di Montezemolo 1996	£ 23.00	S
Very Old Reserve 1972	£ 23.00	S
Moët & Chandon Brut Imperial NV	£ 23.20	S
Vasse Felix Heytesbury 1998	£ 23.30	S
Besserat de Bellefon Cuvée des Moines Rosé NV	£ 23.50	S
Champagne a Margaine Blanc des Blancs 1989	£ 23.50	S
Jacquart Mosaique Millésimé 1992	£ 23.50	S
Pommery Brut Rosé NV	£ 23.50	S
Charles Melton Sparkling Red NV	£ 23.90	S
Osborne Palo Cortado Abocado Solera	£ 24.00	S
Champagne Devaux Cuvée D NV	£ 24.20	S
Blandy's 15 YO Malmsey	£ 24.30	S
Veuve Clicquot Yellow Label Brut NV	£ 24.70	S
Alto 1998	£ 25.00	S
Champagne Pierrel Cuvée Tradition Vintage 1995	£ 25.00	S
Burmester 1997	£ 25.00	S
Warre's 20 YO	£ 25.30	S
La Spinetta Pin 1997	£ 25.40	S
Diamond Valley Estate Pinot Noir 1998	£ 25.50	S
Guelbenzu Lautus 1996	£ 25.50	S
Peter Lehmann Eight Songs Shiraz 1996	£ 26.00	S
Château de Meursault 1er Cru 1996	£ 26.00	S
Charles Heidsieck Brut Réserve Mis en Cave 1993	£ 26.60	S
Barolo Cru la Corda della Briccolina 1995	£ 26.60	S
Riesling Schlossberg Grand Cru Cuvée Ste Cathérine 1997	£ 26.80	S
Arcibaldo 1996	£ 26.80	S
Zwischen Rosé No 4 Nouvelle Vague Beerenauslese 1997	£ 27.00	S
Summus 1997	£ 27.00	S
Roeda Vintage 1997	£ 27.00	S
Hillside Select Syrah 1997	£ 27.50	S
Nicolas Feuillatte Brut 1er Cru Cuvée Speciale 1994	£ 28.00	S
Osborne Pedro Ximénez Viejo	£ 28.00	S
Ruinart Rosé Champagne NV	£ 28.30	S
Moët & Chandon Brut Imperial Vintage 1993	£ 28.80	S
Chardonnay Welschriesling No 4 Nouvelle Vague TBA 1996	£ 29.00	S

SILVER MEDALS

Serpico IGT 1997	£ 29.00	S
Barolo Enrico Vi 1996	£ 29.20	S
Champagne Mumm Cuvée Limitée 1990	£ 29.30	S
Basedow Johannes Shiraz 1996	£ 30.00	S
Terra d'Or 1997	£ 30.00	S
R de Ruinart Champagne 1995	£ 30.00	S
Cecchetti Sebastiani Napa Valley Merlot 1996	£ 30.00	S
Northern Sonoma Cabernet Sauvignon 1994	£ 30.00	S
Rosemount Estate Roxburgh Chardonnay 1997	£ 30.40	S
Réserve Millésimé Brut Philipponat 1991	£ 30.50	S
J Schram Napa Valley 1992	£ 31.00	S
Campbells Merchant Prince Rare Rutherglen Muscat	£ 31.90	S
Welschriesling No 7 Zwischen Den Jeen TBA 1997	£ 32.00	S
Quinta do Silval 1997	£ 32.00	S
Charles de Cazanove Cuvée Prestige Stradivarius 1990	£ 33.00	S
Taittinger Vintage Brut 1995	£ 34.20	S
Pinot Gris Rangen de Thann Grand Cru 1996	£ 35.00	S
Chambolle Musigny 1er Cru les Fuées 1996	£ 35.00	S
Barbera d'Alba Riserva Pozzo dell'Annunziata 1997	£ 35.00	S
Excelsus 1997	£ 35.00	S
Mille e una Notte Rosso 1996	£ 35.00	S
Veuve Clicquot Vintage Réserve 1993	£ 35.40	S
John Riddoch Cabernet Sauvignon 1997	£ 36.20	S
Veuve Clicquot Rosé Réserve 1995	£ 37.30	S
Château Coutet 1996	£ 37.80	S
Corton 1995	£ 38.50	S
Quinta do Vesuvio 1998	£ 39.00	S
Cyril Henschke Cabernet Sauvignon 1996	£ 39.30	S
Grand Blanc Brut Philipponat 1991	£ 41.50	S
Clos de Tart 1996	£ 43.90	S
Clarendon Hills Shiraz Piggott Range 1997	£ 44.50	S
La Grande Cuvée Nicolaine de Jacquart 1990	£ 45.00	S
Château Beausejour-Duffau-Lagarrouse 1996	£ 50.00	S
Bernkasteler Lay Riesling Eiswein 1998	£ 50.00	S
Barolo Cerequio 1996	£ 52.70	S
Quinta do Noval 40 YO Tawny	£ 53.70	S
Gewürztraminer Hengst Grand Cru 1998	£ 56.50	S
Warres Vintage Port 1977	£ 57.50	S
Lanson Noble Cuvée 1989	£ 59.00	S
Veuve Clicquot La Grande Dame 1993	£ 62.00	S
Dom Pérignon 1992	£ 65.80	S
Taittinger Comtes de Champagne Blanc de Blancs Brut 1993	£ 66.20	S
Champage Philipponat Cuvée Clos des Goisses Brut 1990	£ 69.80	S
Château La Mission Haut Brion 1990	£ 132.00	S

STOCKISTS

Every wine in the guide has one or more stockist codes beside its entry, identifying where the wine can be bought. The list below translates the code into the company name, with a telephone number for you to make enquiries.

Where the stockists are stated as Widely Available there are more than 10 outlets who stock this wine. In these cases you should be able to find the wine in most good wine retailers. Every effort has been made to list all the stockists with their relevant wines. Should you encounter any problems with finding a wine listed in this guide, then please contact the IWC at the address on the back page.

3DW	3D Wines	01205 820745
4PL	Four Plus	01892 525733
A&A	A&A Wines	01483 274666
A&N	Army & Navy	0207 834 1234
ABI	ABI Group Ltd	0208 883 9672
ABO	Anthony Borges	01932 853453
ABU	Bodegas Unidas Ltd	01494 676263
ABY	Anthony Byrne Wine Agencies	01487 814555
ACC	Carluccio's	0207 240 1487
ACH	Andrew Chapman Fine Wines	01235 550707
ACQ	Acquivins	01737 212911
ADE	Adel (UK) Ltd	0208 994 3960
ADI	Allders International	01703 644599
ADN	Adnams Wine Merchants	01502 727222
ADW	Andrew Darwin	01544 230534
AFI	Alfie Fiandaca Ltd	0208 752 1222
AGS	Amazing Grapes	0208 202 2631
AHW	AH Wines Ltd	01935 850116
AIL	Annessa Imports Ltd	0208 801 4973
ALA	Australian Premium Wines Ltd	0207 801 9583
ALD	Aldi Stores Ltd	01827 710 871

ALE	Alexander Wines	0141 882 0039
ALI	Alivini Company Ltd	0208 880 2525
ALL	Alliance Wine Company Ltd	01505 506060
ALO	Alouette Wines	0151 346 1107
ALW	AL Wine Services	01792 528 354
ALZ	Allez Vins!	01926 811969
AMA	Amathus Wines Ltd	0208 804 4181
AMW	Amey's Wines	01787 377144
ANT	Anthony & Son	0207 403 4669
APC	Arthur Purchase	01243 783144
AQU	Aquitaine Wines	01347 6612
ARL	Auriol Wines	01252 843190
ARM	Arthur Rackham	01483 458700
ARP	AR Parker & Son	01322 525231
ARR	Arrowfield Wines	01494 678971
ASD	Asda Stores Ltd	0113 241 9172
ASH	Ashley Scott	01244 520655
ASN	André Simon	0207 388 5080
AST	Astley Vineyards	01299 822907
ASW	Ashdown Wine	0208 841 4134
AUC	The Australian Wine Club	0208 538 0718
AUS	Australian Wineries (UK) Ltd	01780 755810
AVB	Averys of Bristol	01275 811100
AVI	Arlington Vintners Int. Ltd	0208 405 6404
AWC	Anthony Wine Cellars	0207 722 8576
AWL	Adriatic Wine Ltd	0191 233 2700
AWM	Albert Wharf Wine Co Ltd	0207 223 8283
AWS	Albion Wine Shippers	0207 242 0873
B&B	Bottle & Basket	0208 341 7018
B&S	Brown & Strauss	01582 834224
BAG	Bacchus Gallery	01798 342844
BAL	Ballantynes of Cowbridge	01446 774840
BAT	Battersea Wine Co	0207 924 3631
BBB	Barnsbury Bottle & Basket	0207 713 0427
BBL	Bat & Bottle Wine Merchants	01785 284495
BBO	Barrels & Bottles	0114 255 6611
BBR	Berry Bros & Rudd	0870 900 4300
BBS	Barton Brownsdon Sadler	01892 824024
BBU	Bruce Burlington	01268 562224
BBV	Breaky Bottom Vineyard	01273 476427

BBZ	Bargain Booze	01270 753001
BCL	Best Cellars	01364 652546
BDG	Bodega Off Sales	0150 553031
BDM	Bodenham Wine	01568 797483
BDR	Bordeaux Direct	0118 903 0903
BDT	Benedict's	01983 529596
BEA	Bella Wines Ltd	01638 604 899
BEC	Beaconsfield Wine Cellars	01494 675545
BEE	The Beer Shop	028 406 24079
BEL	Bentalls of Kingston	0208 546 1001
BEN	Bennetts	01386 840392
BEN	Bennetts	01386 840392
BES	Bestway Cash & Carry Ltd	0208 453 1234
BEX	Bitter Experience	0208 852 8819
BFD	Brian Fords Discount Stores	01271 327744
BFI	Bedford Fine Wines	01234 721153
BFW	Bellefrance Wines Ltd	0207 706 3462
BGL	Bottle Green Ltd	0113 205 4500
BGN	Budgens Stores Limited	0208 864 2800
BHW	BH Wines	01228 576711
BIN	Bin 89 Wine Warehouse	0114 275 5889
BKC	Berkeley Wines (Cheshire)	01925 444555
BKT	Bucktrout	01481 724444
BLA	Blakes & Co Ltd	01292 264880
BLS	Balls Brothers of London	0207 739 6466
BLV	Bacchus Les Vignobles	0208 675 9007
BLW	Blayneys	0191 548 3083
BMK	Benmack International Ltd	01435 866 419
BNC	Bottlenecks (London)	0208 520 2737
BNE	Bin Ends (Rotherham)	01709 367771
BNK	Bottleneck (Broadstairs)	01843 861095
BOB	Booze Brothers	01284 811203
BOD	Bodegas Direct	01243 773474
BOH	La Boheme (London) Ltd	0208 656 7383
BOL	Bacchus Fine Wines	01234 711140
BOO	Booths of Stockport	0161 432 3309
BOR	de Bortoli Wines UK Ltd	01725 516467
BOU	Bouteilles en Fete	0151 346 1107
BOX	The Boxford Wine Co	01787 210187
BRB	Brown Brothers (Europe) Ltd	01628 776446

BRF	Brown-Forman Wines International	0207 323 9332
BRI	Bordeaux Index	0207 7278 9495
BRU	Bruisyard Wines	01728 638 281
BRW	Breckland Wines	01953 881592
BSC	Ben Shaw's Wine Cellar	01484 516624
BSD	Boisdale Wines	0207 730 6922
BSN	Benson Fine Wines	0208 673 4439
BSS	Besos (UK) Ltd	01243 575454
BTH	Booths Supermarkets	01772 251701
BUC	Buckingham Vintners	01753 521336
BUP	Bottoms Up	01707 328244
BUT	The Butlers Wine Cellar	01273 698724
BWC	Berkmann Wine Cellars	0207 609 4711
BWH	Bermondsey Wine Warehouse	0207 231 0457
BWL	Bibendum Wine Ltd	0207 722 5577
BXT	Bay Export Ltd	0207 987 1241
C&B	Corney & Barrow	0207 251 4051
C&D	C&D Wines Ltd	0208 778 1711
C&H	Cairns & Hickey	0113 267 3746
C&W	Carley & Webb Ltd	0207 287 23503
CAM	Cambridge Wine Merchants	01223 568 991
CAR	CA Rookes	01789 297777
CAT	Cantino Augusto	0207 242 3246
CBC	Ciry Beverage Co. Ltd	0207 729 2111
CBK	Cranbrook Wines	0208 554 8050
CCl	Chiswick Cellars	0208 994 7989
CCW	Cachet Wines	01482 581792
CDE	Cote d'Or	0208 998 0144
CDL	California Direct	0207 207 1944
CDM	Caves de la Madeleine	0207 736 6145
CDN	Chiddingstone Vineyards	01892 871400
CDO	Chapel Down Wines Ltd	01580 763033
CEB	Croque-en-Bouche	01684 565612
CED	Cellars Direct (London)	0207 378 1109
CEL	Cellar 5	01925 444555
CEN	Centurion Vintners	01453 763223
CEP	Cert Group	01992 822 922
CER	Cellar 28	01484 710101
CES	Winefinds/Consulate	01722 716100
CFN	Carringtons Fine Wines	0161 446 2546

CFP	Perfect Partners	01580 712633
CFT	The Clifton Cellars	0117 973 0287
CFW	Christchurch Fine Wine	01202 473255
CGW	The Cote Green Wine Company	0161 426 0155
CHF	Chippendale Fine Wines	01943 850633
CHH	Charles Hennings	01798 872485
CHI	Chilford Hundred Limited	01223 892641
CHN	Charles Hawkins	01572 823030
CHS	Quellyn Roberts (Wine Merchants) Ltd	01244 310455
CKB	Cockburn & Campbell	0208 875 7008
CLD	Caledonian Wines	01228 43172
CLP	La Reserve	0207 978 5601
CMI	Charles Mitchell Wines Ltd	0161 775 1626
CML	Chateau Musar (UK) Ltd	0208 941 8311
CNF	Champagne Nicolas Feuillatte UK	01794 507115
CNL	Connolly's	0121 236 9269
COC	Corks of Cotham	0117 973 1620
COD	Coddington Vineyard	01531 640668
COE	Coe of Ilford	0208 551 4966
COK	Corkscrew Wines	01228 543033
COM	Compendium Wine Merchants	0289 079 1197
COT	Cotswold Wine Company	01242 678880
CPD	Food Brands Group	0207 978 5300
CPR	Capricorn Wines	0161 908 1360
CPS	CPA's Wine Ltd	01792 360707
CPW	Christopher Piper Wines Ltd	01404 814139
CRI	Chalié, Richards & Co Ltd	01403 250500
CRL	Wine Centre/Charles Stevenson Wines	01822 615985
CRM	Craven's Wine Merchants	0207 723 0252
CRS	The Co operative Society	01706 891628
CSP	Catherine Scott	0208 305 2787
CSS	Charles Steevenson Wines	01822 626272
CST	The County Stores (Somerset) Ltd	01823 272235
CTC	The Cambridge Wine Warehouse	01954 719090
CTH	Charterhouse Wine Co Ltd	0207 587 1302
CTL	Continental Wine & Food	01484 538333
CTV	Carr Taylor Vineyards Ltd	01424 752501
CVR	Celtic Vintner	01633 430055
CVV	Camel Valley Vineyard	01208 77959
CWA	Cheviot UK Wine Agencies	01925 861 920

STOCKISTS

CWI	A Case of Wine	01558 650671
CWS	The Co-op (CWS Ltd)	0161 827 5492
D&D	D&D Wines International Ltd	01565 650952
D&F	D&F Wine Shippers Ltd	0208 838 4399
DAV	Dartmouth Vintners	01803 832602
DBO	Domaine Boyar Ltd	0207 537 3707
DBS	Denbies Wine Estate	01306 876616
DBW	David Baker Wines	01656 650732
DBY	D Byrne & Co	01200 423152
DEL	Delegat's Wine Estate (UK) Ltd	0208 892 6999
DEN	Dennhofer Wines	0191 232 73242
DIC	Left Bank Village Wines	01432 353720
DIO	Dionysus	0208 874 2739
DIW	Direct Wine Importers	01481 726747
DLA	Daniel Lambert Wine Agenices	02920 666128
DNL	Dunell's Ltd	01534 736418
DVD	Davisons Direct	0208 681 3222
DVP	Davenport Vineyards	01892 852380
DVY	Davy & Co Ltd	0207 407 9670
DWI	Dedicated Wine Importers Ltd	01865 343395
DWL	Darlington Wines Ltd	0208 453 0202
E&J	Ernest & Julio Gallo Winery	01895 813444
EBC	The Exclusive Brandy Club	0169 773744
ECA	Edward Cavendish & Sons Ltd	01794 835800
EDC	Edencroft	01270 629975
EGE	Embassy of Georgia	0207 937 8233
EGG	Ernst Gorge (Wine Shippers) Ltd	01235 538006
EHL	Ehrmanns Ltd	0207 359 7466
EIA	Enoteca Italiana	0207 251 8732
ELL	Ellingham Wines Ltd	0208 892 9599
ELV	El Vino Company Ltd	0207 353 5384
ENO	Enotria Winecellars Ltd	0208 961 4411
EOO	Everton's of Ombersley	01905 620282
EOR	Ellis of Richmond Ltd	0208 943 4033
ESL	Edward Sheldon Ltd.	01608 661409
EST	Estramadura Wines	0208 932 3370
ETM	Elliot & Tatham	0207 349 0884
ETV	Eton Vintners	01753 790188
EUR	Europa Foods Ltd	0208 845 1255
EUW	Eurowines	0208 747 2109

EVE	Everymans	01743 362466
EVI	Evington's Wine Merchants	0116 254 2702
EWC	English Wine Centre	01323 870164
EWD	Euro World Wines	0141 649 3735
F&M	Fortnum & Mason	0207 734 8040
FAB	Fabat UK Ltd	0207 636 7640
FAR	Farr Vintners	020 7821 2000
FCA	Fraser Crameri Assoc.	01284 735907
FCC	The Fine Champagne Company Co	01923 774053
FCV	France Vin	01494 680857
FDB	First Drinks Brands Ltd	01703 312000
FDL	Findlater Mackie Todd	01344 825900
FEN	Fenwick Ltd	0191 232 5100
FLM	Ferrers le Mesurier	01832 732660
FLW	For the Love of Wine	01280 822500
FNZ	Fine Wines of New Zealand	0207 482 0093
FQU	First Quench	1707385110
FRI	Friarwood	0207 736 2628
FRN	Frenmart	01384 892941
FRV	The Four Vintners	0207 739 7335
FRW	Fraser Williamson Fine Wines	01580 200 304
FSA	FSA (Wineshippers) Ltd	0208 201 9096
FSD	Free Spirit (Drinks) Ltd	01702 467224
FSW	Frank Stainton Wines	01539 731886
FTH	Forth Wines Ltd	01577 863668
FTP	Four Throws Post Office	01580 753210
FUL	Fuller Smith & Turner	0208 996 2000
FWC	Four Walls Wine Company	01243 535 219
FWM	Fields Wine Merchants	0207 589 5753
FXT	Freixenet (DWS) Ltd	01344 758 500
G&G	Godwin & Godwin	01225 337081
G&M	Gordon & Macphail	01343 545111
G2W	Grape 2 Wine Limited	01531 670100
GAG	Grape & Grain	0208 426 1562
GAR	Garland Wine Cellar	01372 275247
GBA	Georges Barbier	0208 852 5801
GBY	Elizabeth Gabay & Partners	0208 883 9331
GCF	Les Grands Chais de France	01962 622 067
GCl	Graingers Ltd.	0114 221 0888
GDA	Giada Ltd	01904 691 628

GDM	Giles de Mare	01985 844695
GDS	Garrards Wine Merchants	01900 823592
GEL	Gelston Castle	01556 503012
GER	Gerrys Wines	0207 734 4215
GFT	Guild of French Traditional Wines	01886 832696
GGW	Great Gaddesden Wines	01582 760606
GHC	Goedhuis & Company	0207 793 7900
GHL	George Hill of Loughborough	01509 212717
GIL	GIV UK Ltd	0208 956 2280
GLO	Global Wines	0121 429 1662
GLY	Gallery Wines	01504 48762
GMV	GM Vintners	01392 218166
GNW	Great Northern Wine Co	0113 2304455
GON	Gauntleys of Nottingham	0115 911 0555
GOY	Goyt Wines	01663 734214
GPA	Grapevine (Andover)	01264 737658
GRO	Grog Blossom	0207 794 7808
GRT	Great Western Wine Company Ltd	01225 322800
GSH	The Grape Shop/DP Wines Ltd	0207 924 3638
GSJ	Grants of St James's	01275 890665
GSl	Gerrard Seel Ltd	01925 819695
GTA	Grands Terriors Associés	0207 258 3010
GWC	Greek Wine Centre Ltd	01743 364636
GWF	Gilbey Wine Club	01491 411567
GWI	The General Wine & Liquor Company	01428 722201
H&D	Hicks & Don	01258 456040
H&H	H&H Bancroft	01223 433 660
H&W	Woodhouse Wines	01258 452141
HAC	Hailsham Cellars	01323 441212
HAE	Halewood International Ltd	01924 410110
HAG	The Hanwood Group Ltd	01858 570600
HAM	Hampden Wine Co	01844 201641
HAR	Harrods	0207 730 1234
HAS	Haughton Agencies	01502 727 288
HAW	The Hantone Wine Company	0207 978 5920
HBJ	Heyman, Barwell Jones Ltd	01473 232322
HBR	BRL Hardy Wine Company Ltd	01372 473 000
HBW	H&B Wines Limited	0207 924 2506
HBY	Hall & Bramley	0151 525 8283
HCK	Pierre Henck Wines	01902 751022

HDM	H&D Marketing	01438 820955
HDS	Hedley Wright Wine Merchants	01279 465 818
HDY	Hollywood & Donnelly	01232 799335
HEW	Hein Wines	0207 730 1099
HFI	Hill International Wines (UK) Ltd	01283 217703
HHC	Haynes Hanson & Clark	0207 259 0102
HLV	Halves	01588 673040
HMA	Hatch Mansfield Agencies Ltd	01753 621126
HMC	Hermitage Cellar	01243 373363
HNS	H Needham & Sons (Wines)	01732 740422
HOB	Hobson and Friends Too Ltd	0208 780 3323
HOH	Hallgarten Wines Ltd	01582 722538
HOL	Holland Park Wine Co	0207 221 9614
HOP	Hopton Wines	01299 270734
HOT	House of Townend	01482 326891
HOU	Hoults Wine Merchants	01484 510700
HPD	Harpenden Wines	01923 2527180
HRF	Howard Ripley Select Domaine Imports	0208 360 8904
HSL	Hanslope Wines	01908 510262
HST	La Réserve, Hampstead	0207 435 6845
HSV	Hidden Spring Vineyard	01435 812640
HVN	Harvey Nichols	0207 235 5000
HVW	Helen Verdcourt Wines	01628 625577
HWB	The Bin Club	01454 294085
HWL	HWCG Wine Growers	01279 506512
HWM	Harvest Wine Group	01734 344290
ICL	Italian Continental Food & Wine	01628 770110
IGH	Ian G Howe Wine Merchant	01636 704366
ISA	Camisa Deli	0207 437 7610
ISW	Isis Wines	01628 771199
IVY	Ivy Wines	01243 377883
IWS	International Wine Services	01494 680857
J&B	Justerini & Brooks	0207 493 8721
J&F	Antonia Hadfield Associates	01494 814 804
JAG	JA Glass	01592 651850
JAK	James Aitken & Son	01382 221197
JAR	John Armit Wines	0207 727 6846
JAS	Jascots Wine Merchants Ltd	0208 749 0022
JAV	John Arkell Vintners	0119 382 3026
JAV	John Arkell Vintners	0119 382 3026

JBF	Julian Baker Fine Wines	01206 262 358
JBV	Julian Bidwell Vintner	0208 874 9388
JCB	JC Broadbent	01534 23356
JCK	JC Karn & Son Ltd	01242 513265
JCP	Palmers Brewery	01308 422396
JEF	John E Fells	01442 870900
JEH	J E Hogg	0131 556 4025
JER	JE Ridlington & Son	01205 364747
JFE	James Fearon Wines	01248 370200
JFR	John Frazier	0121 704 3415
JHL	JH Logan	0131 667 2855
JLW	Lay & Wheeler Agencies	01206 713507
JMC	James E McCabe	01762 333102
JNW	James Nicholson Wine Merchant	02844 830091
JOB	Jeroboams	0207 235 1612
JOV	Jolly Vintner	01884 255644
JPL	John & Pascalis Ltd	0208 452 0707
JSM	Sainsbury Supermarkets Ltd	0207 695 6000
JSS	John Stephenson & Sons (Nelson) Ltd	01282 698827
JUS	Just-in-Case	01489 892969
JWB	Jamies Wine Bars plc	0207 242 0421
JWW	Whittaker Wines (Stockport)	0208 878 2302
K&B	King & Barnes Ltd	01403 270470
KEO	Keo UK Ltd	020 7354 3990
KME	Kendal Milne	0161 832 3414
KOC	Kelly of Cults Ltd	01224 867596
KOM	Kingston Estate Wines (UK)	01344 668001
KWI	Kwik Save Stores Ltd	01745 887111
KWS	Kingsland Wines & Spirits	0161 333 4300
L&F	L&F Jones Holdings	01761 417 117
L&S	Laymont & Shaw Ltd	0208 543 2854
L&T	Lane & Tatham	01380 720123
L&W	Lay & Wheeler Ltd	01206 764446
LAS	Havern Wholesales (formerly Liquid Assets)	0116 276 8471
LAU	Lauriston Wines Ltd	01737 814 188
LAV	Les Amis du Vin	0208 451 0469
LAY	Laytons Wine Merchants Ltd	0207 388 4567
LCC	Landmark Cash & Carry	01908 255 300
LCD	Cochonnet Wines	01326 340332
LEA	Lea & Sandeman	0207 244 0522

LFD	Battle Wine Estate	01424 773183
LHP	Laurence Hayward & Partners	01892 544 003
LIB	Liberty Wines	0207 720 5350
LLV	Lakeland Vintners	01539 821999
LLY	Luciana C Lynch	01428 606619
LME	Laurent Mentge	0207 337 9440
LMN	Luxmanor Ltd	0116 2709918
LNR	Le Nez Rouge	0207 609 4711
LOH	Larners of Holt	01263 712323
LOL	Louis Latour Ltd	0207 409 7276
LPD	Laurent-Perrier Distribution	01628 475404
LSH	Laurence Smith	0131 667 3327
LTW	Littlewoods Organisation plc	0151 235 2222
LUC	Luckins Wines	01371 872839
LUD	Luigi's Deli	0207 352 7739
LUV	Lovico International Ltd	01494 511234
LVF	Les Producteurs & Vignerons de France Ltd	01273 730277
LVN	La Vigneronne	0207 589 6113
LWE	London Wine Emporium	0207 587 1302
M&M	M&M Imports UK	01235 813815
M&S	Marks & Spencer plc	0207 268 3825
M&V	Morris & Verdin	0207 357 8866
MAD	Mad About Wine	0208 222 9492
MAK	Makro Self Service	01372 468571
MAR	Marco's Wines	0208 875 1900
MAS	Macs Neighbourhood Centres Ltd.	01707 663366
MAX	Maxxium	0208 747 4843
MAY	F&E May Ltd	08450 661122
MCD	Marne & Champagne Ltd	0207 499 0070
MCL	McLeod's	01507 601094
MCT	Matthew Clark	01275 890678
MER	Meridian Wines	0161 908 1350
MFS	Martinez Fine Wine	01422 320022
MFW	Marcus Fyfe Wines	01546 603646
MHU	Moet Hennessy UK Ltd	0207 235 9411
MHV	Booker Belmont Wholesale Ltd	01933 371363
MHW	Mill Hill Wines	0208 959 6754
MHW	Maidenhead Wine Company	01491 413311
MID	Midnight Communications	01273 666200
MIS	Mistral Wines	0207 262 5437

MIV	Mersea Island Vineyard	01206 385 900
MJW	Michael Jobling Wines	0191 261 5298
MKV	McKinley Vintners	0207 928 7300
MMD	Maisons Marques et Domaines	0208 332 2223
MMW	Michael Menzel Wines	0114 268 3557
MON	Mondial Wine Ltd	0208 335 3455
MOR	Moreno Wine Importers	0208 960 7161
MRL	Mooreland Foods	01625 548495
MRN	Morrison Supermarkets	01924 875234
MTC	Manningtree Wine Cellar	01206 395095
MTL	Mitchells Wine Merchants	0114 274 0311
MTR	Charles Taylor Wines Ltd	0207 928 8151
MTW	Montana Wines Ltd	0208 250 1325
MVG	Mille Vignes	0207 633 0278
MVN	Merchant Vintners Company	01482 329443
MWS	Midhurst Wine Shippers	01730 812222
MWW	Majestic Wine Warehouses Ltd	01923 298200
MYL	Myliko International (Wines) Litd	01204 392222
MYS	Mayor Sworder	0208 686 1155
MZC	Mentzendorff & Co Ltd	0207 840 3600
N&P	Nickolls & Perks	01384 394518
NEG	Negociants UK Ltd	01582 462859
NEI	R&I Neish Ltd	01779 472721
NET	Nethergate Wines	01787 277244
NEV	Neve Agencies	01730 816044
NGS	The South African Wine Centre	0207 224 1994
NHC	NH Creber	01822 612266
NIC	Nicolas UK Ltd	0208 964 5469
NOB	Noblesource Ltd	01780 450 490
NRW	Noble Rot Wine Warehouses Ltd	01527 575606
NTD	Nisa Today's	01724 282028
NUM	Vinum Austria	01234 343 202
NUR	Nurdin & Peacock	0208 971 1638
NWG	New World Wines Ltd	0207 720 0371
NYW	Noel Young Wines	01223 566 744
ODD	Oddbins	0208 944 4400
ODF	Oddbins Fine Wine	0208 944 4400
OFL	Oldacre-Field Ltd	0161 928 4898
OHI	Oakhouse Wine Co	01584 811747
OLS	Old St Wine Co	0207 729 1768

OPW	OP Wine Agencies Ltd	01371 811599
ORB	Orbital Wines Ltd	1858570600
OSW	Old School Wines	01886 821613
OWC	The Oxford Wine Company	01865 301144
OWL	OW Loeb	0207 928 7750
P&R	Peckham & Rye	0141 334 4312
P&S	Philglass & Swiggot	0207 924 4494
PAC	Pacific Wines	01494 680857
PAG	Pagendam Pratt	01937 844711
PAL	Pallant Wines	01903 882288
PAM	Pampas Wines	01707 393 015
PAR	Partridges	0207 730 0651
PAT	Patriarche Père et Fils Ltd	0207 381 4016
PAV	The Pavilion Wine Company Ltd	0207 628 8224
PBA	Paul Boutinot Agencies	0161 908 1370
PDN	"Portal, Dingwall and Norris"	01243 377883
PEC	Pechiney UK Ltd	01753 522800
PEF	Southcorp Wines Europe Ltd	0208 917 4600
PEY	Phillip Eyres Wine Merchant	01494 433823
PFC	Percy Fox & Co	01279 626801
PFT	Parfrements	02476 503 646
PGA	Portugalia Wines (UK) Ltd	020 8997 44 00
PGM	Pengethley Manor	01989 730211
PGR	Patrick Grubb Selections	01869 340229
PGS	Page & Sons	01843 591214
PHP	Phil Parrish	01377 252373
PIC	La Reserve	0207 402 6920
PIM	Vintage Cellars	0207 834 3647
PJN	Pierre Jean	01372 468571
PLA	Playford Ros Ltd	01845 526777
PLB	Private Liquor Brands	01342 318282
PLE	Peter Lehmann Wines (UK) Ltd	01227 731353
PMA	Perry Mill Associates	01256 880611
PMN	Phillip Morgan	01222 231570
PNA	Phillips Newman Agencies	01322 627581
POL	Pol Roger Ltd	01432 262800
POM	Pomona Wines	01634 235658
PON	Peter Osborne & Co	01491 612311
POP	The Pipe of Port	01702 614606
POR	Portland Wine Company (Manchester)	0161 928 0357

POT	Le Pont de la Tour	0207 403 2403
POU	Growers & Chateaux	01372 374239
PRG	Paragon Vintners Ltd	0207 887 1800
PSC	Penistone Court Wine Cellars	01226 766037
PST	Penn Street	01494 715376
PTR	Peter Green	0131 229 5925
PVS	Prestige Vintners	01264 335586
PWI	Portland Wine Cellar (Southport)	01704 534299
PWY	Peter Wylie Fine Wines	01884 277555
QRW	Quellyn Roberts Wine Merchants	01244 310455
QWW	Quay West Wines	01392 410866
RAC	Rackham's Dept Store	0121 236 3333
RAE	Raeburn Fine Wine & Foods	0131 343 1159
RAM	Ramsbottom Victuallers	01706 825070
RAV	Ravensbourne Wine	0208 869 9655
RAW	Richard Ambridge Wines	01903 820143
RBA	Rodrigues Bartholomew	0385 940786
RBS	Roberson Wine Merchants	0207 371 2121
REN	Renvic Wines Ltd	01763 852470
RES	La Reserve	0207 589 2020
REW	La Reserva Wines	0207 978 5601
REY	Raymond Reynolds Ltd	01663 742 230
RHV	Richard Harvey Wines Ltd.	01929 481437
RIC	Richard Granger Ltd	0191 281 5000
RKW	Rickwood of Bearstead Green	01622 737130
RML	Richard Mallinson	01256 770397
RNS	Rex Norris	01444 454756
ROB	TM Robertson	0131 229 4522
ROD	Rodney Densem Wines Ltd	01270 623665
ROG	Roger Harris Wines	01603 880207
ROS	Rosemount Estate Wines Ltd	01483 211466
RS2	Richardson & Sons	01946 65334
RSN	Richard Speirs Wines	01483 537605
RSP	RS Pass Wines	0797 151 2647
RSS	Raisin Social Ltd	0208 686 8500
RSW	RS Wines	0117 963 1780
RTB	Italian Wine Brands Ltd	01992 561888
RTW	The Rose Tree Wine Company	01242 583732
RUK	Ruinart Champagne UK Ltd	0207 416 0592
RVA	Randalls (Jersey)	01534 887788

RVE	Ridgeview Estate Winery Ltd	01444 258039
RWL	Richmonde Wines Ltd	01562 822777
RWR	RW Randall (Guernsey)	01780 460451
S&D	Saltmarsh & Druce	01993 703721
SAB	St Austell Brewery	01726 74444
SAC	La Reserve	0207 381 6930
SAF	Safeway Stores Plc	0208 970 3506
SAN	Sandiway Wine Co	01606 882101
SBS	Sainsbury Brothers	01225 460981
SCA	Scatchard	0151 236 6468
SCK	Seckford Wines Ltd.	01394 446622
SCL	Stephan's Cellar Ltd	01873 850 668
SEA	Seagram UK Ltd	0208 250 1018
SEB	Sebastopol Wines	01235 850471
SEL	Selfridges Ltd	0207 318 3730
SEN	Sensible Wine Services Ltd	01622 832640
SGL	Stevens Garnier Ltd	01865 263300
SHA	Shawsgate Vineyard	01728 724060
SHB	Shaws of Beaumaris	01248 810328
SHE	Andrew Sheepshanks Fine Wines	0207581 9400
SHG	Wine Shop on the Green	01437 766864
SHJ	SH Jones & Company	01295 251179
SHL	Shepherd Love	0208 743 7122
SHR	Sharpham Vineyard	01803 732203
SIA	Siam Winery Co Ltd	0208 674 3182
SKW	Stokes Fine Wines Ltd	0208 944 5979
SLM	Salamis & Co Ltd	0207 609 1133
SMF	Somerfield Stores Ltd	0117 935 9359
SNC	Spedding Nicholson & Co	0122 586 6063
SNO	Snowdonia Wine Warehouse	01492 870567
SOM	Sommelier Wine Co	01481 721677
SPD	Speck Deli	0207 229 7005
SPR	Spar (UK) Ltd	0208 863 5511
STB	Stokes Brothers (UK) Ltd	01303 252178
STE	Stephane Auriol Wines	01252 843190
STG	Tony Stebbings	01372 468571
STH	Hamer Wine	0208 549 9119
STT	Santat Wines	01483 450494
STW	Stewarts Wine Barrels	01232 704434
SVT	Smedley Vintners	01462 768214

SWB	Satchells	01328 738272
SWG	SWIG	0207 431 4412
SWI	Sherston Wine Co (St Albans)	01727 858841
SWN	S Wines	0207 351 1990
SWS	Stratfords Wine Shippers & Merchants Ltd	01628 810606
T&W	T&W Wines	01842 765646
TAN	Tanners Wines Ltd	01743 234500
TAV	Tavern Group Ltd	0161 864 5000
TBO	The Bottle Shop	01925 865 201
TBS	Thomas Baty & Son	0151 236 1601
TBW	TB Watson (Dumfries)	01387 720505
TCV	Three Choirs Vineyards Ltd	01531 890555
TCW	TC Wines	0151 931 3390
TGW	Good Wine Company (London)	0208 858 5577
THC	The Haselmere Cellar	01428 645081
THI	Thierry's Wine Services	01794 507100
THP	Greene King	01580 200304
THS	Thresher	01707 328244
THV	Thwaites Vintners	01254 54431
THW	Southern Wine Brands Ltd	01484 608898
TIB	Talbot Wines	01926 484386
TLS	Tanya Lolonis	0207 229 0976
TMS	Thames Wine Sellers Ltd	0207 928 8253
TMW	Moffat Wine Shop	01683 220554
TNH	Thorman Hunt	0207 735 6511
TNI	The Nobody Inn	01647 252394
TOS	Tesco Stores Ltd	01992 632 222
TOU	Toucan Wines	01232 790909
TPA	The Wine Warehouse	01666 503088
TPW	Topsham Wines	01392 874501
TRO	Trout Wines	01264 781472
TRV	Transit Vin Ltd	0208 674 6344
TVN	The Vintner Ltd	01483 765470
TWB	The Wine Bank	01892 514343
TWC	Wine Cellar (Fareham)	01329 822733
UBC	Ubiquitous Chip	0141 334 5007
UD2	UDV	0207 927 4124
UNS	Unwins Ltd	01322 272711
UWM	United Wine Merchants	01232 231231
V&C	Valvona & Crolla	0131 556 6066

V&V	Vino Vino	0403 436 949
VAL	Valentina Deli	0208 392 9127
VDO	Val D'Orbieu Wines Ltd	0207 736 3350
VDT	Vins Direct	01534 483160
VDV	Vin du Van Wine Merchants	01233 758727
VEX	Vinexports Ltd	01584 811333
VHW	Victor Hugo Wines	01534 32225
VIC	Vica Wines Ltd	01273 477132
VIN	Vinum	0208 840 4070
VIV	Vivian's	0208 940 3600
VIW	Vintage Wines	0115 947 6565
VKW	Vickery Wines	01582 462039
VLW	Villeneuve Wines	01721 722500
VNF	Vinfruco Ltd	01753 712473
VNO	Vinoceros (UK)Ltd	01209 314711
VRL	Verulam Vintners	01784 421822
VRS	Veritaus & Co Ltd	01428 607233
VRT	Vintage Roots	0118 976 1999
VTH	Vintage House	0207 6372592
VTl	Vine Trail	0117 942 3946
VTT	Vinopolis	0207 645 3700
VVS	Valley Vineyards	01189 340176
VWE	Victoria Wine	01483 715066
VXL	Vinexcel Ltd	0161 485 4592
WAA	Warden Abbey Vineyard	01462 811266
WAC	Waters of Coventry Ltd	01926 888889
WAT	Peter Watkins Wine	01604 717700
WAV	Waverley Vintners Ltd	01738 472029
WAW	Waterloo Wine Co	0207 403 7967
WBM	Wine Byre Merchants	01334 653215
WBR	Wadebridge Wines	01208 812692
WBU	Wine Bureau	01403 256446
WCK	Wickham Wines	01237 473292
WCR	Wine Cellar Ltd (Parisa)	01925 454702
WCS	The Wine Cellar (Sanderstead)	0208 657 6936
WDI	Wine Direct Ltd	01932 820490
WDM	Waddesdon Manor	01296 651282
WEK	Wine Emporium/Cockburns	0131 346 1113
WEP	Welshpool Wine Company	01938 553243
WER	Wine Cellar (Douglas)	01624 611793

WES	Wessex Wines	01308 427177
WET	Westbay Distributors Ltd	01703 635 252
WEX	Wine Experience	01949 851495
WFB	Mildara Blass (Europe) Ltd	0208 947 4312
WFL	Winefare Ltd	01483 458700
WGA	Winegrowers Agencies Ltd	01603 410 958
WGG	WG White Ltd	0208 831 1400
WGW	Woodgate Wines	01229 885637
WHS	Wine House	0207 737 0242
WIC	Jolly's Drinks	01237 473292
WIL	Willoughby's of Manchester	0161 834 6850
WIM	Wimbledon Wine Cellar	0208 540 9979
WIN	The Winery	0207 286 6475
WKM	Wickham Vineyard	01329 834042
WLI	Winelink International Ltd	01280 824120
WMK	Winemark	01232 746274
WNC	Winchcombe Wines	01242 604313
WNS	Winos	0161 652 9396
WOA	Wallaces of Ayr	01292 262330
WOC	Whitesides of Clitheroe	01200 422 281
WOI	Wines of Interest Ltd	01473 215752
WON	Weavers of Nottingham	0115 958 0922
WOO	Wooldings Vineyard & Winery	01256 895200
WOW	Wines of Westhorpe	01283 820285
WPL	The Wine Portfolio Ltd	01225 852484
WRC	Wine Rack (First Quench)	01707 328244
WRI	Wrightson Wines	01325 374134
WRK	Wine Raks	01224 311460
WRO	Wroxeter Roman Vineyard	01743 761888
WRT	Winerite Ltd	0113 283 7654
WRU	William Rush Wines	01743 350967
WRW	The Wright Wine Co	01756 700886
WSA	Wineshare Ltd	01306 742164
WSC	Winesource	01225 783007
WSG	Walter S Siegel Ltd	01256 701101
WSO	The Wine Society Ltd	01438 741177
WSP	Barrels & Bottles	0114 255 6611
WST	Western Wines Ltd	01746 789411
WTA	Winetraders (UK) Ltd	0165 251 851
WTD	Waitrose Direct	01344 824694

WTF	Watford Wine Co	0370 533 183
WTH	Withers Agencies Ltd	01273 477132
WTL	Whittalls Wines	01922 36161
WTR	The Wine Treasury Ltd	0207 793 9999
WTS	Waitrose Ltd	01344 424680
WWC	Walmer Wine Company	01472 240558
WWS	Windermere Wine Stores	01539 446891
WWT	Whitebridge Wines	01785 817229
WYW	Wychwood Wines	01932 855323
YAP	Yapp Brothers	01747 860423
YOB	Young's Brewery	0208 875 7007
YOD	Yodeska Ltd	01604 675500
YVM	Tony Stebbings / Yvon Mau	01372 468571
YWL	Yates Brothers Ltd	01204 391777

INDEX

INDEX

INDEX

INDEX

INDEX

INDEX

INDEX

INDEX

INDEX

INDEX

INDEX

INDEX

INDEX

INDEX

INDEX

INDEX

INDEX

INDEX

INDEX

INDEX

INDEX

INDEX

INDEX

INDEX

INDEX

INDEX

INDEX

INDEX

INDEX

INDEX

INDEX

INDEX

INDEX

INDEX

INDEX

INDEX

WINE NAME
STOCKIST
TASTING NOTE

WINE NAME
STOCKIST
TASTING NOTE

WINE NAME
STOCKIST
TASTING NOTE

WINE NAME
STOCKIST
TASTING NOTE

WINE NAME
STOCKIST
TASTING NOTE

WINE NAME
STOCKIST
TASTING NOTE

WINE NAME
STOCKIST

TASTING NOTE

WINE NAME
STOCKIST

TASTING NOTE

WINE NAME
STOCKIST

TASTING NOTE

WINE NAME
STOCKIST

TASTING NOTE

WINE NAME
STOCKIST

TASTING NOTE

WINE NAME
STOCKIST

TASTING NOTE

NOTES ON STOCKISTS AND WINES

WINE NAME
STOCKIST
TASTING NOTE

WINE NAME
STOCKIST
TASTING NOTE

WINE NAME
STOCKIST
TASTING NOTE

WINE NAME
STOCKIST
TASTING NOTE

WINE NAME
STOCKIST
TASTING NOTE

WINE NAME
STOCKIST
TASTING NOTE

ACKNOWLEDGMENTS

Wine, wine and more wine! A whopping 9300 wines were coded, bagged-'n'-tagged and then tasted. It did not end there, but we will not bore you with the whole process. This "impossible" task was all done in record time. It was a phenomenal undertaking completed by a team of dedicated staff and tasters that must be thanked:

• **the International WINE Challenge team** – for committing their time and strength. Their performance under pressure must be applauded. Thanks to the ones who got things started, those who ran, flighted, checked wines, etc during the Challenge and to the ones that stayed behind. To the tasters who gave their expertise and palates, thank you. And we cannot forget Sega Fredo for the espresso that kept us on the go! Eric Duvin from Du pain Duvin for the awesome food . To Hoegaarden Bière, a wonderful refreshing change at the end of the day.

• **from WINE magazine** – Robert Joseph, Charles Metcalfe, Kirsty Bridge and Georgina Severs.

• **for subbing and database management** – the editorial team: Elaine Arnold, Melanie Cook, Nina Pagola, and assisted by Mike and Boz.

Finally, thanks to **publishing editor** James Gabbani and **editor** Nick James-Martin. Their tireless commitment to the Challenge made it a success. They were dedicated to the end! RIP...

HOW YOU CAN HELP US

If you have any ideas about how we can improve the format of the **WINE Magazine Pocket Wine Buyer's Guide** then please write to:
**Nick James-Martin, WINE PWBG, Wilmington Publishing,
6-8 Underwood Street, London N1 7JQ**

The type of subjects we would particularly like to hear about are:
• **Do you prefer to have countries sub-divided by region or grape variety?**
• **Do you find the £5 and Under guides useful?**
• **Would food and wine pairing suggestions be useful?**
• **How else might you like to see the wines sorted or divided?**
• **What other information regarding wines and stockists would be of interest?**
• **Would you prefer the Guide to be ring-bound or loose leafed?**

L'OPPOSITION ANTIGRÉGORIENNE

DU MÊME AUTEUR

Le règne de Philippe Ier, *roi de France* (1060-1108), Paris, Société Française d'Imprimerie et de Librairie, 1922, in-8°.
Ouvrage couronné par l'Académie des Inscriptions et Belles-Lettres, prix Gobert.

Les Vies de Saint Savinien, premier évêque de Sens. Étude critique suivie d'une édition de la plus ancienne *Vita*, Paris, Société Française d'Imprimerie et de Librairie, 1921, in-8°.

Études sur la polémique religieuse à l'époque de Grégoire VII, Les Prégrégoriens, Paris, Société Française d'Imprimerie et de Librairie, 1916, in-16.

Saint Grégoire VII (Collection « Les Saints »), Paris, Gabalda, 1920, in-16.
Ouvrage couronné par l'Académie française, prix Juteau Duvigneaux.

Louvain (Collection « Memoranda »), Paris, 1921.

Aigues-Mortes et Saint-Gilles (Collection « Les petites monographies des grands édifices de la France »), Paris, 1925.

La Réforme Grégorienne, T. I, *La formation des Idées grégoriennes* (Spicilegium Sacrum Lovaniense, fasc. 6), Louvain, Bureaux du Spicilegium, 1924. — T. II, *Grégoire VII* (Spicilegium Sacrum Lovaniense, fasc. 9), Louvain, 1926, in-8°.
Ouvrage couronné par l'Académie des Inscriptions et Belles-Lettres, prix Saintour.

La Chrétienté médiévale (tome VIII de l'Histoire du Monde publiée sous la direction de E. CAVAIGNAC), Paris, 1929.

Saint Roch (Collection « L'Art et les Saints »), Paris, 1930.

L'Europe occidentale de 888 à 1125 (tome II de l'Histoire générale, section moyen-âge, sous la direction de G. GLOTZ), Paris, 1930.

Montpellier (Collection « Les Villes d'art célèbres »), Paris, 1935.

Histoire de l'Église depuis les origines jusqu'à nos jours sous la direction de A. FLICHE et V. MARTIN, tome I, *L'Église primitive*, Paris, 1934 ; tome II, *De la fin du II*^e *siècle à la paix constantinienne*, 1935 ; tome III, *De la paix constantinienne à la mort de Théodore*, 1936 ; tome IV, *De la mort de Théodose à l'élection de Grégoire le Grand*, 1937.